Retheorising capitalism

Retheorising capitalism

Edited by
Anni Kangas, Iuliia Gataulina, Mikko Poutanen,
Anna Ilona Rajala & Henna-Elise Ventovirta

TAMPERE UNIVERSITY PRESS

VERTAISARVIOITU
KOLLEGIALT GRANSKAD
PEER-REVIEWED
www.tsv.fi/tunnus

Cover image by
Natalia Batrakova

Cover design by
Jonna Lahti

Typography by
Markus Itkonen

Layout by
Eija Kylmäniemi

ISBN 978-952-359-062-5 (PDF)
ISBN 978-952-359-063-2 (print, paperback)

Publisher: Tampere University Press, Tampere, Finland
Print service provider: BoD – Books on Demand, Norderstedt, Germany

Suggested citation:
Kangas, A., Gataulina, I., Poutanen, M., Rajala, A. I. & Ventovirta, H-E. (Eds.). (2025). *Retheorising capitalism.* Tampere University Press. https://doi.org/10.61201/tup.981

Contents

Prologue: Capitalism and the spirit of engaged pluralism 7
Iuliia Gataulina, Anni Kangas, Mikko Poutanen, Anna Ilona Rajala & Henna-Elise Ventovirta

1 Introduction: Troubling capitalism 11
Anni Kangas, Iuliia Gataulina, Mikko Poutanen, Anna Ilona Rajala & Henna-Elise Ventovirta

Part I
Representing

2 Reading regenerative vegetable farming for difference 33
Kerry Woodward

3 A proposal for a scatological global political economy: Or, making sense of capitalism through a shit-smeared lens 50
Anna Ilona Rajala

4 The capitalist's apprentice: Employment and the reproduction of capitalist culture 70
Mark L. Young

Part II
Reimagining

5 Re-sensing economies: Artistic and embodied knowing for more-than-capitalist futures 93
Heather McLean, Molly Mullen, Aviv Kruglanski, Leo Hwang & Kelly Dombroski

6 A future worth imagining: Collaging capitalism, expanding political imagination 112
Maria Mäensivu

7 Postcapitalist translations: An experiment with scissors, clippings, and glue 133
Iuliia Gataulina, Anni Kangas, Mikko Poutanen, Anna Ilona Rajala & Tiina Vaittinen

Part III
Repairing

8 Porous boundaries of resistance: Translating an authoritarian-neoliberal university 163
Iuliia Gataulina

9 Resisting academic capitalism with a postcapitalist pedagogy: Healthier universities through antihierarchy, communality, and lived alternatives 183
Iris Pajunen

10 Capitalism as colonialism as capitalism (and the alternatives) 198
Sabaheta Ramcilovic-Suominen

11 A theory of fragmentism 219
Akseli Kettula

Part IV
Reconceptualising

12 (Re)Theorising heterodoxies: Labour in Islamic economic philosophy 245
Mariam Khawar

13 Financialised digitalisation, digitalised financialisation: The inseparability between technological domination and financial hegemony in contemporary capitalism 263
Edemilson Paraná

14 Re-indigenising kuku (green-lipped mussel) economies in Aotearoa (New Zealand) 281
Georgia McLellan, Cory Tuhoro-Bodey & Anataia van Leeuwen

Dialogue: Strings of retheorising capitalism 301
Iuliia Gataulina, Anni Kangas, Mikko Poutanen & Henna-Elise Ventovirta

Contributors 314

Prologue

Capitalism and the spirit of engaged pluralism

Iuliia Gataulina, Anni Kangas, Mikko Poutanen, Anna Ilona Rajala & Henna-Elise Ventovirta

This edited collection participates in the conversation about capitalism. It is the result of an open call inviting submissions from scholars involved in social science debates about capitalism and capitalist practices. The call emphasised that while capitalism remains the dominant socioeconomic model, there is a growing and increasingly vocal demand to rethink and retheorise it. We invited potential authors to explore capitalism theoretically, conceptually, or empirically, emphasising our equal interest in works that seek to address ways to reform capitalism and those interested in envisioning what might come after it. As a result, the book now features a diverse array of contributions. It offers a platform for a multitude of authors to engage with capitalism in a variety of ways.

Assembled in the spirit of engaged pluralism, this book refrains from proposing a single framework for the study of capitalism. Engaged pluralism is an intellectual stance where different viewpoints are actively engaged with to avoid dogmatism and promote deeper understanding and dialogue (Bernstein, 1989). On the pages of this book, this effort takes the following forms: The book not only engages a plurality of voices, but the chapters also explore diverse theoretical and conceptual approaches. Different methodologies, as well as a range of materials, are used to retheorise capitalism. While some chapters are text-based, others turn to visual media or examine capitalism through the practice of pottery making. The book also engages with a variety of audiences whose contributions are relevant to the act of retheorising: among the authors are not only established academics but also university students.

Gataulina, I., Kangas, A., Poutanen, M., Rajala, A. I. & Ventovirta, H-E. 2025. Prologue: Capitalism and the spirit of engaged pluralism. In A. Kangas, I. Gataulina, M. Poutanen, A. I. Rajala & H-E Ventovirta (Eds.), *Retheorising capitalism* (pp. 7–10). Tampere University Press. https://doi.org/10.61201/tup.981

Retheorising, understood within the ethos of engaged pluralism, is a diverse and messy scientific endeavour. It involves embracing variation and difference, while also acknowledging that a pluralistic project is inherently incomplete (Johns & Hall, 2024, p. 2). Instead of providing solace in a coherent theoretical framework, retheorising demands patience to endure the ongoing and evolving nature of inquiry. This is not a new suggestion: The idea of avoiding dogmatism by respecting ideational, theoretical, and methodological diversity has been central to scientific inquiry for centuries (Kurki, 2024). However, in the study of the economy and economic phenomena, the discipline of economics—in its neoclassical form in particular—occupied a hegemonic position for decades (e.g., Amin & Thrift, 2004). This book is part of the continuing effort to challenge this hegemony and expand inquiries in a more pluralist direction.

As a theoretical position, engaged pluralism recognises the multifaceted workings of capitalism. Capitalist social relations manifest in diverse ways within our rapidly changing world. Given the inherent complexity of the social world, engagement with various perspectives and interpretations can be argued to make inquiries more rigorous. This is achieved through the give and take of engagement, which may create momentary tensions but eventually enhances the validity of our conclusions (Box-Steffensmeier, 2022). Such tension is evident throughout the book: some chapters draw on the work of scholars who hold differing views on the nature of capitalism, creating theoretical contrasts with the perspectives presented in other chapters.

However, while the book's pluralist approach to retheorising capitalism may create internal divergence, this can also be understood as an epistemological effort to engage with the widest possible range of plausible alternatives. As pragmatist William James (1909) emphasises in his argument against monism, "something always escapes ... the word 'and' trails along after every sentence. ... Nothing includes everything, or dominates over everything". This resonates with queer scholar Eve Sedgwick's (1994, pp. 5–6) invitation to appreciate the richness of those "junctures" where not everything points in the same direction or signifies monolithically because "such junctures" are the "open mesh of possibilities". On the pages of this book, this pluralist proposition means accepting that various conceptualisations of capitalism—or capitalist and postcapitalist practices—can be simultaneously valid. Some chapters scrutinise the functioning of capitalism as a system, while others focus on how capitalist practices extend into more-than-economic or more-than-human fields like education or excrement. In some chapters the capitalocentrism of inquiries is troubled by illuminating more-than-capitalist or postcapitalist practices already taking place.

Engaged pluralism can also be understood as engagement with ontological diversity, as reflected in the rejection of the singular reality doctrine (Klein Schaarsberg, 2024) or the "one-world world" ontology (Law, 2015). This sort of engaged pluralism takes us beyond the claim that there are various valid perspectives or theoretical and conceptual approaches to capitalism, each representing a different attempt to understand the world. Beyond diversifying ways to know the world, ontological pluralism problematises one of the key assumptions of European or Western cosmologies—the assumption of a singular reality. This assumption, imposed by colonial modernity, has led to the discrediting of other possible ontologies, reducing them to mere beliefs, myths, or legends (Kurki, 2024, p. 6). Examining capitalism in relation to, for example, Indigenous knowledge and Islamic spiritual and ethical development, the chapters in this edited collection can be understood to also foster ontologically and cosmologically pluralistic understandings of capitalism

Experimentation, creativity, and inventiveness are encouraged by engaged pluralism, which invites expanding the methodological routes through which capitalism is approached. While social sciences are generally assumed to be methodologically pluralist, in practice, this pluralism is quite limited. Given the restricted scope of methodological pluralism, inquiries may miss some of the most meaningful aspects of the social world, such as the sensory, tactile, and embodied (Kurki, 2024, p. 2). Recognising this, some chapters in this book call for a renewed methodological imagination, creativity, and inventiveness. They invite us, for example, to think about new ways of sensing the economy or to approach capitalism through the tactile effort of cutting, pasting, and gluing, i.e., collaging.

Engaged pluralism is distinct from alienated pluralism (Young, 2021) or fragmented pluralism that creates a world of separate monisms, or separate monologues (Bernstein, 1989, p. 16). In contrast, this book is a call to an engaged conversation about capitalism and the need to retheorise it. In its Greek origin, the word 'theory' [*theōria*] refers to contemplation, speculation, looking at, viewing, to a sight,, show, spectacle, and things looked at, but also spectator—the English word for theatre being of the same etymology. The Latin prefix re-, on the other hand, connotes words and phrases such as back, back from, back to the original place, again, anew, once more.

Retheorising, then, is all of this and more: to look back, to look again, to think anew, to speculate once more, to sense differently, to engage with the spectacle of capitalism with its various actors. As this book shows, this engagement may happen through various kinds of activities. To reflect this, the book has been structured into four sections entitled "Representing", "Reimagining", "Repairing", and "Reconceptualising". Each part of the book begins with an introduction that provides an overview of the chapters in that part. To underscore the dialogical character of the spirit in which the book has been put together, the book concludes with a 'dialogue of snippets' where the contributors to elucidate their understanding of capitalism and the imperative to engage in theorising it.

Acknowledgements

This book project has been funded by the Research Council of Finland (project no: 325976, project no: 350247) as well as the Kone Foundation (project no: 202204510, project no: 3122801458, and project no: 202105011).

References

Amin, A., & Thrift, N. (2004). Introduction. In A. Amin & N. Thrift (Eds.), *The Blackwell cultural economy reader* (pp. x–xxx). Blackwell.

Bernstein, R. J. (1989). Pragmatism, pluralism and the healing of wounds. *Proceedings and Addresses of the American Philosophical Association*, 63(3), 5–18. https://doi.org/10.2307/3130079

Box-Steffensmeier, J. M. (2022). Engaged pluralism: The importance of commitment. *Perspectives on Politics* 20(1): 9–21. https://doi.org/10.1017/S1537592721003856

James, W. (1909). *A pluralistic universe*. Hibbert lectures at Manchester College on the present situation in philosophy. https://www.gutenberg.org/cache/epub/11984/pg11984.html

Johns, J., & Hall, S. M. (2024). Introducing contemporary economic geographies: An inspiring, critical and plural collection. In *Contemporary Economic Geographies: Inspiring, Critical and Plural Perspectives* (pp. 1–12). Bristol University Press.

Klein Schaarsberg, S. (2024). Enacting the pluriverse in the West: Contemplative activism as a challenge to the disenchanted one-world world. *European Journal of International Relations*, 30(2), 434-460. https://doi.org/10.1177/13540661231200864

Kurki, M. (2024). The limits of pluralism: Pluralism in pluriversal Anthropocene. In J. M. Box-Steffensmeier, D. P. Christenson, & V. Sinclair-Chapman (Eds.), *Oxford Handbook of Engaged Methodological Pluralism in Political Science* (online ed.). Oxford Academic. https://doi.org/10.1093/oxfordhb/9780198861346.013.1

Law, J. (2015). What's wrong with a one-world world? *Distinktion*, 16(1), 126–139. https://doi.org/10.1080/1600910X.2015.1020066

Sedgwick, E. K. (1994). *Tendencies*. Routledge.

Young, K. L. (2021). Progress, pluralism and science: Moving from alienated to engaged pluralism. *Review of International Political Economy*, 28(2), 206–420

VERTAISARVIOITU
KOLLEGIALT GRANSKAD
PEER-REVIEWED
www.tsv.fi/tunnus

1
Introduction
Troubling capitalism

Anni Kangas, Iuliia Gataulina, Mikko Poutanen, Anna Ilona Rajala & Henna-Elise Ventovirta

We chose to entitle this introductory chapter to the book *Retheorising Capitalism* as "Troubling Capitalism". It captures two key features in the approach of the book. On the one hand, it suggests that there is something bothering or even annoying about capitalism: capitalism troubles us, which has given us the motivation to put the book together. On the other hand, the phrase refers to what the chapters in this book are attempting to do: they trouble capitalism in the sense of "stirring it up" or "disturbing it" as implied in the French verb (Larousse, n.d.). Troubling capitalism, then, is about continued conceptualisation, discussion, and debate about capitalism—a sustained engagement with it. The point of troubling, as Donna Haraway suggests, is "to become capable" or "to stir up potent response" (Haraway, 2016, p. 1). Similarly, this book tries to enhance our ability to develop responses to capitalism. This, we believe, is worth the trouble in order not to surrender our agency to the there-is-no-alternative logic of capitalism and to find new ways of living well in the multispecies world.

We are not the first to make the argument that there is a need to discuss, debate, and retheorise capitalism. At once, it may seem the world continues to be gripped by "capitalist realism," suggesting that it is easier to imagine the end of the world than the end of capitalism (Fisher, 2009). However, capitalism has gained renewed interest, particularly since the "global" financial crises of 2007–2012. In stark contrast

Kangas, A., Gataulina, I., Poutanen, M., Rajala, A. I. & Ventovirta, H-E. (2025). Introduction: Troubling capitalism. In A. Kangas, I. Gataulina, M. Poutanen, A. I. Rajala & H-E Ventovirta (Eds.), *Retheorising capitalism* (pp. 11–30). Tampere University Press. https://doi.org/10.61201/tup.981

to the triumphalism associated with capitalism in the 1990s (Fukuyama, 1992) and still in the 2000s (McGuigan, 2009), faith in capitalism has been shaken in different domains of life and in various parts of the world. Often credited for improvements in productivity, longer life expectancies, and availability of consumer goods as well as for improved living standards, capitalism's failure to deliver steady progress for many is increasingly recognised. In high-income countries, its effects can be seen in "soaring inequality, dead-end jobs and macroeconomic instability" (Wolf, 2023, p. 3). While the concentration of wealth in the hands of a few is not historically exclusive to capitalism, it is a strong feature in many capitalist societies (Lierse, Sachweh, & Waitkus, 2022). The fall of extreme poverty over the past two centuries may be attributed, at least partly, to free-market capitalism (Ortiz-Ospina, 2017). Yet, global income and wealth inequalities within countries are at a historic high, and they also remain high between countries, even though the emerging world has somewhat closed the wealth gap during the past four decades (Chancel et al., 2022).

A powerful element that has contributed to capitalism's lost legitimacy is the growing awareness of the connections between the dominant economic model and the environmental catastrophe. The ability of capitalism to provide adequate responses to the climate crisis has been contested by research showing that constant growth—one of the cornerstones of capitalist arrangements—cannot be reconciled with the reduction of greenhouse gas emissions (Nørgård & Xue, 2016). Ecological social movements like Extinction Rebellion and Fridays for Future argue that the end of the world—as we know it—is indeed at hand if capitalism cannot be curtailed. Recognising this, scholars and activists working with approaches such as degrowth (Schmelzer & Nowshin, 2023), *buen vivir* (Duque Acosta et al., 2022), the commons (Perkins, 2023), indigenous economies (Kuokkanen, 2011), and ecological reparation (Papadopoulos et al., 2023) have engaged in the act of rethinking the economy and alternatives to capitalism both in theory and in practice.

Some claim that the root of these problems does not lie in capitalism. For them, the current global economic system is far from what capitalism 'really' is, which has prompted efforts to reimagine capitalism (Henderson, 2020). By contrast, those who operate under the banner of anticapitalism insist that while capitalism has transformed the material conditions of life to the benefit of many, it is a dysfunctional system causing great harm and perpetuating eliminable forms of human and non-human suffering. They remind us that another world is possible—one that would parallel capitalism in its dynamism, innovation, and productivity but not in its harms (Wright, 2019). The dysfunctions of capitalism are also discussed in the literature that draws connections between neoliberal capitalism and the rise of anti-democratic or authoritarian politics (Fabry, 2019; Gataulina, 2024).

Discussions that revolve around capitalism offer a varied landscape. But what is capitalism? As with many concepts in social science, capitalism is a contested term. People use it in a variety of ways, and some scholars refuse to even use the term as it is argued to obscure more than it reveals. Does capitalism refer to the modern economy as a whole, or is it something more specific? Is it broader than the economy as such, a civilisation? Some have suggested that capitalism is so all-encompassing that there is little point in even using the term. Or, as scholars writing about postcapitalist politics have argued, what really needs to be stirred and troubled are the totalising theorisations of capitalism, as they may prevent us from seeing the economy for all its diversity (Gibson-Graham, 2006).

The existence of these debates and more underscores that in the midst of the renewed interest in capitalism, it is quite impossible to find any consensus or generally accepted definitions for the term. To facilitate the effort of retheorising capitalism in the spirit of engaged pluralism outlined in the epilogue, this introductory chapter offers some signposts for navigating these troubled waters. The chapter is structured as follows: First, we detail the genealogy of the term "capitalism". We then move on to consider various ways in which capitalism has been defined: we discuss the treatment of capitalism as a specific kind of economic system as well as suggestions to view it as a societal dynamism that is much broader than the economy. We then scrutinise contributions that highlight capitalism's variable nature, for example, by adding prefixes to the term, as well as efforts to (dis)locate capitalism in time and space. From there, we proceed to the normative debates over whether capitalism should be seen as a force for good or ill. This exploration reveals a landscape that is diverse not just theoretically, epistemologically, and methodologically but also ontologically.

What do we talk about when we talk about capitalism?

As a term, capitalism emerges in the French context. Its origin story is often told in very Eurocentric terms, although the history of capitalism, as much as its current state, is fundamentally global (Anievas & Nisancioglu, 2015). The concept was first used in the middle of the 19th century by French socialists to criticise the practice whereby power was wielded through capital (Sonencher, 2022). Louis Le Blanc, for example, characterised capitalism as "the appropriation of capital by the few, to the exclusion of the many" (Blanc, as cited in Marks, 2016, p. 4). In German, the term capitalism—*Kapitalismus*—was taken into use a few decades later to refer to a specific kind of social system (Krätke, 2020, p. 1).

In the English language, the first use of the term capitalism is also dated to the mid-19th century but to a fiction novel. William Makepeace Thackeray uses the term capitalism in 1854 in the novel entitled *The Newcomes* to refer to the practice of investing in the stock market: the "sense of capitalism", he narrates, "sobered and dignified" a certain character in his novel (Thackeray, 2010; see also Marks, 2016, p. 5). In the digitised Finnish newspaper archives, the first use of the term dates to April 1889: the Berlin correspondent of the bourgeois *Uusi-Suometar* newspaper used the term in a report about German socialists' "wild attacks against monarchy and capitalism". However, in the years that follow, the term is mostly used to describe events outside of Finland. Indeed, while occurrences of the term capitalism can be found in different European language contexts from the mid-19th century onwards, the term is only hesitantly adopted to wider use (see also Krätke, 2020). A Google Ngram search in languages such as English, German, French, and Italian also shows that the use of the term "capitalism" starts to slowly pick up in the 1920s (Google Ngram, n.d.).

It is noteworthy that even if the term capitalism is used increasingly frequently, many scholars relate to the term with hesitation. For example, Daron Acemoglu and James A. Robinson, who are among the most influential contemporary economists, suggest that the term is not very useful in economic or political analysis. They argue that as the concept is associated with the idea of some general laws or dynamics, it easily distracts attention from something more important, which, for them, is the make-up of the political and economic institutions in an economic system (Acemoglu & Robinson, 2015, pp. 4, 24). The term capitalism did not belong to the vocabulary of such classical political economists as Adam Smith, David Ricardo, or Karl Marx either, although they used terms such as "capital" and "capitalist" (Krätke, 2020, p. 2). Karl Marx—the archetypical analyst and critic—only uses the term capitalism a handful of times in his posthumously published writings. In the Economic Manuscripts of 1861–63, "capitalism features just once, in a context where it could signify either the boundless drive of capitalists to enrich themselves and make more capital or the total process of capital accumulation" (Krätke, 2020, p. 2). According to Krätke, this was a conscious choice as Marx detested the moralising uses to which the term had been put. Indeed, the subtitle of Capital is "a critique of political economy", not capitalism. Marx aimed to develop an account of the dynamics and core processes of the capitalist mode of production and, through that, to insert a sense of history into social order. For Marx, the dominant modes of production were the key to the analysis of social change. The capitalist mode of production is one of the modes of production, preceded by primitive communism, slave society, and the feudal mode of production.

Postcapitalist scholars have also problematised the use of the term capitalism, or rather the capitalocentric discourse. Capitalocentrism is an economic discourse centred on capitalism, which marginalises non-capitalist economies. It can be identified not just in the works of the proponents of capitalism but is kept alive also by its critics. As the capitalocentric discourse is actualised, capitalism comes to appear as a totalising force—in good or bad. As a result, non-capitalist practices do not receive the attention they deserve or are designated as somehow subordinate, marginalised, lacking, or insufficient. This means that capitalocentrism has a problematic performative effect: it essentialises capitalism (Gibson-Graham, 1996). In fact, as this short genealogy of the term capitalism shows, it has often served a double function: initially emerging as a polemical and critical concept, it has taken time for it to become a tool of scholarly analysis.

Capitalism as an economic system

One way to define capitalism is to suggest that it is a specific kind of economic system distinctive in its basic institutions. These discussions sometimes evoke Douglass North's (1990, p. 3) definition of institutions as "the rules of the game in a society or, more formally, ... the humanly devised constraints that shape human interaction". Furthermore, institutions "define and limit the set of choices for individuals" (p. 4) and "affect the performance of the economy by their effect on the costs of exchange and production" (p. 5). The argument here goes that capitalism, as an economic system, is qualitatively different from the economic systems of the past or future—central economic planning, feudalism, or slave economy.

What characterises capitalism according to the institutionalist definition is that private owners of capital goods intend to make a profit and then appropriate this profit privately. In this conceptualisation, the main institutions of a capitalist economic system are markets, private property, and business companies. Some scholars emphasise that the financial infrastructure of money and investment are also key capitalist institutions as they enable credit and debt transactions (Hodgson, 2015). In the book *Slavery's Capitalism*, Beckert and Rockman (2016) argue that the institution of slavery was very central to the development of capitalism: Transatlantic slave trade—an economic system based on the enslavement of people of colour and black and indigenous populations—contributed in major ways to industrial development in Europe and the United States. It was this accumulation of wealth that laid the ground for the industrial revolution and the development of capitalism as a dominant economic arrangement in the "western world". Expanding the scope of institutions problematises the Eurocentric origin story of capitalism and reminds us of the importance of analysing the development of capitalism as a global phenomenon (Williams et al., 2021). Moreover, scholars such as Angela Davis (2003) and Genevieve LeBaron (2018) have shown that slavery is not a past phenomenon but, in the form of "modern slavery", continues to thrive in today's advanced capitalist states: the deepening and expansion of capitalism has not weakened reliance on unfree labour but rather reinforced it.

A variable degree of state regulation and involvement has also been a focus of inquiries: in the capitalist economic system, there is typically a degree of state involvement, but no central planning as in some other economic systems (e.g. Kornai, 1992). By contrast, the literature on state capitalism seeks to move beyond "cataloguing national institutional diversity" and scrutinises the role of the state in capitalistically organised social relations. Unlike scholars whose focus is on capitalist institutions, scholars of state capitalism employ a dialectical-historical approach to address the variable roles that state intervention has played in the organisation and reorganisation of capitalism globally (Bair, 2023; cf. Galbraith, 2009).

Capitalism's variable nature

Many scholars who are sceptical toward the concept of capitalism may still see sense in using it with a prefix. This often forms part of efforts to argue that there is not one single type of capitalism; capitalism rather exists in a multiplicity of forms. Examples here include discussions over welfare capitalism, neoliberal capitalism, crony capitalism, necrocapitalism, and racial capitalism. Scholars investing hope in capitalism may use qualifiers such as "rigged" to suggest that the contemporary form of capitalism does not function as capitalism should. Martin Wolf suggests that capitalism has been allowed to "run amok" and that there has been a shortage of effective policy instruments to regulate it (Wolf, 2023, pp. 119, 143). Capitalism seems to have been skewed exactly in the way that such classical political economists such as Adam Smith warned: the powerful have been able to exploit the economic and political systems against the rest of society (e.g. Henderson, 2020).

Excessive rent extraction is one of the reasons why today's capitalism seems not to be able to deliver on its promises. There is a growing consensus that rentier capitalism characterises the contemporary economic system and contributes to widening levels of inequality, falling levels of investment, and economic growth (Mazzucato et al., 2023). Rents are returns that people get simply because of their ability to exert control over a scarce resource. Rent seeking can take on a variety of forms—from the classical political economists' focus on land rent (Stratford, 2023) to the digital economy's "algorithmic control over user attention" (O'Reilly et al., 2024). The term rentier capitalism, then, suggests that the economy's productive capacity is reduced as a result of rent extraction: individuals or groups grab and control surplus value instead of directing it toward new productive investment (Sanghera & Satybaldieva, 2023).

If scholars writing about rentier capitalism focus on the ways in which contemporary capitalism has been skewed, the literature on authoritarian neoliberalism details how capitalism in its neoliberal form skews democratic politics. In it, the dysfunctions of (neoliberal) capitalism are discussed in relation to the politics it propagates. Various scholars argue how capitalism in its neoliberal guise endangers democracy and contributes to the rise of anti-democratic politics and authoritarian governance (Bruff, 2014; Bruff & Tansel, 2019). The intrusion of capitalist logics of extraction, profit-making, managerial control, efficiency, and surveillance into different areas of life beyond material production breeds a political culture that is hierarchical and covert. The mutually enforcing relations between neoliberal capitalism and anti-democratic politics have been scrutinised in the contexts of both liberal democracies (Dean, 2002) and authoritarian regimes (Fabry, 2019; Gataulina, 2024).

If the notions of rentier capitalism as well as authoritarian neoliberalism highlight certain dysfunctions in capitalism as we know it, the concept of racial capitalism works differently: It refers to the entanglements of racialisation and economic systems in the very genesis of capitalism. This concept suggests that capitalism has not only benefited from but also contributed to systemic inequalities that are based on racialisation—and that predate capitalism. In *Black Marxism: The Making of the Black Radical Tradition*,

Cedric Robinson (1983) critiques conventional Marxist interpretations for focusing on class struggle and neglecting the role of racial dynamics in colonisation, slavery, and imperialism.

With various prefixes, capitalism starts to appear less as a system and more like a project continuously under construction. This project can take on a variety of forms. This claim is also made in the literature on the varieties of capitalism (VoC), which scrutinises institutional similarities and differences between capitalist coordinated market economies—originally separated into liberal (i.e. market), mixed, or state-oriented regimes (Hall & Soskice, 2001). The VoC literature has also tried to explain capitalist institutional change from one model to another (Schmidt, 2009), but the variety included in VoC tends to be relatively restricted—or opened up to a degree that clear categorisations lose meaning.

Messy hybridisation could characterise the shifting shapes of capitalism more accurately than static or pure models (see also Ahlqvist & Moisio, 2014). As Coates (2005, pp. 2, 5) explains, the debate on varieties of capitalism has, to a large extent, been an attempt to "grasp why economic performance differs between particular national capitalisms"; it focuses on "why growth rates differ in post-war capitalist economies". The focus in this strand of theorising is typically on nationally bound varieties in the institutional make-up of capitalism. Geographical political economists have recently pointed out that this often assumes "immobile and bounded views of state power and territory" (Alami et al., 2023, p. 631). If the debate has been "territorially trapped" (Agnew, 1994), it should be spatialised to better grasp not just varieties of capitalism but its variegated character. Spatialisation here invites a more nuanced discussion of how capitalism is a phenomenon that is not a 'thing', but a social relation territorialised and scaled in complex ways (Anievas & Nisancioglu, 2015, p. 8).

The time(s) of capitalism

As scholars grapple with the concept of capitalism, their views on the temporalities of capitalism also vary. In some versions of Marxism, for example, capitalist development is easily homogenised: teleological historiographies of capitalism are presumed to proceed through linear stages from primitive communism to slave society and further to feudalist and capitalist modes of production, which were then assumed to evolve further into a mature form of communism (for a problematisation of a teleological interpretation of Marx's view of history, see Rauhala, 2023). Not just Marxists but also others argue that as the dominant and comprehensive form of economic organisation, capitalism is typically argued to be a modern phenomenon. Its emergence is often dated to the 18th century, more precisely to the consolidation of industrial capitalism in the second half of the 18th century. However, features of merchant capitalism existed already in the first millennium, and elements of finance capitalism date back to the high-medieval period. These, nevertheless, were "capitalist islands in a sea of predominantly non-capitalist relationships" (Kocka, 2018, p. 73).

In more nuanced approaches, further periodic concepts are added to describe new forms of capitalist appropriation. Technological developments have, in particular, motivated the periodisation of capitalism: digital capitalism of the 1990s, information capitalism or communicative capitalism of the 2000s, surveillance capitalism of the 2010s, and platform capitalism of the 2020s. All of these can be characterised as diagnoses of changes in the character of capitalist appropriation and circulation (Kornbluh, 2024). They are not qualitative changes to the logic of capitalism, but new introductions and updates to existing frameworks. Surveillance capitalism, for example, means the instrumentalisation of new surveillance technologies for the purpose of commodifying and monetising human activity (Zuboff, 2019). Urban monopoly capitalism, according to Moisio and Rossi (2024), is a contemporary stage in the evolutionary trajectory of capitalism where the corporatised state and tech companies collaborate to extract economic value specifically from urban space.

By contrast to the idea of alternating stages, capitalism can also be viewed as a temporally hybrid phenomenon. Many scholars emphasise that the historical development of capitalism has not proceeded teleologically in one direction. They problematise the idea of evolution or stages in the development of capitalism and shift focus on the entanglements of economic practices. Clear-cut temporal divisions can, indeed, be problematic: historical and institutional diversity is too broad to assume there would not be messy and nonlinear hybrid forms of capitalist and non-capitalist development. That the temporal dynamics of capitalism should be conceptualised as hybrids is a claim made in pericapitalist as well as in postcapitalist approaches. Anna Tsing (2015, p. 132) argues that instead of assuming a forward thrusting "pulse of progress", inquiries into capitalism should pay attention to the polyphonic interplay of temporal rhythms and scales. Similarly, in Yang's (2000, p. 478) research, the trope of hybridity challenges the "strong theory of capitalism", which conceals the fact that capitalism exists in a variety of cultural, political, and temporal forms.

This move decentres capitalism not just temporally but also geographically and shifts the focus of inquiry toward "the postcolonial generation, the offspring of the union of capitalism with native forms of economy" (Yang, 2000, p. 478). In addition to postcolonial contexts, such decentring of capitalism may also bring into play postsocialist dynamics. For example, Ichinkhorloo's (2018) study of 'postsocialist' Mongolia foregrounds the diversity of economic practices that persisted amid the 'transition to capitalism'. Obviously, the view of capitalism offered by the idea of hybridity is very different from narrations where the end of state socialism is told in terms of a triumph and consolidation of capitalism in terms of a more or less systematic adoption of the capitalist institutions.

The idea of hybridity suggests that if we want to understand capitalism, we need to see beyond the logics of capital and capitalists. As Anna Tsing (2015, p. 66) argues, "we need an ethnographic eye to see the economic diversity through which accumulation is possible." Similarly, postcapitalist scholars emphasise that foregrounding the diversity of economic practices enables displacing capitalism from the hegemonic position it has occupied in political-economic analyses. If this is not done, analyses easily reproduce the dominant position of capitalism—they leave us "waiting for the revolution" (Gibson-Graham, 1993).

Decentring capitalism can also mean pluralising ontology and paying attention to socio-economic systems that exist before and/or parallel to capitalism. Scholars seeking to find alternatives to capitalist coloniality have analysed, for example, *buen vivir* (or *sumak kawsay*) in Ecuador (Ranta, 2020). Translated as "good life" or "life in harmony", *buen vivir* is an Andean "cosmovision" that centres the interconnectedness of nature and society, democratic participation, social solidarity, and environmental justice as the basis for socio-economic organisation (Calisto-Friant & Langmore, 2015, pp. 64–65). Emerging as a response to economic and social instability caused by neoliberal and neocolonial reforms of the 1990s, *buen vivir* is thus both the process and the objective of socially and ecologically sustainable economic practices (Villalba-Eguiluz & Pérez-de-Mendiguren, 2019). It is crucial, however, to recognise that, as well-intended as they may be, attempts to diversify and decentre capitalism by foregrounding cultures that manage the economy "differently" are not always unproblematic. Philipp Altmann points out that post-developmental and degrowth movements in the Global North promptly adopted *buen vivir* as "bases for the critique of capitalism and proposing alternatives to it" (Altmann, 2020, p. 83). However, this adaptation has largely rendered the indigenous and grassroots origins of the concept invisible, leading to a well-intended appropriation of the concept (Altmann, 2020).

Attempts to problematise anthropocentric analyses of economic action offer yet another way to decentre the concept of capitalism. This scholarship has pursued two main goals. First, scholars have critically evaluated capitalism's reliance on modernistic logics of environmental exploitation to serve the needs of humanity. They have pointed out how capitalist accumulation, in fact, depends on various non-capitalist forms of life-making, such as photosynthesis and animal metabolism, and then translates them into capitalist commodities (Tsing, 2015, p. 62). Second, scholars have pointed out that capitalism has informed not only such extractive practices but, with the "monoculture" of Eurocentric science and anthropocentric-patriarchal domination of nature, also contributed to the ontology and epistemology where natural environments are approached as commodities and resources freely available for management and exploitation (Oksala, 2023). Thus, this strand of decentring capitalism problematises modernist and anthropocentric knowledge by recentring more-than-human economies and human-nonhuman interactions and collaborations in analyses of economic activity (Jones, 2019; Roelvink et al., 2015).

Decentring capitalism from its human-centrism, however, should not mean that humans are homogenised into one group. Some scholars of capitalism have, indeed, emphasised the importance of acknowledging that climate change is taking the hardest toll on that part of the global population that is the least responsible for the historical greenhouse-gas emissions (Levy et al., 2023; IPCC, 2022). New concepts such as Capitalocene (Moore J., 2017) and Plantationocene (Moore S. et al., 2019) have also emerged to emphasise how various groups of humans are differentially situated within the political-economic systems that drive environmental destruction. They have been put forth to challenge the term Anthropocene, which was coined by certain geologists to emphasise the cumulative impact of human activities on the Earth's climate and ecosystems—and remains a debated concept also among them. With slightly different foci, the terms Capitalocene and Plantationocene remind us that capitalist environmental exploitation has historically intersected with colonial, racial, gender, and class exploitation. Destabilising the idea of a homogenous humanity behind the environmental catastrophe means acknowledging that "environmental problems cannot be decoupled from histories of colonialism, capitalism, and racism" and that these entanglements of extractivism "have made some human beings more vulnerable than others to warming temperatures, rising seas, toxic exposures, and land dispossession occurring across the globe" (Moore S. et al., 2019, para. 3).

The wider context of capitalism

Capitalism, as the discussion above also suggests, may be viewed as a social dynamic going beyond the sphere of exchange and economic contractual practices. Inquiries into the effects of capitalism on social life call attention to what lies beneath the economic surface phenomena. A classic here is Georg Simmel's *Philosophy of Money*. It was published in the early 20th century and examines money as a generalised social fact (Simmel, 2011). Simmel argues that economic phenomena should not be approached as just "economic facts". Rather, the symbolic form of commodities places them firmly in the sphere of culture and social relations affecting all classes in a capitalist economy (Lemert, 2001, p. xi).

Before Simmel, Marx had already emphasised the impact of the capitalist mode of production on social relations. In the third volume of *Capital*, Marx characterises the capitalist mode of production through three key features. First, as production is geared toward the production of commodities, the commodity form comes to define all social relations (Marx, 1991, p. 869). Second, commodity production starts to serve the more overarching goal of the production of surplus-value—this is the rule of capital, which is not the same as the rule of capitalists (Marx, 1991, p. 869). And capital, as Marx writes in *Capital I* (Marx, 1990, p. 932), "is not a thing but a social relation between persons which is mediated through things" (see also Krätke, 2020, p. 7). Moreover, Marx saw the social relation between capital and wage labour as something fundamentally characteristic of the capitalist mode of production (Marx, 2007).

Feminist political economists have further expanded the "hidden abode of production" that, Marx argued, needs to be analysed besides the sphere of exchange to better grasp the capitalist mode of production (Marx, 1990, p. 279). Feminist social reproduction theorists argue that analyses of capitalism need to pay attention not just to its front story but also its societal conditions of possibility: Marx, they point out, may have had a lot to say about the dynamics of production but he did not sufficiently recognise the role of social reproduction (Fraser, 2017). Social reproduction theorists alert us to the fact that for the capitalist economy to function, for people to be able to take up wage work and show up at the gates of factories or office buildings as productive wage labourers, they need to be nourished, nurtured, and socialised. Moreover, this activity often goes unremunerated (Bhattacharya, 2017; Hoppania & Vaittinen, 2015). Feminist political economists underscore that this dynamism has been deeply gendered historically: "the split between 'productive' waged work and unwaged 'reproductive' labour has underpinned modern capitalist forms of women's subordination as reproduction has been associated with women and production with men" (Fraser, 2017, p. 148).

Indeed, there is a plethora of 'non-economic' institutions that are crucial for the functioning of capitalism. For commodities to be sold, they must be appealing to consumers, who in turn need to have the capacity to purchase them. Many scholars have argued that capitalism is animated as much by this "acquisitive manner of life" (Weber, 2001, pp. 33–34) as by the system or mode of production. In 1970, Jean Baudrillard (1998, p. 44) argued that the economy is consumption-based; mass production has led to mass consumption, but crucially, consumer society thrives on our obsession with acquiring things we do not need, which has led to a myth of growth meaning affluence and affluence leading to democracy. Commodities produced for markets include much more than mere 'stuff', for example, mass culture items (e.g. Adorno, 1991), digital technologies and services (e.g. Betancourt, 2016), and services produced by other embodied beings, such as healthcare or beauty services (e.g. McDowell, 2009). This has spawned yet another set of pet names for the capitalist economy and its institutions: mass industry, digital capitalism, and service economy.

Observing the way in which the concept of capitalism has been used by social scientists, we can see that there is generally a recognition of the interconnectedness of the economy to the broader societal fabric or other spheres of life. However, this has sparked criticism that, as the conception of capitalism expands, the economic practices that are specific to capitalist societies may receive too little attention. This point is made, for example, by Jaeggi (2017) in her attempt to renew the *Kapitalismuskritik* tradition associated with the Frankfurt School of Critical Theory through an immanent critique of forms of life organised around a subset of social practices that relate to property, market and exchange, as well as labour and production.

Is capitalism good or bad?

It is sometimes argued that the term 'capitalism' is predominantly used by its critics, inherently implying a critical perspective (e.g. Delanty & Harris, 2023, p. 1). The argument here is that those who relate to this economic system more neutrally or positively would use some alternative terms such as the economy or markets. However, this conception is also worth troubling. Despite his reputation as an archetypical critic of capitalism, Marx saw the bourgeoisie play the most revolutionary part in world history. He was driven by a curiosity to learn how the capitalist mode of production was able to generate massive misery for some and so much wealth for others—or, for "our friend, Moneybag" (Ascher, 2016, pp. 4–5). Marx certainly recognised the social evils associated with capitalism but also saw it as a powerhouse of technological development and scientific discoveries. Michael Krätke (2020, p. 20) argues that Marx "saw capitalism not as a wrong track leading mankind astray from its 'true' destination, but as a necessary and largely progressive stage in human history"—nevertheless, one that would eventually weaken and collapse due to its internal contradictions.

After Marx, many scholars have approached capitalism in a demonstrably positive sense. Joseph Schumpeter's well-known book *Capitalism, Socialism and Democracy,* which dates from 1942, is a defence of capitalism on the grounds that capitalism as an economic system can spark entrepreneurship. Based on a close reading of Marx's work, Schumpeter suggests that capitalism relates to entrepreneurship, as well as innovations. Innovations then lead to tides or what Schumpeter famously referred to as gales of creative destruction. Schumpeter's idea was that this creative destruction at the heart of capitalism causes continuous progress. It was a positive term in the sense that progress would then improve the standards of living for everyone. Also, for Gary Becker, representing the Chicago School of economics, "capitalism with free markets is the most effective system yet devised for raising both economic well-being and political freedom" (Kocka, 2018, p. 84)

Those who emphasize the benefits of capitalism often point out that since the capitalist revolution in the 18th century, increases in living standards have become a permanent feature of economic life in many parts of the world. This is referred to as the "history's hockey stick" to call to mind a graph that takes the shape of a hockey stick lying on the ground with its blade poking up in the air. The handle of the stick represents the centuries of low or no growth, and the upward-pointing blade stands for the sudden speeding up of economic growth after the industrial revolution (Bowles et al., 2017). However, global inequalities persist despite the growth and increase in living standards. As Thomas Piketty (2022, p. 2) notes, the tendency toward equality since the eighteenth century is steady and real. Nevertheless, "different inequalities have persisted at considerable and unjustified levels on all these dimensions—status, property, power, income, gender, origin, and so on—and moreover, that individuals often face inequalities in combination." This leads Piketty (2019) to view capitalism as an ideology that legitimises and perpetuates these inequalities.

There are also other "hockey sticks" in the rink of capitalism. The hockey stick-shaped graph by Mann, Bradley, and Hughes (1999) points out that temperature has risen with industrialisation and the increase in the use of fossil fuels. It shows temperature remaining somewhat flat until about 1900 but then shooting up like the upturned blade of a hockey stick. This has been taken to suggest that while capitalism has, indeed, improved living standards globally, the dependence of economic growth on fossil fuels has left a lasting impact on the planet. Scholars writing about fossil capitalism argue that given the centrality of fossil fuels in the development of capitalism, addressing climate change through decarbonisation would fundamentally disrupt capitalism's ability and necessity to grow. Altvater (2007, pp. 39, 41–42) emphasises that "at the centre of capitalism's relation to nature is its inherent and unavoidable dependence on fossil fuels, particularly on oil"; this manifests in a "perfect congruence" between the physical properties of fossil energy and the political and socioeconomic logics of capitalism.

Recognising that severing the dependence on economic growth requires a massive restructuring of today's capitalist societies, degrowth scholars have put forth proposals about other-than-capitalist institutions, or institutions "beyond growth" (Durand, Hofferberth, & Schmelzer, 2024). Degrowth is not only a strand of scholarly research critiquing the technology-fused promise of "green growth" based on the idea of decoupling economic growth from resource use but also a movement that includes a wide set of grassroots practices of doing economy differently (Kenis & Lievens, 2016) or of pursuing "good life" (Rosa & Henning, 2018). Concerned with the ecological and social toll of capitalist arrangements, Kallis et al. (2018, p. 292) describe degrowth as a way "to organise a transition and live well under a different political-economic system that has a radically smaller resource throughput." Although prominent especially in the academic debate and social movements of the Global North, some scholars have emphasised the importance of bridging the gap between degrowth and Indigenous knowledges and protest movements from the Global South (Nirmal & Rocheleau, 2019). Schmelzer and Nowshin (2023) propose the combination of degrowth in the Global North and ecological reparation to the Global South as a way to address the damage done by capitalism.

By contrast, some have suggested that capitalism might still hold the keys to solving the ecological crisis. Or, given how urgent the task is and how slow socio-techno-political systems are to change, some claim that it is realistic to see capitalism at least as a part of the solution. As Peter Newell and Matthew Paterson (2011, p. 23) suggest in conjunction with their discussion of climate capitalism, "whether we like it or not, for the foreseeable future at least, responses to climate change will be developed in a context of global capitalism." This, however, cannot happen in the context of "capitalism as usual"; capitalism has to transform itself (Newell & Paterson, 2011, p. 25). A new capitalist political economy to ensure the survival of the planet has also been envisaged by Rebecca Henderson (2023). For her, it entails transforming markets, institutions, as well as policy regimes. As Henderson outlines in a book entitled *Reimagining Capitalism* (2020), purpose-driven organisations are at the heart of a reformed capitalism: when building prosperity, business organisations need to put the needs of a liveable planet and a healthy society first, finance needs to be rewired, externalities appropriately priced, cooperation harnessed to solve public goods problems, and governments must find new ways to function.

Cracking open the spaces of capitalism

Motivated by the idea that capitalism is troubling and that this makes its study worth the trouble, this introductory chapter has explored routes through which social scientists have examined capitalism or analysed capitalist practices. Much has been written on how the economics discipline, specifically its neoclassical variant, has occupied a position of hegemony and naturalised a particular set of assumptions and methodologies not only in the scholarly study of the economy but also in policy-making and public perception of economic issues. However, as this chapter shows, a rich and varied body of knowledge is already available for those interested in theorising and retheorising the economy and capitalism otherwise. As Doreen Massey (2014, p. 2041) reminds us, while hegemonies are established by making things seem like a closed space without an outside, they are not totalities, "closed spaces of an immanentist ontology." An effective way to crack open such spaces is to pay attention to the existing diversity. This diversity is not just theoretical, epistemological, and methodological but also ontological, as the preceding mapping of different ways to approach the capitalist economy in research shows.

The chapters in this book further contribute to the task of diversifying the available knowledge. As the book has been assembled in the spirit of engaged pluralism (e.g., Bernstein, 1989), our intention has not been to propose another conceptual framework, theory, or totalising alternative—not to mention another system to "replace" capitalism. What unites the contributions is that they are all motivated by the pressing need to come up with new and inventive ways of studying, analysing, and relating to the economy. Further fostering this diversity, we believe, can make us capable of not only critically scrutinising capitalism but also engaging in acts of imagination and experimentation. Amidst the escalating polycrisis, there is an urgent need for political-economic imaginaries that align with the planet's carrying capacities. The following chapters offer pathways to explore some of them.

References

Acemoglu, D., & Robinson, J. A. (2015). The rise and decline of general laws of capitalism. *The Journal of Economic Perspectives, 29*(1), 3–28. https://doi.org/10.1257/jep.29.1.3

Adorno, T. W. (1991). *The culture industry: Selected essays on mass culture.* Routledge.

Agnew, J. (1994). The territorial trap: The geographical assumptions of international relations theory. *Review of International Political Economy, 1*(1), 53–80. https://doi.org/10.1080/09692299408434268

Ahlqvist, T., & Moisio, S. (2014). Neoliberalisation in a Nordic state: From carter polity towards a corporate polity in Finland. *New Political Economy, 19*(1), 21–55. https://doi.org/10.1080/13563467.2013.768613

Alami, I., Whiteside, H., Dixon, A. D., & Peck, J. (2023). Making space for the new state capitalism, part II: Relationality, spatiotemporality and uneven development. *Environment and Planning A: Economy and Space, 55*(3), 621–635. https://doi.org/10.1177/0308518X231156913

Altmann, P. (2020). The commons as colonisation – The well-intentioned appropriation of Buen Vivir. *Bulletin of Latin American Research, 39*(1), 83–97. https://doi.org/10.1111/blar.12941

Altvater, E. (2007). The social and natural environment of fossil capitalism. *Socialist Register, 43*, 37–59.

Anievas, A., & Nisancioglu, K. (2015). *How the West came to rule: The geopolitical origins of capitalism.* Pluto Press.

Ascher, I. (2016). "Moneybags must be so lucky": Inside the hidden abode of prediction. *Political Theory, 44*(1), 4–25. https://doi.org/10.1177/0090591715613387

Bair, J. (2023). Where is the world in the new state capitalism? *Environment and Planning A: Economy and Space, 55*(3), 770–773. https://doi.org/10.1177/0308518X231160543

Baudrillard, J. (1998). *The consumer society: Myths and structures.* Sage.

Beckert, S., & Rockman, S. (2016). *Slavery's capitalism: A new history of American economic development.* University of Pennsylvania Press.

Bernstein, R. J. (1989). Pragmatism, pluralism and the healing of wounds. *Proceedings and Addresses of the American Philosophical Association, 63*(3), 5–18. https://doi.org/10.2307/3130079

Betancourt, M. (2020). *The critique of digital capitalism: An analysis of the political economy of digital culture and technology.* Punctum Books.

Bhattacharya, T. (2017). *Social reproduction theory: Remapping class, recentering oppression.* Pluto Press.

Bowles, S., Carlin, W., Jayadev, A., & Stevens, M. (2017). The capitalist revolution. In The CORE team, *The economy.* https://www.core-econ.org

Bruff, I. (2014). The rise of authoritarian neoliberalism. *Rethinking Marxism, 26*(1), 113–129. https://doi.org/10.1080/08935696.2013.843250

Bruff, I., & Tansel, C. B. (2019). Authoritarian neoliberalism: Trajectories of knowledge production and praxis. *Globalizations, 16*(3), 233–244. https://doi.org/10.1080/14747731.2018.1502497

Calisto Friant, M., & Langmore, J. (2015). The Buen Vivir: A policy to survive the Anthropocene? *Global Policy, 6*(1), 64–71. https://doi.org/10.1111/1758-5899.12187

Chancel, L., Piketty, T., Saez, E., & Zucman, G. (2022). *World inequality report 2022*. Harvard University Press. https://doi.org/10.4159/9780674276598

Coates, D. (2005). Paradigms of explanation. In D. Coates (Ed.), *Varieties of capitalism, varieties of approaches* (1st ed., pp. 1–25). Palgrave Macmillan. https://doi.org/10.1057/9780230522725

Davis, A. Y. (2003). *Are prisons obsolete?* Seven Stories Press.

Dean, M. (2002). Liberal government and authoritarianism. *Economy and Society, 31*(1), 37–61. https://doi.org/10.1080/03085140120109240

Delanty, G., & Harris, N. (2023). *Capitalism and its critics: Capitalism in social and political theory*. Routledge.

Duque Acosta, C. A., Orozco Holguín, J. L., & Quintero Uribe, V. M. (2022). Cosmovisión, buen vivir y planes de vida. *LumGent, 6*(2), 75–87. https://doi.org/10.52525/lg.v6n2a5

Durand, C., Hofferberth, E., & Schmelzer, M. (2024). Planning beyond growth: The case for economic democracy within ecological limits. *Journal of Cleaner Production, 437*. https://doi.org/10.1016/j.jclepro.2023.140351

Fabry, A. (2019). *The political economy of Hungary: From state capitalism to authoritarian neoliberalism*. Springer International Publishing. https://doi.org/10.1007/978-3-030-10594-5

Fisher, M. (2009). *Capitalist realism: Is there no alternative?* Zero Books.

Fraser, N. (2017). Behind Marx's hidden abode: For an expanded conception of capitalism. In P. Deutscher & C. Lafont (Eds.), *Critical theory in critical times: Transforming the global political and economic order* (pp. 149–159). Columbia University Press.

Fukuyama, F. (1992). *The end of history and the last man*. Penguin.

Galbraith, J. K. (2009). *The predator state: How conservatives abandoned the free market and why liberals should too*. Free Press.

Gataulina, I. (2024). *De/re/composing authoritarian-neoliberal assemblages: Ethnography of Russian universities and beyond* [Doctoral dissertation]. Tampere University.

Gibson-Graham, J. K. (1993). Waiting for the revolution, or how to smash capitalism while working at home in your spare time. *Rethinking Marxism, 6*(2), 10–24. https://doi.org/10.1080/08935699308658052

Gibson-Graham, J. K. (1996). *The end of capitalism (as we knew it): A feminist critique of political economy*. University of Minnesota Press.

Gibson-Graham, J. K. (2006). *A postcapitalist politics*. University of Minnesota Press.

Google Ngram. (n.d.). Capitalism. Retrieved May 1, 2024, from https://books.google.com/ngrams

Hall, P., & Soskice, D. (2001). *Varieties of capitalism: The institutional foundations of comparative advantage*. Oxford University Press.

Haraway, D. (2016). *Staying with the trouble: Making kin in the Chthulucene*. Duke University Press.

Henderson, R. (2020). *Reimagining capitalism in a world on fire*. Public Affairs Books.

Henderson, R. (2023). Moral firms? *Daedalus, 152*(1), 198–211. https://doi.org/10.1162/daed_a_01979

Hodgson, G. M. (2015). *Conceptualizing capitalism: Institutions, evolution, future*. The University of Chicago Press

Hoppania, H.-K., & Vaittinen, T. (2015). A household full of bodies: Neoliberalism, care and "the political." *Global Society, 29*(1), 70–88. https://doi.org/10.1080/13600826.2014.974515

Ichinkhorloo, B. (2018). Collaboration for survival in the age of the market: Diverse economic practices in postsocialist Mongolia. *Central Asian Survey, 37*(3), 386–402. https://doi.org/10.1080/02634937.2018.1501347

Intergovernmental Panel on Climate Change (IPCC). (2022). Summary for policymakers. In H.-O. Pörtner, D. C. Roberts, E. S. Poloczanska, K. Mintenbeck, M. Tignor, A. Alegría, M. Craig, S. Langsdorf, S. Löschke, V. Möller, A. Okem, & B. Rama (Eds.), *Climate change 2022: Impacts, adaptation, and vulnerability. Contribution of Working Group II to the Sixth Assessment Report of the Intergovernmental Panel on Climate Change* (pp. 3–34). Cambridge University Press. https://doi.org/10.1017/9781009325844.001

Jaeggi, R. (2017). A wide concept of economy. In *Critical theory in critical times* (pp. 160–180). Columbia University Press. https://doi.org/10.7312/deut18150-010

Jones, B. (2019). (Com)Post-capitalism: Cultivating a more-than-human economy in the Appalachian Anthropocene. *Environmental Humanities, 11*(1), 3–26. https://doi.org/10.1215/22011919-7349347

Kallis, G., Kostakis, V., Lange, S., Muraca, B., Paulson, S., & Schmelzer, M. (2018). Research on degrowth. *Annual Review of Environment and Resources, 43*(1), 291–316. https://doi.org/10.1146/annurev-environ-102017-025941

Kenis, A., & Lievens, M. (2016). Greening the economy or economizing the green project? When environmental concerns are turned into a means to save the market. *Review of Radical Political Economics, 48*(2), 217–234. https://doi.org/10.1177/0486613415591803

Kocka, J. (2018). Capitalism and its critics: A long-term view. In U. Bosma & K. Hofmeester (Eds.), *The lifework of a labor historian: Essays in honor of Marcel van der Linden* (pp. 71–89). Brill.

Kornai, J. (2021). *The socialist system: The political economy of communism*. Princeton University Press.

Kornbluh, A. (2024). *Immediacy: Or, the style of too late capitalism*. Verso.

Krätke, M. (2020). Capitalism. In M. Musto (Ed.), *The Marx revival* (pp. 1–23). Cambridge University Press. https://doi.org/10.1017/9781316338902.002

Kuokkanen, R. J. (2011). Indigenous economies, theories of subsistence and women: Exploring the social economy model for indigenous governance. *American Indian Quarterly, 35*(2), 215–240.

Larousse. (n.d.). Troubler. Retrieved May 1, 2024, from https://www.larousse.fr/dictionnaires/francais/troubler/80002

LeBaron, G. (Ed.). (2018). *Researching forced labour in the global economy: Methodological challenges and advances*. Oxford University Press.

Lemert, C. (2011). Money? Really! Foreword to the Routledge Classics Edition. In Simmel, G. *The philosophy of money* (pp. iix–xii). Routledge.

Levy, S. R., Gopang, M., Ramírez, L., Bernardo, A. B. I., Ruck, M. D., & Sternisko, A. (2024). A human rights-based approach to climate injustices at the local, national, and international levels: Program and policy recommendations. *Social Issues and Policy Review, 18*(1), 3–30. https://doi.org/10.1111/sipr.12103

Lierse, H., Sachweh, P., & Waitkus, N. (2022). Introduction: Wealth, inequality and redistribution in capitalist societies. *Social Justice Research, 35*, 367–378. https://doi.org/10.1007/s11211-022-00402-6

Mann, M. E., Bradley, R. S., & Hughes, M. K. (1999). Northern hemisphere temperatures during the past millennium: Inferences, uncertainties, and limitations. *Geophysical Research Letters, 26*(6), 759–762. https://doi.org/10.1029/1999GL900070

Marks, S. (2016). *The information nexus: Global capitalism from the Renaissance to the present.* Cambridge University Press.

Marx, K. (1990). *Capital: A critique of political economy. Volume I.* Penguin Classics.

Marx, K. (1991). *Capital: A critique of political economy. Volume III.* Penguin Classics.

Marx, K. (2007). *Economic and philosophic manuscripts of 1844.* Dover Publications.

Massey, D. (2014). Symposium: The Kilburn Manifesto: After neoliberalism? *Environment and Planning A: Economy and Space, 46*(9), 2033–2049. https://doi.org/10.1068/akilburn

Mazzucato, M., Ryan-Collins, J., & Gouzoulis, G. (2023). Mapping modern economic rents: The good, the bad, and the grey areas. *Cambridge Journal of Economics, 47*(3), 507–534. https://doi.org/10.1093/cje/bead013

McDowell, L. (2009). *Working bodies: Interactive service employment and workplace identities.* Wiley-Blackwell.

McGuigan, J. (2009). *Cool capitalism.* Pluto.

Moisio, S., & Rossi, U. (2024). *The urban field: Capital and governmentality in the age of techno-monopoly.* Agenda Publishing.

Moore, J. W. (2017). The Capitalocene, part I: On the nature and origins of our ecological crisis. *The Journal of Peasant Studies, 44*(3), 594–630. https://doi.org/10.1080/03066150.2016.1235036

Moore, S. S., Allewaert, M., Gómez, P. F., & Mitman, G. (2019, January 22). Plantation legacies. *Edge Effects.* https://edgeeffects.net/plantation-legacies-plantationocene/

Newell, P., & Paterson, M. (2011). Climate capitalism. In E. Altvater & A. Brunnengräber (Eds.), *After Cancún* (pp. 23–44). VS Verlag für Sozialwissenschaften.

Nirmal, P., & Rocheleau, D. (2019). Decolonizing degrowth in the post-development convergence: Questions, experiences, and proposals from two Indigenous territories. *Environment and Planning E: Nature and Space, 2*(3), 465–492. https://doi.org/10.1177/2514848618819478

North, D. C. (1990). *Institutions, institutional change and economic performance.* Cambridge University Press.

Nørgård, J., & Xue, J. (2016). Between green growth and degrowth: Decoupling, rebound effects and the politics for long-term sustainability. In T. Santarius, H. J. Walnum, & C. Aall (Eds.), *Rethinking climate and energy policies* (pp. 267–284). Springer International Publishing. https://doi.org/10.1007/978-3-319-38807-6_15

O'Reilly, T., Strauss, I., & Mazzucato, M. (2024). Algorithmic attention rents: A theory of digital platform market power. *Data & Policy, 6*(e6), 1–25.

Oksala, J. (2023). *Feminism, capitalism, and ecology* (1st ed.). Northwestern University Press. https://doi.org/10.2307/jj.2840675

Ortiz-Ospina, E. (2017, September 29). Historical poverty reductions: More than a story about 'free-market capitalism'. OurWorldInData.org. https://ourworldindata.org/historical-poverty-reductions-more-than-a-story-about-free-market-capitalism

Papadopoulos, D., Puig de la Bellacasa, M., & Tacchetti, M. (Eds.). (2023). *Ecological reparation: Repair, remediation and resurgence in social and environmental conflict.* Bristol University Press.

Perkins, P. E. (Ed.). (2023). *Climate justice and participatory research: Building climate-resilient commons.* University of Calgary, LCR Publishing Services.

Piketty, T. (2019). Capital et idéologie. Éditions du Seuil.

Piketty, T. (2022). *A brief history of equality.* Harvard University Press.

Ranta, E. (2020). Toward human/non-human conviviality: Buen Vivir as a transformative alternative to capitalist coloniality. In *The Routledge handbook of transformative global studies* (pp. 419–430). Routledge.

Rauhala, P. (2023). *Marx in the West and in the East: Reading Capital in the divided Germany.* [Doctoral dissertation]. Tampere University. https://urn.fi/URN:ISBN:978-952-03-2802-3

Robinson, C. J. (1983). *Black Marxism: The making of the black radical tradition.* University of North Carolina Press.

Roelvink, G., St. Martin, K., & Gibson-Graham, J. K. (2015). *Making other worlds possible: Performing diverse economies* (1st ed.). University of Minnesota Press.

Rosa, H., & Henning, C. (2018). *The good life beyond growth: New perspectives.* Routledge.

Sanghera, B., & Satybaldieva, E. (2023). Rentier capitalism and global economic imaginaries in Central Asia. *Globalizations, ahead-of-print* (ahead-of-print), 1–21. https://doi.org/10.1080/14747731.2023.2234173

Schmelzer, M., & Nowshin, T. (2023). Ecological reparations and degrowth: Towards a convergence of alternatives around world-making after growth. *Development, 66*(1–2), 15–22. https://doi.org/10.1057/s41301-023-00360-9

Schmidt, V. A. (2009). Putting the political back into political economy by bringing the state back in yet again. *World Politics, 61*(3), 516–546. https://doi.org/10.1017/S0043887109000173

Simmel, G. (2011). *The philosophy of money.* Routledge.

Sonenscher, M. (2022). *Capitalism: The story behind the word.* Princeton University Press.

Stratford, B. (2023). Rival definitions of economic rent: Historical origins and normative implications. *New Political Economy, 28*(3), 347–362.

Thackeray, W. M. (2010). *Newcomes: Memoirs of a most respectable family.* The Floating Press.

Tsing, A. L. (2015). *The mushroom at the end of the world: On the possibility of life in capitalist ruins.* Princeton University Press.

Villalba-Eguiluz, U., & Pérez-de-Mendiguren, J. C. (2019). The social and solidarity economy as a way to "buen vivir." *Revista Iberoamericana de Estudios de Desarrollo, 8*(1), 106–136. https://doi.org/10.26754/ojs_ried/ijds.338

Weber, M. (2001). *The Protestant ethic and the spirit of capitalism.* Routledge.

Williams, E. E., Darity, W. A., & Palmer, C. A. (2021). *Capitalism & slavery.* The University of North Carolina Press.
Wolf, M. (2023). *The crisis of democratic capitalism.* Penguin.
Wright, E. O. (2019). *How to be an anti-capitalist in the 21st century.* Verso.
Yang, M. M. (2000). Putting global capitalism in its place: Economic hybridity, Bataille, and ritual expenditure. *Current Anthropology, 41*(4), 477–494. https://doi.org/10.1086/317380
Zuboff, S. (2019). *The age of surveillance capitalism: The fight for a human future at the new frontier of power.* PublicAffairs.

Part I
Representing

Iuliia Gataulina

Theorising is an act that not only depicts the social world in specific terms; it cuts the world into specific shapes and generates representations with a performative force. The dominant representations of and about capitalism shape not only our theoretical lenses but also socio-political realities themselves (Barad, 2007; Gibson-Graham, 2006, p. xl). The chapters assembled in this part of the book scrutinise and challenge some of the powerful stories that narrate the past, present, and future of capitalism. This may be achieved by bringing to light elements previously outside our theoretical narrations, focusing on lived experiences, exploring the possibilities of experiencing otherwise, or narrating the history of capitalism in different terms. In this sense, the focus on representing also reminds us that the very act of knowledge production is a political terrain—an action, a responsibility, and a creative opportunity. It influences our "possibilities of difference and change, including the potential for successful political interventions" (Gibson-Graham, 2006, p. xl). This part of the book includes three chapters that challenge the prevailing narratives and representations of capitalism, revealing social dynamics that are not determined solely by capitalist forces.

In a chapter entitled "Reading regenerative vegetable farming for difference" (Chapter 2), Kerry Woodward approaches farming as a performative act: it is always in the process of being made and unmade through a multiplicity of human and more-than-human agencies. The question of representation is present here in the sense that the chapter destabilises the monolithic and dominant capitalocentric narrative of agriculture, which typically presents farming as a human-centred enterprise where profit and calories reign supreme. In this task, Woodward draws on the scholarship of diverse economies and illuminates a range of economic, more-than-capitalist, and more-than-human interactions that sustain farming practices.

The chapter "A proposal for a scatological global political economy—or, making sense of capitalism through a shit-smeared lens" (Chapter 3) by Anna Ilona Rajala analyses the political economy of defecation. It demonstrates how that which can be reparative and life-giving in one setting can cause damage and extensive harm in another. In concrete terms, the chapter delves into the human and planetary dimensions of shit. The author's proposal for a scatological global political economy plays with the possibilities of representation by calling attention to those things deemed disgusting, like human excrement, and discusses their importance in retheorising capitalism from the perspective of global (in)equality, relations of care, and ecological crisis. According to Rajala, faeces are central to "both the survival and destruction of life on earth." It is, therefore, essential to take the "position of shit" (Cohen, 2016)—to inquire what economic arrangements and political decisions further the reparative dimensions of excrement and which cause harm to human bodies, communities, and ecosystems.

The chapter entitled "The capitalist's apprentice: employment and the reproduction of capitalist culture" (Chapter 4) by Mark L. Young retheorises employer-employee relations in the Anglo-American context from a historical perspective. The chapter reveals capitalist relations as less emphasised in the era of perceived individual emancipation offered by capitalist employment. It illuminates how social relations under capitalist employment historically carry over many feudal elements, which manifest in paternalistic relations of control, still visible in modern capitalism. This challenges the commonplace representation of a shift from feudalism to capitalism as a democratic system of economic opportunity. It also forces attention on the capitalist dynamics of social control and exploitation.

References

Barad, K. (2007). *Meeting the universe halfway.* Duke University Press.

Cohen, S. (2016). Shit. In M. B. Salter (Ed.), *Making things international 2* (pp. 285–298). University of Minnesota Press.

Gibson-Graham, J. K. (1996). *The end of capitalism (as we knew it): A feminist critique of political economy.* University of Minnesota Press.

2
Reading regenerative vegetable farming for difference

Kerry Woodward

A story about agriculture and capitalism many of us are now familiar with begins with the enclosure of commons in Europe by the nobility and Church. Peasants who had lived with some freedom and ownership over the means of production were locked into servitude, they lost the means of production and the ability to grow food for themselves and their families, while surplus extraction and taxation became significantly easier for the rent-seeking aristocracy and clergy (Hickel, 2021). People in the majority world soon found themselves tied into the insatiable march for land and agriculture from wealthy elites in Europe. Colonial conquests violently extracted agricultural surplus and land from colonised peoples and territories to feed consumers in Europe, and to build colonial wealth (Bellamy Foster, 2016). For food, this meant products such as sugar, tea, and coffee, but also tobacco and cotton for the burgeoning working classes in industrial cities. As part of making territories legible so that they could be controlled and taxed, states undertook to radically simplify a range of socio-economic and ecological processes. Agriculture was standardised and simplified through land consolidation and monocropping (Scott, 1999). This approach to farming lent itself to capture for wealth accumulation and degraded subsistence farming underpinned by disparate local knowledges. Indeed, for centuries, capitalist food production, organised around extracting surplus value from workers and from the land, has continued to displace subsistence agriculture across the globe (Bello, 2009).

Woodward, K. (2025). Reading regenerative vegetable farming for difference. In A. Kangas, I. Gataulina, M. Poutanen, A. I. Rajala & H-E Ventovirta (Eds.), *Retheorising capitalism* (pp. 33–49). Tampere University Press.
https://doi.org/10.61201/tup.981

In the 20th century, the crystallisation of a globalised food system has been characterised by agricultural liberalisation, intellectual property rights, expanding gene revolution technologies, increasing industrial production, land grabbing, and the development of corporate agribusiness monopolies (Holt Giménez & Shattuck, 2011; McMichael, 2012). The global food system specialises in producing commodities. As a commodity, food's primary attribute is price (or its profitability), and the key aim of food production is to sell more in order to make more profit (Magdoff, 2012). Profitability is also affected by smaller margins between the cost of production and the market price of produce. This, in turn, means that corporate actors are implicated in demanding ever cheaper food, which can come at the cost of workers' rights, lower food quality, and environmental degradation.

It is difficult to deny that this story holds up to scrutiny. We only need to look at the extent of land grabs, the dominance that a handful of agribusinesses have over food provisioning across the world, the relentless deforestation to grow more commodity crops for feed, food and industry, or the role that commodity price speculation plays in destabilizing food prices locally in many parts of the world, making basic foodstuffs out of reach for millions.

This story rings true in the Australian context. Indigenous peoples were murdered and displaced, the Country they lived on was taken and parcelled out to or squatted by settlers to raise sheep for wool, and later on wheat, sugar and other grain crops (Bromby, 1989). Today, large farms account for the most market share, as well as productivity gains (narrowly defined in yields and income) in Australia (Jackson et al., 2018). Large farms have increased in number over the past few decades, and their share of output and land has increased even more (Jackson et al., 2018). The increasing corporatisation of farming in Australia has been driven by government policies that favour market solutions and deregulation (Botterill, 2016; Lawrence et al., 2013). While small and medium farms are disappearing, food production and supply chains are increasingly concentrated too. For instance, supermarkets have significant control over food distribution being the chief markets for food sales. Just two supermarket chains account for almost two-thirds of the grocery and food market in Australia (Commonwealth of Australia, 2023).

The chief concern in this story is that capitalist modes of knowing, being and doing drive farming practices that contribute to several planetary and human crises, such as climate change, deforestation, wildlife extinction, and water pollution. The story implores us to look to farming and food provisioning that operate beyond the logic of capitalism.

Telling other tales of agriculture

The evidence for the dominance of capitalist ways of knowing, being and doing agriculture is compelling. Yet, this story is not the whole picture, it does not account for the range of farming and food provisioning practices that are non-capitalist, or perhaps alter-capitalist (e.g. Cameron and Wright, 2014; Goodman et al., 2013; Nelson and Edwards, 2021). There are fewer official data on the extent of non-capitalist food provisioning in Australia than there are on formal, capitalist modes of farming. For instance, the Australian Bureau of Statistics and the Australian Bureau of Agricultural and Resource Economics and Sciences are predominantly concerned with data on farm businesses that have agricultural operations of $40,000 or more. This is no doubt linked to the capitalocentrism of both economic policy and food systems, and reflects an ongoing desire to maximise exports and taxes. Capitalocentrism refers to the way in which we relate all human economic activities to capitalism, they are either capitalist, or they are subordinate to, or in the orbit of capitalism (Gibson-Graham, 1996). In fact, the story that this chapter begins with is a capitalocentric tale, albeit a tale that is critical of capitalism.

A key strand that runs through capitalocentric narratives of farming is that farming is a human enterprise where profits and calories reign supreme. Non-humans, or earth-kin[1], are only acknowledged in as far as they contribute to or disrupt growing. Those that contribute to growing food are commodified or forced into a kind of slavery, those that disrupt food growing are maligned, managed or killed. Yet, earth-kin are integral to farming, without their labour and care, humans would simply not have anything to eat. Indeed, recognition of the agency of non-humans, both animate and inanimate has long been recognised in cultures around the world—such as Aboriginal cultures in Australia (Bawaka Country et al., 2015; Milroy & Milroy, 2008), where this research took place. In more recent times, scholars in science and technology and new-materialist studies have also given attention to the liveliness of things (e.g. Barad 2007, Latour 2007, Bennet 2010).

Objects, animals, microbes, plants and minerals are not simply inert and waiting to be acted upon by humans, they do things in the world, they act on and with others. In farming, tools allow a range of practices to take place, or assemblages to form. For instance, sowing one thousand hectares of wheat would not be possible without a tractor, in this sense the tractor allows a particular form of farming to exist. Buying fresh mangoes in southern or northern cities would not be possible without a range of machines and objects, such as trucks, diesel and boxes. Integrated pest management is not possible without parasitic wasps, hoverflies or ladybugs. Yet at the same time,

1 Karulkiyalu Country et al. (2021, p. 216) use Earth-kin to account for everything they share Country with including "rocks, plants, waterways, animals, fire, weather, seasons, sun, moon, and stars". Inspired by Val Plumwood's notion of earth others, Karulkiyalu Country et al.'s use of earth-kin highlights connection rather than otherness. Country is an Aboriginal English word to speak of the connection, interdependence, liveliness and agency of the places that we inhabit (Bawaka Country et al., 2015). In research undertaken with Country, some researchers include that Country as a co-author. Such a move is an acknowledgement of the agency of Country, and the ways in which it is bound up in the research's becoming.

it is also not possible without mites, thrips or aphids. This last example points to the wanted and unwanted—by humans at least—nature of earth-kin. Humans may do their best to control more-than-human worlds, but we are ultimately only one part of the lively worlds we inhabit, though we are a part that has a significant impact (Puig de la Bellacasa, 2017).

Farming can also be seen as performative. Farming is never given but is always in the process of being made by the intra-action of various constitutive agencies. Barad's (2007) account of performativity holds that worlds are made by the iterative intra-action of entanglements of both material (human and not) agencies and semiotic forces such as discourse, language and representation. Material-semiotic agencies create the worlds they inhabit—there are no given entities or identities that beget their expression. Following this logic, farming can be seen to occur at the interface of diverse more-than-human agencies coming together.

Bringing together the notion of capitalocentrism and plantations, Savinotko (Hyvärinen, 2020)[2] uses the phrase plantationocentrism to highlight the dominance of plantations in food production and the way in which other forms of food production are marginalised or rendered invisible. Most significantly for this chapter, in their work they show how mushroom foraging (a practice that is marginal to plantation production) cannot be separated from plantations; in fact, it is within the plantations that mushroom foraging occurs. Thus, plantation and subsistence, capitalist and non-capitalist are entangled. This is very much the story for many non-capitalist farming practices, they may endeavour to be other than capitalist but must also acquiesce in many ways to always being with capitalist modes of knowing, being and doing. Plantationocentric or capitalocentric narratives of farming can limit transformative possibilities by delegitimising non-capitalist ways of farming, or by failing to see possibilities in farm enterprises supposed to be exclusively capitalist.

This chapter looks beyond lifeless capitalocentric visions of farming to tell another tale. The chapter not only adds to the literature on documenting the diverse economic practices that sustain farming, but also thinks onto-epistemically about farming in a way that challenges the representational and human-centred nature of farming, and draws out the ways in which a single enterprise is un/made of more-than-capitalist and more-than-human entanglements.

Reading for ontological and economic difference on Morning Valley Farm

In reading for economic difference (Gibson-Graham, 2014, 2020) in my fieldwork on a regenerative vegetable farm in Narrm/Melbourne, I position vegetable farming as a more-than-capitalist and more-than-human endeavour, and show how the farmers

2 Pieta Savinotko has changed their surname since the publication of this article.

negotiate living with capitalism, while also enacting values based on conviviality, mutuality and care for the world they live with.

The farm, Morning Valley, is a regenerative vegetable farm on the peri-urban fringe of Narrm/Melbourne. The farm produces a wide range of vegetables that are sold to restaurants, small supermarkets and at a farmer's market. Human labour and hand tools are opted for over heavy machinery—though there is a tractor, no pesticides or herbicides are used, and only limited organic fertilisers and soil conditioners are used, such as feather meal and lime. An important ethical consideration underpinning the farm is to limit the impact of farming on the habitat of which it is part, this ethic has attracted human workers with a similar outlook.

This chapter draws on ethnographic fieldwork that took place over nine months between August 2021 and May 2022. I worked at the farm one day per week for thirteen weeks and conducted interviews with ten human farmers who had a range of experience on the farm, including the owner, farm staff, interns and volunteers. Drawing on these participant observations and interviews, I use Vincent and Feola's (2020) framework for recognising capitalist diversity in agri-food systems (which builds on the work of Gibson-Graham) to highlight the more-than-capitalist and more-than-human nature of the farm. Vincent and Feola's framework adds ontological considerations ('time', 'space', 'human nature' and 'logic of relation') as well as relations to the state ('legitimation' and 'participation') to Gibson-Graham, Cameron and Healey's (2013) economic relations framework (which includes 'transactions', 'enterprise', 'labour', 'finance', 'property'). The addition of ontological considerations in reading for capitalist diversity helps to reveal the more-than-human nature of farming at Morning Valley. Time and space are mediated by, intervened in and co-created by tools, objects, animals, soils and climate. Human nature and logic of relation centre on the relationships between humans and earth-kin, and whether humans dominate or exploit the world around them based on a separation and hierarchy between humans and earth-kin.

Human nature

A longstanding and powerful explanation of human nature is that humans are utility maximisers, driven by individual self-interest (Smith, 1776). This view is linked to capitalist modes of being and doing, and has been contrasted with caring, cooperative, and reciprocal existences (Tronto, 2017). The 'human nature' component of the framework considers human values and actions on Morning Valley. At Morning Valley there were many examples of values grounded in cooperation, reciprocation and care for one another, both from humans and earth-kin. For instance, listening to each other's problems and 'looking out for one another', cooking morning tea and lunch for one another, and supporting each other to complete farming tasks.

The farm was also underpinned by an ethic of sufficiency rather than expansion and accumulation. The owner of the farm, Basil, was happy with the size of the farm as it was. Basil did not want to grow bigger, but did want to be better or more efficient at what they were already doing on the farm. Basil said he would be happy with an income of $50,000–$60,000 annually—which was in line with the median income in Australia (ABS 2019), and he was optimistic about achieving this goal.

Similarly, paid staff acknowledged that they did not work at the farm for the income they earned, and they knew they could get more money doing something else (and some in fact had left higher paid careers to be at the farm). Instead, they pointed to and valued the non-monetary benefits of working at the farm, including conviviality, being outdoors, and working towards something they believed in—farming in a way that minimises its impact on the world around it, while producing nutritious and delicious vegetables.

Morning Valley farmers saw themselves as having concern for the environment, climate change, plastic use, waste, soil health, quality of vegetables, and the animals and insects that also lived in the bounds of the farm. Human farmers were aligned with 'alternative' food systems, and their values were a testament to that. At times, they contrasted themselves and the practices on Morning Valley with conventional farming that was seen to be overly focused on self-interest and profiteering at the expense of the environment and food quality. The superior morality of alternative food systems was at times taken as given. For example, I was told by one farm worker, "you can't buy your vegetables from the supermarket" (Juniper, Field Notes, 2021).

Yet at the same time, some action was driven by efficiency and a desire to profit, highlighting that the farm needed to make money in order to exist given the hegemony of capitalist economic logic the farm operated alongside. Basil opined that "everything has to pay its way" (Basil, Interview, 2021). For instance, he felt that if you want to plant native species as habitat for birds and insects then you would look to cut the flowers and sell them, or if they wanted to beautify the farm, they would then look to run farm tours.

Another common materialisation of the need to be efficient was the practice of minimising walking around the farm. Farmers endeavoured to have all the equipment they needed for their tasks with them so they would not have to walk back to the shed. It was acknowledged that too much walking could eat into the productive labour of human farmers. At times, farmers acknowledged that they could not always care or cooperate with insects and animals, and that they were sometimes killed because they got in the way of human work—which was to produce vegetables to sell. As a farm staff member, Lily admitted, "I guess when I'm working, I have to be efficient, I can't care about each individual being. Which is sad" (Lily, Interview, 2021). Snails and worms were two beings that could find themselves in the way of people's interests. Snails were crushed underfoot or washed down the drain, worms could be sliced by hori hori knives or hoes.

The diverse subjectivities on display at Morning Valley may be inseparable. Drawing on Marcel Mauss, Alain Caille (2013) argues people act out of self-interest, but are also driven by obligation, creativity, and lovingness—self-interest is just one aspect of social relations. An interesting example of the trouble with siloing motives at Morning Valley could be seen in 'giving love' to vegetable beds, which could be understood as providing care for soil and vegetables. However, care was also being provided to increase planting space, to produce more vegetables which leads to profits—so, for profit maximising ends.

Ultimately, the farmers were balancing a desire to limit the destruction to or extraction from others required to grow vegetables, while still making a profit that allowed them to live in a world where money is important. Values and practice of being slow, local and convivial, sat alongside profitability and efficiency. As Ginger put it, it is possible to be "efficiently inefficient" (Ginger, Interview, 2021).

Logic of relation

It is difficult to separate human nature from the logic of relation. From a relational perspective, being in this world is being together. In other words, being in relation to other things, earth-kin, or people, is fundamentally part of our nature. Everything that occurred on Morning Valley was about being in relation. Slugs, snails or birds were never spoken about without their relation to the vegetables that were growing, or human aesthetic perspectives. Tools were always interacting with plants, animals and humans. Fences were only invoked in relation to rabbits, kangaroos or gallina; and hori hori knives intertwined with talk about soil or unwanted plants. Gravel bags did not exist without tarps, nor did tarps exist without weeds and light. This irreducible ecology of interdependence was central to farming at Morning Valley.

Agencies come together or interact in diverse ways; for instance, they might compete, complement or conflict with one another (Mol, 2010). These relationships can be also intertwined with domination or exclusion (Puig de la Bellacasa, 2017). The logic of relation refers to how we are related, whether relationships are hierarchical, involve domination, or recognise interdependence with earth-kin (Vincent & Feola, 2020).

At Morning Valley, interdependence between humans and earth-kin was practiced and recognised at times. Concern for soil biology and rebuilding soils depleted of organic matter could be seen in part as a recognition of the work that soil biology and chemistry did in producing food, and in contributing to a safe climate via carbon sequestration. Plants, insects and soil microbiology were afforded space to live and at times flourish through not tilling soils, not using herbicides or any chemical pesticides, planting native species, and allowing weeds to grow in areas not used for vegetable growing. Similarly, the reduction of industrial inputs and shift towards working *with* ecosystems indicates a move away from an extractivist mindset towards an acceptance of the interconnectedness between humans, earth-kin and the physical, biological and chemical processes of the planet. Human farmers often spoke about and acted respectfully towards earth-kin. Such as being impressed by a 'clever heron' that always knew the right time to show up for an easy feed, or relocating snails from vegetable beds instead of killing them. However, interdependence with earth-kin did not always mean happy mutuality. Farming inevitably involves killing, who or what gets to survive and who or what does not is a decision largely made by human farmers in the farming methods and tools they use, as well as the pressure to harvest a saleable crop within certain timeframes.

As already mentioned, if snails, slugs, or cabbage moth larvae impacted the Morning Valley's profitability too much they would be killed. Some animals were seen as interlopers on the farm, such as the ducks that ate seedlings instead of insects, while other insects scared or repulsed human farmers, such as spiders and slugs. During transplanting or weeding worms were killed by hori hori knives, and weeds were pulled by hand or cut with hoe blades or a string grass trimmer.

Weed and pest management illuminate the way that human farmers control, kill or care for earth-kin. According to Basil, the diversity at Morning Valley protected against pest concerns. Pests were always there, Basil said, but they were not necessarily problematic. Basil had noticed over the years that pests go for weak or sick plants, while the vigorous, healthy and saleable plants (or parts of plants) were often left alone. Still, human farmers occasionally used iron to control and kill snails, while Bt (Bacillus thuringiensis—a biological pesticide) has been used to control and kill caterpillars on brassicas early in the season. Weed management was also driven by a need to control. Couch grass, for instance, was perhaps the most maligned plant on the farm. The grass grows rhizomatically underground, its roots spread deep into the soil and were difficult to remove, requiring significant manual labour.

Some insects, animals, bacteria and fungi were very much welcomed on the farm such as frogs, ducks that ate snails, lacewings, ladybugs, mycorrhiza and rhizobium. Similarly, in some instances plants that would be weeds in one place, were not seen in the same way in another place. Grasses on access tracks were useful for providing habitat for beneficial insects and ensuring the soil did not erode or bake under the sun; these same species of grass in a vegetable bed were unwanted. What is important here is whether the plants were harmful or not to production or to the local ecosystem. For instance, gallina (a sprawling ground plant) had to be removed from wire fences as it slowly pulled the fences down, which might then need to be replaced or repaired. At the same time, native grasses growing along the same fence line were allowed to live as they "aren't doing any harm" (Ginger, Field Notes, 2021).

The farming tools that were used mediated the kind of relationships humans had with earth-kin. For instance, the grass trimmer disconnected humans somewhat from the soil, from plants and insects and from other human workers; farmers had to wear ear-muffs, a head-net and glasses when using it. Moreover, it was more indiscriminate in its killing than hands or hori hori knives. Similarly, the tractor (which had been mostly relegated to use as an oversize wheelbarrow on account of the no-till farming) destroyed soil structure and made it harder for some microbiology to live. This is compared to stirrup hoes, double wheel hoes and hori hori knives which were less invasive and destructive to soil structure and health.

Often the interdependence between human farmers was recognised at Morning Valley and manifested in non-hierarchical convivial relations. The farmers at Morning Valley cooperated, reciprocated and asked each other's opinions about how tasks ought to be completed and whether they need help. They took turns in completing different roles on the farm, such as being in charge of particular crops, or being in charge of packing, organising and delivering vegetables. They also took turns cooking morning tea and lunch for each other. Decision-making was somewhat deliberative. Farmers said things such as "we decided to do something this way" (Field Notes, 2021) as opposed to "I decided that we should do this" Volunteers (who came to work on the farm) were asked what they thought about a particular strategy or approach to a task, and Basil asked for input from others about intercropping. Human farmers at Morning Valley often listened and asked questions instead of, or at least before, telling others what to do.

Still, hierarchical relations also existed as some farmers had more experience, skills and knowledge, worked more often, or were more invested in the farm. The ultimate decisions about the farm operations were made by Basil—each morning he provided the other human farmers with the tasks they would be doing for the day; there was also an assistant manager who helped manage the farm. Basil checked how people were going with the tasks, this could be for seeing if there were any questions alongside 'checking up'. When volunteers came to the farm, paid staff were responsible for overseeing them and providing direction, for instance by testing out the tools before giving them over to volunteers to use or providing demonstrations of how to use tools or how to complete tasks. Some level of hierarchy was necessary for the smooth functioning and profitability of the farm.

Significantly, whether or not interdependence was recognised, interdependence was undeniable. Humans had to negotiate with earth-kin and each other on the farm—whether that was changing how they did a task because a vegetable had grown too large, or because a control method did not work, or because a broken-down tractor had forced a change in how tasks could be done.

Time and space

Time and space can be seen as socio-material constructions, rather than given constants (Puig de la Bellacasa 2017, p. 175). At Morning Valley, time and space were mediated and constructed by the human farmers' values and stories, the tools and methods employed in farming, the vegetables grown, weeds and pests, soil structure, weather, and climate.

Farming practices and methods at Morning Valley slowed time, and worked within seasonal cycles, contrasting with capitalist temporalities. Slow time was achieved through the use of human labour and hand tools. For instance, hori hori knives or hand weeding were much slower than tilling with a tractor. This can be seen as making time to care for the lives of earth-kin on the farm, particularly those that were part of soils (Krzywoszynska, 2019; Puig de la Bellacasa, 2015). The use of hand tools also opened space for convivial relations between farmers by allowing conversation, as well as space for mindfulness.

Basil explained that Morning Valley did not have a 'perennial summer' approach to growing vegetables, an approach which is driven by supermarket and consumer expectations of having the same range of vegetables available year-round. The farm operated in line with the seasons, rather than attempting to transcend or extend seasons using greenhouses or polytunnels. However, succession planting was used as a way to ensure an extended period of crop maturation. On the other hand, time and space were often organised to maximise productivity, in line with capitalist or productivist temporalities (Puig de la Bellacasa, 2015). Farmers tried to organise themselves so they did not have to spend too much time walking around the farm. This was seen as a 'waste' of time; time that could have been used in more productive ways. As Ginger explained, "you're not meant to walk all over the place, you're meant to be efficient" (Ginger, Interview, 2021). Farmers told stories of where they wasted time on doing tasks the wrong way and had to divert labour from other tasks. Again, this was linked to a concern that they could have used the time more productively. There were examples of farming practices that aimed to maximise the use of space and extend time. For instance, intercropping was used to maximise space and linked to productivity and profitability—getting the most out of the vegetable beds. Moreover, the farmers used a cool room, a refrigerated truck and (limited and compostable) packaging was used to extend the shelf life of vegetables.

Ultimately, time and space were understood and performed along capitalist and non-capitalist lines. This was due to the reality that the farm was part of broader capitalist networks. Human farmers needed to be productive to ensure sufficient revenue to cover production costs as well as the wages that sustained their lives. Thus, human farmers were conscious of 'wasting time' and being efficient in their labouring. Yet at the same time, Basil had chosen to stay small and local, to practice no-till farming and use a range of hand tools on the farm. This approach deliberately slowed down the work, contradicting productivist farming logics, and stemmed from an ethical commitment to minimise the farm's environmental impact. Interestingly, human farmers endeavoured to work within these ethical commitments *and* to maximise productivity through practices that cared for earth-kin survival and made productive use of space, such as intercropping.

Relationship with the state, regulation and legitimation

In many ways, Morning Valley farmers desired to escape capitalist modes of being, yet the farm was constantly stratified by the state and capitalist economic relations. Desire, at some level, to oppose 'conventional' food practices was expressed by numerous people who work on the farm—as was wanting a future in which food provisioning was focused on community and sociality. However, these desires came up against the hard reality and acknowledgment that "the farm is operating within the capitalist economy and broken food system... we're entrenched within that realm" (Basil, Interview, 2021). Such realities were, in part, constituted by the state via regulation and legitimation, that support the maintenance of 'free markets', private property, and often view tax paying businesses that contribute to 'jobs and growth' as legitimate enterprises (Vincent & Feola, 2020).

Morning Valley was largely entangled or enmeshed in state regulations. Morning Valley maintained property rights, sold into 'free markets', and paid wages according to labour laws. Playing by the rules of the game allowed human farmers to make a living in a world heavily organised around money. It also allowed the farm to exist over time in a place in which private property rights reign supreme. Concurrently, Morning Valley also participated in alternative capitalist regulation, notably via its organic certification. However, organic certification is unlikely to challenge the state as an alternative vision of regulation. Instead, certification can cede regulatory control to markets, where ethical behaviour is ascribed economic value (Guthman, 2007). Ultimately, certification can be understood as being about making capitalist farming practices better for the health of humans and environment, but certification does not challenge the status quo.

Morning Valley contributed to the 'economy' by paying taxes, employing people and paying wages, and producing goods to sell on the 'free' market. As such, the farm might be seen as legitimate from the perspective of a capitalist state. However, Basil suggested that small, independent farming is not supported enough by institutions or governments in Australia, and this has been a barrier to its proliferation (Basil, Interview, 2021). Indeed, in recent decades the approach from the Australian Government has been to push neoliberal export-oriented farming (Lawrence et al., 2013).

This perceived or real lack of support and government funding for small market farmers in and around Narrm/Melbourne can be seen as a lack of legitimation. I mentioned to Basil that it might be interesting to document the diverse consequences and benefits of the farm enterprise to make a case for more funding for similar endeavours (much like the work of Dombroski et al. (2019) who accounted for diverse non-monetary benefits of an urban farm in Christchurch). Basil appeared interested but clarified that "it would have to be done properly, you couldn't just say 'it's the lifestyle'" (Basil, Interview, 2021). This response suggests that attempts to legitimise ought to fit the expectations of the state, or the status quo. A convivial lifestyle is not sufficient to legitimise an enterprise; the enterprise must show that it is economically viable, and perhaps socially or environmentally responsible.

Ultimately, Morning Valley's relationship with the state, its involvement in regulation and whether it is seen as a legitimate organisation testifies to its entanglement with capitalist modes of knowing, being and doing pushed by the Australian Government. This is despite a desire in many respects to farm in non- or post-capitalist ways.

Knowledge

There were a range of ways in which farmers gained skills and knowledge at Morning Valley. Often the origin of knowledge can be difficult to ascertain, it may come partly or entirely from private enterprise, research at public universities, or via agricultural extension—which can be enmeshed in capitalist modes of existence (Vincent & Feola, 2020), at the same time knowledge can be gained from practice and learning from one another. At Morning Valley, it was much clearer *how* farmers came to learn about farming and gained relevant skills, rather than *where* the knowledge was developed. Farmers learned about vegetable farming from books, podcasts, and online videos. This could be scientific knowledge or about farming practices, and was both paid, shared and open access. While information might have originally come from research institutions or possibly even private enterprises, it was not necessarily capitalist in the way it was accessed and shared.

Farmers had undertaken formal TAFE (Technical and Further Education institutes) and university courses to upskill and build their farming knowledge, including horticulture, fencing, tractor and carpentry courses. At least one farmer paid for a series of online courses in market farming too. Learning from practice on the farm was a key source of knowledge for human farmers. This was through learning from each other, from repetition, and from being close and attentive to soil, weather, insects or plants. Basil said they were happy to learn and reflect and observe and interact while they worked. Several human farmers had undertaken an internship at Morning Valley where they learned intensively over a few months about vegetable farming.

Flora, a farm intern, felt that being out in all seasons, being able to touch, smell, and feel the plants and soil facilitated understanding or respect for soils, insects and plants. Adding to this, Lily believed that through weeding you could observe and learn about the soil, where it was different on the farm, why it might be different and how their farming practices affected soil. Interestingly, learning through observing and interacting directly with soil and plants was seen by Ginger as a better conduit for knowledge than learning through machines or technology. Ginger felt humans were more open to difference or possibility than machines, which can only tell you what you program them to tell you. For some, this practical learning was more accessible than learning from books: "you can always read about something, but I'm someone who really needs to see and do and that's how it probably sticks with me more than just reading" (Rosemary, Interview, 2021). Human farmers also gained knowledge about or relevant to vegetable farming from previous employment or volunteering, such as on other farms or in landscaping. While some farmers have had previous employers act as mentors for them.

Human farmers recognised the importance of agricultural research to inform their work, but also food networks more generally: "I think there's still lots of learning that can be done there for us. Yeah, we could be tuning into some more research and really following best practices and recording what we're doing and then observing what changes are being made" (Lily, Interview, 2022).

Significantly, knowledge about farming was not only seen as relevant for the farmers. Knowledge of farming, of what it takes to grow vegetables in a no-till system, and issues around food waste were seen to be important for non-farmers as well. Such knowledge, or perceived lack of knowledge, impacted what happened on the farm. Moreover, in some ways the farm played a role in educating non-farmers. Basil's communication with buyers about what is available, when, and the seasonal limits to growing vegetables might be seen as a form of knowledge dissemination, helping to educate buyers about the seasonality of food. Similarly, the weekly farmers' market acted as a site of consumer education too, as consumers asked questions about how the vegetables were grown.

Economic relations

There were numerous forms of labour on Morning Valley. There were several paid staff at the farm, though people also volunteered labour, worked as WOOFers (a program that connects people with farms to work and stay on, exchanging labour for food and accommodation), or as interns. Non-monetary forms of compensation included conviviality and friendships, vegetables, enjoyment of work, valuing work, and learning. Hosting WOOFers, volunteers and running an internship program were interesting strategies to overcome labour cost concerns. This revealed how the farm operated within the constraints of capitalist economic relations, and how non-capitalist labour relations were central to Morning Valley's ability to survive—which bears similarity to the way in which care labour has been central to the ability of capitalist economies to exist more broadly (Vogel, 1983).

The transactions that underpinned the farm were largely market transactions, the farm sold produce at a farmer's market, to restaurants, wholesalers, and some small organic supermarkets. Though the outlets they sold to could be seen as valuing more than mere profit or utility, environmental and health concerns also factored in the transactions. At the same time, alternative market transactions supported Morning Valley's operations too. For example, Ginger mentioned that "it is not all about exchanging money, Basil swaps things with people and you get things other ways" (Ginger, Interview, 2021).

The farm had been financed through personal savings, borrowing from family, and government grants, as well as support from the landholder. Thus, finance was drawn from a mix of alternative and non-capitalist relations. Interestingly, Basil told me that he could not get a loan from a bank to support the start-up of the farm and was forced to find some other forms of finance. The landlord assisted by offering reduced rent for the first 18 months of operation, to help the farm get on its feet. A win-win situation, as it helped the farm start up, and has also ensured a long-term tenant for the landlord.

Insecure access to land was seen to be one of the biggest barriers to farming, this is particularly a problem for peri-urban farming which faces incursions from residential development. Basil searched for land to lease using creative strategies, such as printing flyers and leaving them at cafes in regional towns. He ended up leasing land that had been used for organic vegetable farming previously. As such, the land had a water license to pump from the river next to the farm and already had infrastructure, such as irrigation and some washing and processing equipment.

As a private enterprise, decisions about how surplus was managed and put to use at Morning Valley appeared to be largely made by Basil. Unfortunately, there was limited information about how surplus was managed from observations and interviews.

Overall, farmers at Morning Valley practiced and embodied capitalist as well as alternative capitalist and non-capitalist ways of being and doing. Additionally, tools, machines, microbes, animals, soils, plants and climate were all inseparable from growing vegetables at Morning Valley. At times, this inseparability was recognised by human farmers, and there were also examples of where earth-kin were respected and cared for by human farmers. Still, the relationships between farmers and earth-kin also took a pragmatic or utilitarian form.

Making farms beyond capitalism

Reading Morning Valley for ontological and economic difference helps us to move past capitalist ways of knowing and doing farming in at least three significant ways. First, by showing farms are made by more-than-capitalist economic relations. Second, revealing the ways that farms are made through the work of more-than-human entanglements. Third, showing that farms are always in the process of being un/made. These three insights contrast with narratives that see farms as predetermined, discrete, human-centred enterprises that are wholly or inevitably capitalist—accounts that can be termed capitalocentric or plantationocentric (Gibson-Graham, 1996; Hyvärinen, 2020).

Morning Valley was made via a diverse range of economic relations and practices, some of which were capitalist, and others that were not. Human farmers were paid a wage and sold vegetables in markets; they were at times motivated by a desire to be efficient, productive and profitable. At the same time, farmers cooperated, reciprocated and cared for one another's wellbeing and survival. This inventorying of the diverse relations and motivations that make Morning Valley is key to shifting attention from plantationocentric and capitalocentric visions of farming by highlighting the other-than-capitalist relations and practices that are already there.

Capitalist ways of farming are supported by, and support, human dominance over earth-kin, and make farming about making human desires of profit. As Morning Valley shows us, however, humans are not farming alone. The farm would not be possible without the work and support of a diverse range of agencies, such as the tools, soil, insects and plants documented in this chapter. Farming is the collective labour of human/earth-kin entanglements. Looking past the anthropocentrism and static ontologies linked to human/nature; animate/inanimate, and subject/object binaries reveals the complex and fluid entanglements that constitute farming, highlights the lively agencies that are involved in farming, and opens the door for ethical questions about who and what does or does not benefit from farming (as more agencies are acknowledged), and how farming can be more accountable to the lives and well-being of humans and earth-kin.

Thinking about farming as performative, as always in the process of being made and unmade, rather than seeing farms as static predetermined entities, helps us to move beyond plantationocentric and capitalocentric visions of farming. The farm cannot be accounted for by simply adding the various constitutive agencies together—such as soil, plants, humans, or water. Rather, it is work that occurs at the interface of the coming together of these agencies that produce the farm. This insight is significant as it illuminates that farms are made by agencies doing something together, which means that things can be done differently and gives hope for taking up and working with the ways that Morning Valley was made by care, reciprocity, cooperation and sufficiency. Moreover, the performativity of farming allows for performative ethics, as opposed to a predetermined morality. A performative ethics works to shift our attention from what farms *are*, and what farming *should* look like, towards what farming *could* look like. Thus, by troubling the nature of Morning Valley as a static, discrete, human-centred business this chapter shows Morning Valley as a place where human and earth-kin farmers can work towards what farming could look like, rather than what it is, or should be.

References

Barad, K. (2007). *Meeting the universe halfway: Quantum physics and the entanglement of matter and meaning*. Duke University Press.

Bawaka Country, Wright, S., Suchet-Pearson, S., Lloyd, K., Burarrwanga, L., Ganambarr, R., Ganambarr-Stubbs, M., Ganambarr, B., & Maymuru, D. (2015). Working with and learning from Country: Decentring human authority. *Cultural Geographies, 22*(2), 269–283. https://doi.org/10.1177/1474474014539248

Bellamy Foster, J. (2016). Marx as a food theorist. *Monthly Review, 68*(7).

Bello, W. F. (2009). *The food wars*. Verso.

Bennett, J. (2010). *Vibrant matter: A political ecology of things*. Duke University Press.

Botterill, L. C. (2016). Agricultural policy in Australia: Deregulation, bipartisanship and agrarian sentiment. *Australian Journal of Political Science, 51*(4), 667–682. https://doi.org/10.1080/10361146.2016.1239567

Bromby, R. (1989). *Unlocking the land: The saga of farming in Australia* (New ed.). Lothian Publishing Co.

Caillé, A. (2013). Anti-utilitarianism and the gift-paradigm. In *Handbook on the economics of reciprocity and social enterprise*. Edward Elgar Publishing.

Cameron, J., & Wright, S. (2014). Researching diverse food initiatives: From backyard and community gardens to international markets. *Local Environment, 19*(1), 1–9. https://doi.org/10.1080/13549839.2013.835096

Commonwealth of Australia. (2023). *Food and Grocery Code Independent Reviewer Annual 2022–23*. Commonwealth of Australia. https://grocerycodereviewer.gov.au/sites/grocerycodereviewer.gov.au/files/2023-11/fg-ind-reviewer-ar-2022-23.pdf

Dombroski, K., Diprose, G., Conradson, D., Healy, S., & Watkins, A. (2019). Delivering urban wellbeing through transformative community enterprise (National Science Challenge 11). *Building better homes, towns and cities*. https://ir.canterbury.ac.nz/server/api/core/bitstreams/867d806b-4de0-46b2-8b51-5ecf40cd26f7/content

Gibson-Graham, J. K. (1996). *The end of capitalism (as we knew it): A feminist critique of political economy*. Blackwell Publishers.

Gibson-Graham, J. K. (2014). Rethinking the economy with thick description and weak theory. *Current Anthropology, 55*(S9), S147–S153. https://doi.org/10.1086/676646

Gibson-Graham, J. K. (2020). Reading for economic difference. In J. K. Gibson-Graham & K. Dombroski (Eds.), *The handbook of diverse economies* (pp. 476–485). Edward Elgar Publishing.

Gibson-Graham, J. K., Cameron, J., & Healy, S. (2013). *Take back the economy: An ethical guide for transforming our communities*. University of Minnesota Press.

Goodman, D., DuPuis, E. M., & Goodman, M. K. (2013). *Alternative food networks: Knowledge, practice and politics*. Routledge.

Guthman, J. (2007). The Polanyian way? Voluntary food labels as neoliberal governance. *Antipode, 39*(3), 456–478. https://doi.org/10.1111/j.1467-8330.2007.00535.x

Hickel, J. (2021). *Less is more: How degrowth will save the world*. Windmill Books.

Holt Giménez, E., & Shattuck, A. (2011). Food crises, food regimes and food movements: Rumblings of reform or tides of transformation? *Journal of Peasant Studies, 38*(1), 109–144. https://doi.org/10.1080/03066150.2010.538578

Hyvärinen, P. (2020). Sienestystä pohjoisilla puupelloilla: Metsien moninaiset taloudet ja plantaasiosentrismin ongelma. *Alue Ja Ympäristö, 49*(2), 22–43. https://doi.org/10.30663/ay.97101

Jackson, T., Zammit, K., & Hatfield-Dodds, S. (2018). Snapshot of Australian agriculture. *Australian Bureau of Agricultural and Resource Economics and Sciences.*

Karulkiyalu Country, Gordon, P., & Spillman, D. (2021). Embracing Country as teacher in outdoor and environmental education. In G. Thomas, J. Dyment, & H. Prince (Eds.), *Outdoor environmental education in higher education.* Springer Cham.

Krzywoszynska, A. (2019). Caring for soil life in the Anthropocene: The role of attentiveness in more-than-human ethics. *Transactions of the Institute of British Geographers, 44*(4), 661–675. https://doi.org/10.1111/tran.12293

Latour, B. (2007). *Reassembling the social: An introduction to actor-network-theory* (1st publ. in pbk). Oxford University Press

Lawrence, G., Richards, C., & Lyons, K. (2013). Food security in Australia in an era of neoliberalism, productivism and climate change. *Journal of Rural Studies, 29*, 30–39. https://doi.org/10.1016/j.jrurstud.2011.12.005

Magdoff, F. (2012). Food as a commodity. *Monthly Review, 63*(8).

McMichael, P. (2012). The land grab and corporate food regime restructuring. *The Journal of Peasant Studies, 39*(3–4), 681–701. https://doi.org/10.1080/03066150.2012.661369

Milroy, G., & Milroy, J. (2008). Different ways of knowing: Trees are our families too. In *Heartsick for country: Stories of love, spirit and creation.* Fremantle Press.

Mol, A. (2010). Actor-network theory: Sensitive terms and enduring tensions. *Kölner Zeitschrift Für Soziologie Und Sozialpsychologie. Sonderheft, 50*, 253–269.

Nelson, A., & Edwards, F. (Eds.). (2021). *Food for degrowth: Perspectives and practices.* Routledge.

Puig de la Bellacasa, M. (2015). Making time for soil: Technoscientific futurity and the pace of care. *Social Studies of Science, 45*(5), 691–716. https://doi.org/10.1177/0306312715599851

Puig de la Bellacasa, M. (2017). *Matters of care: Speculative ethics in more than human worlds.* University of Minnesota Press. https://virtual.anu.edu.au/login/?url=http://www.jstor.org/stable/10.5749/j.ctt1mmfspt

Scott, J. C. (1999). *Seeing like a state: How certain schemes to improve the human condition have failed.* Yale University Press.

Smith, A. (1776). *The wealth of nations.*

Tronto, J. (2017). There is an alternative: Homines curans and the limits of neoliberalism. *International Journal of Care and Caring, 1*(1), 27–43. https://doi.org/10.1332/239788217X14866281687583

Vincent, O., & Feola, G. (2020). A framework for recognizing diversity beyond capitalism in agri-food systems. *Journal of Rural Studies, 80*, 302–313. https://doi.org/10.1016/j.jrurstud.2020.10.002

Vogel, L. (1983). *Marxism and the oppression of women: Toward a unitary theory.* Rutgers University Press.

VERTAISARVIOITU
KOLLEGIALT GRANSKAD
PEER-REVIEWED
www.tsv.fi/tunnus

3
A proposal for a scatological global political economy
Or, making sense of capitalism through a shit-smeared lens

Anna Ilona Rajala

For the past two decades, excrement and toilets have featured abundantly in research on politics (e.g., Hawkins, 2003; Molotch & Norén, 2010), sociology (e.g., Pickering & Wiseman, 2019; Wiseman, 2019), history and literature (e.g., Penner, 2013; Werner, 2017), philosophy (Žižek, 2017), and anthropology (e.g., Prabaharyaka, 2020). Excrement-related questions have also been of interest in political economy since at least the second agricultural revolution (1830s–1880s), which is characterised by the growth of fertiliser industry and soil chemistry that revolutionised industrial agriculture (see e.g., Foster, 1999). Excretion and how societies deal with it concern a myriad of global political and economic matters such as the global sanitation crisis, sewage dumping from households and industry, agriculture and animal husbandry, food production and food security, ageing societies, intimate care, gut health, more-than-human microbial life, inclusive urban design, public toileting inequalities, and using shit in political protests, to name just a few (see e.g., Baxter & Mtshali, 2020; Black & Fawcett, 2008; Chojnacka et al., 2023; du Plessis, 2023; Gesing, 2023; LaCom, 2007; Ramster, Greed & Bichard, 2018; Riungu, 2021; Smithwick, 2021; Twigg, 2000; Wear, 2019; Wiseman, 2019).

In the age of the Anthropocene—the proposed new geological age of human influence on ecosystems, biodiversity, and natural resources—the above-mentioned scatological matters are more acute than ever. For this reason, I propose in this chapter

Rajala, A. I. (2025). A proposal for a scatological global political economy: Or, making sense of capitalism through a shit-smeared lens. In A. Kangas, I. Gataulina, M. Poutanen, A. I. Rajala & H-E. Ventovirta (Eds.), *Retheorising capitalism* (pp. 50–69). Tampere University Press. https://doi.org/10.61201/tup.981

an approach to global political economy that is specifically tuned to scatological issues. In simple terms, approaching global political economy scatologically means looking at excrement-related questions and how they might be interlaced with politics and the economy on a global scale. This proposal for scatological global political economy (scatological GPE) may sound self-explanatory, marginal and, especially if it concerns *human* excrement, something that can be shrugged off as a private matter. However, as I aim to show throughout, in the age of accelerating anthropogenic climate change, excremental issues cannot be taken merely as a private matter because they are crucial for analyses of how economic and political forces interact with and affect aquatic and terrestrial ecosystems, human and non-human health, and global justice.

I draw on two interrelated research foci, sometimes explicitly and often implicitly. First, Sagi Cohen's (2016, pp. 285–286) abject methodology of "thinking from a position of shit" offers global political economy a specific perspective: it reminds us that something inessential may be essential. As I discuss below, shit may be regarded as inessential waste, but it is absolutely essential for both the survival and destruction of life on Earth. Second, I draw on the inescapably "secretional" reality of embodiment (Rajala-Vaittinen, 2025), or the physiological fact that shitting "critters" (see Haraway, 2016, p. 169, n1) need to defecate to survive, is paramount for understanding the significance of scatology in global political economy.

One of the central themes for scatological GPE is the intricate balancing between excrement as a necessity of life (we all must do it) and excrement as a life destroyer (in the wrong place, it causes diseases and environmental crises). Shit is both life-threatening and life-giving, but neither definition can be fixed as a stable meaning for it. Rather, shit occupies an abject liminal space between fixed meanings, shifting between them depending on context. I discuss this shifting throughout this chapter. The first section delves into the importance of scatological matters for GPE. In the second section, I discuss how shit is both necessary and life-threatening from the perspectives of human health and global justice. I illustrate this with examples, such as constipation, diseases that are transmitted via the faecal-oral route, and care work conceptualised as "dirty". The third section shifts the focus of excremental health from the human to the planetary and the more-than-human. I address anthropogenic nutrient flows and cycling, in which human excreta could offer alternatives to artificial fertilisers instead of ending up in aquatic ecosystems, destroying them irreversibly. In the final epilogue, I conclude with a summary.

A scatological primer

This primer seeks to explain why excrement is such a central matter for all life on Earth, and as such, it also matters greatly for politics and the economy. We all produce excrement, have always done so, and will do so in the future—all 8 billion of us human animals that live on this planet. Some sit on a ceramic seat and flush it with drinking-quality water. There are also dry toilets that use little or no water at all but instead offer an opportunity to put valuable nutrients back to work in food production (see e.g., Aburto-Medina et al., 2020). Some use squat toilets, which are physiologically more beneficial for bowel function, and others do not use toilets at all in the conventional sense but instead use continence technologies that are mostly thrown in the waste bin after use. Some 419 million people, according to the World Health Organization (2024), defecate in the open, meaning anywhere else than toilets or latrines. In the lack of better options, some do it in plastic bags that are flung out in the streets, hence the term "flying toilet". In 2022, only 4.6 billion people used a sanitation service that is safely managed, and over 1.5 billion people do not have private toilets or latrines, which are considered to be basic sanitation services (World Health Organization, 2024). Wherever and however excretion is performed, it is done out of the necessity of survival, because not shitting is not really an option. At the same time, shitting is banal and mundane and often performed without giving it a second thought.

An average adult human person produces 400–500 grammes of faeces per day, which amounts to about 145 kilogrammes per year—"just a little more than an adult panda weighs" (Weisberger, 2018). I do not think I need to point it out, but that is a significant amount of shit on a global scale. Because shit has always been abundant wherever people dwell, the history of human communities, regardless of the prevailing political or economic system, is also the less-talked-about history of the problem of poo and how to deal with it. For example, the Romans built aqueducts and sewer systems and had multi-seat latrines under which flowing water floated human waste away towards more open waters (see e.g. Koloski-Ostrow, 2015, pp. 3–4). The oldest flushing toilet that we know of dates back 2,400 years to a palace in China, although "flushing" was most likely performed by servants who poured water into the lavatory after use (Chen, 2023). Londoners threw and later flushed all their excreta into the Thames, leading to the infamous Great Stink of 1858. This event highlighted the need to construct the then-innovative and oft-copied, but now-inadequate sewage system designed by Joseph Bazalgette, which has for several more recent decades caused raw sewage discharges in the Thames as the system could no longer handle the burden of the rising number of flushers (Jackson, 2014, pp. 97–98). Even the Bible gives a practical tip on how to personally deal with shit:

> Thou shalt have a place also without the camp, whither thou shalt go forth abroad:
>
> And thou shalt have a paddle upon thy weapon; and it shall be, when thou wilt ease thyself abroad, thou shalt dig therewith, and shalt turn back and cover that which cometh from thee. (KJV, Deuteronomy 23:12–13)

Kathleen Myer's (1994/2020) classic *How to Shit in the Woods: An Environmentally Sound Approach to a Lost Art*, the backcountry backpacker's bible on how not to pollute that river from which someone might drink at some point, shares this same age-old wisdom. The problem of how to deal with excrement has always followed human populations out of practical necessity because it cannot be simply left lying around untreated, or else it may end up somewhere it is unwanted. Shit in the wrong place, such as in drinking water or in waterways, is detrimental to both human and non-human health. In turn, shit in the right place can be life-giving: shit is full of microbial life and nutrients that can safely be utilised in food production after having been treated and composted properly.

While excrement in general has less to do with capitalism, shit is increasingly interwoven with capitalism as, on the one hand, capitalist societies and neoliberal policies manage the way in which shit is dealt with and, on the other, the capitalist world-order maintains stark inequalities of wealth and health between human communities. For example, London's super sewer constructed by Tideway, an investor- and pensioner-fund-owned company, is expected to solve raw sewage discharges after 150 years of the completion of Bazalgette's sewage system. Almost a decade in the making, the construction of the massive sewer tunnel was sparked by an EU directive that requires member countries to protect the environment from wastewater pollution. The cost of the construction project "is being paid for by Thames Water's 15 million wastewater customers through their bills, which will rise by no more than £25 per year" (Tideway, n.d.). Customers will have paid £540 million during the tunnel's construction up until the time of its opening, while shareholders have received £298.1 million during the same period. After the tunnel is operational, the customers will continue to pay for the returns of shareholder loans and continuing debt with interest (Plimmer, 2024). Building the so-called super sewer is as necessary as shitting as it is needed to manage sewage safely in the future, and both the tunnel and the return on investment are being paid for by ordinary citizens. This mammoth construction project enables profiting from the physiological necessity of excreting, which demonstrates one possible way to turn inessential waste into profit.

While shit is increasingly tied with how capitalist economies function, it also gives rise to community projects and diverse, other-than-capitalist economies (see Gibson-Graham & Dombroski, 2020). As another contemporary example of how poo is tied to the distribution of wealth, Kenya's Kibera, one of the poorest areas of the world, was once infamously filled with flying toilets. Community-led toilets and bathrooms, biocentres, and biogas production facilities are now replacing them while at the same time creating "opportunities for economic stability through employment, environmental sustainability through waste management and clearance, and social and political stability by providing venues for various social activities that brought the community together" (Wambui, 2020, p. 24). In any community, and especially on a global population level, figuring out how to deal with shit takes a major political effort and economic investment. On the one hand, it offers opportunities for capitalist "salvage accumulation" in which things not dependent on capitalism, like the need to excrete, are translated into capitalist value (Tsing, 2015, p. 53). On the other, it enables people to practise economies otherwise, as shit can also be salvaged in an other-than-capitalist manner: it can be returned to the community, for example, as cooking gas or as nutrient-rich compost. Such alternatives are desperately needed because all life depends on nutrient cycles to which anthropogenic disturbances have been detrimental, and especially the radically unjust and deeply colonial global distribution of excrement-related life-threatening processes, are crises of capitalism and social reproduction (cf. Çelik 2023; du Plessis 2023).

While scatological GPE can address all these matters above and more, my focus in this chapter is on how shit is intertwined with global inequalities of health and wealth on the one hand and with the ecological crisis on the other, both closely related to profit-driven economic growth. This entanglement is complex and works through different interconnections, but there is one thing that stays constant: shitting is a necessity for all critters who shit. Human beings are *visceral*: the interiority of our bodies, the workings of our organs, the oozing of bodily fluids through our skin and orifices are an integral, but often neglected and silenced, part of what it is to be a living organism, but also a political being; a citizen (cf. Montsion & Tan, 2016; Morales et al., 2014; Rajala-Vaittinen, 2025; Tsakiris, Vesar & Tucciarelli, 2021). To be visceral is to acknowledge that we need to eat and defecate, we need care and assistance, and our lives depend on the wellbeing of more-than-human life, such as gut microbiota. Crucially, the necessity of excretion makes shit radically equal; everybody *without exception* does it one way or another, even kings and philosophers, and ladies, as Montaigne (1588/2003) put it. So, we must begin with a simple universal physiological fact: excretion concerns all critters that eat, in all places, throughout history, without exception, and this physiological necessity pertains to the entire history and pre-history of the human species. However, of the 1.2 million animal species we know of on Earth, none other than humans are destroying the planet as they excrete. Defecating, and eating to be able to do so, is a necessity without which there would not be life as we know it but, at the same time, the planet is facing an anthropogenic catastrophe in which poo plays a significant role. Like all human existence, the physiological workings of secretion and excretion are increasingly interlaced with global capitalism, which exacerbates the detrimental consequences of human existence for more-than-human life on the planet and aggravates inequalities between human communities.

Because excretion is radically equal, the threat of radical inequality is always present, and equality can turn into inequality sometimes in an instant. This can happen under many circumstances and be triggered by different events. For example, imagine an able-bodied person who later suffers a severe injury to their spinal cord that causes paralysis that also affects bladder and bowel functions. Then suddenly, something that they used to do independently and in privacy becomes something for which they may need the assistance and presence of another person. Now imagine that this person lives in a conflict area with extremely limited healthcare resources and practically non-existent water and sanitation services or waste management, as all essential infrastructures have been bombed to the ground. Everything they need to be more independent, such as a wheelchair, personal assistance, rehabilitation, incontinence pads, stoma bags, or catheters, is unavailable to them. However, after receiving refugee status in another country with universal access to healthcare, they finally get what they need to take care of their personal hygiene more independently. In other words, equality and inequality related to excreting depend on, for example, where one lives, what one's status in society is, what kinds of things the healthcare system covers, whether one can afford those things that the healthcare system does not cover, and whether one affords professional assistance or has relatives and friends who are able or willing to offer help when needed. Moreover, as the necessity of shitting makes all shitting critters equal, inequalities of wealth and health throw shitting inequalities into even sharper relief: those who cannot excrete independently or those who do not enjoy adequate and safe sanitation are in an unequal and unjust position compared to those who can use the toilet with an adequate level of sanitation, safety, and independence.

With global capitalism and the planetary crisis that we are facing, we no longer have the possibility to think about excretion as something private. Such thinking would be crudely ableist and ignorant of the fact that millions of people do not have the opportunity to excrete in privacy, either due to the lack of sanitation facilities or due to being disabled. Shit is a shared matter when it comes to organising adequate sanitation, care, assistance, and continence technologies, such as incontinence pads, catheters, or stoma bags, for all those in need. Moreover, once poo leaves anyone's body, once it becomes *waste*, it becomes a shared matter of political economy in urban planning, constructing and maintaining sanitation infrastructures, organising waste management and recovery, and protecting the environment from destructive nutrient pollution. In short, even if excretion happens under the privilege of privacy, shit and the continence technologies that are sometimes needed to manage toileting needs end up in aquatic ecosystems and landfills, and so what shit causes to the environment makes it a global, transnational, and shared problem in which the most vulnerable human and other-than-human life tends to draw the shortest straw. To put it bluntly, shit is not merely a shared matter; it is also political (Baxter & Mtshali, 2020; Doron & Raja, 2015; Hawkins, 2003; LaCom, 2007; Wiseman, 2019; see also Vaittinen et al., 2023).

My proposal for scatological GPE is not, of course, exclusive to retheorising capitalism. However, capitalism dominates the economy globally and many of the excrement-related issues discussed in this chapter are closely tied to capitalism and neoliberal policies. Therefore, scatological GPE can be utilised in making sense of capitalism and how wealth is distributed within it. In Anna Lowenhaupt Tsing's (2015) terms, shit could be called pericapitalist: its production is not dependent on capitalism per se—except, of course, through food production—but it can be salvaged for capitalist accumulation (Tsing, 2015, p. 53). Tsing (2015, p. 53) argues that salvage accumulation is an integral feature of how capitalism operates, not just an add-on. London's £4.5 billion super sewer, which finally became operational in 2025 after nine years of construction, is a prime example. This project has enabled shareholders to profit from the physiological needs of citizens and the legal requirement to prevent raw sewage dumping in the River Thames. Conversely, dealing with human waste can also create opportunities for practicing alternative economies. As demonstrated by

Kibera's example, human waste can be returned to a cycle that counters the capitalist exploitation of the soil through artificial fertilisers, which depletes its natural fertility. By doing so, it may begin to repair the "metabolic rift" between humans and the soil, where the metabolic exchange of material between humans and the soil is based on a capitalist exploitative interaction that leaves the soil depleted (see Foster, 1999, pp. 383–384).

How a necessity of life becomes the making of a disaster

In this section, I discuss how excrement constitutes a persistent question of global justice. This question is currently closely tied to global capitalism as the dominant economic system, in which inequalities of wealth and health feature in many harmful ways, including the way in which inequalities cause population health and wellbeing to worsen (Wilkinson & Pickett, 2010). Achieving global justice and mitigating the persisting inequalities of wealth and health (see e.g. Balakrishnan & Heintz, 2019; Cash-Gibson et al., 2018; Jumbri et al., 2019; Lynch, 2019) add to the challenge of dealing with excrement. For example, these inequalities exacerbate the burden of faeces-related diseases in financially disadvantaged areas due to the unjust distribution of wealth that capitalism thrives upon.

While there are also positive applications for faecal matter in healthcare, such as treating ulcerative colitis with faecal transplants (e.g., Laperrousaz, 2024), it poses many serious life-threatening risks. Shit may contain pathogens that are lethal when consumed, in addition to being unpleasant and transgressive to the senses. Shit in the wrong place, such as in food or drinking water, poses a serious threat to health. For example, since cholera first spread across the globe in the 19th century, millions of people have died in the consequent six pandemics. The current seventh cholera pandemic started in 1961, and in many parts of the world, the disease is now endemic. It is estimated to kill around 21,000 to 143,000 people each year (World Health Organization, 2023b). Cholera is only one of several diseases that are transmitted via the faecal-oral route. While the burden of diarrhoeal disease attributable to inadequate water, sanitation, and hygiene (WASH) has dropped significantly during the past 20 years, unsafe drinking water was accountable for 35% of human diarrhoea deaths in lower and middle-income countries in 2019, which equals more than 505,000 deceased (World Health Organization, 2023a). Poor sanitation is also a major contributor to malnutrition and several debilitating and lethal tropical diseases. Higher-income countries are not, of course, immune to diseases of faecal origin. For example, foodborne Shiga toxin-producing Escherichia coli (E. coli O157: H7 or STEC) outbreaks are not uncommon (Yang et al., 2017). An infection may lead to a life-threatening condition, but as E. coli usually responds to antibiotics, poorer countries and conflict areas again bear the greatest burden as basic medicines, such as antibiotics, are not always available (Knowles et al., 2020). So, while shit does not depend on any particular political or economic system per se, global inequalities exacerbated by capitalism cause shit to become an even more life-threatening issue in the poorer areas of the world.

Accidents and illnesses that affect mobility and hence also the way one uses the toilet concern all people. Such illnesses and accidents include, for example, having a stroke that causes paralysis, living with debilitating pain that makes moving about more laboursome, breaking a leg or a finger, having major surgery that can cause difficulties with independent mobility, having a spinal cord or head injury, having a mobility-affecting neurological condition that may cause the loss of dexterity of hands to wipe, or just simply getting older and frailer. These are just a few causes for possibly needing assistance to use the toilet or continence technologies independently, and sometimes it is temporary and other times permanent. Furthermore, even if a disability does not cause loss of independence in toileting, public toilets, in particular, can be hostile environments that do not accommodate the needs of disabled people (Wiseman, 2019).

Needing assistance with toileting concerns millions of people across the world. If assistance is scarce, then not being able to defecate on one's own or to clean afterwards becomes a question of life and death. When I embarked on my postdoctoral research on the politics of excrement in 2022, one of the first stories I was told was about the loss of an elderly but still very much independent parent due to a minor incident. This incident had caused a temporary restriction on independent walking and toileting, and it should have been a case of a relatively short hospital stay. Due to chronic understaffing, this person was not assisted to use the toilet often enough, and they ended up contracting bacterial sepsis of faecal origin, which cost their life. Soiling oneself is not simply incredibly uncomfortable and inconvenient, it may end lives. Similarly, not being able to excrete can end tragically. A young British man, Mr. Richard Handley, lost his life suddenly in 2012. Aged just 33, he suffered a heart attack. Having lived with chronic constipation all his life, his bowel was severely obstructed by faecal impaction, which caused him to vomit up liquid faeces and inhale it. Behind the abject medical cause of death, however, there is another more tragic one: Mr. Handley's death was ultimately caused by factors that led to his constipation to worsen. There had been changes to his diet and the monitoring of his bowel movements at his care home, both of which are against the recommended medical care of chronic constipation (Hill, 2018).

The examples in this section about how shit may constitute a threat to life globally are tragic because most of them are avoidable. In the case of understaffing and lack of due care, such as monitoring the bowel movements of a care home resident, the solution is not blaming staff who are often already underpaid, work under limited resources, and suffer repeated moral injury for not being able to do their work as ethically as they would like to—as is often the case in healthcare organised according to neoliberal principles (see e.g., Whiley & Grady, 2022). Such moral violence was even more prevalent among nursing staff during the COVID-19 pandemic (Liang et al., 2023). Care work has been conceptualised as dirty work because it deals with bodies and their fluids, and it is often gendered and devalued both economically and in social status because of this (Twigg, 2000; Wibberley, 2013). The stigma of dirty work, perceived as social and moral taint, and poor occupational conditions—the stigma can also be internalised and (re)produced among nursing professionals—negatively predicts willingness to work especially in institutional aged care (Manchha et al., 2022). Intimate care, such as toileting or bathing, always requires a lot of professional skill, sensitivity, and connectedness, but it may be considered "common-sense" and thus it does not receive much attention on a policy level (Göransson, Larsson & Carlsson, 2023; Twigg, 2000). Reversing the stigma of dirty work would be to recognise that it is not only necessary and lifesaving, and should be compensated accordingly, but that it can also be perceived positively and as rewarding for both caregivers and care receivers (Meldgaard Hansen, 2016).

In the case of poor sanitation and diseases transmitted via the faecal-oral route, the solution is better sanitation. This is easier said than done, because the contemporary flushing toilet, which has become a metonym for good sanitation in popular imagination, is not a sustainable solution—at least not in its current state and form. This brings us to a segue between human health and planetary health, which I address in the following section.

Going around in circles: from the colon to the table

The global sanitation crisis discussed above is also a crisis of planetary health, because the crisis is not only about open defecation and how people needlessly die of diseases of faecal origin. It is also about the metabolic rift between humans and the soil (Foster, 1999): vast masses of nutrient-rich human waste end up in places where they are harmful rather than useful, and this affects planetary health, on which all life on Earth depends. Nutrient-rich waste is detrimental when consumed, for example when consuming food irrigated by untreated wastewater, but life-giving when used safely in food production. In this section, I discuss how scatology might guide us to rethink our relationship with biochemical flows. The necessity of eating and defecation and the consequent necessity of the existence of vast amounts of nutrient-rich flows tie our existence on this planet to the visceral guts of the earth, the soil: "We are humus, not Homo, not anthropos; we are compost, not posthuman" (Haraway, 2016, p. 55). However, our current capitalist relationship with nature and the soil is one of estrangement rather than kinship (Foster, 1999).

Let us begin with flushing. The undeniable fact is that as the use of flushing toilets increased in different societies, it became necessary to build more comprehensive sewage systems, and consequently the streets were cleaned of faecal waste. Where comprehensive sewage systems exist, problems with open defecation are not widespread, although open defecation is often the only option for homeless populations. In areas with sewage systems, cases of sanitation-related diseases are fewer (see e.g.

Tiwari, Tirumala & Shukla, 2022). The problem, however, was usually not eliminated but merely transferred elsewhere. For example, in the Finnish capital Helsinki in the late 19th century, flushing toilets were at first either illegal or exceptional luxury items, but as legislation changed, they became more common in households, ending many infectious diseases of faecal origin as the city sewage infrastructure caught up. The downside was that all the sewage was dumped in Töölö Bay, destroying its ecosystem for decades to come. In the summer of 1910, local newspapers recorded a large fish kill and the smell of the bay as so disgusting that even train passengers passing by Helsinki had to hold handkerchiefs over their noses (Laakkonen, 2001, p. 178).

The planet cannot handle the current nutrient pollution. Nutrient-rich excreta are extremely harmful in aquatic ecosystems, which are essential in stabilising the climate (Häder et al., 2020). The widespread use of flush toilets is among the reasons for the pollution, as sewage infrastructures and water treatment facilities are inadequate or lacking in many areas globally. The environmental cost of flushing is growing. For example, in the UK, flushing the toilet accounts for nearly a third of household drinking-quality water consumption. According to a Guardian article, water treatment is responsible for about 1% of UK greenhouse gases (Saner, 2019). Options for the flushing toilet exist. For example, dry toilets turn waste into compost when used correctly, thus enabling users to put nutrients back to use, either in food production or landscaping. They can also be integral in community-building, as the case of Kenya's Kibera demonstrates. They can also offer a means of enacting countercultures (Kuhn et al., 2022, p. 73). There are also low-flow toilets and toilets that use little to no water. All these types of sanitation systems can be installed in urban areas and even in blocks of flats. However, for some, there is just something about the apparent efficiency of those toilets that use a whole bucketful of water, allowing them to avoid looking at their faeces or facing the shame of the next person finding something floating around the bowl.

A good example of the love for flushing efficiency is the United States Energy Policy Act of 1992 (EPACT92) and its aftermath. It set household toilet flush volume to 1.6 gallons, effectively banning the installation of the monumental 3.5-to-7-gallon (13–26.5 litres) flushers (GovTrack.us., 2024), which created a new market demand for importing used and now illegal 3.5-to-7-gallon toilets from Canada. This case demonstrates the lengths to which people are prepared to go just to evade environmental policies (Perman, 2000) and to manage the shame and stigma that pertains to the functions of our bladder and bowels.

The politics of flushing, from ending open defecation to protecting aquatic ecosystems, is an important consideration in discussions about the Anthropocene that is entangled with disturbances in nature's biochemical cycles, such as enhancing nutrient-rich flows that exchange and transform organic matter in ecosystems. Human influence has been disturbing nature's biogeochemical cycles for millennia; for example, by putting nutrients (i.e. animal and human waste) in concentrated areas for farming and growing crops, as well as through landscaping, building dwellings, and redirecting waterways. The current scale of anthropogenic disturbance is a more recent phenomenon. Human action has accelerated the magnitude and rate of nutrient flows, such as the flow of nutrients between soil and water (e.g. through leaching) or soil and atmosphere (e.g. carbon cycling and aeolian transport of dust), and the movement of minerals (e.g. the physical shipping of phosphate rock), as well as plants and animals to some extent (Smithwick, 2022, pp. 140–142). While all greenhouse gases exist and cycle naturally, human actions have increased their amounts in natural biochemical cycles, with numerous adverse effects on the planet (Olah, Prakash & Goeppert, 2011; Raimi et al., 2021). Human influence on biogeochemical cycles is so significant that we can talk about anthrobiochemical cycles (Fairchild et al., 2022).

The current large-scale disturbance is largely attributable to industrial agriculture driven by capitalist means of production, which currently depends on chemically produced artificial fertilisers (see Foster, 1999). The replacement of guano (bird droppings) and manure with such fertilisers has had many adverse effects. First, it has increased nitrous oxide (N_2O) emissions beyond natural atmospheric levels during the past century (Gmitrowicz-Iwan & Ligęza, 2023). N_2O is the third largest anthropogenic greenhouse gas emission after methane and carbon dioxide, with its human-related sources mainly being agricultural production processes, industrial production, and livestock emissions (Hu, 2021). Second, the Haber-Bosch process of synthesising ammonia from atmospheric nitrogen by reacting it with hydrogen is essential for artificial fertilisers and it has made agricultural land use significantly more efficient, but also increased soil acidification, increased the formation of fine particulate matter in the atmosphere, accelerated the eutrophication of semi-natural ecosystems, and altered the global greenhouse balance (Sutton et al., 2008). Third, in addition to synthesising ammonia, artificial fertilisers depend on the mining of rock phosphate, which is the source of raw phosphorus used in mineral fertilisers. Phosphorus plays a key role in energy transformation, enzyme activation, photosynthesis, the formation of nucleic acid, and adenosine triphosphate (ATP) synthesis in plants (Plaxton & Tran, 2011). It is an essential and irreplaceable mineral for all life on Earth, but deposits of minable raw phosphorus sources are becoming increasingly scarce. The European Commission (2023) has listed phosphorus and phosphate rock as critical raw materials. Their demand will increase in the future. In 2040, the global supply of phosphorus will fall below the global requirement, while the climate impact from mining and processing the mineral sources of phosphorus will double between 2000 and 2050 (Nedelciu et al., 2020).

Urine and faeces are full of nutrients and there is significant potential in the safe recovery of nutrients from sewage sludge or animal by-products to address the current and future fertiliser crisis (Chojnacka et al., 2023; Koskue et al., 2022; Samoraj et al., 2022; Sichler et al., 2022). Wastewater and sewage sludge are notable and more sustainable sources of nitrogen and phosphorus compared to using atmospheric nitrogen in the Haber-Bosch process and mining for phosphate rock (Kar et al., 2023; Sichler et al., 2022). According to different scenarios, the phosphorus potential in all human urine and faeces accounts for a total of 13–22% of the global fertiliser demand (Kok et al., 2018). In Europe, approximately 25% of phosphorus from human excreta is already recycled back to agriculture, all via the application of sewage sludge (Cordell et al., 2011). While this may not seem like much, it is likely that there is much more potential in sludge recycling as recovery methods and technologies improve. The efficiency of recovery also depends on improving sewage infrastructure and water treatment processes globally. According to the United Nations (2023), of the household wastewater generated globally, 42% is discharged without safe treatment. Of the total wastewater nitrogen pollution in coastal areas, 63% comes from sewage waste (Tuholske et al., 2021). If solids and wastewater were to end up in sewers, treatment plants, and other places where they could be recovered, there would be more to recover.

Legal, political, and economic accountability for discharging untreated wastewater is needed. For water companies operating on a for-profit basis, sewage dumping may be a more lucrative option than environmental protection, even when legislation is in place. For example, several privatised water companies in the UK periodically dump raw sewage into rivers and coastal waters. Discharges of raw sewage are allowed to be released from storm overflows on the UK network, but only in exceptional circumstances, for example due to unusually high rainfall. This is to release pressure in the sewage system, which is designed to take in both wastewater and rainfall, thus causing overflows and discharges. This dual system, dating back to the design of Joseph Bazalgette, is also the reason for building London's super sewer discussed above. In 2021, raw sewage was dumped in the UK 372,533 times over 2.7 million hours, and in 2022, 301,000 times over 1.75 million hours. The vast majority of these raw sewage discharges were illegal cases of dumping on dry days (Laville & Horton, 2023). In 2021, the water company Southern Water pleaded guilty to discharging vast volumes of raw sewage into coastal waters for close to six years, causing "very considerable environmental damage" while reaping "considerable financial advantage"—and because it was cheaper than treating it (Laville, 2021).

Nutrients in soil, working together with more-than-human microbes that transform biochemicals into forms that plants can use to grow, are essential for feeding the global population. However, as discussed above, capitalism and its industrial-scale agriculture are not succeeding in this task, as the consequences for the environment have been detrimental. Moreover, as Uma Lele writes:

> The world has produced enough food since the Second World War to feed itself despite rapid population growth, owing to extraordinary technological and institutional change. The rise in world food production, however, has been accompanied by unequal access to that abundance, as well as soil degradation, loss of biodiversity, and growing water scarcities. (Lele, 2021, p. 1)

Rethinking our relationship with biochemical flows is not merely about replacing one harmful industrial-scale process with another of the same scale, just more sustainable, while maintaining the unjust distribution of its products and letting "cannibal capitalism" continue to devour everything on its path with its voracious appetite (Fraser, 2022). Rather, it must bring us back to the question of global justice, both distributive and environmental, because the planet is quickly becoming inhospitable for all life—including human life, whose excremental existence plays a significant part in the climate crisis.

Epilogue

Thinking from the position of shit demonstrates that shit is both inessential waste and something essential and salvageable. Both in the context of global justice and the ecological crisis, shit is caught up in an infinite inversion in which its necessity to life never escapes the fact that, in the wrong place, it is potentially hostile to life. What we have is a kind of Schrödinger's cat's poo situation: shit is both potentially destroying and preserving life at each moment. To put it concisely, we all must do it to survive, but some of our shit ends up in places it does not belong, and so what was a necessity may end up killing you while destroying whole ecosystems, even though those nutrients could be put to better use in more sustainable fertiliser production. Shit is tied to politics and the economy in many ways globally, because human communities have always had to deal with their waste either by recycling it into something useful or by treating it as just that: waste.

In discussing inequality of wealth and health, I aimed to show that where injustice is allowed to exist, shit often poses a threat to well-being and even to life. I also discussed how the way shit is dealt with, or not dealt with, can be detrimental to the environment. Its value could be salvaged for something other than shareholder profits by recycling excreta into fertilisers, instead of letting the nutrients end up in the environment. The common denominator between human and more-than-human health is solving the sanitation crisis, which I argue includes both inadequate sanitation (human health) and inadequate wastewater treatment (more-than-human health). This is one of the most urgent crises of global justice that must be solved. However, the adverse effects do not happen due to some natural order of things or necessary causes; behind them are policies, profit-seeking, and active and conscious human decisions to act one way rather than the other. This is crucial because of what I referred to as radical equality and radical inequality: while we all must do it to keep alive, the very necessity of life is also vastly unjust to those living in the poorest areas of the globe. Understanding this offers ways to make sense of capitalism and its machinery of inequality.

Acknowledgements

This research is funded by the Research Council of Finland (project no: 350247). I would like to thank Henna-Elise Ventovirta for numerous helpful comments to make this text so much better, and Anni Kangas and the *Assembling Postcapitalist International Political Economy* (Research Council of Finland project no: 325976) team for numerous discussions that have shaped my thinking. As always, this is dedicated to Timo Uotinen whose commentary and support are invaluable.

References

Aburto-Medina, A., Shahsavari, E., Khudur, L. S., Brown, S., & Ball, A. S. (2020). A review of dry sanitation systems. *Sustainability (Basel, Switzerland), 12*(14), 5812. https://doi.org/10.3390/su12145812

Baxter, V., & Mtshali, M. N. (2020). "This shit is political; shit is real." The politics of sanitation, protest, and the neoliberal, post-apartheid city. *Studies in Theatre and Performance, 40*(1), 70–82. https://doi.org/10.1080/14682761.2019.1689755

Black, M., & Fawcett, B. (2008). *Last taboo: opening the door on the global sanitation crisis.* Earthscan. https://doi.org/10.4324/9781849776325

Balakrishnan, R., & Heintz, J. (2019). Human rights in an unequal world: Structural inequalities and the imperative for global cooperation. *Humanity: An International Journal of Human Rights, Humanitarianism, and Development 10*(3), 395–403. https://dx.doi.org/10.1353/hum.2019.0017.

Cash-Gibson, L., Rojas-Gualdrón, D. F., Pericàs, J. M., & Benach, J. (2018). Inequalities in global health inequalities research: A 50-year bibliometric analysis (1966–2015). *PloS One, 13*(1), e0191901–e0191901. https://doi.org/10.1371/journal.pone.0191901

Çelik, C. (2023). Global food insecurity as a crisis of social reproduction for the classes of labour. *Human Geography, 16*(2), 193–199. https://doi.org/10.1177/19427786231153052

Chen, M. (2023, February 16). Unearthed flush toilet dates back 2,400 years. *China Daily.* https://global.chinadaily.com.cn/a/202302/16/WS63ed04ada31057c47ebaf009.html

Chojnacka, K., Skrzypczak, D., Szopa, D., Izydorczyk, G., Moustakas, K., & Witek-Krowiak, A. (2023). Management of biological sewage sludge: Fertilizer nitrogen recovery as the solution to fertilizer crisis. *Journal of Environmental Management, 326,* 116602–116602. https://doi.org/10.1016/j.jenvman.2022.116602

Cohen, S. (2016). Shit. In Salter, M. B. (Ed.), *Making things international* 2, pp. 285–298. University of Minnesota Press.

Cordell, D., Rosemarin, A., Schröder, J. J., & Smit, A. L. (2011). Towards global phosphorus security: A systems framework for phosphorus recovery and reuse options. *Chemosphere, 84*(6), 747–758. https://doi.org/10.1016/j.chemosphere.2011.02.032

Doron, A., & Raja, I. (2015). The cultural politics of shit: class, gender and public space in India. *Postcolonial Studies, 18*(2), 189–207. https://doi.org/10.1080/13688790.2015.1065714

du Plessis, G. (2023). Destructive plasticity and the microbial geopolitics of childhood malnutrition. *Review of International Studies, 49*(2), 300–318. https://doi.org/10.1017/S0260210522000328

European Commission. (2023). *Critical raw materials.* Directorate-General for Internal Market, Industry, Entrepreneurship and SMEs. https://single-market-economy.ec.europa.eu/sectors/raw-materials/areas-specific-interest/critical-raw-materials_en

Fairchild, I., Cearreta, A., Summerhayes, C., Gałuszka, A. & Wagreich, M. (2022, April 22). *The Anthropocene signal amidst the noise.* In Rosol, C. & Rispoli, G. (Eds.), Anthropogenic markers: Stratigraphy and context. Max Planck Institute for the History of Science (MPIWG). https://www.anthropocene-curriculum.org/anthropogenic-markers/anthrobiogeochemical-cycles/contribution/the-anthropocene-signal-amidst-the-noise

Foster, J. B. (1999). Marx's theory of metabolic rift: Classical foundations for environmental sociology. *The American Journal of Sociology, 105*(2), 366–405. https://doi.org/10.1086/210315

Fraser, N. (2022). *Cannibal capitalism: How our system is devouring democracy, care, and the planet and what we can do about it.* Verso.

Gesing, F. (2023). The material politics of slurry: Mobilisations and transformations along the waste–fertiliser continuum. *Political Geography, 101*, 102832-. https://doi.org/10.1016/j.polgeo.2023.102832

Gibson-Graham, J. K., & Dombroski, K. (2020). *The handbook of diverse economies.* Edward Elgar Publishing. https://doi.org/10.4337/9781788119962

Gmitrowicz-Iwan, J., & Ligęza, S. (2023). Floodplain lakes as an indicator of increasing industrial pollution – Case study from a fertilizer factory in Poland. *Environmental Research, 238*, 117278–117278. https://doi.org/10.1016/j.envres.2023.117278

GovTrack.us. (2024). H.R. 776 — 102nd Congress: Energy Policy Act of 1992. https://www.govtrack.us/congress/bills/102/hr776

Göransson, C., Larsson, I., & Carlsson, I. (2023). Art of connectedness: Value-creating care for older persons provided with toileting assistance and containment strategies—A critical interpretive synthesis. *Journal of Clinical Nursing, 32*(9–10), 1806–1820. https://doi.org/10.1111/jocn.16216

Haraway, D. J. (2016). *Staying with the trouble: Making kin in the chthulucene.* Duke University Press.

Hawkins, G. (2003). Down the drain: Shit and the politics of disturbance. In Hawkins, G. & Muecke, S. (Eds.), *Culture and waste: The creation and destruction of value*, pp. 39–52. Rowman & Littlefield.

Hill, A. (2018, February 8). 'Gross failure' in man's care led to death from constipation. *The Guardian.* https://www.theguardian.com/uk-news/2018/feb/08/gross-failure-in-mans-care-led-to-death-from-constipation

Hu, S.-M. (2021). Trace gas measurements using cavity ring-down spectroscopy. In W. W. Chen, D. S. Venables, & M. W. Sigrist (Eds.), *Advances in spectroscopic monitoring of the atmosphere* (pp. 413–441). Elsevier.

Häder, D.-P., Banaszak, A. T., Villafañe, V. E., Narvarte, M. A., González, R. A., & Helbling, E. W. (2020). Anthropogenic pollution of aquatic ecosystems: Emerging problems with global implications. *The Science of the Total Environment, 713*, 136586–136586. https://doi.org/10.1016/j.scitotenv.2020.136586

Jackson, L. (2014). *Dirty old London: The Victorian fight against filth.* University of Yale Press.

Jumbri, I. A., Ikeda, S., Jimichi, M., Saka, C., & Managi, S. (2019). Inequality of health stock and the relation to national wealth. *International Journal for Equity in Health, 18*(1), 188–188. https://doi.org/10.1186/s12939-019-1096-x

Kar, S., Singh, R., Gurian, P. L., Hendricks, A., Kohl, P., McKelvey, S., & Spatari, S. (2023). Life cycle assessment and techno-economic analysis of nitrogen recovery by ammonia air-stripping from wastewater treatment. *The Science of the Total Environment, 857*, 159499. https://doi.org/10.1016/j.scitotenv.2022.159499

KJV. (2008). *The Bible: Authorized King James version.* Oxford University Press.

Knowles, R., Sharland, M., Hsia, Y., Magrini, N., Moja, L., Siyam, A., & Tayler, E. (2020). Measuring antibiotic availability and use in 20 low- and middle-income countries. *Bulletin of the World Health Organization, 98*(3), 177–187C. https://doi.org/10.2471/BLT.19.241349

Kok, D.-J. D., Pande, S., van Lier, J. B., Ortigara, A. R. C., Savenije, H., & Uhlenbrook, S. (2018). Global phosphorus recovery from wastewater for agricultural reuse. *Hydrology and Earth System Sciences*, 22(11), 5781–5799. https://doi.org/10.5194/hess-22-5781-2018

Koloski-Ostrow, A. O. (2015). *The archaeology of sanitation in Roman Italy: Toilets, sewers, and water systems.* The University of North Carolina Press.

Koskue, V., Monetti, J., Rossi, N., Nieradzik, L., Freguia, S., Kokko, M., & Ledezma, P. (2022). Fate of pharmaceuticals and PFASs during the electrochemical generation of a nitrogen-rich nutrient product from real reject water. *Journal of Environmental Chemical Engineering, 10*(2), 107284. https://doi.org/10.1016/j.jece.2022.107284

Kuhn L., Kayser M., Aue R., Bongers-Römer S. (2022). Notdürftige Infrastrukturen: Öffentliche Toiletten zwischen Neoliberalisierung und Utopie. *B&S Öffentliche Infrastrukturen - Die politische Gestaltung der vernetzten Gesellschaft (LpB) 1*(2), 69–75.

Laakkonen, Simo. (2001). *Vesiensuojelun synty: Helsingin ja sen merialueen ympäristöhistoriaa 1878–1928.* Gaudeamus.

LaCom, C. (2007). Filthy bodies, porous boundaries: The politics of shit in disability studies. *Disability Studies Quarterly*, 27(1–2). https://doi.org/10.18061/dsq.v27i1/2.11

Laperrousaz, B., Levast, B., Fontaine, M., Nancey, S., Dechelotte, P., Doré, J., & Lehert, P. (2024). Safety comparison of single-donor and pooled fecal microbiota transfer product preparation in ulcerative colitis: systematic review and meta-analysis. *BMC Gastroenterology, 24*(1), 402–412. https://doi.org/10.1186/s12876-024-03487-2

Laville, S. (2021, July 6). Southern Water dumped raw sewage into sea for years. *The Guardian.* https://www.theguardian.com/environment/2021/jul/06/southern-water-dumped-raw-sewage-into-sea-for-years

Laville & Horton, H. (2024, March 26). 4m hours of raw sewage discharges in England in 2023, data expected to show. *The Guardian.* https://www.theguardian.com/business/2024/

mar/26/4m-hours-of-raw-sewage-discharges-in-england-last-year-figures-expected-to-show

Laville, S. & Horton, H. (2023, July 4). Water firms discharged raw sewage 300,000 times last year, court hears. *The Guardian.* https://www.theguardian.com/environment/2023/jul/04/thames-water-fined-33m-for-pumping-sewage-into-rivers

Lele, U. (2021). Introduction. In Lele, U. J., Agarwal, M., Baldwin, B., & Goswami, S. (Eds.), *Food for all: international organizations and the transformation of agriculture* (First edition.). Oxford University Press.

Liang, T., Kaka Mirza, H., Malakoutikhah, A., Dehghan, M., Mokhtarabadi, S., Behzadi Fard, S., & Al-Amer, R. (2023). Moral injury and its correlates among Iranian nurses in the second year of the COVID-19 pandemic: A multicenter cross-sectional study. *Journal of Religion and Health, 62*(6), 3979–3994. https://doi.org/10.1007/s10943-023-01938-w

Lynch, J. (2019). *Regimes of inequality: The political economy of health and wealth.* Cambridge University Press. https://doi.org/10.1017/9781139051576

Manchha, A. V., Way, K. A., Tann, K., & Thai, M. (2022). The social construction of stigma in aged-care work: Implications for health professionals' work intentions. *The Gerontologist, 62*(7), 994–1005. https://doi.org/10.1093/geront/gnac002

Meldgaard Hansen, A. (2016). Rehabilitative bodywork: cleaning up the dirty work of homecare. *Sociology of Health & Illness, 38*(7), 1092–1105. https://doi.org/10.1111/1467-9566.12435

Molotch, H. L., & Norén, L. (2010). *Toilet: public restrooms and the politics of sharing.* New York University Press.

de Montaigne, M. (2003). On experience. In Michel de Montaigne, *The complete works* (pp. 922–1045). Translated by Donald M. Frame. Everyman Library. (Original work published 1588).

Montsion, J. M., & Tan, S. K. (2016). Smell this: Singapore's curry day and visceral citizenship. *Singapore Journal of Tropical Geography, 37*(2), 209–223. https://doi.org/10.1111/sjtg.12143

Morales, M. del C., Harris, L., & Öberg, G. (2014). Citizenshit: The right to flush and the urban sanitation imaginary. *Environment and Planning. A, 46*(12), 2816–2833. https://doi.org/10.1068/a130331p

Myer, K. (2020). *How to shit in the woods: An environmentally sound approach to a lost art.* Ten Speed Press. (Original work published 1994).

Nedelciu, C. E., Ragnarsdottir, K. V., Schlyter, P., & Stjernquist, I. (2020). Global phosphorus supply chain dynamics: Assessing regional impact to 2050. *Global Food Security, 26,* 100426–100426. https://doi.org/10.1016/j.gfs.2020.100426

Olah, G. A., Prakash, G. K. S., & Goeppert, A. (2011). Anthropogenic chemical carbon cycle for a sustainable future. *Journal of the American Chemical Society, 133*(33), 12881–12898. https://doi.org/10.1021/ja202642y

Penner, B. (2013). *Bathroom.* Reaktion Books.

Perman, S. (2000, April 3). Psst! Wanna Buy an Illegal Toilet? Americans travel to Canada to get around a conservation law. *Time.* https://content.time.com/time/subscriber/article/0,33009,996507,00.html

Pickering, L., & Wiseman, P. (2019). Dirty scholarship and dirty lives: Explorations in bodies and belonging. *The Sociological Review, 67*(4), 746–765. https://doi.org/10.1177/0038026119854244

Plaxton, W. C., & Tran, H. T. (2011). Metabolic adaptations of phosphate-starved plants. *Plant Physiology, 156*(3), 1006–1015. https://doi.org/10.1104/pp.111.175281

Plimmer, G. (2024, April 26). Thames Water customers will have paid £540mn for London's 'Super Sewer'. *Financial Times.* https://www.ft.com/content/1b58a0f7-cf7a-4d39-9ebb-93db7172ece3

Prabaharyaka, I. (2020). Shit, shit, every where (or: notes on the difficulties of classifying shits). *International Development Planning Review, 42*(3), 295–313. https://doi.org/10.3828/idpr.2020.12

Raimi, O. M., Ilesanmi, A., Alima, O., & Omini, D. E. (2021). Exploring how human activities disturb the balance of biogeochemical cycles: Evidence from the carbon, nitrogen and hydrologic cycles. *Research on World Agricultural Economy,* 2(3), 23–44. https://doi.org/10.36956/rwae.v2i3.426

Rajala-Vaittinen, A. (2025). Secretional care and non-ableist postgrowth: Taking the diverse needs of urination and defecation seriously. [Manuscript submitted for publication]. Tampere University.

Ramster, G., Greed, C., & Bichard, J.-A. (2018). How inclusion can exclude: The Case of public toilet provision for women. *Built Environment, 44*(1), 52–76. https://doi.org/10.2148/benv.44.1.52

Riungu, J. N. (2021). *Off-Site enhanced biogas production with concomitant pathogen removal from faecal matter.* CRC Press. https://doi.org/10.1201/9781003174196

Samoraj, M., Mironiuk, M., Izydorczyk, G., Witek-Krowiak, A., Szopa, D., Moustakas, K., & Chojnacka, K. (2022). The challenges and perspectives for anaerobic digestion of animal waste and fertilizer application of the digestate. *Chemosphere, 295,* 133799–133799. https://doi.org/10.1016/j.chemosphere.2022.133799

Sichler, T. C., Adam, C., Montag, D., & Barjenbruch, M. (2022). Future nutrient recovery from sewage sludge regarding three different scenarios—German case study. *Journal of Cleaner Production, 333,* 130130-. https://doi.org/10.1016/j.jclepro.2021.130130

Smithwick, E. A. H. (2022). Nutrient flows in the landscape. In Francis, R. A., Millington, J. D. A., Perry, G. L. W., & Minor, E. S. (Eds.), *The Routledge handbook of landscape ecology* (pp. 140–158). Routledge. https://doi.org/10.4324/9780429399480-9

Sutton, M. A., Erisman, J. W., Dentener, F., & Möller, D. (2008). Ammonia in the environment: From ancient times to the present. *Environmental Pollution, 156*(3), 583–604. https://doi.org/10.1016/j.envpol.2008.03.013

Tideway. (n.d.). *About us.* Retrieved May 17, 2024, from https://www.tideway.london/about-us/

Tiwari, P., Tirumala, R. D., & Shukla, J. (2022). Household choices of sanitation infrastructure and impact on disease in India. *Environment and Planning. B, Urban Analytics and City Science, 49*(8), 2054–2071. https://doi.org/10.1177/23998083221088293

Tsakiris, M., Vehar, N., & Tucciarelli, R. (2021). Visceral politics: a theoretical and empirical proof of concept. *Philosophical Transactions of the Royal Society of London. Series B. Biological Sciences*, *376*(1822), 20200142–20200142. https://doi.org/10.1098/rstb.2020.0142

Tsing, A. L. (2015). *The mushroom at the end of the world: on the possibility of life in capitalist ruins*. Princeton University Press.

Tuholske, C., Halpern, B. S., Blasco, G., Villasenor, J. C., Frazier, M., & Caylor, K. (2021). Mapping global inputs and impacts from of human sewage in coastal ecosystems. *PloS One*, *16*(11), e0258898-. https://doi.org/10.1371/journal.pone.0258898

Twigg, J. (2000). *Bathing—The body and community care*. Routledge. https://doi.org/10.4324/9780203190876

United Nations. (2023). *Blueprint for acceleration: Sustainable development goal 6 synthesis report on water and sanitation 2023*. https://www.unwater.org/sites/default/files/2023-08/UN-Water_SDG6_SynthesisReport_2023.pdf

Vaittinen, T., Koljonen, K., Tella, S., Asikainen, E., & Laatikainen, K. (2023). Holistically sustainable continence care: A working definition, the case of single-used absorbent hygiene products (AHPs) and the need for ecosystems thinking. *Proceedings of the Institution of Mechanical Engineers. Part H, Journal of Engineering in Medicine*, https://doi.org/10.1177/09544119231188860

Wambui, J. M. (2020). A cosmopolitan ghetto: The shifting image of Kibera Slum from 'Flying Toilets' to a centre for metropolitan innovation. *Thinker, 85*, 20–35. https://doi.org/10.36615/thethinker.v85i3.379

Wear, S. L. (2019). Battling a common enemy: Joining forces in the fight against sewage pollution. *Bioscience*, *69*(5), 360–367. https://doi.org/10.1093/biosci/biz02

Werner, F. (2017). Excerpts from "Dark Matter: The history of shit" by Florian Werner (transl. Tereza Kuldova). *Journal of Extreme Anthropology*, *1*(1), 63–80. https://doi.org/10.5617/jea.4520

World Health Organization. (2023a). *Burden of disease attributable to unsafe drinking-water, sanitation and hygiene: 2019 update*. https://iris.who.int/bitstream/handle/10665/370026/9789240075610-eng.pdf?sequence=1

World Health Organization. (2023b, December 11). *Cholera*. https://www.who.int/news-room/fact-sheets/detail/cholera

World Health Organization. (2024, March 24). *Sanitation*. https://www.who.int/news-room/fact-sheets/detail/sanitation

Weisberger, M. (2018, March 21). *How much do you poop in your lifetime?* Live Science. https://www.livescience.com/61966-how-much-you-poop-in-lifetime.html

Whiley, L. A., & Grandy, G. (2022). The ethics of service work in a neoliberal healthcare context: doing embodied and "dirty" emotional labor. *Qualitative Research in Organizations and Management*, *17*(1), 136–157. https://doi.org/10.1108/QROM-08-2020-2005

Wibberley, G. (2013). The problems of a 'dirty workplace' in domiciliary care. *Health & Place*, *21*, 156–162. https://doi.org/10.1016/j.healthplace.2013.01.014

Wilkinson, R., & Pickett, K. (2010). *The spirit level: Why equality is better for everyone*. Penguin.

Wiseman, P. (2019). Lifting the lid: Disabled toilets as sites of belonging and embodied citizenship. *The Sociological Review, 67*(4), 788–806. https://doi.org/10.1177/0038026119854255
Yang, S.-C., Lin, C.-H., Aljuffali, I. A., & Fang, J.-Y. (2017). Current pathogenic Escherichia coli foodborne outbreak cases and therapy development. *Archives of Microbiology, 199*(6), 811–825. https://doi.org/10.1007/s00203-017-1393-y
Žižek, S. (2017). Knee-Deep in ideology. *Journal of Extreme Anthropology, 1*(1), 82–83. https://doi.org/10.5617/jea.4475

4
The capitalist's apprentice
Employment and the reproduction of capitalist culture

Mark L. Young

On the eve of the Industrial Revolution Adam Smith (1776) reflected on emerging employment relations and how they would affect the cognitive ability of workers. Observing that one's "understandings" were "necessarily formed by their ordinary employments," Smith (1776) warned that the restricted ambit of the workplace dulled the employee's intellect by limiting opportunities to "exert [their] understanding or exercise [their] invention" (p. 336). Subsequently, he observed, the structure of the workplace impaired the employee's capacity to effectively function in social and political life. But Smith was careful to preserve the assumption that employment under capitalism was a departure from the past by locating the cause of these conditions in the seemingly objective, technical division of labour rather than in relations of domination. A few years later, John Millar (1803) connected the psychosocial implications of employment with workplace subordination. He observed that labourers are "placed in a state of inferiority" through which they "acquire habits of submission" (Millar, 1803, pp. 115–116). Consequently, "[b]y living in a state of inferiority and dependence, the mind is inured to subjection. . ." (Millar, 1803, p. 291). Neither Smith nor Millar drew a direct connection to a historic feudal power structure, even as they described relations of dominion over labour. Yet, no matter how much early economists brushed aside the feudal legacy within employment relations, this legacy was clearly inscribed in English common law and its influence can be traced well into the liberal-capitalist era.

Young, M. L. (2025). The capitalist's apprentice: Employment and the reproduction of capitalist culture. In A. Kangas, I. Gataulina, M. Poutanen, A. I. Rajala & H-E. Ventovirta (Eds.), *Retheorising capitalism* (pp. 70–90). Tampere University Press. https://doi.org/10.61201/tup.981

This chapter examines the persistence of a feudal legacy of hierarchy and paternalism in the Anglo-American workplace. Because of its relevance to modern employment, this chapter focuses on the evolution and influence of paternalism within "free" labour rather than the undisguised domination associated with chattel slavery. But just as coerced servitude is often assumed to have disappeared with the abolition of chattel slavery, feudal forms of domination are perceived as relics of a past that gave way to the emancipatory spirit of capitalism and wage labour. Consequently, the persistence of workplace paternalism and hierarchy offers a basis for rethinking the purportedly liberalising dimensions of occupational freedom by positing that all employment is a form of domination. This, in turn, supports a reassessment of capitalism, from a democratic system productive of economic opportunity to one of social control and exploitation. I argue that employment perpetuates the spirit of apprenticeship by limiting employee autonomy and requiring submission to authority within a hierarchic framework. By tracing the historic endurance of apprenticeship-like power relations into the modern institution of employment, I uncover the feudal legacy of wage labour. The psychosocial effects of employment that Smith and Millar identified remained relevant throughout industrialisation and continue into the seemingly liberalising era of the modern gig economy.

Workplace domination continues to cultivate authoritarian personality traits which suppress critical thinking, rationalise domination and subordination, and encourage political apathy and conformity (Fromm, 1941/1994; Jost & Hunyady, 2002).[1] These traits arise from a psychological need to assuage and rationalise feelings of powerlessness engendered through workplace subordination. For many, the rationalisation of subordination takes the form of a self-narrated fantasy of freedom and autonomy realised through conformity to workplace culture. This phenomenon has long been studied by psychologists. But while earlier researchers located the origins of authoritarian traits in childhood development (Adorno et al., 1950; Lipset, 1959), later scholarship has focused attention on continued socialisation in adulthood (Mortimer & Simmons, 1978) and on the workplace as the most important theatre of this process (Kohn & Schooler, 1983; Stanojevic et al., 2020). Traits acquired in the workplace transfer to other social contexts (Gini, 1998; Marcuse, 1964; Solt, 2012). Subjection to workplace authority, I contend, fosters submission in the consumer and political spheres. Submission through participation in consumeristic behaviour supports concentrations of wealth and power that wield influence in the political sphere. Acceptance of a commercially driven political sphere, in turn, fosters public consent to law and policy which underpin a capitalist agenda. Thus, submission and consent to economistic ideology, hierarchy, and extremes of inequality in wealth and power support a unified capitalist culture.[2] And by creating conditions that make the

---

1 I am not arguing that employment fosters the authoritarian personality in toto but rather highlighting research that associates submission and conformity with chronic domination.

2 *Capitalist culture* is herein defined as culture reflective of the relations of production which are defined by Althusser (1971/2014) as "relations of exploitation" (pp. 27–34).

wage relationship virtually unavoidable, these features of capitalist cultural generate their own reproduction.

Capitalism has historically been posited as a departure from feudalism, associated with market freedom and individual liberty. Likewise, employment is characterised as a source of freedom in the choice of occupation.[3] But the break from feudalism was not as complete as some have asserted. When viewed historically, employment relations reveal the persistence of a feudal power structure within the modern capitalist framework. While industrial capitalism gained ascendency in the early nineteenth century, the legal doctrine of master and servant that once regulated relations between apprentice and master, was applied to wage workers in both England and America. And even as the enforcement of this legal doctrine began to disintegrate by the mid-nineteenth century, its spirit remained embedded in Anglo-American workplace culture, institutionalising the attitudes and conventions of apprenticeship but without its traditional path to independence. The subsequent history of employment has been the history of a persistent paternalism that elicits and normalises workplace discipline, obedience, and fidelity alongside a discourse of freedom and opportunity—the rationalisation of domination and dependency within an illusion of agency and independence.

Feudalism persisted in both Britain and America through the paternalism embodied in the doctrine of master and servant. This doctrine, handed down from medieval times with few alterations, was used to define and delimit worker freedom (Horwitz, 1977; Steinfeld, 1991; Tigar & Levy, 1977). Indeed, the first printed version of master and servant by the seventeenth-century jurist Sir Matthew Hale (1713/1820) retained a feudal vocabulary. By the eighteenth century, master and servant served to regulate the institutions of bound labour and apprenticeship—both, *temporary* forms of unfreedom. Its core principles, according to jurist Mathew Bacon (1740, p. 544), created a "superiority of power" over the servant in which was demanded "duty, subjection," and "allegiance." When a nascent wage regime emerged in America at the end of the eighteenth century, the doctrine's jurisdiction was expanded to include free labour. At which time, asserted Tomlins (2010), "the ambit of master and servant law steadily widened until it absorbed the employment contract as a whole . . ." (p. 330).

What were once temporary conditions of the dependent apprentice became the perpetual reality of the permanent employee. Employment continued to resemble apprenticeship through the circumscription of autonomy and habitual subjection to employer domination, leaving many to rationalise dependency and subordination by associating freedom with conformity to paternalistic authority (Fromm, 1941/1994).

This cultural environment of employment helps to perpetuate obedience to paternalistic authority outside of the workplace in economic, political, and social spheres. Three hallmarks of apprenticeship, *discipline*—adoption of the methods, rules, procedures, and technical values of production, *obedience*—a priori recognition of the master's authority, and *fidelity*—commitment, and faithful identification with

[3] Throughout this chapter the term employment will denote work performed for wages or salary exclusively.

the interests of master and trade, characterised classic apprenticeship. These features persist within the institution of employment, cultivating transferable behaviours. Capitalist culture is reflected and reinforced when *discipline* becomes the internalised adoption of corporate/capitalist methods and values (Graeber, 2018; Hochschild, 1983; Mills, 1951); *obedience* is exhibited in apathetic political conformity and deference to authoritarian hierarchy (Elden, 1981; Jackall, 1988; Pateman, 1970; Solt, 2012); and *fidelity* is manifest in personal identification with power, corporate or political, which rationalises a restricted interpretation of one's agency and freedom (Casey, 1999; Fromm, 1941/1994; Jost & Hunyady, 2002; Marcuse, 1964; Willmott, 1993). These conditions, in turn, influence the behaviour of employees in other social spheres (Gini, 1998; Jackall, 1988; Marcuse, 1964). In this way a persistent paternal-feudal influence within the modern workplace paradoxically contributes to the reproduction of a culture thought to be liberal and democratic.

From feudal law to management discourse

Master and servant law, argued Orren (1991), represented an unbroken chain of feudal discipline stretching from its misty beginnings in fourteenth-century Britain into nineteenth-century America. Orren observed this feudal artefact, where it resided for so many centuries, in the hands of local jurists serving as an instrument of power and control. She argued that master and servant law met its demise in 1930s America with a series of federal acts through which the regulation of workers by common law was repudiated in favour of a legislative approach that would address labour in broadly political and anonymous terms.[4] But already by the end of the eighteenth century the exercise of disciplinary power had evolved from physical compulsion to more indirect, psychological forms of coercion (Elias, 1939/2000; Foucault, 1995; Gellner, 1983/2006). This trend was reflected in workplace discipline in which direct compulsion was abandoned in favour of economic coercion (Young, 2023). As nineteenth-century economic conditions increasingly made wage work unavoidable, the locus of discipline passed from law, imposed by jurists, to anonymous economic power commanded by employers.

Consequently, what Orren (1991) saw as the decay and ultimate demise of master and servant signalled its completed transfer to more indirect modes of enforcement rather than the end of feudal power over workers. Her assessment inadvertently implies an association of freedom with wage labour by positing the end of feudal employment relations. But while the mechanisms of disciplinary power were no longer legible in the official documents of the state, the persistence of the master-apprentice power relationship may be traced through employment-management discourse into modern times as it gradually migrated from law to a more general and rationalised workplace culture—a migration that only *appeared* to leave feudal forms behind.

---

4 Orren (1991) posits the end of feudalism in America with the demise of master and servant through the 1937 Supreme Court ruling in *National Labor Relations Board* v. *Jones & Laughlin Steel Corp.*

Originally, the relationship of master and apprentice was more than economic; it prepared the apprentice for an independent assimilation into society. Paternalistic power was legitimised by the master's function as role model and educator, *in loco parentis*. The apprentice studied the techniques of a trade in its entirety but also, as a member of the master's family, received training in self-discipline and moral comportment (Laslett, 1965; Rorabaugh, 1986). And while the apprentice was expected to conform to strict hierarchy under the master's command, once their term was completed and after a period of journeyman status, the former apprentice ideally became an independent, autonomous member of society (Morris, 1946).[5] Apprenticeship remained the dominant form of vocational training throughout eighteenth-century Anglo-America. With the advent of industrialisation, however, social conditions began to change.

In the late eighteenth-century, following the American revolution and independence, a new spirit of individualism initiated a decline in the master's authority. Lured by immediate economic autonomy and a chance to participate in rising consumerism, many young workers chose wage-paying jobs over apprenticeship (Rorabaugh, 1986). At the same time owners of capital and champions of laissez-faire economic policy, annoyed with the old guild craftsmen's power to regulate labour and set their own wages sought to supplant trade masters. "[C]ertain employers, calling themselves masters, after the fashionable aristocratick slang of the day," fumed one group of New York carpenters, in 1836, "have unwisely pretended to regulate the price of journeymen's labour, and if possible set aside our regulations..." (House carpenters, 1836). Eventually the capitalist-masters succeeded in weakening traditional craft associations and the artisan became the "permanent journeyman" of capital (Mill, 1848, p. 283; Ware, 1924).

Lost with the guild tradition were provisions for education and training that prepared the apprentice for independence. The (capitalist) master and servant relationship became strictly pecuniary. But those who objected to this new relationship were often not disputing the economic dimension of wage labour. Instead, they were protesting, as Ware (1924, p. xiv) noted, "a loss of dignity and independence." Dependency, described in the nineteenth century as "industrial feudalism" (Chevalier, 1839, p. 204), has characterised employment ever since, manifest in the paternalistic hierarchy of the modern workplace which, as Jackall (1988) observed, resembles the feudal structure of a medieval fiefdom.

Under such circumstances it was difficult to equate freedom with employment. To legitimate conditions under which the apprentice as employee would no longer progress to independent status, freedom had to be *discursively* connected to employment. This was accomplished, in the nineteenth century, by redefining

[5] Eighteenth-century indentures (contracts) stipulated that the graduated apprentice would receive not only tools of their trade but in many cases clothing and farm animals. These stipulations demonstrate that apprenticeship was not intended to merely produce industrious workers but to provide a foundation for independence.

freedom as a *chance* of freedom, an unfalsifiable lottery of independence.[6] This discourse of opportunity would legitimise domination under wage labour with the implication that employment was only a temporary prelude to freedom, substituting the apprentice's path to independence with vague and imprecise notions of striking it rich.

The transition from a discourse of individual independence to one of opportunity is illustrated in an 1842 legal treatise which obscured the distinction between apprentice and worker, implying that hired servitude (employment) under a paternalistic master, like apprenticeship, was merely a temporary condition. "As a permanent arrangement, where servitude is the *unchanging* and inevitable lot of one class," insisted Silas Jones (1842), "it cannot be justified, but what is more rational than that the young man ... should contract to serve and assist the gentleman of wealth, until he can safely command the means of being his own master!" (p. 81). It is here we see the shifting locus of feudal authority as it began to leave the legal domain and gradually take the form of management discourse. The abstraction of opportunity veiled the incremental establishment of permanent worker servitude as it was ideologically transfigured into a kind of freedom to participate in an uncertain, but ostensibly democratic, chance. Opportunity helped to relocate the locus of power, from direct, legally supported, discipline to the indirect, psychological coercion of an abstract economic system. In so doing, it accommodated a growing reliance, by the end of the nineteenth century, on workplace discipline through psychological manipulation. This manipulation included the characterisation of the employer, first as an individual, later as company, as a paternal figure whose authority was validated through implications of moral and intellectual superiority. The employer thus assumed the permanent role of master in the master/apprentice relationship.

The changing face of paternalism

Early examples of workplace paternalism were directly related to authority figures who saw themselves as moral superiors whose rule was supported by law. They regarded their employees, much like the apprentices of the past, as "dependent and requiring the moulding influence of a benevolent owner" (Anthony, 1977, p. 75). Directly analogous to the proscriptions written into the old indentures, employees were characterised as incapable of self-discipline and independence. Throughout the nineteenth century paternalism was facilitated by the worker's increasing dependency on wage labour. Employers exercised control either as a condition of employment or through the restriction of wages. A common attitude of the time was expressed by a British employer who insisted that if he paid workers more than subsistence wages, they would only waste their money on "bottles of whiskey, bags of sweets, or fat geese for Christmas" (George, 1909, p. 196). Paternalism in Britain also took the form of factory

[6] It was a common belief of the age that most individuals held, as Smith (1776, p. 155) remarked, an "absurd confidence" in "their own good fortune," making this discourse readily acceptable.

festivals and group excursions. These precursors of modern, corporate-sponsored events included ritual enactments of obedience and fidelity which diffused the feudal-like hierarchy of the workplace into a more general community culture. In these group activities workers publicly honoured employers with song, poetry, or gifts, mimicking feudal patronage, "affirming their unwavering allegiance ... and their acceptance of paternalistic practices" (Moine, 2023, p. 214). These activities also inspired the fantasy of illusionary participation in the personal lives of their employers which encouraged fidelity and diverted attention away from class conflict and oppression.

Paternalism was enthusiastically adopted in America and implemented in factory towns such as Lowell, Massachusetts, where employee's non-working hours were subject to strict regulation. When the economist Richard Ely (1885) visited the company town of Pullman, Illinois, he encountered a "dependent and servile people" living under a "benevolent, well-wishing feudalism, which desires the happiness of the people, but in such a way as will please the authorities" (pp. 464–465). Direct interference with employee's personal lives persisted into the twentieth century. As late as 1914, Henry Ford, under what one newspaper called "Ford's Feudal System," employed a squadron of investigators to visit employee's homes and determine if their marital status, hygiene, and moral comportment conformed to company standards ("Ford Methods of Handling Men," 1914; Watts, 2005, p. 220).[7]

Modern employers continue to "regulate workers' off-hour lives," observed Anderson (2017), "—their political activities, speech, choice of sexual partner, use of recreational drugs, alcohol, smoking, and exercise" (p. 39). But many rationalise or are unaware of the extent of this power as it has assumed a less obtrusive, benevolent character. In the early days of industrialisation such presumption was regarded as an affront to worker independence and dignity, outrage that is conspicuously absent from modern employee attitudes. Early nineteenth-century English workers openly rebelled against paternalistic intrusion into their private lives (Alton, 1824). These employees were not protesting low wages or long working hours but, rather, assumptions that they were not capable of self-governance. By the mid-nineteenth century, however, in many American and British centres of industrial activity, criticism and strikes were more likely directed towards technical aspects of work such as length of workday or rate of pay as paternalism was gradually rationalised within workplace culture.

In both Britain and America, master and servant law underpinned the paternalism and authority of the employer. Within nineteenth-century American courts, Groat (1911) observed: "The spirit of medievalism with its antagonism to the working classes and its ingrained feeling that in some way the labourer must be controlled by his employers, somewhat after the manner of a serf by his lord or an apprentice by his master, survived" (p. 50). But by the end of the century, master and servant was less frequently evoked to discipline workers. Discipline shifted to more abstract and anonymous forms of economic coercion. At the same time the exercise of power

---

7 Here the mass production and standardisation associated with Fordism was applied to the social lives of employees. And even as the overt practice of paternalism under Ford was short-lived, it demonstrated that the standardised, mass-produced (conforming) employee was becoming a desideratum of the large organisation.

within the workplace became increasingly indirect, a matter of procedure, policy, and economic rationalities.

By the end of the nineteenth century disciplinary power, in a general context, was no longer personal but had become an anonymous machine (Foucault, 1980). This was reflected in the twentieth century exercise of company power through which paternalism was realised in seemingly innocuous benefits such as company meals, vocational guidance, savings plans, health care, guaranteed employment, and other services and incentives (Devinatz, 2012; Mayo, 1933). Still, these less intrusive forms of paternalism continued to encourage dependency and legitimate employer authority, throughout the twentieth century, operating on the old assumptions that characterised employees as irresponsible and untrustworthy. Peters and Waterman (1982) underscored the continued prevalence of these assumptions insisting that most modern "organizations are governed by rules that assume that the *average* worker is an incompetent ne'er-do-well, just itching to screw up" (p. 236). Recent scholarship echoes these themes observing that employees continue to be the targets of routine manipulation and deception (Gottschalk, 2018).

The transformation of paternalism to an anonymous system of rules and policy obscured the locus of authority, blunting the ability to effectively recognise or challenge conditions of dependency. When an early nineteenth-century factory town in England was criticised as a "nursery for men" it was because the paternalistic employer, whose workplace authority was supported by local law, directly sought to regulate workers' private lives as if they were his apprentices or wards (Wooler, 1817, p. 469). But an eerily similar characterisation was repeated over a century and a half later in a poem by an American auto worker: "Are these men and women Workers of the world? Or is it an overgrown nursery with children ... What is it about the entrance way, those gates to the plant ... that instantaneously makes a child out of a man?" (Jones, 1977, p. 30). In the latter critique the authority of the master is replaced with an ambiguous, indefinable spirit, one that was no longer challenged but accepted with resignation. The direct paternalism of the earlier employer was gradually subsumed by a permeating employment ethos, no longer enforced by authoritative figures or conspicuously supported by legal doctrine. Criticism therefore lost its target, and its vitality melted into cynicism and submission. Dependency on an anonymous system masked the domination that was once so poignant under direct, personal control.

"Humane" paternalism legitimises permanent apprenticeship

By the early 1900s it could no longer be claimed that employment was a temporary stop on the way to personal independence. Growing class consciousness and increasing economic inequality demanded new methods of employee pacification. Industrial psychologist Charles Myers (1922), speaking before a group of British elites alarmed by the rise of Bolshevism in Russia, insisted that, in the twentieth century, "the mind of the worker would receive paramount attention." (p. 62). Industrial psychologists sought to encourage solidarity among workers and between owners and workers through the manipulation of emotion. But this strategy was not only intended to improve workplace harmony but to foster broader social cohesion (Myers, 1922). The intent was to ameliorate potential class conflict by connecting the capitalist mode of production to the well-being of the country. As another industrial psychologist put it, in their work "the social well-being of the nation is the only legitimate end" (Farmer, 1924, p. 78).

One way to promote social well-being, it was thought, was through paternalism. Workers identified with companies that promoted a "humane," paternalistic image (Mayo, 1933). Morale (fidelity) could be improved by artificially cultivating meaning and cohesion within the workplace and beyond. It was an attempt, observed C. Wright Mills (1951), to paradoxically "conquer work alienation within the bounds of work alienation" (p. 235). The serf was connected to the manor; the apprentice was part of the master's family; the modern employee would become part of the company team under leadership that was no longer repressive but caring. Originally, within apprenticeship, discipline and obedience were emphasised and fidelity grew naturally as the apprentice identified with the master and other workers in pursuit of a common trade (Wilentz, 2004). But industrial psychologists reversed this sequence with a manipulated fidelity (morale) to foster obedience (reliability) and discipline (increased production). Around the same time, much as the demise of apprenticeship signalled an expansion of feudal authority over adults, changes in twentieth-century management introduced a new class of employee to the lockstep of workplace discipline.

At mid-century Mills (1951) raised the alarm: white-collar and professional workers were gradually sinking into the quicksand of what he called the "managerial demiurge" (p. 77). These workers were increasingly disciplined through management manipulation and subjected to the bureaucratic rules of business and government. The locus of industrial authority became more integrated, nebulous, and anonymous. And as more people were subject to psychological management, social interaction outside the workplace was increasingly influenced by a corporate-commercial morality.

The cultural effects of the managerial demiurge emerge, not only from the subordination of the employee, but through the mercenary ethic it elicits. Salesmanship, argued Mills (1951), became an essential personal ethic for those on the company payroll. The worker's very identity was subsumed by false politeness and calculated interest in others (Bagraim, 2001; Fromm, 1941/1994; Hochschild, 1983; Schachtel, 1961). Consequently, "[t]he managerial demiurge extends to opinion and emotion and even the mood and atmosphere of given acts" (Mills, 1951, p. 110). This phenomenon, observed Mills (1951) like Smith long before him, arises from the daily experience of employment. And it is a powerful influence in capitalist culture as values acquired in the workplace are transferred to other social contexts. As Stanojevic et al. (2020) have argued, conditions in the workplace such as task structure, authoritarian rule, and restricted autonomy, influence employee behaviour in society at large. The disciplined use of emotion and affection; a cultivated obedience to rules, policies, and hierarchy; and fidelity to company ethics and mores condition one's approach to life to be performative, uncritical, conforming, habituated to fantasy and illusion—not only a disciplined employee but an obedient consumer target and faithful political subject (Barber, 2007; Shankar et al., 2006; Solt, 2012).

Manufacturing freedom in the workplace

As more and more professionals during the second half of the twentieth century sacrificed autonomy to company discipline, management looked for ways to disguise domination by restoring the employee's sense of control—to vanquish servitude without challenging authority. "Managed autonomy" became the watchword of a new age of illusional freedom (Wallace, 2022, p. 32). Researchers rediscovered the problems associated with workplace domination that Smith (1776) and Millar (1803) had identified and set about finding ways to empower employees by *simulating* autonomy in the workplace (Wallace, 2022).

Influenced by Abraham Maslow, who demonstrated the importance of individual freedom and autonomy in psychological development, management scholars hoped to improve productivity by providing workers with a scripted path to self-actualisation (Wallace, 2022). But beneath the surface of this stylised freedom remained the paternalism of the old apprentice's master—the company, *in loco parentis*. In fact, Peters and Waterman (1982), in their influential analysis of management strategies, used the analogy of a schoolroom to underscore the importance of *disciplined* autonomy in the workplace. Worker autonomy, they explained, must be "simulated" along lines of shared company values. A mid-level manager is "anything but a swashbuckling entrepreneur," they elucidated, but the company's socialising process "is aimed at making him believe that that's exactly what he is, a hero" (Peters & Waterman, 1982, p. 213). At the same time, however, "his autonomy is in reality extraordinarily limited" (Peters & Waterman, 1982, p. 214). Employee freedom, once circumscribed through the discipline of legal proscription, was now restricted through a psychological feudalism in which autonomy, as it was within apprenticeship, would be permitted only under disciplined circumstances. Autonomy became associated with the internalisation of capitalist-economic rationalities, broadly, and company aspirations, more narrowly. Individual freedom thus became synonymous with disciplined conformity. When company values become worker values their observance is, in a formal sense, autonomous.

The exercise of this type of power parallels what Foucault (1991, p. 102) referred to as "governmentality." Governmentality operates on individuals to promote an agenda through standardised systems and diverse channels of discourse that encourage self-regulation in conformity with political, economic, and cultural norms (Miller & Rose, 1990). Employee autonomy based on this premise anonymises power to obscure domination. The instrumentalisation of individual aspirations of freedom confuses freewill with conformity, removing vitality and force from critical thinking. "By defining autonomy as obedience to the core values of corporate culture," argued Hugh Willmott (1993, p. 527), "the meaning and possibility of freedom is tightly circumscribed ..." (p. 538). In this way, argued Wallace (2022), "employee self-fulfilment becomes a means of their subjection" (p. 34).

And this subjection encourages conformity beyond the workplace. Management theorists, like earlier industrial psychologists, attempting to make their work relevant connect their strategies for governing individuals with national economic concerns and the aspirations of industrial leadership (Miller & Rose, 1990). This type of self-regulated freedom conditions the subject to conformity, not only in the workplace but in the consumer and consent-based political spheres in which the exercise of freewill is restricted to carefully curated choices. "Industrial psychology," asserted Marcuse (1964), "has long since ceased to be confined to the factory" (p. 10). The ethos and structure of employment influence ethical norms beyond the workplace, shaping morality of society at large (Gini 1998; Jackall, 1988). The ethic that management cultivates is submission to authority, both legitimated and obscured through psychological manipulation, whether in the workplace, the marketplace, or the polling place.

Rehearsing subjection

Even as the apprentice's path to freedom was substituted with the simulated independence of managed autonomy, employer paternalism continued to shape the employment relationship as one of master and servant. Late twentieth-century corporate executives raved about the "wonderful" "paternalism and discipline of the Japanese companies" that American firms were adopting (Friedman, 1981, p. D2). At the same time, dependency was obscured through contrived competitions that psychologically replaced the substantive progression towards independence that the apprentice formerly experienced. Within the workplace, meaning was artificially introduced with superfluous awards, false status symbols, and theatrical elements that Peters and Waterman (1982), referred to as "hoopla and razzle-dazzle" (p. 241). Group events that glorify the company's mission or its products, often taking the form of child-like theme parties, both trivialised and normalised employee subordination while diverting attention away from dependency and domination. And those employees who were not deceived by such manipulation but, nevertheless, endured management practices embraced a subculture of cynical submission. This performative adaptation, much like the identity-alienating salesperson ethic observed by Mills (1951), influenced social interaction outside of the workplace.

During the final decades of the twentieth century growing employee cynicism encouraged indifferent obedience to company culture, a fantasy orientation to workplace reality. Corporate culture, according to Willmott (1993), inspires workplace dramaturgy in which employees instrumentally conform to expected roles and thought while internally rejecting them. According to Berger and Luckmann (1966), this phenomenon generates a culture of reciprocal manipulations among workers. "What is obscured, if not lost from such consciousness," argued Willmott (1993), "is a capacity to reflect critically upon the sense and impact of being in control" (p. 538). This fantasy orientation not only encourages a dramaturgical approach to the workplace, but also the adoption of a self-alienating, instrumental posture in other social contexts (Berger & Luckmann, 1966).

Self-alienation supports capitalist culture outside the workplace by encouraging the acceptance of performative reality—a reality scripted through public political and marketing discourse. This "controlling" language, argued Marcuse (1964), manipulates reality by "denying or absorbing" opposing facts and contradictions: "it does not search for but imposes truth or falsehood" (p. 103). And however dismissive the public may be of this ritualised discourse, they, nevertheless, play their expected roles and conform to its directives.

This acceptance of manipulative discourse facilitates compliance to a "designed" workplace culture (Casey, 1999, p. 159) which, like early twentieth-century industrial psychology, cultivates fidelity through emotional manipulation to simultaneously drive and obscure discipline and obedience. Intense allegiance to the company is fostered through a discursively constructed corporate family and team-based work configuration which purportedly levels hierarchy (Bagraim, 2001; Casey, 1999). But behind this discourse of equality is a powerful mechanism of neo-feudal domination. Many employees demonstrate intense corporate loyalty and adopt a paternalistic fantasy of corporate compassion that they steadfastly maintain even when faced with factual evidence to the contrary (Casey, 1999, 1996; Jost & Hunyady, 2002). And in conditions analogous to nineteenth-century industrial workers who vicariously shared in the personal lives of wealthy company owners, many modern employees display a sense of fealty through their identification with the wealth and power of the corporation. "Identification with the greatness of [the company], even when self-narrated as 'maturity' displays a dependent, narcissistic, effect of corporate culture on employees" (Casey, 1999, p. 165). This sense of fidelity and obligation cultivates an intense desire to compete with other workers through performances of self-sacrifice, such as working overtime and weekends, which are conspicuously displayed before peers and superiors. Through these ritualised performances employees attempting to assuage their own feelings of powerlessness conform to company culture, identify with corporate power, and submit to workplace authority (Fromm, 1941/1994). Thus, a cultivated fidelity delivers production-increasing discipline and unquestioning obedience. The feudal residue of apprenticeship persists in a corporate culture that elicits and demands discipline, obedience, and fidelity. But perhaps more telling evidence of feudal power relations within employment is found in the *non-productive* exercise of power.

In the late nineteenth century Thorsten Veblen (1899, p. 78) identified a penchant among the wealthy for employing honorific "henchmen and retainers" to bolster their status as employer/patron. Over a century later, the employment of superfluous staff continues to represent a sort of organisational conspicuous consumption. Like symbolic feudal retainers, many modern workers enact a daily fiction within which they understand their job to be completely without meaning or value, and yet, are compelled to *pretend* that it has both. David Graeber (2018) estimated that 37–40% of employees in the northern Atlantic world hold what he called "bullshit jobs." Meaningless employment becomes a degrading drama of workplace discipline, obedience to rules and procedures, and fidelity to a culture of fantasy. "Being forced to pretend to work just for the sake of working ... [is] the pure exercise of power for its own sake ... the purest expression of lack of freedom" (Graeber, 2018, p. 85). Previously, workplace domination was obscured under the thin veil of psychological manipulation. But in the "bullshit job" the employee has no choice but to rehearse their own subjection, apprenticed to a "make-believe" world that celebrates submission and dependency from which "the overwhelming majority of us" will be freed only "on retirement, if at all" (Graeber, 2018, pp. 85, 256). Consequently, the employee becomes habituated to ignore meaning in life tasks, embracing a ritual acceptance of hierarchy and authority. This workplace dramaturgy prepares the employee to interpret the world, both inside and outside of the workplace, as an illusion in which she has no agency, a spectator who only finds meaning in obedient and faithful conformity to the discipline of capitalist culture.

Servant-entrepreneurship

Pointless employment may represent the apotheosis of subordination and dependency, but it is the new digital work frontier and the rapidly emerging gig economy that promise new extremes of illusional freedom under a paternalism that shifts authority to the anonymous sphere of computer-generated discipline. Here, domination is once again characterised as independence through the anonymisation of disciplinary power (Foucault, 1995; Habermas, 2005). And the same old legitimising discourse of the nineteenth century—of freedom through opportunity—is recycled as if new. "No boss, No shifts, No limit" boasted one platform company succinctly associating freedom, autonomy, and opportunity with employment that enforces discipline and obedience automatically through an algorithmic digital master (Ravenelle, 2019, p. 269; see also Wood et al., 2019).

Gig work offers the appearance of freedom combining indirect management with the internal discipline of governmentality (Schor, 2020). It accommodates a psychologically defensive, ego-saving interpretation of domination as *liberation* (Thompson, 2019). What Vallas and Schor (2020, p. 282) called "permissive power," is a digitally surveilled variation of managed autonomy. It creates the illusion of autonomy, the illusion that the worker is an entrepreneur (Ravenelle, 2019). Control is "radically redistributed" but still governed by "centralized power" (Kornberger et al., 2017, p. 79). "The growing literature on deteriorating conditions for workers in ride-hail and delivery suggests the exercise of power, rather than a shift to a new kind of peer-based capitalism" (Vallas & Schor, 2020, p. 278). Yet, the discourse of freedom and opportunity persists to legitimise what might be called servant-entrepreneurship. Once again, the discourse is focused on the production of the elusive, self-actualised employee through an entrepreneurial fantasy—pretend autonomy masking the dominion of apprenticeship.

And once again this approach, insofar as it is applied to other spheres of activity, shapes and influences society. Working under digital surveillance and algorithmic management habituates one to an illusional conception of freedom, permitted only within prescribed parameters. Such conditions promote a culture in which independence and autonomy are reduced to the choice of servile roles or the selection of consumer products. If one's orientation to life is dramaturgical, as Maslow's (1954) scholarship demonstrated, self-actualisation becomes as meaningless as it is unattainable. Concepts such as managed autonomy and servant-entrepreneurship, as modes of identity-alienating conformity, do not promote but suppress the individual's capacity for truly autonomous agency.

The reproduction of capitalist culture

Ironically, management psychologists, addressing the demoralising effects of workplace domination, seemingly ignored Maslow's assertion that freedom and autonomy cannot be manufactured. "Self-actualization," according to Maslow (1954), "is more akin to growth and maturation than it is to habit formation or association via reward, that is, it is not acquired from without ... it is the contradiction of motivation" (p. 296). The very definition of self-actualisation precludes the acceptance of paternalistic authority and describes one who is resistant to "fantasy" and manipulation (Maslow, 1959, p. 24; 1954). Much as Smith (1776) before him, Maslow (1954) argued that the "overcoming of obstacles" and the development of "potentialities like intelligence" are indispensable to psychological development (p. 340; see also Fromm, 1941/1994). Modern scholarship has confirmed that truly self-directed or entrepreneurial work promotes psychological well-being even when financial rewards are lower than those under similar employment (Shir et al., 2019). But autonomy cannot be managed or corralled within company policy. Self-actualisation, therefore, is incompatible with employment.

Employment, as a never-ending apprenticeship of circumscribed freedom and imaginary autonomy, fosters authoritarian personality traits which facilitate acceptance of the political, economic, and social domination associated with capitalist culture (Fromm, 1941/1994). There is a reciprocal relationship between these traits and the reproduction of relations of domination within the workplace and beyond (Kohn & Schooler, 1983). According to Maslow (1954), those unable to achieve self-actualisation see reality less clearly and are prone to over-socialisation and conforming behaviour. Employment, by preventing self-actualisation through the restriction of true autonomous agency, reproduces and secures the acceptance of domination. Indeed, Maslow (1954) warned that psychopathology has been "produced in intelligent people leading stupid lives in stupid jobs" (p. 95). Recent scholarship only emphasises the modern-day salience of Maslow's assessment (Graeber, 2018; Gottschalk, 2018). And the ubiquity of this individual psychopathology influences behaviour in other domains to produce a broader *social* pathology (Thompson, 2019). When individuals are guided by others, insisted Maslow (1954), they increasingly adopt feelings of powerlessness and lose confidence in their ability to make decisions. In this way, workplace hierarchy contributes to a society-wide pathological sense of powerlessness.

Populations plagued by feelings of powerlessness are more likely to rationalise and accept further authoritarianism and domination while believing they are free (Fromm, 1941/1994; Lipset, 1959; Maslow, 1954; Solt, 2012; Yost & Hunyaday, 2002). Employees whose workplaces in many ways "resemble the religious orders [and] totalitarian parties" of the past (Bagraim, 2001, p. 47) become accepting targets of authoritarianism outside the workplace. "It is difficult," argued Frederick Solt (2012), "to view one's employer as a superior whose orders must be obeyed without question without viewing government officials similarly" (p. 704). Authoritarianism, within the hierarchy of employee-apprenticeship, no matter how indirect, obfuscated, or rationalised, encourages passivity, political apathy (Elden, 1981; Napier & Jost, 2008; Pateman, 1970), and cultivates a pervasive ethos of conformity and subordination (Thompson, 2016).

Domination associated with hierarchy, argued Thompson (2019), supports a reification of consciousness that inhibits critical thinking and simplifies cognition. Consequently, a unidimensional world view undermines the capacity for complex reasoning in a way that, much as Smith (1776) implied, is incompatible with democratic citizenship. The ability to safeguard and participate in democracy is threatened when one spends the bulk of their waking hours acting out prescribed behaviour under a regime of authority and hierarchy. Such conditioning supports a cultural atmosphere in which the struggles and burdens of democracy are permitted to degenerate into the comfortable repetition of simplistic slogans and platitudes.

The workplace, for many, is the most important influence on adult conceptions of political, economic, and social reality (Kohn & Schooler, 1983; Stanojevic et al., 2020). And "exposure to hierarchical experiences ... is complemented by more complete cultural domination" (Solt, 2012, p. 704). Feudal discipline persists in an ethos of apprenticeship which confines the individual's freedom to paths of innocuous action worn smooth by workplace ritual (Roth, 1995; Smith & Stewart, 2011). Fidelity, cultivated through company allegiance, resurfaces as dedication to the brand, whether as a product or political party. Discipline emerges as behavioural compliance with party dogma or advertising slogans. Obedience is manifest through deference, respect, and adulation for political figures or celebrity marketeers. Bonds of paternalism are cemented through fantasised solidarity and vicarious participation in the agenda of the wealthy, powerful, and popular. The employee's rationalised dependency is exploited through the marketplace that treats its customers as "needy children" (Barber, 2007, p. 316) and the political arena where leaders assert authority by cultivating a parental image (Lakoff, 2005; Marcuse, 1964; Moses & Gonzales, 2015). Habits of submission seamlessly integrate with institutional regimes of compliance and conformity that reproduce the relations of production throughout capitalist culture (Mortimer & Simmons, 1978; Shepard, 1987).

By tracing the historic evolution of paternalism, this chapter advanced two theses. First, vestiges of feudalism shaped employment relations under capitalism throughout the history of modern wage labour. This phenomenon casts doubt on popular assumptions that employment, and capitalism more broadly, are engines of democratic freedom and economic opportunity. Second, authoritarian personality traits, developed under employment, influence social behaviour beyond the workplace, supporting the reproduction of capitalist culture by discouraging critical analysis and fostering compliance and conformity within social institutions that mirror the hierarchic and authoritative structures of employment. Thus, the apprentice of the workplace becomes the apprentice of capitalist culture. At one time apprenticeship was an education in agency and independence, but when its power relations were made permanent, workplace training became always and everywhere a lesson in domination. "[A]n apprentice is a servant for a time," wrote the early-American jurist Tapping Reeve (1816), "and the slave is a servant for life" (p. 341).

References

Adorno, T. W., Frenkel-Brunswick, E., Levinson, D, & Sanford, N. (1950). *The authoritarian personality.* Harper & Brothers.

Althusser, L. (2014). *On the reproduction of capitalism: Ideology and ideological state apparatuses.* Verso. (Original work published, 1971)

Alton, J. (1824). *A refutation of Mr. Owen's system.* James Robertson.

Anderson, E. (2017). *Private government: How employers rule our lives (and why we don't talk about it).* Princeton University.

Anthony, P. D. (1977). *The ideology of work.* Tavistock.

Bacon, M. (1740). *A new abridgement of the law* (Vol. 3). Nutt and Gosling.

Bagraim, J. J. (2001). Organisational psychology and workplace control: The instrumentality of corporate culture. *South African Journal of Psychology 31*(3), 43–49. https://doi.org/10.1177/008124630103100306

Barber, B. (2007). *Consumed: How markets corrupt children, infantilize adults, and swallow citizens whole.* W. W. Norton.

Berger, P., & Luckmann, T. (1966). *The social construction of reality: A treatise in the sociology of knowledge.* Doubleday.

Casey, C. (1996). Corporate transformations: Designer culture, designer employees, and 'post occupational' solidarity. *Organization, 3*(3), 317–339. https://doi.org/10.1177/135050849633002

Casey, C. (1999). "Come, join our family": Discipline and integration in corporate organizational culture. *Human Relations, 52*(2), 155–178. https://doi.org/10.1177/001872679905200109

Chevalier, M. (1839). *Society, manners, and politics in the United States.* Weeks, Jordan & Company.

Devinatz, V. (2012). Reevaluating US company paternalism from the nineteenth to the twentieth centuries. *Labor History, 53*(2), 299–304. https://doi.org/10.1080/0023656X.2012.679407

Elden, J. M. (1981). Political efficacy at work: The connection between more autonomous forms of workplace organization and more participatory politics. *American Political Science Review, 75*(1), 43–58. https://doi.org/10.2307/1962158

Elias, N. (2000). *The civilizing process: Sociogenic and psychogenic investigations* (E. Jephcott, Trans.). Blackwell (Original work published, 1939)

Ely, R. T. (1885). Pullman: A social study. *Harper's New Monthly Magazine, 70*(417), 452–466.

Farmer, E. (1924). The interconnection between economics and industrial psychology. *Journal of the National Institute of Industrial Psychology, 2*(2), 78–83.

Ford methods of handling men. (1914, July). *Factory: The Magazine of Management, 13*(1), 46–50.

Foucault, M. (1977). *Discipline and punish: The birth of the prison,* (A. Sheridan, Trans.). Vintage Books.

Foucault, M. (1980). *Power/knowledge: Selected interviews & other writings, 1972–1977,* (C. Gordon, L. Marshall, J. Mepham, & K. Soper, Trans.). Pantheon.

Foucault, M, (1991). *The Foucault effect: Studies in governmentality.* (G. Burchell, C. Gordon, & P. Miller, Eds.). University of Chicago.
Friedman, T. L. (1981, June 9). Talking business with Lewis W. Lehr and John M. Pitblado of 3M; New approach for the 80s. *New York Times*, D2.
Fromm, E. (1994). *Escape from freedom.* Henry Holt. (Original work published, 1941)
Gabel, J. (1975). *False consciousness: An essay on reification.* Harper & Row.
Gellner, E. (2006). *Nations and nationalism.* Oxford University Press. (Original work published 1983)
George, W. L. (1909). *Labour and housing at Port Sunlight.* Alston Rivers.
Gini, A. (1998). Work, identity and self: How we are formed by the work we do. *Journal of Business Ethics, 17,* 707–714.https://doi.org/10.1023/A:1017967009252
Gottschalk, S. (2018), *The terminal self: Everyday life in hypermodern times.* Routledge. https://doi.org/10.4324/9781315555010
Graeber, D. (2018). *Bullshit jobs: A theory.* Simon & Schuster.
Groat, G. G. (1911). *Attitude of American courts in labor cases: A study in social legislation.* Columbia University.
Habermas, J. (2005). *Legitimation crisis.* (T. McCarthy, Trans.). Beacon.Original work published 1973)
Hale, M. (1820). *The history of the common law of England.* Henry Butterworth. (Original work published 1713)
Hochschild, A. (1983). *The managed heart: Commercialization of human feeling.* University of California.
Horwitz, M. (1977). *The transformation of American law, 1780–1860.* Harvard University.
House carpenters. (1836, March 7). *Evening Post* (New York).
Jackall, R. (1988). *Moral mazes: The world of corporate managers.* Oxford University.
Jones, D. L. (1977). *Horizons of industrial productivity.* University of Michigan.
Jones, S. (1842). *An introduction to legal science.* John S. Voorhies.
Jost, J., & Hunyady, O. (2002). The psychology of system justification and the palliative function of ideology. *European Review of Social Psychology, 13,* 111–153. https://doi.org/10.1080/10463280240000046
Kohn, M. L., & Schooler, C. (1983). *Work and personality: An inquiry into the impact of social stratification.* Ablex.
Korberger, M., Pflueger, D., & Mouritsen, J. (2017). Evaluative infrastructures: Accounting for platform organization. *Accounting, Organizations and Society, 60,* 79–95. https://doi.org/10.1016/j.aos.2017.05.002
Lakoff, G. (2005). *Don't think of an elephant! Know your values and frame the debate.* Scribe.
Laslett, P. (1965). *The world we have lost: England before the Industrial Age.* Charles Scribner's Sons.
Lipset, S. M. (1959). Democracy and working-class authoritarianism. *American Sociological Review,* 23(4), 482–501. https://doi.org/10.2307/2089536
Marcuse, H. (1964). *One dimensional man.* Beacon.
Maslow, A. H. (1954). *Motivation and personality.* Harper.

Maslow, A. H. (1959). Critique of self-actualization. I. Some dangers of being cognition. *Journal of Individual Psychology, 15*(1), 24–32.
Mayo, E. (1933). *The human problems of industrial civilization.* MacMillan.
Mill, J. S. (1848). *Principles of political economy* (Vol. 2). John W. Parker.
Millar, J. (1803). *An historical view of the English government* (Vol. 4). J. Mawman.
Miller, P. & Rose, N. (1990). Governing economic life. *Economy and Society 19*(1), 1–31. https://doi.org/10.1080/03085149000000001
Mills, C. W. (1951). *White collar: The American middle classes.* Oxford University.
Moine, F. (2023). Worker's responses to paternalism in British factory-based events. *Journal of Victorian Culture, 28*(2), 209–226. https://doi.org/10.1093/jvcult/vcad016
Morris, R. B. (1946). *Government and labor in early America.* Columbia University.
Mortimer, J., & Simmons, R. (1978). Adult socialization. *Annual Review of Sociology 4*(1), 421–454. https://doi.org/10.1146/annurev.so.04.080178.002225
Moses, J. F. & Gonzales, M. H. (2015). Strong candidate, nurturant candidate: Moral language in presidential television advertisements. *Political Psychology, 36*(4), 379–397. https://doi.org/10.1111/pops.12160
Myers, C. (1922). The mansion house meeting. *Journal of the National Institute of Industrial Psychology, 1*(2), 59–67.
Napier, J. L., & Jost J. T. (2008). The "Antidemocratic personality" revisited: A cross-national investigation of working-class authoritarianism. *Journal of Social Issues, 64*(3), 595–617. https://doi.org/10.1111/j.1540-4560.2008.00579.x
Orren, K. (1991). *Belated feudalism: Labor, the law, and liberal development in the United States.* Cambridge University.
Pateman, C. (1970). *Participation and democratic theory.* Harvard University.
Peters, T., & Waterman, R. (1982). *In search of excellence: Lessons from America's best-run companies.* Harper & Row.
Ravenelle, A. J. (2019). "We're not Uber:" Control, autonomy, and entrepreneurship in the gig economy. *Journal of Managerial Psychology, 34*(4), 269–285.https://doi.org/10.1108/JMP-06-2018-0256
Reeve, T. (1816). *The law of baron and femme.* O. Steele.
Rorabaugh, W. J. (1986). *The craft apprentice: from Franklin to the Machine Age.* Oxford University.
Roth, A. L. (1995). "Men wearing masks": Issues of the description in analysis of ritual. *Sociological Theory, 13,* 201–227. https://doi.org/10.2307/223300
Schachtel, E. G. (1961). On alienated concepts of identity. *The American Journal of Psychoanalysis, 21*(2), 120–127. https://doi.org/10.1007/BF01873114
Schor, J. B. (2020). *After the gig: How the sharing economy got hijacked and how to win it back.* University of California.
Shankar, A., Cherrier, H., & Canniford, R. (2006). Consumer empowerment: A Foucauldian approach. *European Journal of Marketing, 40*(9/10), 1013–1030. https://doi.org/10.1108/03090560610680989
Shepard, R. (1987). Toward a universal law of generalization for psychological science. *Science 237*(4820), 1317–1323. https://doi.org/10.1126/science.3629243

Shir, N., Nikolaev, B., & Wincent, J. (2019). Entrepreneurship and wellbeing: The role of psychological autonomy, competence, and relatedness. *Journal of Business Venturing, 34,* 1–17. https://doi.org/10.1016/j.jbusvent.2018.05.002

Smith, A. (1776). *An inquiry into the nature and causes of the wealth of nations* (Vol. 2). Strahan & Cadell.

Smith, A., & Stewart, B. (2011). Organizational rituals: Features, functions and mechanisms. *International Journal of Management Review 13,* 113–133. https://doi.org/10.1111/j.1468-2370.2010.00288.x

Solt, F. (2012). The social origins of authoritarianism. *Political Research Quarterly, 65*(4), 703–713. https://doi.org/10.1177/1065912911424287

Steinfeld, R. (1991). *The invention of free labor: The employment relation in English and American law and culture, 1350–1870.* University of North Carolina.

Stanojevic, A., Akkerman, A., & Manevska, K. (2020). The oppressive boss and workers' authoritarianism: Effect of voice suppression by supervisors on employees' authoritarian political attitudes. *Contemporary Politics, 26*(5), 573–595. https://doi.org/10.1080/13569775.2020.1801168

Thompson, M. J. (2016). The rise of the servant society. *New Politics, 15*(4), 27–35.

Thompson, M. J. (2019). Hierarchy, social pathology and the failure of recognition theory. *European Journal of Social Theory, 22*(1), 10–26. https://doi.org/10.1177/1368431018768625

Tigar, M., & Levy, M. (1977). *Law and the rise of capitalism.* Monthly Review Press.

Tomlins, C. (1993). *Law, labor, and ideology in the early American republic.* Cambridge University. https://doi.org/10.1017/CBO9780511583643

Tomlins, C. (2010). *Freedom bound: Law, labor, and civic identity in colonizing English America, 1580–1865.* Cambridge University. https://doi.org/10.1017/CBO9780511778575

Vallas, S. & Schor, J. B. (2020). What do platforms do? Understanding the gig economy. *Annual Review of Sociology, 46,* 273–294. https://doi.org/10.1146/annurev-soc-121919-054857

Veblen, T. (1899). *The theory of the leisure class: An economic study in the evolution of institutions.* MacMillan.

Wallace, J. (2022). Making a healthy change: A historical analysis of workplace wellbeing. *Management and Organizational History, 17*(1–2), 20–42. https://doi.org/10.1080/17449359.2022.2068152

Ware, H. (1924). *The industrial worker 1840-1860: The reaction of American industrial society to the advance of the Industrial Revolution.* Houghton Mifflin Company.

Watts, S. (2005). *The people's tycoon: Henry Ford and the American century.* Alfred A. Knopf.

Wilentz, S. (2004). *Chants democratic: New York City and the rise of the American working class, 1788–1850.* Oxford University.

Willmott, H. (1993). Strength is ignorance, slavery is freedom: managing culture in modern organizations. *Journal of Management Studies, 30*(4), 515–552. https://doi.org/10.1111/j.1467-6486.1993.tb00315.x

Wood, A. J., Graham, M., Lehdonvirta, V., & Hjorth, I. (2019). Networked but commodified: The (dis)embeddedness of digital labour in the gig economy. *Sociology, 53*(5), 931–950. https://doi.org/10.1177/0038038519828906

Wooler, T. J. (1817, August 20). Mr. Owen's plan for the growth of paupers. *The Black Dwarf, 1*(30), 465–476.

Young, M. L. (2023). Equality and corporal punishment: Wage labor's crisis of legitimation, 1795-1835. *Journal of the Early Republic, 43*(3), 427–454. https://doi.org/10.1353/jer.2023.a905096

Part II
Reimagining

Anna Ilona Rajala

Reimagining the future is one way to retheorise capitalism. In a world that hangs in the balance, it has become critical to think about how to hold aspirations and visions of more compelling futures (Donnelly & Montuori, 2022, p. 3). Imagination, as Ruha Benjamin (2024) has recently argued, is a powerful tool to rid our social and mental structures of the dominating imaginaries that are destructive for living well. Imagining a future in which more-than-human thriving becomes possible calls for *re*-imagining, or imagining anew, the futures that now seem either bleak and destructive or reparative but impossible. The three chapters in this part seek to reimagine the future in different ways: re-sensing the economy, rediscovering a future worth imagining, and reimagining academic work.

In the chapter "Re-sensing economies: Artistic and embodied knowing for more-than-capitalist futures" (Chapter 5), Kelly Dombroski, Leo Hwang, Aviv Kruglanski, Heather McLean, and Molly Mullen problematise the way in which the economy is often theorised; economic theories come to make and remake the world in their image. According to the authors, the rationalist, discursive theorisation and the privileging of abstracted forms of knowing and representing economies is part of the historical milieu that resulted in the violence of colonisation, in extractive and oppressive regimes of labour, and in the separation of humans from the environment or "natural resources". By appealing to the necessity of responding to the various eco-social crises at hand, the chapter asks what alternative modes of theorising might be suited to imagining and enacting more-than-capitalist futures? Reflecting on practices such as performance art, comedy, alternative community spaces, gardening, and improvisational music, the authors explore approaches to re-sensing economy that value the body, senses, and relationships, promote connectivity and interdependence, and embrace pluriversal ways of knowing.

A call for reimagining is also put forth in Chapter 6, entitled "A future worth imagining", where Maria Mäensivu emphasises the importance of enhancing our abilities to engage in utopian thinking. To enable good and dignified lives, we need to be able to imagine alternatives to the status quo. Collages and other forms of crafting, Mäensivu suggests, present a fruitful arena to reinvigorate political imagination. The chapter is organised around three collages and a "failed" pottery experiment. Through them, Mäensivu engages some key themes in social science literature on contemporary capitalism: the body, social reproduction, violence, and failure. However, the larger, utopian theme of a "future worth imagining" runs through the treatment of these themes. This is exemplified, for example, by the play of images and counter-images in the collage that analyses how bodies are made to conform to certain societal expectations but, at the same time, reminds us of the possibilities of emancipation.

The chapter "Postcapitalist translations in four capitalist worlds: An experiment with scissors, clippings, and glue" (Chapter 7) is an example of what reimagining academic work through playfulness, love, and humour can yield. The authors, Iuliia Gataulina, Anni Kangas, Mikko Poutanen, Anna Ilona Rajala, and Tiina Vaittinen, present an assemblage of collages and mined poetry as an experimental translation of post/pericapitalism(s). Through craft as research, the authors invite the reader to actively explore and interpret the compositions and related retheorisations of postcapitalist universities, postcapitalist scholarship in the post-socialist/post-Soviet context, and to interrogate the connections between pericapitalism and dementia. Through the strangeness and unexpected connections evoked by the collages, the chapter inspires the "reader to imagine what capitalism(s), its traces, translations, frictions, and interstices are and could be."

References

Benjamin, R. (2024). *Imagination: A manifesto.* Norton Shorts.

Montuori, A. & Donnelly, G. (2022). *Routledge handbook for creative futures.* Routledge.

5

Re-sensing economies

Artistic and embodied knowing for more-than-capitalist futures

Heather McLean, Molly Mullen, Aviv Kruglanski, Leo Hwang & Kelly Dombroski

Can we think our way out of the current climate and political crises with human and ecological health intact? Or, perhaps thinking alone is not enough to get us out of the harmful extractive economic systems that shape our life-worlds from the intimate to the global. In this chapter, we propose the need to open up our ways of knowing beyond the rationalist abstract ways economic theorists have been known for. We draw on art and embodied creative practice to seek out and generate new ways of attending and attuning to the world. What insights would emerge if we were to consider theory as an artistic practice and artistic practice as theory? One insight is that we can connect economic theorising to important but overlooked bodies of knowledge, including knowledge in bodies, which may hold transformative economic potential for shaping wiser economic (and environmental) futures.

Arts practices offer strategies for practising radical tenderness and the embodied presence to work with the tensions, difficulties, and pain of historical and ongoing colonial modes of thinking and being (Machado de Oliveira, 2021). This chapter explores economic theorising through a patchworking of artistic and embodied practices. Beginning with the body, the local, and the more-than-rational, we offer some tentative insights into re-sensing economies towards postcapitalist interdependencies.

But first, who are we—these bodies re-sensing economies? We are a group of scholars, artists, and makers from different places in the world. We know each other through the Community Economies Institute, an organisation that theorises and

McLean, H., Mullen, M., Kruglanski, A., Hwang, L. & Dombroski, K. (2025). Re-sensing economies: Artistic and embodied knowing for more-than-capitalist futures. In A. Kangas, I. Gataulina, M. Poutanen, A. I. Rajala & H-E. Ventovirta (Eds.), *Retheorising capitalism* (pp. 93–111). Tampere University Press.
https://doi.org/10.61201/tup.981

practices diverse and community economies thinking and hosts the Community Economies Research Network. Building on J.K. Gibson-Graham's (1996, 2006) feminist critique of political economy, the diverse economies (DE) approach challenges mainstream, overdetermining and capitalocentric framings of 'the economy'. Capitalocentric framings understand 'the economy' as inevitably and always capitalist. A DE approach instead thinks of economic practices as sites of politics and transformation that might be postcapitalist (Gibson-Graham, 2006) or even just "more-than-capitalist" (Gibson-Graham & Dombroski, 2020, p. 11). Rather than retheorising capitalism per-se, we draw on DE scholarship to retheorise economy in a way that decentres capitalism. In orthodox economics and in much everyday discourse, 'the economy' is typically represented as predominantly, or even singularly, capitalist, which has made it almost impossible to imagine alternatives (Gibson-Graham, 1996).

Even the anti-capitalist imagination can position capitalism as the central, all-determining force or structure that needs to be resisted or overthrown. From the anti-essentialist perspective of DE thinking, there is no privileged centre nor one primary determining force or structure of transformation. As DE scholars and practitioners, we aim to approach economies as sites of diverse, vital and abundant economic practices (Gibson-Graham et al., 2021). We amplify the work of artists, activists, and communities who are enacting economic, social and ecological change in multiple ways (McLean, 2022). Working with communities in all kinds of teaching, research and activist projects, we experiment with and practice more-than-capitalist alternatives (Gibson-Graham et al., 2017).

We want to be upfront here; if you are looking for a chapter that comprehensively sets out how DE thinking is theorising capitalism, this is not it.[1] But the practices and approaches presented in this chapter have grown from our engagement with DE thinking and its performative ontology. For over three decades, DE scholars have highlighted that the way the economy is theorised is performative; economic theories come to make and remake the world in their image (Gibson-Graham, 1996). Starting with performative ontology involves seeing theory as more than a tool for explaining economy. Instead, theory plays a part in making particular economies possible or not. What would it look like then to refuse to retheorise capitalism once again, and instead theorise or re-sense something else—something at the very edges of our abilities to think, rationalise and understand? And how might art and embodied practice help us to do this?

Gibson-Graham make some space for exactly this in their shift from DE thinking to community economies (CE) thinking. In their 2006 book *A Postcapitalist Politics*, they sketch the outlines of an ethical space of negotiation in which new forms of economy might arise in sporadic yet ubiquitous and punctiform ways. Rather than defining what such a new form of economy might look like, they outline four ethical coordinates around which such an economy might negotiate ways of being together and three

---

1 You might like to try Gibson-Graham, J. K., & Dombroski, K. (Eds.). (2020). The Handbook of Diverse Economies. Edward Elgar.

sets of politics that might help diverse, place-based groups get there. Gibson-Graham (2006, p. 88) suggest that a community economy might organise around questions of:

- what is *necessary* to personal and social survival;
- how social *surplus* is appropriated and distributed;
- whether and how social surplus is to be produced and *consumed*; and
- how a *commons* is produced and sustained.

For Gibson-Graham (2006, (pp. xxxiv-xxxvii), "negotiations around these key coordinates and the interactions between them could inform an ethics and politics of community economy" (p. 88), which is indeed what we see in the art and embodied practices we outline in this chapter. The politics of imagining and enacting new economies, as outlined by Gibson-Graham (2006), consist of:

- A politics of language
- A politics of the subject
- A politics of collective action

For us, these points of ethical negotiation and politics of imagining and enacting new economies cannot just be projects of *thinking* but must be projects of embodied experimentation and sensing new ways of being in the world. Our language intervention then, is to shift from *rethinking* and *retheorising capitalism* to a language of *re-sensing economies.* Our intervention in the politics of the subject is to engage with the embodied subject in its fullness, including *more-than-rational embodied engagement and experimentation* with postcapitalist ways of being in the world. Our intervention in collective action is to quilt *an assemblage of artistic and embodied practices together*—to bring together unlikely bedfellows, enabling a collective re-sensing of what economies have been and could be. For those of us in academic positions, working as scholars, it is hard to be comfortable with such loose quilting, to not have everything tied up and to "mean the same thing" (Sedgwick, 1994, p. 6), or to have a sense of mastery on a subject. But that is precisely the kind of uncertainty we need to practice and cultivate in order to be open to multiplicity, possibility, and to wide pluriverses of reality where things can be something other than what they are now (Escobar, 2018). It is these "richest junctures" that Sedgwick (1994, p. 6) is referring us to—but we must first cultivate ourselves as subjects that can let this be. And this is where we think art and embodied practice are essential to imaging and enacting economies differently.

The chapter proceeds as follows. In section 2, performing artists Molly Mullen and Heather McLean contribute two critical pieces to our quilt, sharing and reflecting on projects that they have worked on. Both Molly and Heather engage in performance, comedy and satire to critique capitalist and colonial systems and structures, as well as to 'co-sense' alternative economies with their communities. In section 3, Aviv, Kelly and Leo contribute experimental quilt pieces, experiments with community gatherings, gardens and improvisational music. We then reflect on how these three divergent practices offer strategies for imagining and enacting postcapitalist possibilities.

Embodying playful economic critique

The first two quilt patches describe projects that invite participants and audiences to experience and participate in the ridiculousness of capitalist imaginaries. In these projects, a politics of language and the subject is performed in light hilarity. Rather than using negative affect to problematise and educate about capitalism and colonialism, the artists draw on a sense of the ridiculous to provoke generative critique.

Molly: The devaluation station in Aotearoa New Zealand

I have been questioning the relationship between capitalism, value and evaluation in the context of community/participatory arts since the late 1990s. In 2014, having just submitted my PhD thesis (which interrogated this relationship through the lens of feminist and diverse economies thinking), I saw a call for proposals for the Festival of Uncertainty at the Auckland Old Folks Association (OFA) in Tāmaki Makaurau Auckland in Aotearoa New Zealand.

Figure 1. Old Folks Association Hall, 2024, photo by Molly Mullen

The OFA is an incorporated society founded in 1945. Its hall still stands, but in 2011 the purposes of the association were extended to include supporting intergenerational exchange through arts and culture. The OFA committee has since experimented with new ways to enact service and generosity to its communities, including arts communities, by, for example, hosting unfunded or un-fundable projects for little or no cost.

The call for participation in the Festival of Uncertainty, organised by Feasting House, read as follows,

> ...If excellence, market value and profile were set aside and money were not an issue, what else might be possible? What projects might emerge and where could art go?
> Feasting House seeks projects that foster art as an activity of radical uncertainty.
> This is a platform for the entirely unachievable, non-viable projects and career death experiments. Art that slips by, that fails to eventuate, that lacks quality or craft, that is impossible to find, that plays out in isolation, or in a social crowd; ideas, sketches, hopes, obsessions, all as simply a process of continued and unstoppable practice...
> https://ofa.org.nz/festival-of-uncertainty/

I felt compelled to respond. I had had no time or head space for creative practice since starting my PhD, and was fed up with writing and talking about 'what else might be possible' in articulating the value of participatory and community arts. I wanted to involve others, generate possibilities, and perhaps some joy. My partner Tom Beeston and I responded to the call:

> ...with the ethos of your festival, you're probably not planning to collect feedback or to conduct an evaluation. While you have put market value, excellence and profile aside, we'd like to bring it back to the fore in our perhaps absurd, slightly satirical 'devaluation' process. Evaluation (in the most basic sense) is about measuring something's worth/effectiveness against specific prescribed standards for some utilitarian purpose, e.g. to improve practice and provide evidence of 'performance' or success.
> We propose to design and conduct a thoroughly pointless exercise in evaluation that may, at the same time, invite people to think in different ways about 'value'.

I was inspired by the concept of 'bullshit' in relation to social impact evaluation in the arts (Belfiore, 2009). Eleonora Belfiore proposes that, in the UK in the 2000s, pressure to justify public funding of the arts resulted in the idea that the socio-economic value of the arts could be measured using impact assessment tools. Belfiore unpacks the political bullshitting that went on at this time, with ministers stating in one sentence that it was essential to use quantified measurements to convince the 'system' of the value of the arts and in the next, acknowledging such evidence to be meaningless. But the centripetal dynamic of capitalocentrism kicked in, and impact became a proxy for value, with value standing for 'value for money'. The popularity of impact evaluation is rooted in the anxiety of justifying the value of the arts and the assumption this must be done using the assumed-to-be-universal language and tools of capitalism (Belfiore, 2009). What is overlooked is the way the arts generate contextually and culturally relevant methodologies for sensing and articulating diverse forms of value. How might evaluation be reimagined, remade, as a *pluriversal* practice, in which multiple notions of value and practices of value are made possible and can co-exist?

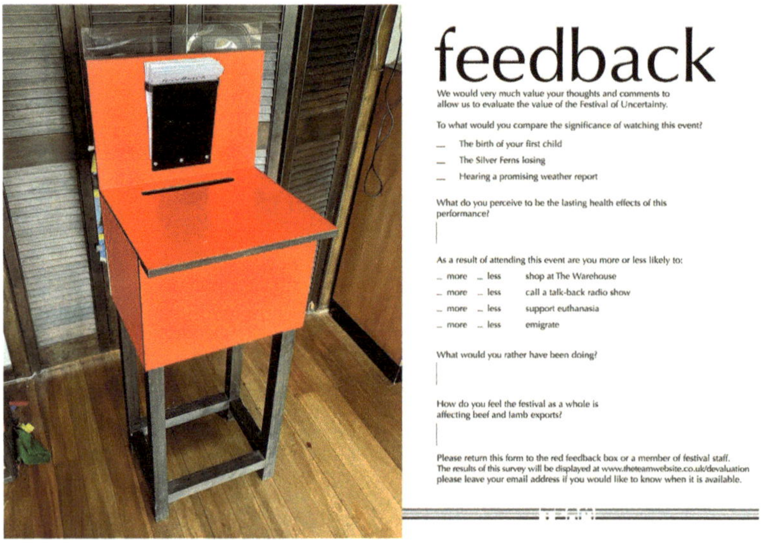

feedback

We would very much value your thoughts and comments to allow us to evaluate the value of the Festival of Uncertainty.

To what would you compare the significance of watching this event?

_ The birth of your first child
_ The Silver Ferns losing
_ Hearing a promising weather report

What do you perceive to be the lasting health effects of this performance?

As a result of attending this event are you more or less likely to:

_ more _ less shop at The Warehouse
_ more _ less call a talk-back radio show
_ more _ less support euthanasia
_ more _ less emigrate

What would you rather have been doing?

How do you feel the festival as a whole is affecting beef and lamb exports?

Please return this form to the red feedback box or a member of festival staff.
The results of this survey will be displayed at www.theteamwebsite.co.uk/devaluation
please leave your email address if you would like to know when it is available.

Figure 2. The Devaluation Station and feedback form, images by Molly Mullen

Tom designed and made the Devaluation Station: a bright red laminate box, raised, plinth-like, on long timber legs. It was placed at the entrance to the OFA hall for the festival's duration. To complete the form and return it through the narrow slot is to participate in an individualised, predetermined practice of valuing. One form, one pen, one slot, one measure of value, a universal singularity. Form-filling is, typically, deeply mundane, and because of this, it can seduce us uncritically into a practice of judging value by arbitrarily capitalocentric measures. But the bright red box and ridiculous questions playfully call attention to and defamiliarise this practice.

When audiences received the form, there would be a slight shoulder sag, eye roll, or eyebrow raised at being asked to evaluate this event. The invitation to evaluate in this way was at odds with the Festival of Uncertainty, which eschewed market value. Some people discarded the form immediately. When others read the questions, though, they gave a slight smile, a laugh, or turned to check whether it was for real. Some completed the form, drew on it, wrote poems, or made paper aeroplanes.

There is no shortage of art that is critical of capitalism, but the Devaluation Station might be understood specifically as a practice of generative critique. Lea Schick (2021) proposes the term generative critique, drawing on the work of Latour (2004) and Verran (2014) who "formulate a kind of critique [. . . that] aims at 'adding to' or generatively help develop the subject matter" (Schick, 2021, p. 484). Schick argues that some art practices go beyond revealing/exposing a problem and instead encourage people to engage with it in critical *and* productive ways. The devaluation station playfully engaged people with the bullshit of measurement, inviting the audience to recognise it, to get a feel for it, to laugh at it and reconsider their participation in it. Looking back, I wonder whether the devaluation station inadvertently recentred capitalism by making capitalocentric concepts and practices the focus. I am also uncertain if, ultimately, it was both critical *and* productive. We tried to catalyse a shared process of deconstructing the concept and practice of impact evaluation, but could we have done more to prompt reimagining or collective experimentation with postcapitalist alternatives? As people participated in and responded to the Devaluation Station, whether they completed and returned a form, turned it into a paper aeroplane, or simply laughed at it, were they, if only in a small way, putting ideas, imaginings, of economy and capitalism into motion in different, unexpected ways? Through prompting a sense of hilarity and playful participation, perhaps this work did do more than just inflame people's negative feelings about capitalocentric evaluation in the arts, generating, at a more-than-rational level, some sense that evaluation could be otherwise (Schick, 2021), it could be fun, funny, collective, creative, embodied, non-representational.

Heather: Honey Bucket Housing in Secwepemculecw British Columbia

As I reflect with DE co-conspirators on the ways that arts practices can foster sensing more-than-capitalist futures, I see how, like Molly, my performance-based work is also a form of generative critique. As Schick (2021) argues, "art as generative critique may provide a productive and vital mode for intervening into [energy] futures in-the-making" (p. 483). For the artists I work with, generative critique takes the form of a satirical planning workshop that includes a portable toilet and a lot of laughing.

I am a white settler of Scottish, Irish and English descent who researches mutual aid and the arts in Secwepemculecw, a territory colonially named British Columbia, Canada. This is where I grew up. Since 2020, I have been meeting with Mi'kmaq musician and comedian Nakuset Gould and Secwepemc and Nlaka'pamux comedian, poet and visual artist Chris Bose online and in person to create comedic responses to the escalating climate and housing crisis impacting our communities. Through improv games, collage making, and performing as our alter-egos, we co-create surreal, satirical urban planning projects.

My alter-ego is Toby Sharp, a self-proclaimed world leader in innovation and creativity. I originally created Toby when I was working as a community development planner in Tkaronto (colonially named Toronto) and performing with Dirty Plotz, a cabaret collective that shared stories about the historic and ongoing erasure of women, 2-Spirit, non-binary people, and trans women in arts scenes. Toby was my response to the proliferation of expert consultants charging municipal governments and nonprofit organisations exorbitant fees to learn how to be more 'creative' while working with increasingly cut back resources. Because Toby recently decided to become a 'world leader' in research on Indigenous entrepreneurs, he is now collaborating with Nakuset's Skus Akwesan, a drag-king Instagram influencer, and Chris's Donny Dreamcatcher, a leg wrestling coach and property developer. Honey Bucket Housing is one project that emerged from Toby, Skus and Donny's collaborations. This initiative, which encourages people to move into the plastic portable toilets often found on construction sites, is Donny's response to the growing housing crisis across so-called British Columbia.

While working online for Thompson Rivers University in Tk'emlúps te Secwépemc, a city colonially named Kamloops, I connected with Chris, an old friend from the local art and punk scene. Stuck in our hometown for the first few months of Covid, we met for walks around the city. As our alter ego characters, we filmed each other discussing urban development and oil pipeline expansion. Unintentionally, we were engaging in what Gómez-Peña et al. (2021) refer to as the anti-colonial research practice of alter ego performance art. The local landscape shaped by colonial and capitalist expansion, as well as more-than-capitalist community building and care, offered endless topics to investigate and discuss on our performance walks. For example, we walked on the beach where the Royal Canadian Mounted Police had recently arrested Indigenous Elders and women Water Protectors. These groups had set up an encampment to protest the drilling of the TMX oil pipeline to transport Alberta tar sands sludge under the local river. We also stopped in to chat with neighbours working for a grassroots mutual aid organisation run by moms and Elders responding to the city's opioid crisis.

A friend at the University of Northern British Columbia (UNBC) asked me if Chris and I would like to perform in a small online conference on women and environmental research. We reached out to Nakuset, who I had been following on social media since meeting her while working with the Toronto Free Gallery, an artist-run centre that supported underrepresented Indigenous, Black and People of Colour artists, 2-Spirit and LGBTQIA+ artists. Nakuset, Chris and I started to meet on Zoom to create the UNBC talk, which led to us creating more comedy videos. We drew attention to the voracious forest fires and intense flooding that have impacted our communities over the past few years. We also made connections between the climate crisis, increasing gentrification and precarious work in the arts, university and community development sectors. As Indigenous land defenders, water protectors, artists and scholars point out, these ecological disasters and power asymmetries signal historic and ongoing settler colonial violence across so-called Canada (Elliott, 2020; Farrales et al., 2022).

When we discussed the Honey Bucket project, Chris joked that living in a small portable toilet makes sense because it feels like we live in increasingly irrational and dystopian times. For Chris, his puerile humour is an effective way to respond to the growing number of families living in caravans, mobile homes, and temporary modular homes after forest fires and floods have devastated communities across Secwepemcúl̓ecw. He also shared how his mom's ancestral village, Camchin, colonially named Lytton, completely burned down in 2021 after the area was enveloped in a 50-degree Celsius heat dome, the hottest recorded temperature in the Northern Hemisphere that day.

In 2023, we further developed the Honey Bucket project for a satirical urban planning workshop for the rEvolver Festival of Performance's Indigenous Emergence Triple Feature and Community Gathering in East Vancouver (Up in the Air Theater Company, 2023). In this performance, participants planned their own Porta Potti housing. As Skus, Donny and Toby, we facilitated a collaborative session where participants created collages with cut-out images of police, high-end art, designer beer, flowers, various critters, and many other images. As participants created their collages, we discussed the ridiculous state of urban politics in Vancouver, including how the current Mayor, Ken Sim, was endorsed by billionaire Chip Wilson, the owner of Lululemon yoga pants. Implementing his law and order platform, since 2022, Sim has aggressively worked with police to harass the growing unhoused population in a violent clean the streets campaign. In the rEvolver gathering, participants responded to Mayor Sim by creating their own Porta Potti plans that poked fun at policing and gentrification with collages featuring cops in expensive yoga pants serving expensive craft beer and high-end art found in some of the city's trendy neighbourhoods.

As we develop our alter-ego performance research, I see how our toilet humour and comedic collage-making foster sensing more-than-capitalist futures in small ways. Alter-ego and comedy provide us with tools to engage in generative critique. First, in performing Toby, Skus and Donny, we unsettle power hierarchies perpetuated through embodied gestures and how these repetitions universalise white supremacist, ableist, and heteropatriarchal economic discourses and structures (Lane & Mancini, 2021; Stephens, 2012). Comedic alter ego performance also offers us ways to undo mastery, or the expertise of planners, developers and researchers upholding colonial and neoliberal policies and practices (Machado de Oliveira, 2021). Moreover, in collaboration with rEvolver participants, we co-created a space to laugh at, learn from and be with "the precarity, brokenness and imperfection of our collective existence" (Machado de Oliveira, 2021, p. 53) in increasingly gentrified and policed cities in so-called Canada.

Importantly, the satire of Honey Bucket Housing also echoes feminist DE calls for embodied and slow scholarship that takes time to grow. While practising this work, Chris and Nakuset have reflected on the many times university researchers have approached them to provide land acknowledgements and create Indigenous curriculum or to create art projects with minimal financial support. Their insights have taught me to slow down and practice hyper-reflexivity as a white cis-gendered settler researcher with ongoing complicities in colonial, neoliberal systems and structures. Taking inspiration from DE thinkers and practitioners collaborating with Indigenous, Black and People of Colour scholars, queer and feminist scholars, I take cultivating networks of interdependence and care seriously as we create more projects. With our crappy creations, we aim to laugh, dream and stumble towards more abundant, wise and kind futures.

Experiments in sensing postcapitalist economies

In the following three examples, Aviv, Kelly and Leo narrate experiments with sensing postcapitalist and community economies. Leo's band Vimana gives insight into the politics of collective action and a community formed through commoning in their album *Space Triangle of Love*. In this case, the collective making of music enabled a deeply embodied experience of what it means to do things together. Aviv's intervention of the open door invites a politics of the subject built on the concept of 'swerve' where new subjects emerge briefly and unexpectedly (Gibson-Graham, 2006), perhaps literally swerving through an open door and into a new way of being in the economy. Kelly's garden began as an experiment in embodied knowledge production and transfer between herself, a new environment and her children. It also performs a politics of language, where *thinking* of economies as gardens with both flourishing surplus and overdetermined crop fails involves *sensing* economies differently. Each of these quilt pieces is an experiment: partial, transient, not fully rationalised or given meaning, but they offer some tentative re-sensing of what different forms of economy could look like. As adrienne maree brown reminds us: "experiment, gather feedback, experiment again. That is how we learn" (brown, 2017, p. 106).

Leo: Space Triangle of Love

In the midst of the pandemic in July 2022, Vimana, the band I play guitar in, along with Brian Rodriguez on bass and Bruce Todd on drums, went into the studio to record our first album. While this is our first official recording, we have been performing together for over ten years. We play all original instrumental music, which at times veers towards jazz, psychedelic rock, or a little bit of funk and blues. Whatever it is, it is esoteric, so in some ways having 220 copies of an album pressed onto vinyl seems like a highly questionable enterprise. But in other ways, the music we create is beyond the simple calculations of production. It is beyond enterprise.

Our particular kind of instrumental music is simultaneously rooted in structure and improvisation. The songs have a firm foundation, a pattern, specific phrases, and then over many weeks, we learn how to embellish that structure through improvisation. We try different textures, different colours, different patterns until the song takes shape and becomes something less ephemeral and more like an object you can touch and feel with your hands.

Sometimes, we have remarked how playing music together is our form of therapy or meditation or prayer. It is something centring for each of us, it provides a space where we can exist on a different plane than our ordinary work or home life planes. We have to be open to our nonverbal communication with one another. We have to awaken different aspects of our selves.

Before the pandemic, the band would perform in public about once a month, but once the pandemic hit, all public performances ceased. As a local band with few diehard fans, when we play at local establishments, we are typically bartering our services for free drinks, sometimes dinner, plus tips. A few venues will add a little bit of money ranging from fifty to a few hundred dollars. But we are not focused on music making as commerce. The real objective of this endeavour is to share our music with other people. The National Endowment for the Arts (2010) notes, "it has been fruitful to consider not only attendance—visiting museums or going to ballet, for example—but also arts creation or performance (...). This latter type of activity (...) represents a phenomenon often labelled as the 'informal' arts" (p. 2).

A year into the pandemic the Massachusetts Cultural Council released a grant focused on helping artists who had been impacted by the pandemic. We applied and received one of the grants to enable making a record. Suddenly, our little basement trio was able to book time in a local studio, Sonelab, with a well-known engineer, Justin Pizzoferrato. We had the tracks mastered by Carl Saff in Chicago and finally pressed onto vinyl by Citizen Vinyl in Asheville, North Carolina. The cover art was done by Bruce's teenage daughter. My son Simon appears on a few tracks on keyboard, and my father Bo Youp also appears on a track on violin. A local graphic designer and friend, Max Germer did the final layout of the album cover, and local photographer Julian Parker Burns took the photo on the back.

The result is 220 copies of our album, *Space Triangle of Love*, many of which will be gifted to family, friends, and people we want to impress. And the rest we hope to sell at gigs or record stores, with a hope to seed some of the funding for the next album, but primarily our hope is to get our music out into the world and listened to.

In many ways, this would be considered a broken economic model. It is not a business model in the traditional sense where profit is extracted from the production. Yet, the endeavour, this rural activity, has produced something in this world that did not exist before. The value, intrinsically rural, intrinsically personal, and lacking a commercial market in the capitalist sense, is nevertheless transformative in its small scale. We might say "when the 'informal' arts are considered, however, the urban arts primacy generally fades. Metro and non-metro residents tend to engage in these activities at the same rate" (National Endowment for the Arts, 2010, p. 3). The creativity is still production, whether it is in a small rural town or a large metropolitan city.

I think back to my very first conversation with Julie Graham[2] where she dared me to define an economy. What we came up with was that an economy is a system designed to improve the quality of life for people. In that regard, *Space Triangle of Love* qualifies as economic activity. It is non-capitalist in its endeavour and its expectations. The album emerges from what Jay Salinas calls Cultureshed:

1. A geographic region irrigated by streams of local talent and fed by deep pools of human and natural history.
2. An area nourished by what is cultivated locally.
3. The efforts of writers, performers, visual artists, scholars, farmers and chefs who contribute to a vital and diverse local culture

(Salinas, 2012, as quoted by Barrett, 2012, p. 1).

[2] Julie Graham, with Katherine Gibson, wrote under the pseudonym J.K. Gibson-Graham. We draw on their shared work in diverse and community economies throughout this chapter.

The album is the product of a local ecosystem of exchange, some in currency (including a pandemic relief grant), some through gifting of time or talent. While the additional gift economy created through pandemic relief funds was instrumental in the production of a physical product, the ecosystem of local artists, musicians, restaurants, bars, local festivals, art galleries, and audience members created an economy that is more than capitalocentric, it is centred and reliant on community. As musicians, we are interested in the transformative nature of art production, how it changes the artist, the audience, and the environment in which we exist.

Aviv: Economies as sculptures, physical objects in space

Famously annoying artist Richard Serra created the "Tilted Arc" in Foley Federal Plaza in Manhattan in 1981. People had to walk around it. It blocked their way, creating much controversy. This particular work of macho metalwork can help me make a point: art objects form part of public/social space, of people's daily lives. Unlike the typical functional objects that surround us, they inhabit space differently, leaving room for ambiguity, posing questions. Every office worker passing through the plaza had to engage their body with the questions posed by the imposing and annoying Serra. The economic/artistic projects I would like to discuss are not there to annoy or provoke, but like Serra's arc, they are physically, socially and economically present in the space of daily life. What kind of *economic* sculptures can we create in our neighbourhoods? Two elements are important in this story: the provocation of open doors and some experiences of meandering paths.

In 2009 Adrian[3] signed a lease on the ground-floor storefront in Santa Dolors Street, (Maricel, Spain). They drippily painted the name of the project on its big green doors. At the end of a cul-de-sac, these doors opened to create one big space, half of it inside and half outside, in the shade of a tall Tipuana Tipu tree. Once open, five years of dinners, workshops, meetings, film screenings and other kinds of loitering commenced. Everyone who drifted in was offered a cup of tea. These were years of gratifying social activity, sharing, celebrating, questioning, debating, inviting. They were also years of not knowing, doubting, waiting. They ended with a couple of years of getting in debt and collectively, exuberantly responding to crisis. This storefront was an attempt to create community economies in a street corner lacking much social infrastructure. The big open doors were central to its functionality, nourishing its program with new ideas, letting activities spill out onto the street.

Years later, Adrian and his collaborator Adel were walking around the Avenue neighbourhood in Whykham, the northern British city in which they now lived. On this particular day, they bumped into a small one-story building, a village hall. In it, they met Kid, a fifty-something hippy with a goatee beard, long hair, and an ironic sense of humour imbued with a generous sense of humanity. He ran the space, referring to himself alternately as the mis-manager or the dictator of the hall. The hall was a hub of activity, diverse cultural groups using it for a variety of purposes during the week.

3 Pseudonyms used in this vignette.

The story of the hall also involved the two elements discussed here: the meandering paths of not knowing and the porosity of boundaries in open doors. The hall existed for about 15 years, a grassroots form of social infrastructure. Reflecting back, Kid says, "I opened the door and thought, 'will anybody come in?'" Kid's words describe a state of not-knowing: not knowing who will come through the door, not knowing what proposals they might bring with them, not knowing what direction the character of the hall might take. The hall counted on people's trajectories meandering through the open doors and populating its calendar, creating the activities that flavour the space, bringing the income that paid expenses. At the same time, it was not 'anything goes'. Both had a certain ethics, a certain aesthetic, that helped them drift in a particular way, enabling community economies in the neighbourhood around them.

Adel and Adrian started a weekly online community radio show from the hall. Defined as a radio/teahouse, it was an open space for people to wander in, interview, get interviewed, request a song, have a warm beverage. After several years, it expanded into a weekly market. But when the owners of the building wanted it back, the hall was shut down, and the projects abruptly ended. Adel and Adrian started a market/radio/teahouse in an old abandoned Victorian church recently acquired by a local housing charity, and the cycle began again.

In these stories, open doors are physical embodiments of the porous boundaries of community economies. People and ideas wander in, and encounters occur. The other element present in all of these stories is their drifting around in a state of not-knowing for long stretches of time. These projects are vulnerable explorations, aiming to create grassroots social infrastructure for neighbourhoods that need them. Could they have materialised in the way they did had they followed a concrete plan (a business plan)? Probably not. Could they have gained a higher level of stability, taking root and staying for longer in service of the communities in which they were entangled? Probably. But what we have instead are experiments in doing economies in community.

Kelly: Retheorising and re-sensing economies through the garden

I moved to a new town a little over a year ago. In the first few weeks, I started a vegetable garden. With the cost of living crisis in Aotearoa New Zealand, there had been a lot in the news that year about how vegetable gardening was not really a solution to food insecurity—it was a rich people's activity in that people could spend so much money setting up a garden and only get a few vegetables right at the time they were cheapest in the supermarket. My garden began with some gifted plants and some found materials. I want to tell you about two different beds in my garden.

For the first garden, I repurposed some wood from a fallen tree and old bricks to make a low garden. I covered it all with half-ready compost, buried some more food waste in it, then a bit of commercial compost and pea straw. In this garden, my aim was to firstly build the relationships of microorganisms in the soil to support nutrition for both the plants and our family, and secondly, to create a beautiful display of vegetable plants in a mixed planting and multi-layered arrangement that was attractive to the children (aged between 4 and 16). I wanted a range of spring and summer plants that would pique their interest giving them an embodied sense of where food came from and helping them form relationships with soil and place and food.

In early spring, with my preschooler, I planted corn plants along the back. My teenager pitched in with a story of the 'three sisters' (corn, squash and beans) she had heard in the audiobook version of "Braiding Sweetgrass" (Kimmerer, 2013). So, we planted small cucurbit plants, including cucumber, zucchini and small pumpkins. And we planted borlotti beans, to experiment with drying and preserving them for winter consumption. We also planted some gifted climbing beans that had been continuously cultivated by Italian immigrants and never commercialised. We planted tomatoes that my son had grown from seed—a heritage range of different colours, sizes and shapes, including some shaped like bums, much to the delight of the younger two children. We planted herbs and cultivated a spearmint that just popped up in the middle of it all. The youngest child took delight in trying all the leaves and experiencing the different flavours, while another child started making herbal teas. The corn began to grow tall, the tomatoes growing up the corn, developing in beauty and productivity.

Later in the spring, my husband dug a sandpit for the children. He piled all the topsoil to create another bed. He broke up the clods, but it was hard and dry. I did not really have much of a plan but wanted to use the space to grow more food somehow. My son and I had already planted a whole packet of pumpkin seeds we had been gifted into old plastic planters. We decided to use the pumpkin seedlings to break in the garden since I figured they are usually resilient. We watered the spot and planted them all out in the poor soil, adding a little compost as we planted each plant. We covered it over with a thin layer of bark mulch sourced from a friend. Soon, the whole garden was covered with prolific pumpkin vines. Yet, after a few weeks of this insane growth, I noticed some spots of powdery mildew on the pumpkin leaves. I called my dad and brother, who work in horticulture. They agreed I should remove all the infected leaves and then spray all the plants with garden oil.

Figure 3. The garden at its peak growth, photo by Kelly Dombroski.

I follow their advice that same day, but by the next week, the mildew has spread to the whole bed and started into a few plants in the other beds. I use eco-fungicide, which is made of potassium bicarbonate. Despite all that prolific growth, there are actually only about five pumpkins growing. I had now spent about $45 trying to control the mildew. The following week, I again cut out all the infected leaves, and this time I harvest four of the larger pumpkins. Another one has rotted already from disease, and two small ones I leave on the vine hoping it might recover. The plot looks devastated, the ground dry and lumpy, the plants all white, yellow, and disintegrating before our eyes.

Meanwhile, the other garden is also partly full of dead plants—but dead plants at the end of a good life. We have harvested and eaten all the corn but leave the stalks standing as they still support tomatoes. I harvest all the borlotti beans, which come to about half a jar, possibly enough for one meal—or enough for a crop next year. The tomatoes are coming to the end of their time, and we are collecting bowls of them and using them to make pasta sauce. The zucchini still produce each day and have been resistant to the spots of mildew, unlike their sisters in the other garden nearby. The herbs are flowering, the marigolds around the edge are enjoying a comeback as the vegetable plants die back. It is ready for an autumn planting.

What does all this have to do with retheorising economy? J.K. Gibson-Graham, Cameron and Healy (2013) discuss how we often think of the economy as some kind of machine with levers to pull and inputs and outputs. They give us the example of the Moniac machine, built to replicate and predict the effects of interest rates and savings on the national economy. The machine represents ordinary people interacting with the economy as a set of variables who respond in predictable ways—saving when interest rates are high, borrowing when they are low, and just generally responding predictably to the levers pulled by the 'real economists'. Gibson-Graham et al. (2013) invite us to think of the economy as something much bigger than the Moniac machine—and also much smaller. They invite us to think of the economy as a community garden, where the inputs of sunlight, rain, people's time and energy, gifting, harvesting, composting and more represent the interactions and complexity of the economies we are all living in. In that economy, we all have agency to do things together to make something different, and we all participate in a variety of ways. As I work in the garden, I begin to re-sense the economy as something I participate in with some agency.

Like many in urban settings, I have experienced metabolic rift, embedded in a 'throw it away' economic rationality, unable to see where our waste goes. Aotearoa New Zealand produces masses of food for places around the world. The food waste is thus often returned to the soil—or landfilled in anaerobic purgatory—somewhere else in the world (Goburdhone & Dombroski, 2023). We extract from our soils to feed the world, and then we have had to extract fertilisers from countries like Nauru to replenish our soils enough to continue to produce food. While a machine model of the economy treats all inputs and outputs as much the same (standardised as money), sensing the economy as a garden allows us to see that it really matters where the inputs and outputs come from and where they go to. My gardens worked in small-scale experimental ways to nurture my family and close some of the metabolic rift. We ate the produce, and we learned about what works in our area. We returned our waste to the soil. While I was hoping to use the cheap and free pumpkin plants to do the work of breaking up the soil for me, of establishing the relationships of fungi, microbes and rhizomes in the soil, these plants succumbed to disease, and I spent a lot of money on outside inputs to try and fix it.

In all this, the children are watching and sensing and learning. One asks, "Why did the pumpkin patch all die off, and the other patch produce so much food?" My other children note how you get sick of eating to the seasons—the in-season vegetables losing their relative value. But how this means we easily give them away to others, too. My son bikes around the neighbourhood gifting people grapefruit and zucchini. The garden is our theory of the economy and also allows us to interact with the economy differently. Our experiments in feeding ourselves are experiments in closing the metabolic rift and nurturing different kinds of active economic subjectivities.

Sensing as theory

Our patched-together quilt of creative interventions does not fit within a tidy summary or conclusion. Rather, in the spirit of the DE approach that encourages embodied, material, creative, and contextualised theorising, our quilt of creative practices in this chapter offers a glimpse into some ways our work helps us experiment and practice more-than-capitalist economies. Reflecting on our quilt, we also draw from performance studies and DE thinking. Both draw on the concept of performativity to consider how discourse, texts and practices go beyond representing 'the world' or 'the economy' and, instead, can bring particular worlds or economies into being, making them more or less possible. When assembled together, the quilt patches of practice in Parts 1 and 2 offer a sense of the 'both/and' relationship between anti-capitalist and postcapitalist thinking and action proposed by DE scholar Ethan Miller (2015). Miller asks, "[c]an we not construct forms of action and subjectivity in which both critique and experiment, rage and hope, opposition and possibility, co-exist and even co-constitute one another?" (p. 3). We contend that creative and artistic practices can offer such forms of action and subjectivity because of their capacity to bring together elements that might be viewed as incoherent or incompatible in other contexts. Also central to this chapter is the idea that embodied and sensorial experiences have a crucial but overlooked role in sensing, imagining, enacting and embodying more-than-capitalist economies.

Molly and Heather's comedic interventions satirised the ridiculousness of capitalist imaginaries that have been taken very seriously across the arts, education, and urban planning sectors. Their examples show how satirical arts interventions that measure impact, or the value of art, and promote Porta Potti living can provide some hilarious, somatic release. These interventions create opportunities to laugh with and learn from glitches and failures in neoliberal logics and practices and to envision alternatives with communities. Both Molly and Heather's practices point to the potential of generative critique that can spur new possibilities rather than imposing change with negative affect. Leo, Aviv and Kelly's quilt pieces offer glimpses into learning from improvisational music-making, experimental community gathering spaces and home gardening. These examples shine a light on the ways that each co-creative practice fosters interdependent economies and economic subjects through embodied and improvisational experiences. These community and diverse economies are being continuously theorised and retheorised, as much through bodies, feelings and relationships as they are through thoughts and words.

For each of us, the activities and experiments we share in this chapter propel us to feel and sense beyond the abstract and rational economic theory that tends to dominate theory and mainstream popular discourse. These adaptive, decentralised, interdependent, relational and transformative (brown, 2017) practices strengthen our ability to engage fully with the world and, practice radical tenderness and hold space for difficulties, tensions, and contradictions. Our practices also help us dream and build economies that forefront interdependence and care with our local communities and beyond, including our international community economies research network (CERN).

To conclude, we hope that, like Kelly's garden patch, this chapter will sprout more heterogenous, fertile and resilient spaces to co-sense and co-practice economies differently. Maybe we will experience glitches, blunders and failure. But, as we face accelerating socio-ecological crises globally, we can learn from missteps and co-imagine more healthy futures.

References

Barrett, S. (2012, November 13). Rebuilding the front porch: An interview with Patrick Overton. *Art of the Rural*. Available at: http://theruralsite.blogspot.com/2012/11/rebuilding-front-porch-interview-with.html

Belfiore, E. (2009). On bullshit in cultural policy practice and research: Notes from the British case. *International Journal of Cultural Policy*, 15(3), 343–359. https://doi.org/10.1080/10286630902806080

brown, a. m. (2017). *Emergent strategy: Shaping change, changing worlds*. AK Press.

Elliott, A. (2020, March 26). After the crisis, what kind of world do we want? Post-apocalyptic novels hold lessons—and warnings. *CBC Arts*. CBC. https://www.cbc.ca/arts/after-the-crisis-what-kind-of-world-do-we-want-post-apocalyptic-novels-hold-lessons-and-warnings-1.5509721

Escobar, A. (2018). *Designs for the pluriverse: Radical interdependence, autonomy, and the making of worlds*. Duke University Press.

Farrales, M., Hoogeveen, D., Sloan Morgan, O., De Leeuw, S., & Parkes, M. (2022). Framing futurities in photovoice, health, and environment: How power is reproduced and challenged in arts-based methods. *GeoHumanities*, 8(2), 415–434. https://doi.org/10.1080/2373566X.2022.2080095

Gibson-Graham, J. K., Cameron, J., Dombroski, K., Healy, S., & Miller, E. (2021). Cultivating community economies: Tools for building a livable world. In J. G. Speth & K. Courrier (Eds.), *The new systems reader: Alternatives to a failed economy* (pp. 410–432). Routledge.

Gibson-Graham, J. K. (1996). *The end of capitalism (as we knew it)*. University of Minnesota Press.

Gibson-Graham, J. K. (2006). *A postcapitalist politics*. University of Minnesota Press.

Gibson-Graham, J. K., Cameron, J., & Healy, S. (2013). *Take back the economy: An ethical guide for transforming our communities*. University of Minnesota Press.

Gibson-Graham, J. K., & Dombroski, K. (2020). Introduction to the handbook of diverse economies: Inventorying as ethical intervention. In J. K. Gibson-Graham & K. Dombroski (Eds.), *The handbook of diverse economies* (pp. 1–25). Edward Elgar.

Goburdhone, S., & Dombroski, K. (2023). Thinking with soils: Can urban farms help us heal metabolic rifts in Aotearoa? *New Zealand Geographer*, 79(2), 127–131. https://doi.org/10.1111/nzg.12363

Gómez-Peña, G., Martinez-Cruz, P., & García-López, S. (2021). *La Pocha Nostra: A handbook for the rebel artist in a post-democratic society*. Routledge.

Kimmerer, R. (2013). *Braiding sweetgrass: Indigenous wisdom, scientific knowledge and the teachings of plants*. Milkweed Editions.

Lane, J., & Mancini, L. (2021). The clowns are here. *Canadian Theatre Review*, 183, 5–7.

Latour, B. (2004). Why has critique run out of steam? From matters of fact to matters of concern. *Critical Inquiry*, 30, 225–248.

Machado de Oliveira, V. (2021). *Hospicing modernity: Facing humanity's wrongs and the implications for social activism*. North Atlantic Books.

McLean, H. (2022). Creative arts-based geographies: Some cautionary and hopeful reflections. *ACME: An International Journal for Critical Geographies*, 21(3), 311–326.
Miller, E. (2015). Anticapitalism or postcapitalism? Both! *Rethinking Marxism*, 27(3), 364–367.
National Endowment for the Arts. (2010). *Come as you are: Informal arts participation in urban and rural communities.*
Schick, L. (2021). The power of generative critique in art-energy projects. In H. S. Rogers (Ed.), *Routledge handbook of art, science, and technology studies* (pp. 469–487). Routledge.
Sedgwick, E. K. (1994). *Tendencies.* Routledge.
Stephens, L. (2012). Rethinking the political: Art, work and the body in the contemporary circus [Doctoral dissertation]. University of Toronto.
Up in the Air Theater Company. (2023). *rEvolver Festival.*
Verran, H. (2014). Working with those who think otherwise. *Common Knowledge*, 20(3), 527–539.

VERTAISARVIOITU
KOLLEGIALT GRANSKAD
PEER-REVIEWED
www.tsv.fi/tunnus

6
A future worth imagining
Collaging capitalism, expanding political imagination

Maria Mäensivu

In International Politics and International Political Economy, images and creative forms of data are often valued solely for their representational function, rather than being appreciated as creative processes in their own right. Consequently, they are rarely engaged with on their own terms. However, by incorporating emotional and embodied experiences and representing them through material dimensions, creative methods can effectively convey issues that cannot be fully understood through text or words alone (Ristovska, 2018). The use of creative methods can also encourage researchers to pursue multisensory and multimodal forms of reasoning (Andrä, 2022). This contribution extends these perceptions to examine and retheorise capitalism through the use of visual images and creative methods.

This chapter on collaging capitalism is structured around collages, a zine, and a pottery experiment. The themes revolve around the future, the individual body and social reproduction, violence, and the strength of failure. Through each of these themes, the chapter engages with academic debates on the character of capitalism. The conclusions attempt to bring all these seemingly separate themes together, and can also be understood as a collage in itself.

Mäensivu, M. (2025). A future worth imagining: Collaging capitalism, expanding political imagination. In A. Kangas, I. Gataulina, M. Poutanen, A. I. Rajala & H-E. Ventovirta (Eds.), *Retheorising capitalism* (pp. 112–132). Tampere University Press. https://doi.org/10.61201/tup.981

Collaging as an arena for retheorising

As an act that involves composing various materials in new and imaginative ways through gluing, drawing, cutting, ripping, and more, collaging arguably offers a fruitful arena for retheorising capitalism. Kangas et al. (2019) propose that collaging involves breaking established structures, becoming aware of boundaries and rules, and reaching beyond them. They point out that creating surprising connections and challenging power relations is central to collaging. They suggest that this form of rule-breaking through theorising and collaging can expand our thinking in "queer ways". The potential of collaging to expand boundaries is not limited to visuality, as collages can also incorporate other senses such as hearing and touching (Kangas et al., 2019).

Creative methods also relate to the corporeal and tactile as they are brought to existence through manual doing and embodied sensations that intertwine with abstract and reflective thought (Andrä, 2022). The corporeal nature of art is further exemplified by the fact that creating art inevitably involves leaving traces of oneself in it (Rippin & Vachhani 2018). The collages that this chapter discusses were made in a workshop discussing capitalism. They contain traces of me, as well as my peers with whom I spent time discussing and exchanging cutouts during the collaging process. These collages would not have been as they are now without the collaborative effort and ideas coming together on a single piece of paper. As Gauntlett (2011, p.2) argues, "making is connecting", and these collages also connect the corporeal to the social realms of art. While this aspect of collaging cannot be fully translated into the two-dimensional pages of a book, the collages I created also embrace the sensory and playful nature of collaging.

In addition, collages can serve as a space for retheorising due to their utopian characteristics, which relate to the ability to expand our political imagination. The concept of 'utopia' carries dual meanings: no-place and good-place (Eskelinen et al. 2020a, p.7). However, the concept has been increasingly critiqued in recent years. Eskelinen et al. (2020a) argue that in much of the criticism utopias are seen as a static blueprint for a society. Central to these criticisms is the fear that such a society is only achievable through absolutist, totalitarian and authoritarian means, and consequently the anti-utopian sentiments have grown especially in the era of liberal capitalist democracies.

Contrary to this belief, Eskelinen et al. (2020a) demonstrate that utopias should be seen as vital for the expansion of our political imagination. This is where they resonate with the idea of collaging. Instead of approaching utopias through a static model, they should be seen as relational and heuristic tools that can serve social and political imagination. Consequently, they help in critically examining our current reality. Thus, utopias and collages should be approached as counter-images that reflect current societal problems, or as a compass that shows there are alternatives, and we can navigate towards them. Utopias should also be approached as reflexive rather than static, as the relationship between utopia and reality is dynamic and constantly changing. Furthermore, even though imagination and dreaming might seem like solitary activities, the transformative power of utopian thinking can only be understood if it is fostered and practiced collectively—treated as a skill (Eskelinen et al., 2020a, pp.7, 11–12, 14).

According to Eskelinen et al. (2020a), the loss of the critical function of utopias and political imagination is an alarming symptom, as it inhibits our ability to conceive of different worlds. They argue that the inability to dream is the antithesis of both utopias and dystopias. Moreover, they suggest that by fostering political imagination, we can recognise ever-expanding opportunities beyond capitalist realism and challenge the current status quo. Therefore, utopian thought is vital for challenging and retheorising capitalism, and collaging, as I propose in this chapter, offers a specific arena for this.

Indeed, visual methods are important not only because they expand our understanding of what can be studied and discussed, but also because they expand our imagination. Ristovska (2018) argues that the distinction between imagination and reasoning needs to be questioned, as cultivating imagination—new perspectives and imaginative practices—are needed to address the sociopolitical crises that are unfolding globally. Visual arts have the capacity to challenge linearity, fixed identities, and conventional interpretations, while also accommodating different, relational modes of engagement with sociopolitical issues (Kangas et al., 2019; Ristovska, 2018). Since visual arts involve creation, they can also be described as world-making projects (Kangas et al., 2019). Moreover, visual arts and utopian thought can be engaged with cooperatively to expand political imagination. The following sections propose one way to achieve this.

Thoughts about the future

Figure 1. Ajatuksia tulevaisuudesta [Thoughts about the future], photo by Visa Keskinen.

Questioning our biases of what kind of a future is achievable and worth working towards is vital for utopias—for reconstructing and retheorising the current status quo. The collage "Thoughts about the future" (Figure 1) was inspired by the way in which utopias are taken up in certain post-structural, feminist and decolonial approaches that question what is seen as natural or taken for granted. It experiments with the idea of an ideal future. The text at the bottom-left of the collage reads "ajatuksia tulevaisuudesta" in Finnish, which translates to "thoughts about the future" and also serves as the title of the piece. The collage is a representation of one utopia and attempts to show a world beyond capitalist economic systems: a world where there is no need for constant growth and people and nature coexist as equals.

The collage has been glued to a dark green canvas, parts of which are visible beneath the ripped images. The left side of the collage consists of a three-dimensional weaving pattern where a starry and a blue sky alternate. The woven pattern represents the interconnected nature of efforts to achieve a better future. The starry pattern serves as a reminder to reach for the stars, while the blue pattern ties the piece together. Weaving symbolises the importance of creating things by hand and fostering a connection to the items we own through repairing and upcycling. It is also associated with contemporary forms of craft-based activism, described as a "gentle revolution" that occurs quietly and rarely disturbs others, yet critiques mass production and capitalist structures (Rippin & Vachhani, 2018, p. 236).

Additionally, the yellow flowers growing in between rocks serve as a reminder of the resilience of nature: how dandelions and tree roots have the power to grow through concrete roads and thrive despite human attempts at removing them. For this motif, I also took inspiration from Zen Buddhist art in which there is little differentiation between natural accidents and human control and which contrasts with the Western need for symmetry and orderliness (Watts, 1957/1973, pp. 205, 211). Rather than focusing on controlling nature and creating neat grid-like landscapes and concrete cities, what if we worked with nature and built cities that grew alongside it? The idea of coexistence between humans and nature is further emphasised by the images of a forest with only a small human-made church peeking from behind the trees.

On the right side, there is a text about the nature of Vietnam. The text is interesting in the way it describes living beings as valuable, even if they do not contribute to economic growth. It mentions "the trees, water buffalo and wild dogs—ancient lands of Ba Be National Park—endless rice paddies." Originally from a late 20th-century travel booklet, I encountered it accidentally but wanted to add it to my collage to create a contrast with mainstream economic thinking, which often views nature as a resource for humans. Here, however, all mentions of human intervention have been removed from the text, emphasising the need to see nature as valuable in its own right. Similarly, reciprocity between humans, the land, and the spirit world are key principles in indigenous economies, as Rauna Kuokkanen (2011) points out. In literature about indigenisation and postcolonial studies, Western hegemony and its exploitative relationship with nature are heavily questioned (Gray & Coates, 2010). Indigenous economic ideas can be valuable in our quest to rethink capitalism and expand our understanding of the relationship between humans, the economy, and nature.

On top of that text, I added the word "Degrow" and a chart with a descending line to remind of the contemporary degrowth scholars' ideas about the necessity of redesigning the economy and society to reduce production and energy use, and a (re) politicisation of the economy (Kallis et al., 2018; Akbulut, 2021). The word degrow refers to the possibility of organising the economy in a way that is not reliant on constant growth to function: staying still and being content is enough. Akbulut (2021) points out that degrowth scholarship also needs to account for principles such as solidarity, justice, and democracy, since the basic needs of many people are not yet met.

Furthermore, above the words signalling toward degrowth thinking, there is an image of a pristine lake and some islands with a rainbow at the centre. To the right bottom side, I added some red background and write the word "burn" on it. This reflects my personal worries over our planet, but it is also intended to act as a warning of inaction. It represents my frustrations over current climate policies and the increasing pessimism and passivity towards defending nature. These worries and frustrations find an echo in academic literature. For example, Ekberg et al. (2022) explore the multiple ways in which (meaningful) climate change policy has been and still is obstructed. For example, climate change denial that has been forcefully promoted by the fossil fuel industry and additionally, many actors call to stall climate action with claims of alleged costs. Therefore, even the most well-meaning individuals are unable to contribute to curbing emissions both at the individual and societal level. Similarly, Hornsey and Fielding (2020) remind that progress on climate change mitigation is hampered by both climate scepticism and failure of nonsceptics to engage in meaningful climate action despite concern about climate change.

Throughout the collage, I drew red flowers with spiral centres (Japanese *hanamaru*) as well as some insects such as butterflies and bumblebees. Humans, whether we like it or not, are dependent on nature. We cannot live without plants that provide us with oxygen and food, but nature can live and go on without humans. Similarly, Anna Tsing (2013) points out how capitalism is also dependent on nature both by producing resources that capitalism alone cannot create and by giving value to capitalist commodities trough non-capitalist social relations.

Additionally, the bugs scattered throughout the collage represent this dependence. I chose pollinators specifically to show that even the smallest of creatures can have huge impacts on our entire society. Humans have been reliant on bees throughout history, even prior to agriculture (Ellis, 2022). Many studies have also highlighted the global importance of bees in combatting climate change and have expressed worry over their declining populations (see e.g. Brown & Paxton, 2009; Hung et al., 2018; Madras-Majewska & Majewski, 2016). Furthermore Ellis (2022) argues that capitalist agriculture is the biggest threat to bees despite it being heavily reliant on the indispensable little pollinators. The *hanamaru* is a Japanese symbol, which is often used similarly to a golden star, or to signal a "job well done". In the collage, it represents hope for the future and the belief that a better future can still be achieved.

The collaging exercise described above resonates with Eskelinen et al.'s (2020a, p.7) approach where utopias are a heuristic tool for improving social and political imagination. I believe that my way of working with the collage material shows that collages—as a form of or method for utopian thought—can serve a critical function in relation to our present reality. However, the fact that this collage allowed me to juxtapose themes resonates with the idea that utopias are societal counter-images: utopian thought not only highlights problems of its own time but also investigates, analyses and reconstructs existing historical conditions to inspire new possibilities (p. 22). For example, the discussion around human reliance on nature and bees both highlights the current issues but also allows us to imagine different futures where these issues are faced. The images of future do not necessarily need to be the most realistic or absolute, but they need to show us that there are more options than to continue as-is and hope for the best.

Body in capitalism

Figure 2a. A detail from the zine entitled "Body, body, body", photo by Visa Keskinen.

The zine entitled "Body Body Body" (Figures 2a–e) explores the relationship of capitalism to the body trough images revolving around the themes of reproduction, labour, gender-roles, racism, beauty, and liberation. Bodies are an interesting entry point to retheorisations of capitalism as they are at the centre of both human life and societal control. The zine consists of multiple yellow pages. There is an image of a naked baby with the word "body" written all around it in red, green and black crayon (Figure 2a). Around the baby, a red halo is drawn in a child-like manner. The image of the baby can serve as a motif for the beginning of the life cycle and the first steps of humanity. On the other hand, it can represent innocence prior to being 'tainted', objectified, and exploited by the capitalist systems.

Observed as a whole, the zine deals with the theme of capitalist reproduction. It develops into a commentary on the centrality of labouring bodies and labour power in capitalism. On one of its pages, I placed newspaper cut outs that discuss the declining fertility rate with text written over them that says: "Not enough white babies" (Figure 2b). This references the ways in which many industrialised Western countries seem to be ever-so-focused on declining birth rates and its effects on the working populations—on the availability of the kind of labour that capitalism needs to reproduce itself (Ross, 2023; Jones, 2022; Weiss, 2021)

Indeed, the motif of a body is in a key role in capitalism and its analyses: David McNally (2017, p.1) links the working body under capitalism to sub-Saharan African and Haitian mythos of zombies as "unthinking, body-machines, lacking identity, memory and consciousness - possessing only the physical capacity to labour". He further argues, through Marxist theory, that capitalism is dependent on the exploitation of the human labourer, but also that liberation of the body struggles against the abstract nature of capitalism and cannot be done without radically transforming the relationship between persons and things.

Moreover, scholars of racial capitalism have also reminded that the concern over the declining birth rate mostly applies to white people and is a concern because it is a threat to white supremacy. As Riley et al. (2022) note, abortion and control over reproductive health can be rooted in racism and white supremacy. Since access to safe abortion is a vital part of healthcare, attempts to control them can show us critical information about the fragile nature and developments in societal power structures. For example, Sudenkaarne and Blell (2022) argue that healthcare and healthcare politics needs bioethical consideration of power-structures such as racism and sexism.

Figure 2b. A detail from the zine entitled "Body, body, body", photo by Visa Keskinen.

The text "murdered and missing indigenous babies" (Figure 2b) provides a reference to the epidemic of Missing and Murdered Indigenous Women (MMIW) in Canada and the United States, which further highlights the racist structures behind justice systems (Joseph, 2021). As Rauna Kuokkanen (2008) has argued, global capitalism represents a multifaceted attack to indigenous women's existence as it furthers their marginalisation and undermines indigenous peoples' right of self-determination. I placed a reference to MMIW here to illustrate that despite the capitalist focus and interest toward labouring bodies, not all bodies are treated equally. This text highlights the ways in which racialised bodies are seen as "less" important than white bodies. This point is also made by racial capitalism scholars who argue that capitalist accumulation requires disposability and unequal differentiation of human value, most often through racism and white supremacy (Melamed, 2015).

In the zine, there is a page discussing reproductive rights as well as women's role as homemakers (Figure 2c). It contains text cut from a *Time* magazine from around the 1970s criticising women's liberation, which encouraged rejection of "traditional roles as mother and homemaker". On top of the text cut out I wrote the words "Labor for labor" and "Nurture love care". "Labor for labor" is a wordplay on homophones of labour as an act of giving birth and labour as in working (using the American variant of the word labour). By placing it there, I wanted to draw attention to how reproduction can be tied to the need for a steady supply of workers as social reproduction feminists have highlighted (Weiss, 2021). For example, Weiss (2021) shows how social reproduction exposes tension between the reproduction of capitalist society and the wellbeing of people in it but also rests on structures of inequality both domestically and globally.

Figure 2c. A detail from the zine entitled "Body, body, body", photo by Visa Keskinen.

The text "Nurture love care" as well as the drawn vaginas and the bleeding flower all tie into gender roles—especially the traditional notions of women as homemakers.

It resonates with Schult's (2006) idea of how reproductive labour, while necessary, is often overlooked and unpaid, but also manifests in different ways across the categories of race, class, and gender. Additionally, Tronto (1993) and Kuokkanen (2011) point out how care-work, such as work done by stay-at-home parents, is often undervalued in comparison to wage labour and production.

In the zine, there is also a pull-tab with an image of a man with x's for eyes and a text: "in the end we die". In the composition of the zine, this closes the circle of reproduction and serves as a reminder that death will come to everyone equally. However, in capitalist societies, even death is not truly equal. For example, Mezzadri (2022) demonstrates, how marginalised bodies were over-exposed to health and economic impacts of the COVID-19 pandemic, but also how the role of these 'surplus lives' is to be disposable under racial capitalism and neoliberal regime. As Mezzadri (2022, p. 390) notes, "the dehumanising narrative of given people as less worthy of being saved in a context of limited resources was presented as rational choice."

While political economists and social reproduction feminists have highlighted that the body is a way to produce and reproduce labour, it is also tied to capitalist dynamics as a vital support for consumerist and capitalist cycles. With this zine, I also wanted to explore the role of the body in capitalism by prompting questions such as*:* How are the ways in which we are displeased with ourselves artificially reproduced by capitalist structures and how do they support capitalist functions? The zine also features an image of a naked woman with red markings around her and covering her eyes as well as highlighting different parts of her body (Figure 2d). It brings attention to the ways in which the sexualised and objectified person is often also dehumanised (Bernard & Wollast, 2019; Wollast et al. 2018). This is not to say that sexuality and sex are inherently harmful, but we need to carefully examine the power structures that are reproduced through capitalist sexualisation and the commodification of marginalised bodies.

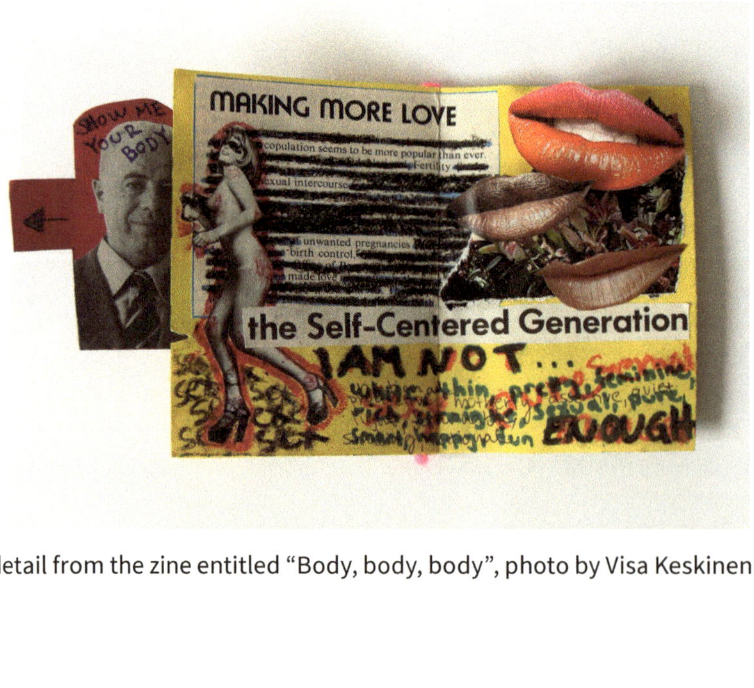

Figure 2d. A detail from the zine entitled "Body, body, body", photo by Visa Keskinen.

Feminist scholars have also pointed out how subjects are enmeshed in cycles of desires in patriarchal capitalism (Lewis & Hames, 2011). Halberstram (2011, p.95) argues that the commodification (of feminine bodies) depends on hetero-normative visual and erotic desires, which are deployed for example in advertisements. Furthermore, in the current digital age, sexualised labour, self-commodification, and pornographisation affect cultural consumption practices, for example, in social media (Drenten et al. 2020). The image of the naked woman then, on the pages of the zine, suggests that these changing dynamics should be further examined in relation to capitalism and its entanglement with the sexualised body.

Beside the woman there is a text "The Self-Centered Generation" and "I am not (white, thin, pure, smart...) enough" (Figure 2d). Written in different colours of crayon with the words overlapping each other, the text is intentionally difficult to read. With these words, I wanted to highlight the conflicting ways in which capitalism affects self-image: on one hand, bodies are sexualised and made the object of desire, but, on the other hand, consumerism thrives on the idea that a person is not "enough". For example, under patriarchal capitalism, women are often driven to transform their bodies and themselves to be perfect and desirable (Lewis & Hames, 2011).

Expanding the notion of beauty to include marginalised bodies might seem like a worthy goal, but Snider (2018) reminds us that 'beauty' is a socially constructed exclusionary category that upholds power hierarchies. They further argue that expanding the notion of 'beauty' to include different types of bodies such as fat, old, and disabled is often just a way for corporations to increase their consumer-base and profits. This understanding of beauty is represented by the image of an old man peeking with the text "show me your body" above it (Figure 2d). I chose to include this motif in the zine to represent the hidden forces that drive the sexualisation and dissatisfaction of bodies that are marginalised in the sense of not being considered beautiful in conventional thinking. The text "Making more love" as well as the three-dimensional lips that pop out of the page almost attacking the viewer represent how sexualisation is often non-consensual and forced onto people (Figure 2d). It also highlights the different ways in which different bodies are sexualised and others even fetishised (see Benard, 2016).

Furthermore, the zine features a page with an image of three women dressed in white reaching for the sky with their upper bodies rising from the paper (Figure 2e). They are decorated with red crayons and green glitter with the text "Rise" written above them. This final page of the zine represents the possibility of emancipation. It suggests rising beyond and not accepting the capitalist control over one's body. The last image originally represented women doing an "anti-fertility dance", representing their denial of societal norms and expectations placed on women. Within the zine, it can also be understood to represent other ways people can deny capitalist and neoliberal expectations aimed towards bodies. One such way could also be rejection of beauty and embracing ugliness as a political tool.

Figure 2e. A detail from the zine entitled "Body, body, body", photo by Visa Keskinen.

Because beauty is a neoliberal concept that is culturally created, the concept of ugliness is also tied to different structures of power and systemic oppressions that include issues of race, weight, dis/ability and wealth (Snider, 2018). Utilising ugliness can be both a way to mobilise transgressive politics, but also to showcase the dissatisfaction towards social standards that encourage self-hatred (Fanghanel, 2020; Eileraas, 1997). As Snider (2018, p. 343) remarks, "ugliness doesn't sell like beauty". Hence, actively becoming ugly, grotesque, and unmarketable can be a form of liberating oneself from the objectification and demands of capitalism.

Capitalism and violence

Are humans naturally selfish and violent as Hobbesian and neoliberal economic interpretations might lead us to conclude? The idea that human action is motivated by self-interest is also known as "psychological egoism" and has been widely accepted by political economists, psychologists, and philosophers alike (Feinberg, 2012). For example, Hobbes proposes in his classic work *Leviathan*: the natural condition of mankind is that beyond states the law of nature compels that men are enemies to one another (Hobbes, 1996).

The collage (Figure 3) entitled "The big headache" explores the different ways in which capitalism is reliant on the various forms and structures of violence and how they reinforce one another. Max Weber famously argued that: "a state is a human community that (successfully) claims the monopoly of the legitimate use of physical force within a given territory" (Weber 1991, p. 1). If this defines states, then our baseline understanding of states as international actors shows how fundamentally reliant the international status quo is on violence.

Figure 3. The big headache, photo by Visa Keskinen.

The collage consists of multiple different elements. It has been built from ripped pieces of paper glued onto a red background. In the right corner, there is a large text "the big headache", which serves as the title of this collage. It also references the way in which violence is often thought to be annoying, but inevitable—like a headache, some approach it as a natural function of human body. But headache should not be the natural state or the norm of how a human body functions.

On the left side there is an image of the world's atomic resources with a red text "Doom is acceptable for the economy" written over it. This brings attention to the ways in which capitalism, militarism and power-structures are intertwined. Previously, Rosa Luxemburg (1951 p.454) argued that capitalism in reliant and inseparable from colonialism and militarism. Similarly, Mrozowski (2019) links capitalism and colonialism throughout historical processes, making Luxemburg's abstract arguments more concrete. In addition, Antal (2018) argues that the new forms of militarist capitalism incorporate aspects of warfare to our everyday life through hybrid-forms of warfare created especially by right-wing populist regimes. Furthermore, Onbaşı (2016) analyses the ways in which capitalism, nationalism, militarism, and patriarchal structures are merged, and how its hegemony is felt in daily routines. The collage visualises the links between capitalism and oppressive structures of power while also prompting reflection on whether peace is compatible with the capitalist economy.

Below, there is a text that says "more bombs than ever" as well as an image of a war airplane and a tank behind it. Over this, there is a text "war is a child's play", which I wrote in crayon. On one hand, this is a way to challenge the assumption of war as something inevitable by pointing out the immaturity of aggressive responses. Even children can resolve their issues by violence, but it takes time to learn to handle conflicts constructively. On the other hand, it shows that war affects children's development and, for example, what kind of games they play (Bankova, 2017).

With these motifs in the collage, I wanted to bring attention to the concept of violence beyond direct physical harm. My idea was that this allows us to better understand the functions of our global society that cause harm to different populations. For example, through Johan Galtung's (1969; 1990) concepts of direct, structural, and cultural violence or Rob Nixon's (2011) notion of 'slow violence' (covert violence that occurs out of sight), the mechanisms of violence can be understood. By scrutinising multiple concepts of violence, we can recognise the different structures that capitalism can use to ensure access to cheap labour and natural resources as well as combat resistance and encourage consumerism.

The point that I wanted to make in this collage is that retheorising capitalism also requires us to rethink our approach and stance on violence. The collage attempts to simultaneously make visible and denaturalise the role of violence in capitalism. Taking a suggestion from Rob Nixon's (2011, 13) idea of a "representational bias against slow violence", it says that we need to critically engage with the notion that violence is a "necessary evil" or something natural. Finally, in addition to retheorising our dependence on violence, we need to actively engage with initiatives that challenge these norms and values. When the structures of society are intertwined with violence, it is no surprise that advocating for peace and ending violence is seen as controversial. Nixon (2011, p.15) further proposes that we need imaginative measures that helps us make the insidious and imperceptible tangible. While Nixon refers to imaginative writing, another way to do this could be by collaging or using other creative methods.

There is also a ripped piece of paper depicting a graph of the stock market in the collage. This piece extends beyond the boundaries of the paper. The ripped pieces remind of the way paper cutting machines cut paper into thin strips. Behind the ripped paper, some images of coins can be seen. They indicate how the neoliberal economic order itself can be seen as a form of violence (Nixon, 2011, p.10). At the centre of the piece, there are cigarettes that represent the way capitalism's "addiction" to violence, and the harm it causes, tends to remain hidden. As Nixon (2011) suggests with the notion of slow violence: it is something more insidious and deceptive than direct forms of violence such as wars.

To the upper corner of the page, I placed an image of a monstrous-looking bug. It creates a contrast to the Nixonian idea of the 'slowness' and 'hiddenness' of violence and, through its spectacularity, reminds us of the horrible nature of violence and war. Below the bug, there is a green image of Uncle Sam balancing on top of stilts and creating a shape similar to a dollar symbol ($). This is an attempt to show how fragile capitalism is. Rather than being a mere "bug" in the system, uncertainty and economic collapses are a feature of capitalism. As political economists remind us, capitalism is built on contradictions that incite a broad range of complex societal struggles (Fraser, 2017)

Much of neoclassical economic analysis also relies on the assumption that individuals rationally pursue their interests egotistically (Bowie, 1991). Some traditions adopt egoism itself as an ethical position, and assume that by pursuing their own happiness, general happiness can also be achieved (Spencer, 1881; Bowie,

1991). These understandings of humans are often used as an explanation for the ongoing violence in our lives. The traditions of economics and politics both rely on assumptions of selfishness in humans. But what if this was not the case? Bowie (1991) challenges egocentric paradigms and argues that these models are seriously flawed. This also ties into Eskelinen et al.'s (2020a) idea of utopias as counter images. If we limit our understanding of humans to violent egoistical creatures, we fail to seek out alternatives to our current systems.

To give alternatives to egoism-based economic models, we can listen to and learn from, for example, indigenous communities. Many indigenous communities rely on subsistence based economic systems that do not centre around exchange for profit, but rather the sustenance of the community and the surrounding environment through endless circulation of goods. However, these models are often dismissed as "primitive", and they have been actively restricted by colonial powers alongside the active eradication of indigenous people. (Kuokkanen, 2011). By beginning to question our perceptions of human nature as selfish or violent, we can both question the necessity of war and violence as pillars of economy and widen our perception of the possible utopian futures.

What do ugly plates teach us about capitalism?

When making clay plates as a Christmas present for my brother, I had no intention of them looking like I had smeared ketchup all over them. When I finally saw the final product and the terrifying massacre forever immortalised on three small plates, I wanted to close my eyes and forget ever making them. It was not an educational moment in which I could learn to make better plates in the future. To me, it just felt like a punch in the gut. After all my hard work, I produced pieces that I was ashamed to show anyone.

The Western idea where 'failure is not an option' (Smith & Henriksen, 2016) is not the only way to approach mistakes. For example, in Navajo communities, the spirit line or *ch'ihónít'i* can represent purposeful mistakes that create a symbolic path for the survival of the weaving tradition (Yohe, 2012, p.28). The Japanese idea of *wabi-sabi* refers to a feeling when we encounter unpretentious, imperfect, and essentially authentic beauty (Kempton, 2018). I do not think that my ketchup-plates evoke any feeling of *wabi-sabi* nor is it a cultural tradition to be kept alive, however, in some sense, their imperfection can teach us about how to approach societal transformation.

Capitalism and failure are connected through the idea that for one to win, someone else must fail, as Halberstam (2011) suggests. Halberstam also connects failure to queerness, as homosexuals embody a failure in production and reproduction. In contrast: "The queer artist works with rather than against failure and inhabits the darkness" (Halberstam, 2011, p.96). Similarly to collages, my way of making ceramics is undisciplined and, as such, queer (Kangas et al., 2019). The ugly plates I made truly fail to embody the neoliberal standards of consumer culture: they are an eyesore and are made without profit orientation.

Figure 4. Ugly plates, photo by Visa Keskinen.

The plates also call to mind the way Osborne (2018) writes about accepting failure and loss. They argue that feminists, anti-racists, and queer activists are constantly losing to the rising forces of the alt-right, white supremacy, and heteropatriarchal capitalism. Instead of taking this message as a sign to finally give up—and maybe do some mindfulness exercises to become happier—Osborne suggests embracing this loss and finding the transformative power of failure. They argue that loss, negative feelings, and trauma should be felt because they are political and rich with possibilities (and impossibilities): "I dig ashes, blood, bone, and shit into my garden bed. They help things grow" (Osborne, 2018, p. 5).

Tackling an issue as vast as retheorising capitalism can be a daunting task that leaves one feeling completely incompetent to take even one step forward. Even smaller tasks like taking a shower, getting out of bed, or beginning to write can feel so impossible that it is easier to do nothing and stare at the ceiling for hours. If I cannot do it perfectly, then what is the point? If I cannot change everything, then why even bother? We are so unaccustomed to the thought of failure that it is easier to do nothing than to do something imperfectly. That is where the political power of failure comes from. It mobilises us and helps us act even if the outcome is not what we had originally planned. To be comfortable with failure means having the ability to do things, to create, and to try. Smith and Henriksen (2016) argue that failure—more specifically, the ability to try again despite failure—is essential for creative thinking. While creativity can be a way to uphold neoliberal values such as risk-taking or individualisation (Smith & Henriksen, 2016), it also has value in disturbing neoliberal hegemony. When we understand utopian thought as a creative practice (Eskelinen et al., 2020a), using that imagination for concrete societal change requires us to also accept failing time and time again. In this sense, making ugly plates repeatedly can be a valuable tool in generating transformative politics.

Osborne (2018) also encourages us to turn and listen to people who have already experienced catastrophic losses but still live and nurture the world around them: indigenous people. They remind us that we should not appropriate or centre ourselves in the conversation of failure and should be aware of the ways others' worlds have been destroyed for our benefit. Instead of looking for a revolution in Western monorealism, we should take the time to cultivate a space to care for the multiple subaltern worlds that already exist in the cracks of urban spaces and where those excluded from society converge (Osborne, 2018). Capitalism is built on exclusionary power structures. Therefore, it is vital to care for and empower the spaces excluded from neoliberal society also in order to retheorise capitalism.

We need to breathe life into creating spaces that are gentle and offer us moments of counter-hegemonic warmth and kindness, care, nurturing, affection, and make the utopian alternative concrete (Osborne, 2018). We can learn to love and care for the imperfect by crafting failed pieces. When handing my clay plates as a gift to my brother, he was visibly happy and spent time carefully wrapping them so they would not be damaged when returning home. This interaction changed the plates from being only a representation of my incompetence to a gift capable of bringing joy and connecting people together.

Growing up as a perfectionist, allowing myself to accept failure was never an option. However, by giving myself the space and opportunity to enjoy failing, I find that I am also reclaiming my time and my body. By challenging the values of productivity and efficiency, failure itself can be a revolutionary act against capitalism. Therefore, as Halberstam (2011, p. 110) suggests,

> If we want to make the antisocial turn in queer theory we must be willing to turn away from the comfort zone of polite exchange in order to embrace a truly political negativity, one that promises, this time, to fail, to make a mess, to fuck shit up, to be loud, unruly, impolite, to breed resentment, to bash back, to speak up and out, to disrupt, assassinate, shock and annihilate.

The final collage

The collages and the bowl experiment demonstrate how utopian thought and the active rejection of neoliberal values can be useful in retheorising capitalism. In the first collage, I illustrated how utopian imagination can provide us with alternatives to current society. The second collage explored the ways in which capitalism controls bodies and how this can be challenged by rejecting beauty as an ideal. The third collage attempted to denaturalise the role of violence in capitalist societies and proposed that, to see alternatives to the violent status quo, we need to question what we perceive as natural human behaviour. Finally, the bowl experiment highlighted the importance of failure and imperfection in beginning to build alternatives to capitalism in our contemporary society.

My experimentation with collages was based on the idea that seemingly in compatible themes can be connected in surprising ways. It also shows that, when looking for alternatives to the current status quo, we cannot focus on individualised issues. This resonates with Eskelinen et al. (2020b), who point out the rise in private forms of hope. This means that people aim to change their current situations for the better, for example, by turning to entrepreneurship or by escaping the daily grind by choosing a simpler life. However, this is a form of false emancipation lacking transformative power. It is no surprise that popular escapist fantasies rely on individualism. Like individualistic hope, the neoliberal and capitalist emphasis on mindfulness—also referred to as 'McMindfulness'—is an attempt to reach individual fulfilment without societal transformation (Hyland, 2017). As Wrenn (2022) argues, due to the neoliberal focus on individual accountability, society also becomes comprised of self-interested individuals who seek to forward their own agendas. These self-centred modes of transformation cannot change the societal dynamics that cause dissatisfaction in the first place.

Instead, the solutions for transformative utopias can be found in social and collective hope that presents alternatives to the current status quo. The question remains: Where and how the skills related to utopian imagination can be fostered? How to identify common aspirations for collective action among diverse groups of people (Eskelinen et al., 2020b)? David Gauntlett (2011) suggests that making and creating can connect people, ideas, and materials within social and physical environments. Craft is, indeed, often associated with women coming together, and can rarely be done completely alone, detached from any communal activity, because even the manufacturing of materials often requires multiple skills and forms of labour (Rippin & Vachhani, 2018). The ways in which making and crafting can bring communities together could also be a way to foster collective utopian imagination and transformative politics, as exemplified by collaging. After all, making and crafting is not only connecting and social, but also embodied. As Rippin and Vachhani (2018, p.213) write: "We seem to be surprised by our own delight in our ability to make things ourselves." In crafting, we leave traces of ourselves in the things we make, and therefore crafting becomes both personal and embodied (Rippin & Vachhani, 2018). Expanding this idea to collaging shows us how it can be used to make the collective utopia into something concrete.

References

Akbulut, B. (2021). Degrowth. *Rethinking Marxism, 33*(1), 98–110. https://doi.org/10.1080/08935696.2020.1847014

Andrä, C. (2022). Crafting stories, making peace? Creative methods in peace research. *Millennium, 50*(2), 494–523. https://doi.org/10.1177/03058298211063510

Antal, A. (2018). The new form of capitalist militarism: The permanent state of exception. *Draft paper* presented at the Luxemburg and Her Ideas Conference, Rosa Luxemburg Stiftung–New York Office and International Rosa Luxemburg Society.

Bankova, P. (2017). Children play war. *The Belogradchik Journal for Local History, 8*(1), 113–132.

Benard, A. A. F. (2016). Colonizing Black female bodies within patriarchal capitalism: Feminist and human rights perspectives. *Sexualization, Media, & Society, 2*(4), 2374623816680622. https://doi.org/10.1177/2374623816680622

Bernard, P., & Wollast, R. (2019). Why is sexualization dehumanizing? The effects of posture suggestiveness and revealing clothing on dehumanization. *Sage Open, 9*(1), 2158244019828230. https://doi.org/10.1177/2158244019828230

Bowie, N. E. (1991). Challenging the egoistic paradigm. *Business Ethics Quarterly, 1*(1), 1–21. https://doi.org/10.2307/3857590

Brown, M. J. F., & Paxton, R. J. (2009). The conservation of bees: A global perspective. *Apidologie, 40*(3), 410–416. https://doi.org/10.1051/apido/2009019

Drenten, J., Gurrieri, L., & Tyler, M. (2020). Sexualized labour in digital culture: Instagram influencers, porn chic and the monetization of attention. *Gender, Work & Organization, 27*(1), 41–66. https://doi.org/10.1111/gwao.12354

Eileraas, K. (1997). Witches, bitches & fluids: Girl bands performing ugliness as resistance. *TDR (1988-), 41*(3), 122. https://doi.org/10.2307/1146612

Ekberg, K., Forchtner, B., Hultman, M., & Jylhä, K. M. (2022). *Climate obstruction: How denial, delay and inaction are heating the planet.* Routledge. https://doi.org/10.4324/9781003181132

Ellis, R. (2022). *Capitalist agriculture and the global bee crisis.* Routledge. https://doi.org/10.4324/9781003142294

Eskelinen, T., Lakkala, K., & Laakso, M. (2020a). Introduction: Utopias and the revival of imagination. In T. Eskelinen (Ed.), *The revival of political imagination: Utopia as methodology* (pp. 3–19). Bloomsbury Academic & Professional.

Eskelinen, T., Lakkala, K., & Pyykkönen, M. (2020b). The privatization and recollectivization of hope. In T. Eskelinen (Ed.), *The revival of political imagination: Utopia as methodology* (pp. 37–53). Bloomsbury Academic & Professional.

Fanghanel, A. (2020). On being ugly in public: The politics of the grotesque in naked protests. *Hypatia, 35*(2), 262–278. https://doi.org/10.1017/hyp.2020.5

Feinberg, J. (2012). Psychological egoism. In R. Shafer-Landau (Ed.), *Ethical theory: An anthology* (pp. 498–507). John Wiley & Sons.

Fraser, N. (2017). Behind Marx's hidden abode: For an expanded conception of capitalism. In P. Deutscher & C. Lafont (Eds.), *Critical theory in critical times: Transforming the global political and economic order* (pp. 141–159). Columbia University Press.

Galtung, J. (1969). Violence, peace, and peace research. *Journal of Peace Research, 6*(3), 167–191. https://doi.org/10.1177/002234336900600301

Galtung, J. (1990). Cultural violence. *Journal of Peace Research, 27*(3), 291–305. https://doi.org/10.1177/0022343390027003005

Gauntlett, D. (2013). *Making is connecting.* John Wiley & Sons.

Gray, M., & Coates, J. (2010). 'Indigenization' and knowledge development: Extending the debate. *International Social Work, 53*(5), 613–627. https://doi.org/10.1177/00208728 10372160

Halberstam, J. (2011). *The queer art of failure.* Duke University Press.

Hobbes, T. (1996). *Hobbes: Leviathan: Revised student edition* (R. Tuck, Ed.). Cambridge University Press. https://doi.org/10.1017/CBO9780511808166

Hornsey, M. J., & Fielding, K. S. (2020). Understanding (and reducing) inaction on climate change. *Social Issues and Policy Review, 14*(1), 3–35. https://doi.org/10.1111/sipr.12058

Hung, K.-L. J., Kingston, J. M., Albrecht, M., Holway, D. A., & Kohn, J. R. (2018). The worldwide importance of honey bees as pollinators in natural habitats. *Proceedings of the Royal Society B: Biological Sciences, 285*(1870), 20172140. https://doi.org/10.1098/rspb.2017.2140

Hyland, T. (2017). McDonaldizing spirituality: Mindfulness, education, and consumerism. *Journal of Transformative Education, 15*(4), 334–356. https://doi.org/10.1177/1541344617696972

Jones, C. I. (2022). The end of economic growth? Unintended consequences of a declining population. *American Economic Review, 112*(11), 3489–3527. https://doi.org/10.1257/aer.20201605

Joseph, A. S. (2021). A modern trail of tears: The missing and murdered Indigenous women (MMIW) crisis in the US. *Journal of Forensic and Legal Medicine, 79*, 102136. https://doi.org/10.1016/j.jflm.2021.102136

Kallis, G., Kostakis, V., Lange, S., Muraca, B., Paulson, S., & Schmelzer, M. (2018). Research on degrowth. *Annual Review of Environment and Resources, 43*, 291–316. https://doi.org/10.1146/annurev-environ-102017-025941

Kangas, A., Krivonos, D., Perheentupa, I., & Särmä, S. (2019). Smashing containers, queering the international through collaging. *International Feminist Journal of Politics, 21*(3), 355–382. https://doi.org/10.1080/14616742.2018.1535249

Kempton, B. (2018). *Wabi sabi: Japanese wisdom for a perfectly imperfect life.* Hachette UK.

Kuokkanen, R. (2008). Globalization as racialized, sexualized violence: The case of Indigenous women. *International Feminist Journal of Politics, 10*(2), 216–233. https://doi.org/10.1080/14616740801957554

Kuokkanen, R. (2011). Indigenous economies, theories of subsistence, and women: Exploring the social economy model for Indigenous governance. *American Indian Quarterly, 35*(2), 215. https://doi.org/10.5250/amerindiquar.35.2.0215

Lewis, D., & Hames, M. (2011). Gender, sexuality and commodity culture. *Agenda, 25*(4), 2–7. https://doi.org/10.1080/10130950.2011.633393

Luxemburg, R. (1951). *The accumulation of capital.* Rosa Luxemburg Internet Archive. https://www.marxists.org/archive/luxemburg/1913/accumulation-capital/

Madras-Majewska, B., & Majewski, J. (2016). Importance of bees in pollination of crops in the European Union countries: Economic science for rural development conference proceedings. *Economic Science for Rural Development Conference Proceedings, 42*, 114–119.

McNally, D. (2017). Ugly beauty. Monstrous dreams of utopia. In S. J. Lauro (Ed.), *Zombie theory: A reader*. U of Minnesota Press.

Melamed, J. (2015). Racial capitalism. *Critical Ethnic Studies, 1*(1), 76–85. https://doi.org/10.5749/jcritethnstud.1.1.0076

Mezzadri, A. (2022). Social reproduction and pandemic neoliberalism: Planetary crises and the reorganisation of life, work and death. *Organization, 29*(3), 379–400. https://doi.org/10.1177/13505084221074042

Mrozowski, S. A. (2019). Violence and dispossession at the intersection of colonialism and capitalist accumulation. *Historical Archaeology, 53*(3–4), 492–515. https://doi.org/10.1007/s41636-019-00205-8

Nixon, R. (2011). *Slow violence and the environmentalism of the poor*. Harvard University Press.

Onbaşı, F. G. (2016). Paid military service at the intersection of militarism, nationalism, capitalism, and (hetero)patriarchy: Escaping without leaving 'manhood'. *Citizenship Studies, 20*(6–7), 883–898. https://doi.org/10.1080/13621025.2016.1191436

Osborne, N. (2018). For still possible cities: A politics of failure for the politically depressed. *Australian Geographer, 50*, 1–10. https://doi.org/10.1080/00049182.2018.1530717

Riley, T., Zia, Y., Samari, G., & Sharif, M. Z. (2022). Abortion criminalization: A public health crisis rooted in white supremacy. *American Journal of Public Health, 112*(11), 1662–1667. https://doi.org/10.2105/AJPH.2022.307014

Rippin, A., & Vachhani, S. (2018). Craft as resistance: A conversation about craftivism, embodied inquiry and craft-based methodologies. In E. Bell, G. Mangia, S. Taylor, & M. L. Toraldo (Eds.), *The organization of craft work* (pp. 217–234). Routledge.

Ristovska, S. (2018). Imaginative thinking and human rights. In S. Ristovska & M. Price (Eds.), *Visual imaginary and human rights practice* (pp. 311–320). Global Transformations in Media and Communication Research - A Palgrave and IAMCR Series. Palgrave Macmillan, Cham. https://doi.org/10.1007/978-3-319-75987-6_18

Ross, L. J. (2023). Birth justice and population control. In *Birthing justice* (2nd ed.). Routledge.

Schult, S. (2006). Dissolved boundaries and "affective labor": On the disappearance of reproductive labor and feminist critique in empire (F. Peters, Trans.). *Capitalism Nature Socialism, 17*(1), 77–82. https://doi.org/10.1080/10455750500505473

Smith, S., & Henriksen, D. (2016). Fail again, fail better: Embracing failure as a paradigm for creative learning in the arts. *Art Education, 69*(2), 6–11. https://doi.org/10.1080/00043125.2016.1141644

Snider, S. (2018). On the limitations of the rhetoric of beauty: Embracing ugliness in contemporary fat visual representations. In S. Rodrigues & E. Przybylo (Eds.), *On the politics of ugliness* (pp. 337–365). Springer International Publishing. https://doi.org/10.1007/978-3-319-76783-3_16

Spencer, H. (1881). *The data of ethics*. Williams and Norgate.

Sudenkaarne, T., & Blell, M. (2022). Reproductive justice for the haunted Nordic welfare state: Race, racism, and queer bioethics in Finland. *Bioethics, 36*(3), 328–335. https://doi.org/10.1111/bioe.12973

Tronto, J. C. (1993). *Moral boundaries: A political argument for an ethic of care.* Psychology Press.

Tsing, A. (2013). Sorting out commodities: How capitalist value is made through gifts. *HAU: Journal of Ethnographic Theory, 3*(1), 21–43. https://doi.org/10.14318/hau3.1.003

Watts, A. (1973). *Zen* (R. Lehtonen, Trans.). Otava. (Original work published 1957)

Weber, M. (1991). *From Max Weber: Essays in sociology.* Taylor & Francis Group.

Weiss, H. (2021). Social reproduction. *The Open Encyclopedia of Anthropology.* https://www.anthroencyclopedia.com/entry/social-reproduction

Wollast, R., Puvia, E., Bernard, P., Tevichapong, P., & Klein, O. (2018). How sexual objectification generates dehumanization in Western and Eastern cultures. *Swiss Journal of Psychology, 77*(2), 69–82. https://doi.org/10.1024/1421-0185/a000209

Wrenn, M. V. (2022). Corporate mindfulness culture and neoliberalism. *Review of Radical Political Economics, 54*(2), 153–170. https://doi.org/10.1177/04866134211063521

Yohe, J. A. (2012). Situated flow: A few thoughts on reweaving meaning in the Navajo spirit pathway. *Museum Anthropology Review, 6*(1), Article 1.

7

Postcapitalist translations

An experiment with scissors, clippings, and glue

Iuliia Gataulina, Anni Kangas, Mikko Poutanen, Anna Ilona Rajala & Tiina Vaittinen

This chapter reports on an experiment using the collage method to analyse post- and pericapitalist academic literature. The experiment was motivated by a methodological approach that understands research as a craft involving the production of various artefacts. Based on cutting, pasting, and overlaying, the collage offers a particularly interesting method for analysing post- and pericapitalist material (see also Särmä, 2014; Choi et al., 2023).

The terms 'postcapitalist' and 'pericapitalist' relate critically to portrayals of capitalism as an all-encompassing monolith. They strive to demonstrate the diversity of the economy by challenging arguments based on categorisations, such as the binary of capitalism and noncapitalism. The term postcapitalist refers to an approach developed particularly by J.K. Gibson-Graham (1996; 2006). The related framework of diverse economies rejects conventional notions of where, how, and by whom the economy is practised. Postcapitalist approaches also criticise capitalocentric perspectives. Capitalocentrism refers to the dominant economic discourse that is unable to discuss the economy with reference to anything but capitalism. Found in the mainstream economic discourse as well as in its critical analyses, it conceals the actual diversity and indeterminacy of economic activity (Gibson-Graham, 2006, p. 56).

The term pericapitalist originates from Anna Tsing's (2015) analyses of how the harvesting of matsutake mushrooms becomes part of the capitalist production of value. Tsing uses the concept of salvage accumulation to describe the ability of capital to amass value produced without its temporal or spatial control. Matsutake

Gataulina, I., Kangas, A., Poutanen, M., Rajala, A. I. & Vaittinen, T. (2025). Postcapitalist translations: An experiment with scissors, clippings, and glue. In A. Kangas, I. Gataulina, M. Poutanen, A. I. Rajala & H-E. Ventovirta (Eds.), *Retheorising capitalism* (pp. 133–160). Tampere University Press.
https://doi.org/10.61201/tup.981

mushrooms are products of nature, and their harvesting has been organised in a way that could be called noncapitalist. However, through the supply chains, the value of the mushrooms is "translated" into capitalist form. In this context, the term pericapitalist stands for activities taking place both inside and outside capitalism. It is not an attempt to outline alternative economic forms but rather a way to shed light on capitalism's dependence on noncapitalist activities (Tsing, 2015, p. 66).

Although Tsing analyses activities in remote areas where matsutake mushrooms can be found, she suggests that "'noncapitalist forms' can be found everywhere in the midst of capitalist worlds" (Tsing, 2015, p. 66). In our experiment, we tested the terms post- and pericapitalist in four different worlds: the Finnish university, the post-Soviet legacy, postsocialist transitions, and dementia care. The purpose was to explore, with the help of dialogue between visual and verbal expression, the forms of life that break through the cracks and splits where capitalist accumulation does not fully succeed or even fails. The experiment was conducted at a retreat for slow research organised on 16–17 March 2022. Our toolbox included scissors, pencils, paper of different colours, felt-tip pens, feathers, glitter, clippings, and academic literature we had brought with us to the retreat. We cut and pasted images and sentences from newspapers, magazines, and academic journals into collages. From time to time, we would return to reading academic articles—or cutting and crossing out parts of them. We underlined and crossed out text to make space for life pushing through: past, current, and future.

We treated our collage work as a translation across different materials and registers. The activity of translation has a special role in pericapitalist as well as in postcapitalist research. Anna Tsing (2015) suggests that translation is a pericapitalist activity. The accumulation of wealth "requires acts of translation across varied social and political spaces" (Tsing, 2015, p. 62). In turn, Tuomo Alhojärvi and Anna Tuomikoski (2022, pp. 246–247) describe the term *postcapitalist* as a "translation problem"—for example, in the Finnish language, the word for postcapitalism can refer to the last stage of capitalism and society after capitalism. Alhojärvi and Tuomikoski suggest that such "a difference in a single word" or the irreversibility of translation is an expression of postcapitalism: it reminds us that in translations between systems, something remains uncontrollable (Alhojärvi & Tuomikoski, 2022, p. 247). Postcapitalist translations could help renounce the simplified differentiations between capitalism and noncapitalism.

The retreat lasted for two days, and in between, dreams and the subconscious influenced the collages (see Figure 7). The shared time-space gave rise to a special kind of inquiry. Exclamations, jokes, and play intertwined with academic work, often considered a serious activity. The shock and melancholy caused by the recently started full-scale war in Ukraine was in the background. Similar affective connections would hardly have emerged had this co-authored chapter been written in separate physical and material time-spaces, with everyone working on separate assignments and commenting on each other's outputs afterwards. In the process, collages evolved into clusters and collections of collages—and this chapter was simultaneously being formed into a collage of its own.

Each member of the group cut out pictures for their collages from magazines that had been collected from the university library's disposals: they had turned into a burden of capitalism that the university library system, struggling with a lack of space, could no longer accommodate. With their help, we dwelled on the troubles of postcapitalism (cf. Haraway, 2016). As Alhojärvi (2021a) suggests, capitalocentrism was initially introduced as a problematic and as a prompt to reinvent how the economy is analysed. However, it is now often treated as "a problem of others, and a problem out there", not as a "thorny issue within our projects" (Alhojärvi, 2021a, p. 62: emphasis added). Keeping this in mind, we also wanted to trouble postcapitalist inquiries by posing questions such as: What are the silences of this research approach and who are the subalterns whose voices must be made heard (cf. Spivak, 1988)? While working on the material, we also considered the internal power relations of the postcapitalist discourse: cutting, pasting, reading, colouring, and conducting serious academic work interspersed with carnivalesque banter.

This textual collage proceeds in the following order. In the first section, Mikko Poutanen uses the collage method to map a postcapitalist university. In the following two sections, Anni Kangas and Iuliia Gataulina focus on the contributions of postcapitalist scholarship in the post-Soviet and postsocialist contexts. The collage of Anna Ilona Rajala, in turn, examines pericapitalism and dementia. Our research report is rounded off by the poem of Tiina Vaittinen, 'mined' from an article by Gayatri C. Spivak (2000), "Translation as culture". In the poem, Spivak's lecture to another audience over twenty years ago is translated into a fractal commentary on both capitalism and the research group's collaging experiment.

Mikko: "Mapping a postcapitalist university"

In my experiment (Figure 1), I used the collage method to map the postcapitalist university. I sought material from inspiring international research, which could illuminate the struggles with intensifying capital(ist) cycles within academia in contexts where this process is further along than it is currently in my own national context—Finland. The universities of Anglophone countries are often presented as desirable benchmarks for other counries (Kivistö et al. 2019, p. 59). It felt like a predictive translation for the future.

As part of my collage work, I found myself reflecting on the language of the postcapitalist university. After all, not only was I primarily relying on examples from Anglophone countries but also on English-language research literature. The hegemony of the English language, fuelled by academic capitalism, had *colonised* my work dealing with the postcapitalist university. I was conscious of becoming trapped in the *anglo*cene (cf. Alhojärvi & Hyvärinen, 2020, pp. 467–470). I chose to consciously lean into this in search of a different perspective in the "predictive translation" of my collage.

I ended up linking my collage work to two books by Richard Hall, a British researcher. The books deal with the strain and alienating impact of academic work (Hall, 2018a) and the need for new initiatives (Hall, 2021). Hall's approach is openly Marxist, which tends to lead to capitalocentric readings of postcapitalism as something that merely follows capitalism. This is different than what research engaged with diverse economies envisions (e.g. Gibson-Graham, 1996, 2006). However, I also wanted to avoid reductive interpretations. Departing from Hall's works, I first sought to define the structural problems of the university. Defining and identifying these problems makes it important and desirable to outline a different, postcapitalist university. Based on Hall's works, I created a textual spiral (Figure 1).

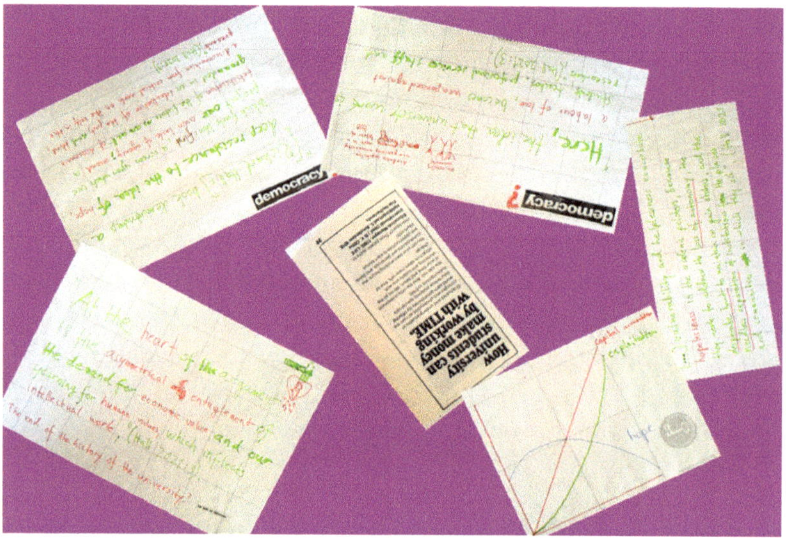

Figure 1. Mapping a postcapitalist university, photo by Mikko Poutanen.

The spiral shape was motivated by Hall's metaphor of an academic exercise bike that members of the University community pedal frantically—only to remain stationary. The spiral shape is built using slips of paper with quotes from Hall's book (Hall, 2021). I chose to make the background violet, which was the colour of my "own" university at the time. Colours also play a role on the slips of paper: I used red, associated with emotions, for texts representing negative structures of hopelessness such as lack of agency, academic work becoming instrumentalised, and critical fractures in the construction of self-image. In turn, green was a colour I found to represent more neutral texts. At the centre of the spiral, I pasted a clipping from an old *Time* magazine, which announced that university students could earn money by working for the magazine—the spiral of writing about universities revolves around making money.

One of the goals of my collage work was to bring out both a paranoid and a reparative reading of the material. Paranoid reading seeks to reveal and criticise a subject matter, but easily gets stuck in its own negativity. It needs to be supported by reparative reading, which allows multiple interpretations, including hopeful ones (Sedgwick,

2003). This approach appears to be typical of the postcapitalist research tradition. Thus, I did not attempt to create an entirely unambiguous collage but wanted to leave the reader room for interpretation and positive motivation. It is true that my collage fuels a certain degree of paranoia, as Hall (2021) effectively describes the current British university as a *hopeless* place that exhausts students and staff. According to him, until the inhumanity of this structure is identified and acknowledged, it will be impossible to move past it (Hall, 2018b). The present-day university inevitably creates dissatisfaction and ill-being (Erickson et al., 2020; see also Kuusela, 2020). The capitalist university turns academic labour of love against the university community as exploitation (Hall, 2021, pp. 25–26). Hall has borrowed the concept of "labour of love" from Silvia Federici (1975), who used it to refer to domestic work ignored in value calculations. The academic identity turns into a unilateral commitment that gives rise to pathological anxiety and despair. Hope for a better future supports conditions that make the hopeful targets of exploitation (Iorio and Tanabe, 2019). In other words, hope turns against itself.

The university has become a hostile place for intellectual work. Making universities part of the generation of capital is essentially linked to the increased ill-being of students and staff, which has been discussed critically and plentifully in the UK over the past several decades (e.g., Fleming, 2021; Reading, 1996), but also increasingly in Finland (Rinne et al., 2014). The university community suffers from the epistemological burden of higher education policy—the continuous methodological control, measurement and assessment, drawing on the managerialism exercised in the spirit of new public management (Fleming, 2021, pp. 40–42; Kuusela et al., 2021; Lorenz, 2012). The Finnish university funding model, which is heavily based on performance and productivity, is one of the most competitive in Europe (Kivistö et al., 2019). When competing, the goal is to secure a position in the hierarchy of academic competition, not to be free from hierarchies (Hall, 2021, p. 134). With the vicious nature of the spiral, I also sought to express that the university community is ensnared in the logic of capitalist realism (Fisher, 2009) just like any other actor in the capitalist society (see also Chapter 8 in this volume).

As part of my collage, I drew a graph in which hopefulness about academic work turns downward as the degree of exploitation increases. I wanted to play with the capitalocentric universal language of numbers, indicators, and graphs (cf. Raworth, 2017, pp. 12–14). In my graph, as capital accumulates, the degree of exploitation at the university increases—and hope for a better future collapses.

To depict labour of love turning against the university community, I drew a detail for my collage, in which—drawing on Hall (2021)—the weaponised labour of love shoots 'love' at members of the university community, who have already surrendered. The bullets are heart-shaped, but destructive (Figure 2). In another detail of my work (Figure 3), the heart of the capitalist university is broken—shattered with a hammer featuring the euro currency symbol, which is more relatable to me than the dollar or the pound. The drawing illustrated my reaction to Hall's hopeless and joyless analysis of a university permeated by capitalism.

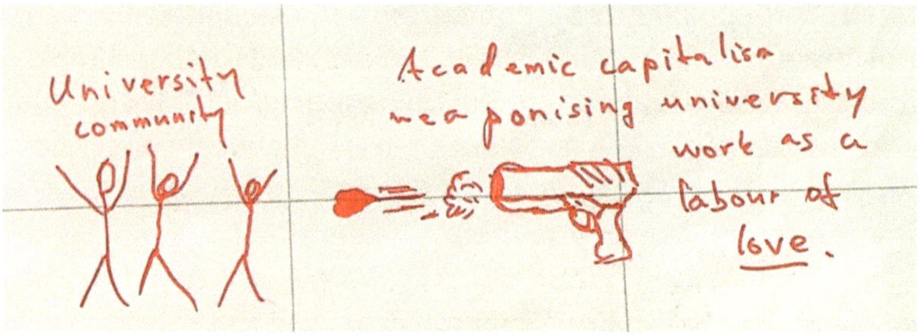

Figure 2. A detail from the collage "Mapping a postcapitalist university", photo by Mikko Poutanen.

Figure 3. A detail from the collage "Mapping a postcapitalist university", photo by Mikko Poutanen.

However, postcapitalist literature points out the importance of reparative reading: we are not meant to get stuck in hopelessness. According to Anna Tsing (2015), the cracks of the capitalocentric world contain space that may easily remain hidden but is not determined by capitalism. While Hall's analysis can justifiably be described as being paranoid, it also contains reparative elements. For example, Hall suggests that we can free ourselves from capitalist realism's impact restricting the imagination by giving up any nostalgic yearning for a romanticised university or a career achieved through self-sacrifice. It is possible to truly imagine and strive for something else.

Hall (2021, pp. 227, 250) emphasises that his book does not offer straightforward answers or a plan for measures with which the university community can free itself from the structures of an oppressive university. Working with detailed plans and schedules is specifically part of the operating model followed by the present-day university overrun by capitalism. When identifying and outlining postcapitalist paths, it is necessary to accept incompleteness and imperfection. It is not a question of translating one static model into another, but of working with an incomplete dialogue between dynamic translation processes. Gibson-Graham (2006) also emphasise that a policy probing new postcapitalist initiatives and opportunities is inevitably incomplete or imperfect. If capitalocentrism can only be challenged with perfect, deployable alternatives, we are stuck.

Fixing the university could mean, for example, granting the university community real ownership of their work, workplace and social relationships (Kociatkiewic et al., 2020, p. 19; see also Poutanen, 2023). The capitalocentrism of the present-day Finnish university can also be challenged through democratic practices although academic democracy has also suffered from neoliberal control and the related managerialism (Poutanen et al., 2022). Joan Tronto has suggested that universities are platforms for strengthening the caring democracy in society (Tronto, 2018). Such tools can be used to build postcapitalist opportunities in Finnish universities, as well.

Easier said than done, however. The spiral in my collage reflects this reality: it is difficult to discern a way up in a spiral winding deeper and deeper. Indeed, we do not only fall into the trap of academic capitalism, but walk into it, even as we are aware of it. This makes it necessary to cast our eyes outside the spiral. Working on this topic in different ways—verbally or visually—involves a continuous dialogue between paranoid and reparative readings.

Anni: "The 'post-Soviet' in the postcapitalist scene"

The collage (Figure 2) examines the term 'post-Soviet' in the postcapitalist scene. It is motivated by the increasingly critical discussion around the term, especially since Russia's invasion of Ukraine. These discussions typically suggest that the term 'post-Soviet' comes with baggage: it reinforces a colonial mindset and obscures the diverse and multifaceted legacies of the Soviet Union (Koplatadze, 2019). With the collage, I wanted to inquire what kind of life the post-Soviet legacy lives in the postcapitalist scene. My presumption was that the prefix 'post-' is used to stand for the legacy of the Soviet project. I wanted to find out how the wildly heterogeneous character of this legacy is treated in the articles that try to fit it into the postcapitalist scene (cf. Alhojärvi, 2021b, p. 173).

The word 'scene' refers to a group of people who are interested in the same topics and exercise influence in matters related to them. The punk scene and start-up scene are examples of this. The postcapitalist scene is similarly formed by academic figures discussing what lies beyond capitalism (see also Alhojärvi, 2017). In it, capitalism is typically treated as a destructive or violent legacy—a failure on a cosmic scale (Alhojärvi, 2021b, p. 167). In terms of destructiveness, the Soviet project does not pale in comparison to capitalism. Its multifaceted legacy contains elements of Soviet-driven ideas of progression, violence against humans and the environment, and Russian colonialism, but also of kleptocracy fed by the neoliberal shock therapy following the collapse of the Soviet Union. This heterogeneous legacy forms various kinds of traces and layers to the 'post-Soviet space' imagined stretching from Estonia to Ukraine and across Azerbaijan to Kyrgyzstan.

Figure 4. Collage "Come to where the flavor is", photo by Anni Kangas.

Collaging is movement between different forms and methods of expression (Kangas et al., 2019). It is translating. The hypothesis of my collaging experiment was that as the post-Soviet is translated into a form suitable to the postcapitalist scene, something worth examining happens. In previous research, Alhojärvi and Hyvärinen (2020, p. 467) have approached translation from one natural language to another as a site of ethico-political challenges and opportunities. They point out that the meaning of the Finnish word for translate (*kääntää*) is partly different from its English equivalent. In addition to signifying the converting of a linguistic expression from one language to another, *kääntää* can also mean reversing, ploughing, bending, changing direction, twisting (the meaning of words), and stealing (Itkonen & Kulonen, 2012, p. 483).

For collage material, I chose academic journal articles where the terms 'post-Soviet' and 'postcapitalist' were used. As belonging to the postcapitalist scene is indicated especially through references to the writings of J.K. Gibson-Graham, I conducted searches in the university library's database using the terms 'post-Soviet' and 'Gibson-Graham'. The search produced 188 results. I excluded the articles that did not seem adequately postcapitalist—they did not seem to be 'in' the scene, as their reference to the postcapitalist literature seemed only superficial. I then printed the articles that had passed the screening. Reflecting the fact that the postcapitalist scene is mainly constructed through written expression, I had at my disposal a stack of white sheets of paper lined with black text.

The etymology of the word 'scene' also refers to a view, a stage (see also Koskinen, 2020). In addition to the journal articles, I used US *Time* magazines from the 1970s that I had found on the university library's shelf for disposed material. *Time* being an extremely visual medium, it also meant that collaging became a translation from the textual to the visual, and back. Through their visual and colourful layout, the issues of *Time* magazine questioned the written, black-and-white, minimalistic aesthetics of academic expression.

For the background of my collage, I used aerial images from magazines. These images symbolise the sense of distance or unfamiliarity with which the articles I analysed approach the post-Soviet legacy. Rather than sensing its multiplicity, the post-Soviet legacy is treated as an object of rationalist remote sensing (cf. Paasi, 2000). In remote sensing, an aeroplane or satellite carries a measuring device that observes a target from afar. Similarly, the articles I examined employ various data collection and research methods, along with gibsongrahamesque language and categorisations, to characterise the post-Soviet legacy in a rationalist manner. This results in the dilution of the inherent messiness of the legacy as the authors, presumably, try to translate it into a form expected in academic publications.

The collage also portrays the practices that Lisa Tilley (2017) refers to as "academic piracy" and "extractivism". To maximise value in the machinery of academic capitalism, multifaceted legacies must be filtered and processed in English, predominantly in the West (cf. Tilley, 2017). To communicate this idea, I framed the collage by curled strips of paper where the viewer can read the names of prestigious academic publishers: *Cambridge University Press, Macmillan, Pennsylvania State University Press, Indiana University Press.* The curled strips call to mind the bending that these legacies, in all their complexities, needs to go through in order to fit into categories such as the 'post-Soviet' or into the semiotic and material order of the Anglocene (Alhojärvi, 2017, p. 41). In a more reparative reading, however, the curls may also be associated with unruliness—with the ever-present possibility of knowing and being otherwise. Paper is a fragile material. When I curled it with scissors, some of the strips tore, which brought to my mind how Sara Ahmed (2017, p. 171) evokes the idea of fragility of things not as a problem but as something to stay with.

There is a closed mouth at the centre of the collage. I cut it out of an old advertisement depicting a stereotypically Asian-looking female member of an aeroplane cabin crew. The figure has cast her eyes down and says that she is ready to serve. As part of the collage, the closed mouth of this orientalised figure expresses the trouble of knowing whose voice is heard when the diverse post-Soviet legacy is adapted to the postcapitalist scene. The closed mouth symbolises the epistemic burden manifested as the loss of voice (cf. Tlostanova, 2015). At the bottom of the collage, a self-assured middle-aged white male figure is casually examining a geometric diagram on the computer screen. He describes it to another figure who is leaning forward to curiously scrutinise the diagram. In contrast to the post-Soviet subject, this man has a voice. This refers to the impulse to strive for certainty in academic research. In his discussion of postcapitalist research practice, Alhojärvi (2021b, p. 173) points out that from a derridaesque perspective, the heterogeneous character of any legacy makes it difficult to manage and calculate. However, the articles I worked with seemed to attempt to render the diverse post-Soviet legacy into something more manageable. To achieve this, they employed various epistemic techniques such as calculations, categorisations, and surveys. These methods were presumably guided by another persistent legacy—that of empiricism and positivism—which suggests that knowledge is effectively constructed by measuring or categorising observational data and identifying generalisable patterns within it (Kurki, 2024, p. 2).

My collage 'concludes' that the multifaceted character of the post-Soviet legacy is easily truncated and diluted by established epistemic, methodological, and publication practices. This issue persists even in the postcapitalist publication scene, despite the literature's strong focus on diversity. However, the collage's cigarette advertisements and their flavoursome promise from 'Marlboro land' ("Come to where the flavour is!") point to a utopian horizon in theorising, to the possibility of knowing otherwise. Its emphasis on flavour foregrounds the role of various senses, suggesting that knowing is not exclusively a matter of thinking (on sensing, see Chapter 5 in this volume). The collage as a whole, then, can be read as an invitation to reimagine ourselves—academic knowers—as playful subjects engaging in experimentations that enhance our capacity to be open to the pluriversal diversity of legacies.

Iuliia: "Enlivening the postsocialist for postcapitalism"

When doing research on postsocialist neoliberalism(s) (Gataulina, 2024), it became evident to me that the Western categories of capitalism, neoliberalism, and liberal democracies have become the starting point for explaining postsocialist realities. What would happen if we examined postsocialism in all its variety, enlivened it, and allowed it to speak for itself? With the help of my collages, I analyse the contribution of postsocialist translations to (post)capitalism.

I started my collage work by thinking about the place of postsocialism in postcapitalist scholarship. Saying that postsocialism is completely absent from theorisations of capitalism and postcapitalism is not accurate. It is present but silent. As phrased by Martin Müller (2020, p. 736; emphasis added), in writings about "the heartlands of democracy and of market capitalism, *the East is the silent bystander*". The diversity of the postsocialist "East" is ignored (see also Cima & Sovova, 2022). Postsocialism may have a place, but it is often discussed in the alien voice of Western categories. Postsocialism is a target of theorisation but not a point of departure (cf. Connell, 2007). In scholarship on capitalism and, consequently, postcapitalism, silence makes postsocialism into the conceptual Other of postcapitalism. Recently, postcapitalist scholarship has made a turn to postsocialism, and these discussions seek to portray postsocialism in its diversity (e.g. Pavlovskaya, 2015; Cima & Sovova, 2022).

The essentialising categories applied to postsocialism are both economic (market capitalism) and political (liberal democracy). As a result of their application, the distinctiveness of more than 70 years of state socialist governance has been erased (Müller, 2020, p. 736). Recognising the uneven histories and geographies of state socialism emphasises the need to make sense of postsocialism in a way that acknowledges its diversity, imperfection, hybridity and lack of teleology (Stenning and Hörschelmann, 2008, p. 330). However, despite being hegemonic, these essentialising categories are not universal. The erosion of distinctiveness produces epistemological blindness to the diversity of postsocialism and its ability to enrich the discussion about capitalism and postcapitalism. Theorisations related to capitalism—including postcapitalism—often operate in a pot of knowledge production linked to academic capitalism, unable to escape or suggest new ingredients, new perspectives.

How, then, has postsocialism been theorised if its distinctiveness has been erased? Postsocialist realities have been marked by a "transition" discourse: a move towards capitalism and liberal democracy. The discourse of transition, however, leads us to believe that there is a "capitalism original" and that the linear translation process from socialism to capitalism has an ideal destination. The transition discourse also implies that the transition as such carries no value. It is simply the path that must be taken to achieve the desired goal of market capitalism. Such a discourse prevents us from seeing postsocialist spaces in all their diversity: as hybrids of socialist legacies, neoliberal capitalism, and informal and patrimonial practices (Müller, 2020, p. 739). A complete transition is only possible for those capable of integration into the global capitalist system: for acultural and ahistorical subjects of oligarchy (on the "emptiness" of globalisation, see Ritzer & Ryan, 2002).

It is not surprising that such a transition remains unfinished. Postsocialism is stuck in an eternal transition towards capitalism and an "elusive modernity" (Müller, 2020, p. 736). Being stuck in a state of transition makes postsocialist spaces fall out of time and space (Müller, 2020, p. 741) or defines them as political or economic failures (Cima & Sovova, 2020, p. 1372). Viewed from this epistemological perspective, postsocialism is in an interstitial position unable to escape its past. It still carries its socialist legacy but is unable to achieve the promised future of market capitalism and liberal democracy. The "post" prefix refers to the past as if the postsocialist East has not yet found its way into the present after nearly 30 years (Müller, 2020, p. 741).

Postsocialist spaces have been dropped out of time and place to become signifiers of emptiness: they are "a 'grey place' that evokes no emotion at all—the terra incognita of the world, where Macedonia, Moldova, Montenegro and Molvanîa[2] blend into an amorphous mass" (Müller, 2020, pp. 737–738). The greyness of postsocialist landscapes is a negation: it is the lack of a feature; it is emptiness, darkness, and the past (Choi, 2016, p. 106). The affective imagery of emptiness and greyness cannot offer any diversity, innovation, usefulness, or hopefulness. A grey place must be either abandoned or changed into something "more flavourful"—in this case, liberal democracy or market capitalism. Halauniova (2022) points out that postsocialist material realities are referred to as "unaesthetic" products of imperfect modernity, void of quality and beauty, in need of upgrading. In her study, Trnka (2012, p. 19) describes the colourless nature of memories related to state socialism: when looking back on the 1989 Velvet Revolution in Czechoslovakia, the participants of Trnka's study used colours to draw temporal and geographic differences. The grey zone of communist Czechoslovakia was compared to the world in colour of, for example, Austria.

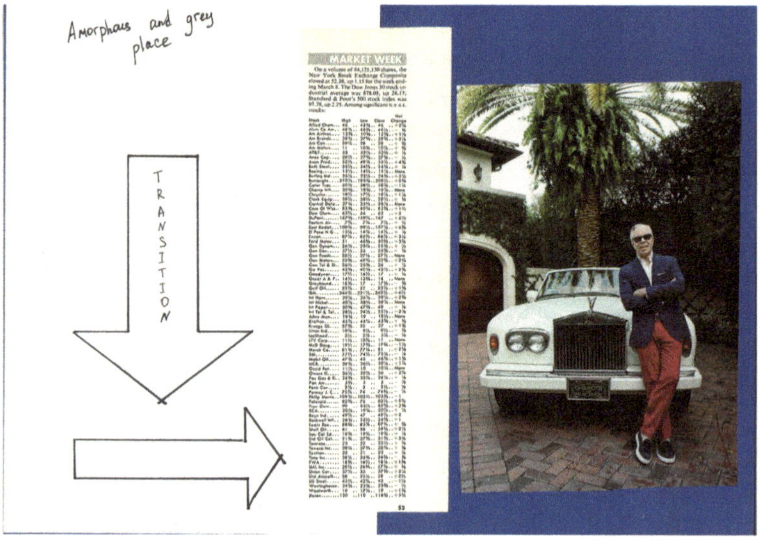

Figure 5. Collage "Amorphous and grey place", photo by Iuliia Gataulina.

The goal of my first collage was to depict postsocialist spaces as grey and empty while playing with the resulting imagery (Figure 5). I placed a white sheet of paper on the left side of my collage and left it empty, as it represents the triviality of postsocialist spaces. Only the two arrows break up the emptiness. They represent the "transition" towards market capitalism. The arrows point towards the desired goal: the affluence of the capitalist market economy, depicted in my collage by a picture of a wealthy, stylishly dressed older white man happily leaning against his luxurious car in the yard of his estate. Capitalism stands for colours, wealth, and joy. These two pictures are separated by a third one: a clipping with share price data from the New York Stock Exchange, which serves as a capitalist translation machine in the collage, translating postsocialism into added value, the universal language of capitalism (Alhojärvi & Tuomikoski, 2022, p. 243).

How about trying to enliven postsocialist spaces and incorporating the diversity of postsocialism into theorisations of capitalism, including postcapitalism? Instead of assuming that capitalism wanders into and settles down in the postsocialist space, this would mean recognising not only the diversity of capitalism but also the hybrid nature of postsocialism. Making the postsocialist diversity a premise of theorisation offers the opportunity to see differences instead of monolithic entities. This also enables us to enrich our understanding of postcapitalism. We need to abandon the epistemology of transition and recognise the richness and uniqueness of (post) socialism (e.g. Stenning & Hörschelmann, 2008).

Instead of examining capitalism as a machine performing an endless transition and translation, postcapitalism invites us to accept the opportunities offered by postsocialist translations in analyses of global capitalism and its frictions (Tsing, 2005). It is interesting to examine how capitalism generates frictions when it is intertwined with the practices, ethics, and ideology of the state socialist era. The research focused on the hybrid nature of postsocialism suggests where these frictions might be. For example, Jennifer Patico (2009) has studied how postsocialist subjects incorporated socialist ethics into capitalist relationships. Elizabeth Dunn (2004) has analysed how postsocialist workers converted individual performance, posited by capitalism, into collective responsibility. Seen from this epistemological perspective, postsocialist translations are endless. However, they do not aim for a specific goal ("capitalism original"), but are instead part of an ongoing translation process, change, and movement.

Figure 6. Collage (untitled), photo by Iuliia Gataulina.

In my second collage (Figure 6) I tried to reverse greyness and emptiness by imagining bright and colourful postsocialist spaces anchored in time and place. I chose a yellow background and, at the centre of it, I glued the front page of Martin Müller's (2020) article, which I used as one of the starting points for my piece. The heading of Müller's article refers to the search of the Global East. By placing this search attempt at the centre of my work, I attempted to visualise the epistemic move of positioning postsocialist hybrid realities in time and place. I also decorated the image with feathers and glitter to symbolise the richness and colourfulness of postsocialist spaces. Collaging, as a method of arranging objects into new relationships and constellations, creates space for the art of noticing (Tsing, 2015) and showcases the richness, hybridity, and diversity of postsocialism.

Anna Ilona: "Dementia as a site of pericapitalist translation"

My collage (Figure 7) came into being through the invariably masculine clippings of 1970s *Time* magazines and a dream I had the night between our two days of collage work. In the dream, my subconscious wanted me to reorganise my output from the first day, and during the second day I did what I saw in the dream, an essential part of which was the abundant use of glitter and the concealing of quotes from Anna Lowenhaupt Tsing's book (2015) behind flaps, just like in Eric Hill's Spot books familiar from my childhood.

Figure 7. Collage "What language do we speak", photo by Anna Ilona Rajala.

Pictures of older people. Pronouns—except it was manifestly impossible to find feminine pronouns in *Time* magazines dating back to the 1970s. A depressed old possum. Big losers. A stranger. "Citizen". The tender embrace of a human animal and chimera. References to the economy: can we afford, or can we afford not to? My day one mosaic of elderly care in which everyone is taken care of, cut and pasted on yellow and pink paper, based on my dream vision. The politics of suspicion and indifference: "Each minute, each day, something happens somewhere". A utopistic or *eutopistic* collage of bell hooks's (2000, p. 88) love ethic, in which our lives and destinies are always connected to other lives, animals and destinies on this planet. *Amor vincit omnia*—love conquers all (Figure 8)?

Figure 8. Detail from the collage "What language do we speak", photo by Anna Ilona Rajala.

What language do we use when we talk about dementia as a pericapitalist site? How could Tsing's (2015) concept of 'pericapitalism' and the related concepts of 'salvage accumulation' and 'translation' be used in research on political economy and dementia (see Rajala, 2022)? What kinds of pericapitalist sites, points of interaction between capitalist and noncapitalist economies, are found in daily care? How can nature, independent of capitalism, such as bodily functions or the need for care and assistance, be translated for the needs of capitalism, which depends on salvage accumulation?

What happens to translation when the context of language use changes and the power carried by words is directed into new areas? *Is it permissible* for anything to happen to the translation? Postcapitalist translation is qualified by the tension between the context-dependent plasticity of language and the history-bound nature of language. On the one hand, language and translation must remain alert and malleable to avoid narrowness: postcapitalist language must be capable of looking beyond this moment in history and the economic system. On the other hand, language and translation are bound to this moment in history because, as the hopelessly material beings we are, the only way we can hurl ourselves into the future is like Walter Benjamin's (1980, pp. 697–698) angel of history: our faces turned toward the past to witness the catastrophe we have caused, which keeps piling wreckage at our feet.

Dementia creates a special need for care and assistance due to deteriorating memory and cognition, linguistic challenges, and a progressive deterioration of mobility, daily functioning (including getting dressed, eating, going to the toilet independently), and the ability to perceive time and space. The part of my collage with a white background reflects the need for care and ways to address it, as well as the intertwining of care with questions concerning the economy. On the flap at the top of my collage (Figure 9), nurses and doctors are working around a patient cut out of the picture to save their life. When you turn the flap, the necessary life-maintaining work gives way to the precariousness of life and the need for care, which all of us will come across at some point in our lives. Nevertheless, care is mainly considered an expense item, and the hurry (that is, reduced resources and performance pressures) is always explained by the legacy of financial crises. This very same legacy can be seen behind the marketisation of care.

Figure 9. A detail from the collage “What language do we speak”, photo by Anna Ilona Rajala.

In the field of care, capitalist value is produced by way of translation from noncapitalist value production systems: care needs and meeting them—an unavoidably corporeal activity—are not produced by capitalism, but the value they generate is continuously salvaged to amass capitalist wealth. This is also the case in dementia care, even though the material reality of the need for care arising from dementia and the actions taken to answer the need are too complex to be labelled under simple service products that lend themselves to pricing (Rajala, 2016). In the words of Silva Tedre (2004, pp. 47–48, composition in verse is mine):

> Care is embodied encounters and more,
> unavoidable embrace of bodies, as in a wrestling hold.
> Care is embodied evasions, choices
> of gaze direction, working hands,
> bodies lifting, settled and situated
> in physical spaces, corporeal beings
> turning, getting up and walking with the assistance
> of another corporeal being, using physical spaces
> and moving from space to space.

Care in Finland is a billion-euro business (e.g., Harala, 2015). Since the late 1980s, boosted by the recession of the 1990s, Finnish social policy has been guided by the ideology, theories, and approaches of neoliberalism (Koskiaho, 2008). As a result, the public sector’s responsibility has been reduced, the number of private for-profit service providers has increased, and services have begun to be produced and provided on a market basis (Viva Collective, 2022). In the past three decades, elderly care has increasingly evolved into marketised care, not as the result of some passive processes but as conscious political choices. Dementia is multifaceted and complex, and it is caused by various pathologies, yet in marketised care, answering the need for dementia care must be simplified into a priceable item. This requires translation, in which care is converted into a commodity, and the person needing care into a manageable unit (Diamond, 1992, p. 209; Rajala, 2016).

Figure 10. A detail from the collage "What language do we speak", photo by Anna Ilona Rajala

In my collage, this simplification process leading to a priceable format is represented by a flap with a picture from which people have been cut out (Figure 10). The caption reveals that they are disabled people waiting in a line like everyone else (waiting for what?). On the flap, the people have been replaced with text that is decorated with glitter, but sounds indifferent: "Each minute, each day, something happens somewhere". However, the flap reveals room for resistance, as the crisis can be made political. As expressed in the quote from Tsing (2015, p. 65), found under the flap, "[p]ericapitalist economic forms can be sites for rethinking the unquestioned authority of capitalism in our lives". Tsing's observation of the capitalist logic of salvage also applies in the context of care: for-profit care is dependent on noncapitalist value production systems, and salvage is an unavoidable and intrinsic part of capitalist operating principles, not an add-on (Tsing, 2015).

Tsing (2015) emphasises that her study cannot be scaled to other contexts without changes being made to the research framework. Nevertheless, I find that Tsing's methodological concepts are useful in the analysis of the political economy of dementia care. However, the non-scalable terminology must be partly retranslated. One option is to take back economic language to open ethical and political possibilities, to explore the possibilities of linguistic interventions that benefit exercising the economy otherwise (Alhojärvi & Hyvärinen, 2020). My linguistic intervention, with which I seek to build a different political economy for dementia, makes capitalism's dependency on noncapitalist value production systems visible.

Salvage accumulation is an example of how a new context requires translation. The concept fits in contexts where something that exists outside and despite the capitalist value production system is salvaged and made a part of the capitalist supply chain. The economy built around matsutake mushrooms—a product of nature that cannot be commercially cultivated—is a good example of this. The context of dementia care obviously differs from mushroom picking, because similar directly salvageable and priceable material does not exist in that context. The bodies of those living with dementia, of course, produce as they consume like anyone else's, but the material is not something that is currently incorporated into global capitalist supply chains (cf. Rajala, 2022). The material that bodies produce is, however, essential for salvage accumulation indirectly: it enables capitalist service economy to be set up around bodily fluids and secretions—from commercial care, global care chains, and reproductive labour to death cleanup. Corporeality always means the existence of needs as well as answering to them, which can be harnessed, for example, to accumulate profit in care services. In this sense, 'salvage' and 'salvage accumulation' must also lend visibility to the pericapitalist sites created by vulnerability and life's precarity in the care context. In these pericapitalist sites of care, the salvaging of noncapitalist value, such as answering the needs of care that exist despite of capitalism, is made possible by translating needs into services.

Words and concepts are not identical with their objects (Adorno, 1970, p. 17). As words and concepts never entirely capture the thing they refer to, providing detailed definitions of things by attaching concepts to them is always a violent act. Like Procrustes, conceptualisation forces an object to fit under an umbrella term regardless of what is lopped off. This is why 'salvage' needs a complementary constellation of words and meanings that characterise the topic examined without creating an identity between it and a concept (Adorno, 1970, p. 164; Benjamin, 1963, p. 16).

As a form of translation, collage work inspires to group meanings into constellations or at least arrange them in a way that differs from the source material's "traditional" academic reading, interpretation, and referencing. When working on my collage, I found my thoughts revolving around Tsing's (2015) terminology in different languages. I conclude with twisting and turning the word 'salvage' back and forth. However, these twists and turns did not end up as such in my collage; their meaning was not revealed to me until I examined my collage at a later point.

The word salvage refers to the act of saving and rescuing the cargo of a drifting or sunken ship. While the corporeality of the needs for care does not involve the salvaging of a concrete load or harnessing it for the needs of capitalism, the word salvage, from the Latin *salvare*, is an apt choice in the context of care. It is apt not only because care keeps those in need of it alive but also because all of our lives are precarious, even those of us living in abundance (Tsing, 2015, p.2). The precarity of life is a consequence of both the financial and the ecological crises, as well as a simple fact of life: without care, there is no life, human or otherwise. To survive among the wreckage that humanity has accumulated at our feet, we need one another. Each of us is dependent on other living beings, and any one of us can suddenly become fully dependent on the help, care, and attention of others. In other words, any one of us can unexpectedly find themselves in need of rescue and thus form a site for pericapitalist translation, where our need for help can be linked to the capitalist value production system, especially in marketised health and social welfare systems.

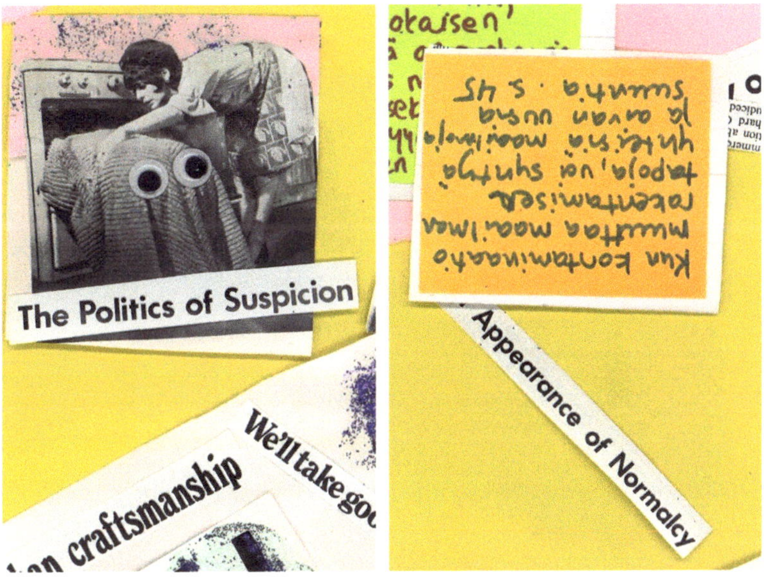

Figure 11. A detail from the collage “What language do we speak”, photo by Anna Ilona Rajala.

Thus, colliding Tsing’s pericapitalist set of concepts with other contexts contaminates it, to use Tsing’s own terminology, imbuing it with new meanings (Rajala, 2022). After being contaminated, nothing is the same (Figure 11). Something necessarily happens to the translation when the language user and the context of language use change, and the power carried by words is directed into new areas. The word ‘contamination’ carries the connotation of something dirty, lethal, abject—from the Latin *contamen*, contact, contagion—but it also carries hopeful tones: *con-* “together”, *tangere* “touch”. In other words, contamination also communicates cooperation, dependence on others, care, being in each other's arms, touching and being touched, joint movement, shared space, physical contacts, evasions, and collisions—and much more. However, this constellation does not translate the word salvage into salvation but leaves it in a flickering space between salvation and precarity. In such an interstitial space, drawing up a postcapitalist future image as a site of salvation is not the solution, as proclaiming salvation when wreckage is still accumulating is premature. This leaves us with iconoclastic utopia, finding postcapitalist cracks in the here and now, opportunity, messianic hope, love, and radical (from the Latin *radix,* roots) conclusions that are still being written. As it states on the very edge of my collage: The conclusion was obvious

(Figure 12). And it is: solutions that are more radical than usual (*ratkaisuja, jotka ovat tavanomaisia keinoja radikaalimpia*, in Finnish).

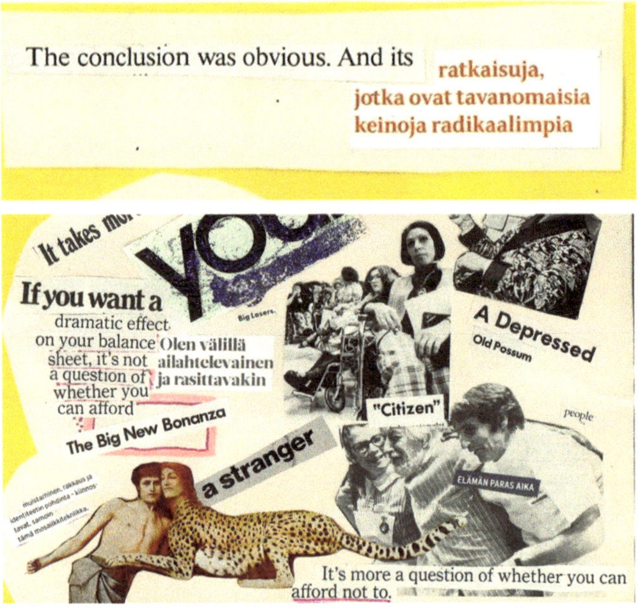

Figure 12. A detail from the collage "What language do we speak", photo by Anna Ilona Rajala

A poem "mined" from Spivak (2000)

Translation is necessary but impossible
grabs on to some one thing and then things
neverending weaving, violence,   this natural machine,
programming the mind

Translation   is a reparation
that constitutes the subject in responsibility
the play   of the ethical as such
a reader   the ethical subject
it is not under the control of the *I* that we think of as the subject
            the body itself is a script – of perhaps one should say a ceaseless inscribing instrument.

The expression 'lost our language' does not mean
that the persons involved do not know their mother tongue.
It means they no longer compute with it,
it is not their software.
English understood as the semiotic as such
idiom that we must honorably establish so that we can 'perform' it as art
            'the global interdependence of human hearts and minds',
   double-talk for the financialisation of the globe,
            alibi for the contemporary new world order,
post-Soviet exploitation.

The international book trade is a trade in keeping with the laws of world trade.
At one end, the coming into being of the subject of reparation.
At the other end, generalised commodity exchange.
We translate somewhere in between.

Translation was the most intimate act of reading
to transfer from one   to the other
relating to the other as the source of one's utterance *is*
the ethical as being-for.
listening
with care and patience, in the normality of the other,   enough to notice
that the other has already silently made that effort.

Translation is   not only necessary but unavoidable.
And yet   it is impossible.
            the contradiction,
            the counter-resistance, that is
            at the heart of love.
            the pleasure of the text.

Tiina: Rounding off with peek-a-boo flaps and wormholes within and beyond post/peri/capitalist imaginations

The words in the poem on the previous page are not mine. I borrowed them from Gayatri Chkraworty Spivak (2000), utilising a method of close reading/writing, where the words of academic articles are used in a new verse text that seeks to interpret—translate—the original text. The method originates from the long tradition of alternative academic writing, where creative writing is used as a method of analysis (e.g. Bochner & Bochner, 1996; Puumala, 2007).

The poem was created while listening to our co-creative discussions on collaging post- and pericapitalism(s). I first highlighted in yellow those parts of Spivak's article that, in my mind, spoke with my co-authors' collages. I then used a black felt-tip to cross out those parts of the article that I had not highlighted, leaving only the ingredients of the poem visible. Finally, I copied the highlighted parts to a Word file, where I reorganised the extracts into an interpretation of the post- and pericapitalist translations produced in our retreat. The first version of the poem was long. After reading the analyses of my co-authors, I distilled the poem by picking out its most essential elements, eventually merging it digitally with my collage, created from the clips from *Time* magazines (Figure 13).

I came to the poetic method at a point when I was stuck with my own erratic collaging with scissors and glue. My collage was about 'translating translations.' Our experimentation's original aim was to write a special issue article on 'capitalist translations' and, instead of peri/post/capitalism(s), my mind was focused on thinking about translations. Also, the political economy of the neoliberal university had concretely intervened in my work: As academic precariat working on temporary contracts in various projects, I had had little (no) time to do my homework of reading prior to the workshop. But I had read Spivak on translation years ago, and it returned to me. And I to it.

Eventually, I turned to exploring our very experiment of collaging as a peri- or postcapitalist activity within the neoliberal university. I flitted through our shared space filled with felt-tip pens, coloured papers, and shredded magazines, examining the emergent connections between our collages, looking over my co-authors' shoulders, and interrupting their work with poor jokes. I sought to read from the evolving collages their novel notions of peri- and postcapitalism, gradually being carved—or glued—into existence, with traces of erasure in their paths of emergence, as the collages made their messages meaningful—to me (cf. Derrida, 1978). I became enchanted by how collages gradually revealed the potentialities of alternative ways of living in the fractured world(s) of post/peri/capitalism(s)—including those that previous post- and pericapitalist discourses might have silenced.

Perhaps you can read these potentialities, too? Although the traces of erasure and emergence were likely different for you than they were for me. That may well be how the hide-and-seek playfulness of the collage works. Now, with the reader of this textual collage having joined along, our experiment continues.

This chapter has been about academic work of humour and love that never fully yields to the productive rules of the neoliberal university. For sure, this chapter is an 'output' subordinate to the project economy. But it is not only that. It is also a product of doing things differently, by shredding articles into strips, curling and glueing them, turning them into poems in between dreams turned into peek-a-boo flaps without a pre-set vision or purpose. Academic texts always include various 'peek-a-boo flaps'. Their wormholes can whisk the reader off to unplanned and surprising places. However, in academic writing, attempts are often made to hide and seal any wormholes and peek-a-boo flaps to make sure the reader stays on the path marked out by the author and follows their argumentation. While there is a place for such academic writing and related methods of thought and analysis, creative methods are also needed at the university—which perhaps is not entirely hopeless.

This chapter is a maze of collages that, we hope, has taken the reader to imagine what capitalism(s), its traces, translations, frictions, and interstices are and could be. Where the linear academic prose invites readers to explore the world from a carefully defined and straightforward perspective, collage-like academic argumentation works differently. In collages, smoothing the reader's path is not an end. Collage is a technique where seemingly unrelated topics or objects are placed in a frame that is equally strange to them all, resulting in an ambiguous composition that defers from unanimous messages (Sylvester, 2007, p. 571; Särmä, 2014). The viewer—or reader—then must actively participate in the practices of assigning meaning, while exposing themselves, their own interpretation to and relatedness with the elements in the collage.

Thus, a collage is an experiment that continues in each reading, articulating meanings that neither the individual elements nor the collagist can articulate on their own. By combining poems, imagery, magazine clippings, Post-it notes, shredded paper, and glitter with academic analysis, this chapter—our experiment that started in spring 2022—emerged as a collage comprising various text types: as a cluster of collages, it makes an assemblage of post/peri/capitalism(s). It forms a non-linear 'architectural space' (van Alphen, 2005), where the reader can wander and get lost—only to find their way out through new peek-a-boo flaps and wormholes within and beyond post/peri/capitalist imaginations.

References

Adorno, T. W. (1970). *Negative Dialektik/Jargon der Eigentlichkeit*. Suhrkamp.

Ahmed, S. (2017). *Living a feminist life*. Duke University Press.

Alhojärvi, T. (2017). Yllättymisiä: antroposkenen paranoia ja tiedon tilanteinen ongelma. *Tiede & Edistys, 42*(1), 36–56. https://doi.org/10.51809/te.105246

Alhojärvi, T. (2021a). For postcapitalist studies: Inheriting futures of space and economy. *Nordia Geographical Publications, 50*(2), 1–230. https://doi.org/10.30671/nordia.103117

Alhojärvi, T. (2021b). Kohti jälkikapitalistista tutkimusta: tilan ja talouden tulevat perinnöt. *Poliittinen talous,* 9(1), 167–176. https://doi.org/10.51810/pt.107659

Alhojärvi, T., & Hyvärinen, P. (2020). Translating diverse economies in the Anglocene. In J. K. Gibson-Graham & K. Dombroski (Eds.), *The handbook of diverse economies* (pp. 467–475). Edward Elgar Publishing.

Alhojärvi, T., & Tuomikoski, A. (2022). Käännös kapitalismin jäljissä. *Tiede & Edistys, 47*(4), 243–250. https://doi.org/10.51809/te.125854

Benjamin, W. (1980). *Gesammelte Schriften. Band I, Teil 2*. Suhrkamp.

Benjamin, W. (1963). *Ursprung des deutschen Trauerspiels*. Suhrkamp.

Bochner, A. P., & Ellis, C. (1996). *Composing ethnography: Alternative forms of qualitative writing*. Altamira Press.

Choi, S. (2016). Grey. In M. B. Salter (Ed.), *Making things international 2: Catalysts and reactions* (pp. 106–121). University of Minnesota Press.

Choi, Shine, Särmä, S., Masters, C., Zalewski, M., Brown, M. L., & Parashar, S. (2023). *Ripping, cutting, stitching: Feminist knowledge destruction and creation in Global Politics*. Rowman & Littlefield Publishers.

Cima, O., & Sovová, L. (2022). The end of postsocialism (as we knew it): Diverse economies and the East. *Progress in Human Geography, 46*(6), 1369–1390. https://doi.org/10.1177/03091325221127295

Connell, R. (2007). *Southern theory: The global dynamics of knowledge in social science*. Polity.

Derrida, J. (1978). *Of grammatology*. Johns Hopkins University Press.

Diamond, T. (1992). *Making gray gold: Narratives of nursing home care*. University of Chicago Press.

Dunn, E. C. (2004). *Privatizing Poland: Baby food, big business, and the remaking of labor*. Cornell University Press.

Erickson, M., Hanna, P., & Walker, C. (2020). The UK higher education senior management survey: A statactivist response to managerialist governance. *Studies in Higher Education, 46*(11), 2134–2151. https://doi.org/10.1080/03075079.2020.1712693

Federici, S. (1975). *Wages against housework*. Falling Wall Press.

Fisher, M. (2009). *Capitalist realism: Is there no alternative?* Zero Books.

Fleming, P. (2021). *Dark academia – How universities die*. Pluto Press.

Gibson-Graham, J. K. (1996). *The end of capitalism (as we knew it): A feminist critique of political economy*. Blackwell.

Gibson-Graham, J. K (2006). *A postcapitalist politics*. University of Minnesota Press.

Halauniova, A. (2022). Good and bad concrete: Fugitive modern and the aesthetics of renovation in Poland. *City: Analysis of Urban Change, Theory, Action, 26*(1), 28–50. https://doi.org/10.1080/13604813.2021.2019490

Hall, R. (2018a). On the alienation of academic labour and the possibilities for mass intellectuality. *tripleC, 16*(1), 97–113. https://doi.org/10.31269/triplec.v16i1.899

Hall, R. (2018b). *The alienated academic – The struggle for autonomy inside the university.* Palgrave Macmillan.

Hall, R. (2021). *The hopeless university: Intellectual work at the end of the end of history.* Mayfly Books.

Harala, S. (2015, August 21). Talouselämä: Yksityisistä hoivayrityksistä on tullut jo miljardibisnes. *YLE News.* https://yle.fi/uutiset/3-8244734

Haraway, D. (2016). *Staying with the trouble: Making kin in the Chthulucene.* Duke University Press.

hooks, b. (2000). *All about love: New visions.* William Morrow.

Iorio, J. M., & Tanabe, C. S. (2019). *Higher education and the practice of hope.* Springer. https://doi.org/10.1007/978-981-13-8645-9

Itkonen, E., & Kulonen, U. M. (2012). Kääntää. In E. Itkonen & U. M. Kulonen (Eds.), *Suomen sanojen alkuperä: Etymologinen sanakirja.* Finnish Literature Society.

Kangas, A., Krivonos, D., Perheentupa, I., & Särmä, S. (2019). Smashing containers, queering the international through collaging. *International Feminist Journal of Politics, 21*(3), 355–382. https://doi.org/10.1080/14616742.2018.1535249

Kivistö, J., Pekkola, E., Nordstrand Berg, L., Foss Hansen, H., Geschwind, L., & Lyytinen, A. (2019). Performance in higher education institutions and its variations in Nordic policy. In R. Pinheiro, L. Geschwind, H. Foss Hansen, & K. Pulkkinen (Eds.), *Reforms, organizational change and performance in higher education: A comparative account from the Nordic countries* (pp. 37–69). Palgrave Macmillan. https://doi.org/10.1007/978-3-030-11738-2_2

Kociatkiewicz, J., Kostera, M., & Parker, M. (2021). The possibility of disalienated work: Being at home in alternative organizations. *Human Relations, 74*(7), 933–957. https://doi.org/10.1177/0018726720916762

Koplatadze, T. (2019). Theorising Russian postcolonial studies. *Postcolonial Studies, 22*(4), 469–489. https://doi.org/10.1080/13688790.2019.1690762

Koskiaho, B. (2008). *Hyvinvointipalvelujen tavaratalossa.* Vastapaino.

Koskinen, K. (2020). Antroposkenen ekosysteemi: Pohjoinen metsä villin luonnon näyttämönä. *Lähikuva: Audiovisuaalisen Kulttuurin Tieteellinen Julkaisu, 33*(2), 25–41. https://doi.org/10.23994/lk.97383

Kurki, M. (2024). The limits of pluralism: Pluralism in pluriversal Anthropocene. In J. M. Box-Steffensmeier, D. P. Christenson, & V. Sinclair-Chapman (Eds.), *Oxford handbook of engaged methodological pluralism in political science* (online ed.). Oxford Academic.

Kuusela, H. (2020). Kuuleeko strateginen johto? Katsaus yliopistojen työhyvinvointikyselyjen tuloksiin. *Tiedepolitiikka, 45*(2), 30–35.

Kuusela, H., Kaleva, V., Tomperi, T., Poutanen, M., & Tervasmäki, T. (2021). Korkeakoulupolitiikan muuttuvat valtasuhteet Suomessa: Säätiöyliopiston synty ja kamppailu yliopistodemokratiasta. *Politiikka, 63*(2), 158–187. https://doi.org/10.37452/politiikka.101246

Lorenz, C. (2012). If you're so smart, why are you under surveillance? Universities, neoliberalism, and new public management. *Critical Inquiry, 38*(3), 599–629. https://doi.org/10.1086/664553

Müller, M. (2020). In search of the global east: Thinking between north and south. *Geopolitics, 25*(3), 734–755. https://doi.org/10.1080/14650045.2018.1477757

Paasi, A. (2020). Book review: Rethinking geopolitics. *Environment and Planning D: Society and Space, 18*(2), 282–284.

Patico, J. (2009). Spinning the market: The moral alchemy of everyday talk in postsocialist Russia. *Critique of Anthropology, 29*(2), 205–224. https://doi.org/10.1177/0308275X09104006

Pavlovskaya, M. (2013). Between neoliberalism and difference: Multiple practices of property in Post-Soviet Russia. *Europe-Asia Studies, 65*(7), 1295–1323. https://doi.org/10.1080/09668136.2013.822708

Poutanen, M. (2023). Breaking bonds: How academic capitalism feeds processes of academic alienation. In R. Hall, I. Accioly, & K. Szadkowski (Eds.), *Palgrave international handbook of Marxism and education* (pp. 71–92). Palgrave Macmillan.

Poutanen, M., Tomperi, T., Kuusela, H., Kaleva, V., & Tervasmäki, T. (2022). From democracy to managerialism: Foundation universities as the embodiment of Finnish university policies. *Journal of Education Policy, 37*(3), 419–442. https://doi.org/10.1080/02680939.2020.1846080

Puumala, E. (2017). *Asylum seekers, sovereignty, and the senses of the international: A politico-corporeal struggle*. Routledge.

Rajala, A. I. (2016). Pitkäaikaishoivan ruumiillisuuden arvosta. In J. Parviainen, T. Kinnunen, & I. Kortelainen (Eds.), *Ruumiillisuus ja työelämä: Työruumis jälkiteollisessa taloudessa* (pp. 132–145). Vastapaino.

Rajala, A. I. (2022). Olipa kerran sieni kapitalismin raunioissa. *Poliittinen Talous, 10*. https://doi.org/10.51810/pt.112312

Raworth, K. (2017). *Doughnut economics: Seven ways to think like a 21st-century economist*. Chelsea Green Publishing.

Readings, B. (1996). *The university in ruins*. Harvard University Press.

Ritzer, G., & Ryan, M. (2002). The globalization of nothing. *Social Thought and Research, 25*(1/2), 51–81. https://doi.org/10.17161/STR.1808.5196

Rinne, R., Jauhiainen, A., & Kankaanpää, J. (2014). Surviving in the ruins of the university? Lost autonomy and collapsed dreams in the Finnish transition of university policies. *Nordic Studies in Education, 34*(3), 213–232.

Spivak, G. C. (1988). Can the subaltern speak? In C. Nelson & L. Grossberg (Eds.), *Marxism and the interpretation of culture* (pp. 271–313). University of Illinois Press.

Spivak, G. C. (2000). Translation as culture. *Parallax, 6*(1), 13–24. https://doi.org/10.1080/135346400249252

Stenning, A., & Hörschelmann, K. (2008). History, geography and difference in the post-socialist worlds: Or, do we still need post-socialism? *Antipode, 40*(2), 312–335. https://doi.org/10.1111/j.1467-8330.2008.00593.x

Sylvester, C. (2007). Whither the international at the end of IR? *Millennium: Journal of International Studies, 35*(3), 551–573.

Särmä, S. (2014). *Junk Feminism and Nuclear Wannabes: Collaging Parodies of Iran and North Korea* [Doctoral dissertation]. University of Tampere. https://urn.fi/URN:ISBN: 978-951-44-9535-9

Tedre, S. (2004). Tukisukkahousut sosiaalipolitiikkaan. Inhomaterialistinen hoivatutkimusote. In E. Jokinen, M. Kaskisaari, & M. Husso (Eds.), *Ruumis töihin! Käsite ja käytäntö* (pp. 41-64). Vastapaino.

Tilley, L. (2017). Resisting piratic method by doing research otherwise. *Sociology, 51*(1), 27–42. https://doi.org/10.1177/0038038516656992

Tlostanova, M. (2015). Can the post-Soviet think? On coloniality of knowledge, external imperial and double colonial difference. *Intersections. East European Journal of Society and Politics, 1*(2), 38-58. https://doi.org/10.17356/ieejsp.v1i2.38

Trnka, S. (2012). When the world went color: Emotions, senses and spaces in contemporary accounts of the Czechoslovak Velvet Revolution. *Emotion, Space and Society, 5*(1), 45-51. https://doi.org/10.1016/j.emospa.2011.05.001

Tronto, J. C. (2018). Higher education for citizens of caring democracies. *South African Journal of Higher Education, 32*(6), 6–18. http://dx.doi.org/10.20853/32-6-2710

Tsing, A. L. (2005). *Friction: An ethnography of global connection*. Princeton University Press.

Tsing, A. L. (2015). *The mushroom at the end of the world: On the possibility of life in capitalist ruins*. Princeton University Press.

van Alphen, E. (2005). *Art in mind: How contemporary images shape thought*. University of Chicago Press.

Viva Collective, Zechner, M., Näre, L., Olli Karsio, Antero Olakivi, Liina Sointu, Hanna-Kaisa Hoppania, & Tiina Vaittinen. (2022). *The politics of ailment*. Policy Press.

Part III
Repairing

Henna-Elise Ventovirta

Retheorising capitalism may also take the form of repairing, as understood by Eve Kosofsky Sedgwick (2003). Sedgwick distinguishes reparative readings from paranoid readings, which tend to engage with the subject matter by exposing its shortcomings. Paranoid readings scrutinise the harmful or problematic aspects of capitalist arrangements, running the danger of reproducing them as "inevitable" (Sedgwick, 2003, p. 147), while reparative readings are grounded in the ability to be surprised: they centre around the question *"what else is there already"*. The aspect of surprise is also where reparative readings conceptualise hope, grounding it on the notion that "the future may be different from the present" (Sedgwick, 2003, p. 146). The multiple crises of our time have given impetus to efforts to rethink and even repair capitalism. However, in many cases, it may be more appropriate to speak about repairing political economies rather than capitalism. This means paying attention to the "life-enhancing" and generative aspects and practices of various political economies already present today (Penttinen, 2013). This part of the book comprises four chapters, each engaging in the reparative task in a distinct manner.

The chapter "Porous boundaries of resistance" (Chapter 8) by Iuliia Gataulina retheorises capitalism through diverse forms of resistance against it. It focuses on how the authoritarian-neoliberal regime is challenged in the university context as well as on efforts to rethink and repair the university. Based on ethnographic research at Russian universities, Gataulina details how the power of both transnational neoliberalism and the authoritarian state is not just resisted, but also how "more hopeful recompositions" emerge. The verticality of power is replaced by collegiality, fear by joy, and state borders are challenged through deterritorialised academic activities. However, Gataulina also points out that there is no "utopian outside" to escape to. This means that we need to accept a certain messiness and patchiness in attempts to repair what has been ruined by the forces of capitalism and authoritarianism.

A (post)capitalist university is also reimagined in the chapter "Resisting academic capitalism with a postcapitalist pedagogy" (Chapter 9) by Iris Pajunen. Drawing on feminist scholarship, among others, Pajunen drafts a suggestion for a postcapitalist university pedagogy whilst critically reflecting on its limits within the confines of neoliberal academia. For those of us working in contexts dominated by academic capitalism, the chapter is a reminder of the importance of seeing what else is already there. The chapter first revisits previous scholarship on academic capitalism and its repercussions both in the context of Finland and globally. Based on autoethnography as a university student and, more specifically, as a participant in a participatory workshop tasked with retheorising capitalism, Pajunen puts forth a suggestion for a postcapitalist pedagogy that centres on "methodological and epistemological diversity, communality and collegiality, as well as inclusion and antihierarchy" rather than competition, fear, and hierarchy.

The chapter by Sabaheta Ramcilovic-Suominen (Chapter 10) is entitled "Capitalism as colonialism as capitalism (and the alternatives)." It reflects on the shared temporal and historical pathways of capitalism and colonialism. Ramcilovic-Suominen argues that colonialism permeates every aspect of capitalist societies in both the Global North and the Global South. This also means that colonialism—and the violent and extractive structures it produces—is not a thing of the past. However, the chapter is also reparative: it explores collective responses and pathways towards futures that could be post- and anti-colonialist-capitalist and concludes on a hopeful note: "the solutions are indeed already here, and not only some but all are needed."

This part of the book concludes with a chapter entitled "A theory of fragmentism" (Chapter 11), which examines capitalism as something repairable. In this chapter, Akseli Kettula argues that capitalism must take a new path because the age-old debate between market failure and government failure has proved useless. Kettula presents a theory of fragmentism that focuses on the root causes of these failures rather than the debate about the failures themselves. In this sense, the theory of fragmentism seeks to "escape the debate between market failure and government failure", as Kettula suggest. At the core of the theory is the diversification of markets, aiming at a better-functioning market economy while mitigating systemic risks. Kettula's chapter attempts to offer a corrective to the prevailing flaws of the current economy by theoretically restructuring capitalism.

References

Penttinen, E. (2013). *Joy and international relations: A new methodology*. Routledge.

Sedgwick, E. K. (2003). *Touching feeling: Affect, pedagogy, performativity*. Duke University Press.

VERTAISARVIOITU
KOLLEGIALT GRANSKAD
PEER-REVIEWED
www.tsv.fi/tunnus

8

Porous boundaries of resistance

Translating an authoritarian-neoliberal university

Iuliia Gataulina

The task we set ourselves is to build the university afresh in a way that will free teachers from the directives of administrators.
If the university cannot be free anymore, we need a new free university.
This is where the paths of the university and the state part.

Manifesto of the Free University

As the intrusive powers of capitalism penetrate different areas of life, causing dispossession and exploitation, numerous attempts have been made to rethink economic-social relations anew. However, since capitalism is itself a multitude, as the introduction to this edited volume demonstrates, opposition to its workings can be imagined and acted upon in diverse ways. While it is important to capture the workings of capitalism, I believe it is equally important to analyse—and possibly learn from—different projects that actively resist the ruination of socio-economic realities created by capitalism in its various constellations.

In this chapter, I specifically focus on diverse forms of resistance to neoliberal capitalism, particularly when it couples with the oppressive powers of a state (Fabry and Sandbeck, 2019; Fabry, 2019; Dönmez and Duman, 2021) and propagates anti-democratic and authoritarian politics (Bruff, 2014; Bruff and Tansel, 2019). As the epigraph to this chapter demonstrates, I analyse different forms of resistance to the neoliberalisation of universities—one of the sites where the logics and practices of neoliberal capitalism have intruded. In this chapter, I approach neoliberalism as an economic and political formation that generates extraction, profit-making,

Gataulina, I. (2025). Porous boundaries of resistance: Translating an authoritarian-neoliberal university. In A. Kangas, I. Gataulina, M. Poutanen, A. I. Rajala & H-E. Ventovirta (Eds.), *Retheorising capitalism* (pp. 163–182). Tampere University Press. https://doi.org/10.61201/tup.981

managerial control, efficiency, and surveillance over performance (Harvey, 2005; Giroux, 2014). It reinforces itself through administrative and legal mechanisms, limiting spaces of resistance (Bruff and Tansel, 2019). Thus, despite the widespread idea that neoliberalism can build a world of peace and freedom, this notion has faced solid scholarly critique (Harvey, 2005, Chapter 1). Neoliberalism itself can engender authoritarian governance, which reproduces inequalities of power in capitalist societies and breeds a hierarchical and covert political culture (Bruff and Tansel, 2019; Dean, 2002).

Moreover, previous research has shown that the workings of neoliberal capitalism extend beyond liberal democracies, manifesting its consequences in other political regimes, such as authoritarian states. The authoritarian power of the state can synchronize with the neoliberal regime of New Public Management to build hierarchies of power and control. This is visible, for example, in the centralisation of political power in Russia through authoritarian-neoliberal governance, often referred to as the "vertical of power" (Gel'man and Ryzhenkov, 2011), which can also be realised in the context of universities (Gataulina, 2025 Forthcoming; Gerashchenko, 2022).

Analysing resistance to the authoritarian-neoliberal regimes of governance, control, and dispossession is important to understand how the intrusive powers of both transnational neoliberalisation and the state are resisted and can possibly be translated into more hopeful recompositions. Therefore, in this chapter, I seek to retheorise capitalism through diverse forms of resistance against it. My understanding of capitalism and resistance to it is inspired by the assemblage approach, which emphasizes their constant movement, reordering, and connections (Higgins and Larner, 2017; Deleuze, 2004; Acuto and Curtis, 2014). My inquiry is motivated by the following questions: How are resistances to the authoritarian-neoliberal regimes of governance imagined and acted upon? What are the capabilities and limitations of those projects of resistance? What are the ontological relations between the intrusive powers of capital and the state and diverse forms of resistance to them? What can we learn from these projects of resistance to better understand how more hopeful worlds can be actualised?

Pondering these questions, I investigate Russian universities where the oppressive powers of neoliberalisation and the authoritarian state entangle (Gataulina, 2025 Forthcoming; Minina, 2017; Mäkinen, 2021; Dubrovsky and Kaczmarska, 2021; Forrat, 2016). I also pay attention to how different projects of resistance to the authoritarian-neoliberal regime arise. The analysis in this chapter is based on ethnographic data generated for my PhD project in 2019–2021, which included university visits, observations of academic events, interviews, media publications, and my own autoethnographic experience of studying in Russian universities and participating in alternative academic projects analysed in this chapter. Russian universities and alternative academic projects by Russian academics beyond institutionalised universities became fruitful sites to interrogate diverse forms of resistance to authoritarian-neoliberal governance, as well as the possible tensions, contradictions, and limitations of their work. While focusing solely on Russian universities, my intent is to go beyond the specificities of the Russian situation and make wider claims about authoritarian-neoliberal control and its possible subversion.

My interest in critically investigating resistance to authoritarian-neoliberal regimes does not stem from a desire to devalue their efforts; I respect and am often inspired by their work. Rather, my aim is to contribute to a shared understanding of how oppressive powers can be contested, subverted, and resisted - and what our limitations in doing so might be. Here, I see research as secondary to direct political action. As Hardt and Negri (2000, p. 206) claim, theory is only capable of providing analysis; resistance and liberation are essentially born through practice.

The authoritarian-neoliberal university

The intrusive powers of capitalism penetrate university spaces, and this intrusion is often described with the concept of neoliberalisation (Giroux, 2014; Connell, 2019; Olssen and Peters, 2005; Hall, 2018a; Cannella and Koro-Ljungberg, 2017). In this literature, neoliberalisation is closely connected to the rise of "knowledge economies" or "knowledge capitalism," which are defined as the latest, post-Fordist phase of capitalism associated with the technological revolution in the 1990s (Peters, 2021). Neoliberalisation of academia refers to the subjection of higher education and research to the logic of markets by replacing the "traditional professional culture of open intellectual inquiry" with institutional stress on performance, audit, competitiveness, and the economic efficiency of university activities (Olssen and Peters, 2005, p. 313). Research on the neoliberalisation of universities often emphasizes its negative impacts on higher education and research, such as the dissipation of academic freedom (Dönmez and Duman, 2021, p. 4; Peters, 2021), precarisation of academic work (Borovskaia et al., 2014; Loveday, 2018), and erosion of critical thinking due to the subjugation of the curriculum to perceived market needs (Ashwin, 2020). Moreover, the neoliberalisation of universities leads to the rise of hierarchical, covert, or even authoritarian governance (Belina et al., 2013; McCann et al., 2020).

However, analyses of how universities operate beyond the contexts of liberal democracies and the Global North emphasize that universities are equally becoming subjected to the oppressive powers of the state, including authoritarian state governance. The intrusive powers of the state often entangle with neoliberal reforms, creating a new composition of oppressive forces (Coşar and Ergül, 2015 on Turkey; Dönmez and Duman, 2021 on Turkey and Hungary; see also Bruff, 2014). Similar developments are visible in Russian universities, where the authoritarian-neoliberal control of the state regime engenders control and dispossession (Gataulina, 2025 Forthcoming; Minina, 2017; Mäkinen, 2021; Dubrovsky and Kaczmarska, 2021; Forrat, 2016). Russian development cannot be characterised simply as privatisation and deregulation. Neoliberal ideas such as competition, cost-efficiency, managerial control, and economic growth thrive when attached to the authoritarian governance of the Russian state (Gataulina, 2025 Forthcoming; Smolentseva et al., 2018).

The effects of neoliberal-authoritarian governance of Russian universities have often been referred to by the academic community as processes of ruination: the "destruction" of higher education (Sidorov, 2021) or a "guillotine" for academics (Konkurs..., 2020). The salvage accumulation on which capitalism breeds produces ruination (Tsing, 2015, p. 5; Pyyhtinen et al., 2022, p. 3). Authoritarian-neoliberal governance similarly intrudes into academic worlds and translates them into a power- and profit-making assemblage. While universities are not abandoned, academic worlds are ruined through this intrusion. In this chapter, my aim is to analyse the resistance to hierarchical, covert, and extractive practices that neoliberal capitalism cultivates through its attachment to the authoritarian state. I demonstrate how, in the Russian context, resistance is formed against the neoliberal-authoritarian university and, subsequently, the Russian state, which complicates the scenario of solely resisting marketisation or privatisation.

Resistance

The intrusive powers of capital and the state penetrating universities prompt different forms of resistance and attempts to transform an authoritarian-neoliberal university into something more liveable (Wullf-Wathne, 2020; Peters, 2021). During my fieldwork in 2021, I participated in a panel discussion where two Russian professors pointed out that alternative, horizontal projects are a way to disseminate knowledge in society, as the university, functioning as an authoritarian-neoliberal bureaucratic "machine," fails to do so:

> There is a demand for the dissemination of knowledge in society, but the university as a structure is not moving forward with this demand. Firstly, the university is a huge bureaucratic and supervisory machine; thus, to get some new courses or any new undertakings started, a lot of approvals are needed. Second, university is there to a great extent to "feed" the university management, fulfil the requirements and chase the rankings. If we want to spread knowledge, we need to work on horizontal projects.

The quotation suggests that struggles against neoliberalisation should be analysed in a complex manner: while resistance against neoliberalisation often equals resistance against marketisation, this might not be the case in every time and place (Bruff and Tansel, 2019, p. 241). Neoliberalisation takes different forms. Those interested in mutations of capitalism should also pay attention to localised projects of resistance and the imagining of alternative futures. Moreover, resistance to neoliberalisation in academia rarely takes place solely around university operations but instead stands against the wider political context (Dönmez and Duman, 2021, p. 10).

My analysis draws on the assemblage-inspired view of theorising and conceptualising resistance. Assemblage-inspired analysis suggests that any politico-economic formation, including capitalism, authoritarianism, or their hybrids, is characterised by constant movement, change, and (de)stabilisation. These assemblages are composed of human and more-than-human elements, such as human subjectivities, institutionalised regulations, and material objects (Higgins and Larner, 2017; Deleuze, 2004; Acuto and Curtis, 2014). This suggests that changes and ruptures of these oppressive systems are not always controllable by human intentions. Nevertheless, in this chapter, I specifically analyse those projects that intentionally attempt to subvert and decompose authoritarian-neoliberal powers. To analyse their workings and limitations, I invoke Anna Tsing's concept of translations.

Translations

Translation is the process of "drawing one world-making project into another" (Tsing, 2015, p. 62). Anna Tsing uses the concept of translation primarily to analyse the liability of contemporary capitalism. She argues that contemporary capitalism is based on acts of translation, where non-capitalist value systems are drawn into capitalist accumulation (Tsing, 2015, p. 43). Capitalism, in all its variety, stabilizes itself by being "a translation machine for producing capital from all kinds of livelihoods, human and non-human" (Tsing, 2015, p. 133). The spaces where such acts of translation happen are pericapitalist sites: they are simultaneously inside and outside capitalism (Tsing, 2015, p. 63). While Tsing focuses mostly on how non-capitalist sites are translated into profit-making in these pericapitalist sites, she leaves room for other kinds of translations: "[p]ericapitalist economic forms can be sites for rethinking the unquestioned authority of capitalism in our lives" (Tsing, 2015, p. 65).

While Tsing specifically looks into translations for the capitalist accumulation, I develop this concept further by theorising different forms of resistance which attempt to translate, subvert, and transform the authoritarian-neoliberal assemblage of extraction and dispossession. The projects that I analyse in this chapter initially sprang out of institutionalised universities and work to translate academic production into a form based on collegiality and openness. This is where the idea of a pericapitalist site becomes enriched by layers of oppressive state power and resistance to it: I trace how resistance to neoliberalisation of universities become merged with resistance to the authoritarian state. These sites of translation attempt to subvert hierarchical and surveillant political culture which both neoliberalisation and authoritarianism bolster through their contamination.

Sites of translation: FEM TALKS, Free University, DOXA

In the following, I analyse three academic projects where the translation of authoritarian-neoliberal governance has taken place: FEM TALKS, Free University, and DOXA. These are sites of knowledge production that escape institutionalised university boundaries and show resistance to authoritarian-neoliberal control and dispossession. They can be thought of as attempts to translate the processes of ruination into liveable projects and to reclaim academia that has previously been alienated by the authoritarian-neoliberal accumulation of power and resources.

FEM TALKS is an educational project organised by three early-career researchers in 2018. FEM TALKS consists of various activities: mini-conferences, a course on feminist theory, translation and writing of feminist texts, and a podcast. The goal of the project is "to enable people to talk and learn about [feminism] in the language of current research": "[f]rom an initiative to popularise feminist philosophy within academia, FEM TALKS has grown into a broad educational project" (FEM TALKS, n.d.). The organisers of the FEM TALKS project openly stated that it was very unlikely they would be able to institutionalise their activity within a contemporary Russian university contaminated by authoritarian-neoliberal governance: "We would not be given a position at the university, even if we all received a degree, and hardly any of us needs it anyway" (Danilov, 2020).

Another translation site, the Free University, was established in 2020 by a group of Russian academics whose work contracts were not renewed by the Higher School of Economics in Moscow. The university administration laid off opposition-minded academics, citing the need to secure the university's business reputation (Golubeva, 2020). The format of free universities has been known since the 1960s and is "built on a rich tradition of feminist, anti-racist, and working-class struggles to create spaces of autonomous learning and empowerment" beyond the institutional confines of the public and private university (Erdem, 2020, pp. 316–317). Free Universities are usually organised against the commodification of higher education and become grassroots initiatives aimed at the development of "postcapitalist imaginaries in academia" (Erdem, 2020, p. 317). However, the extractive and ruinative workings of capitalism beyond the contexts of the Global North imply resistance to both capitalism and other forms of oppressive power, such as the authoritarian state, as demonstrated by the case of the Free University organised by Russian academics.

The third site of translation, DOXA, was initially started as a student media publication at the Higher School of Economics in Moscow but rapidly became one of the strongest voices of political opposition in Russia. DOXA covered university news, published academic texts, and organised support for students who had been persecuted and detained due to their political activities (DOXA, n.d.). Because of these activities, DOXA's official status as a student organisation was revoked. As explained by the university administration, DOXA's activities were "harming the business reputation of the university" (VshE lishila zhurnal..., 2019).

All three projects are sites of authoritarian-neoliberal translations: they have been in contradiction with, and ruined by, authoritarian-neoliberal governance and, through their activities and ethos, have attempted to translate the extraction, control, and hierarchies of authoritarian-neoliberal governance into something different. The ensuing analysis is organised around the following themes: spatialities of resistance and the imagination of freedom outside of authoritarian-neoliberal dictate; collegiality, horizontality, and joy in academic projects; reclaiming the university; and, finally, the limitations and paradoxes of such acts of translation.

Aiming outside: Spatialities of resistance

Being in contradiction with the authoritarian-neoliberal nature of contemporary institutionalised universities, these projects, in their aim to find the opportunity and space for translations, have deterritorialised academic knowledge production and attempted to form connections outside the institutionalised university architecture.

The organisers of FEM TALKS, who initially started their project within the boundaries of a university, realised that these boundaries became pressing on them:

> We really lacked feminist theory at Moscow State University. We wanted to make ourselves known and arrange events, lectures, and seminars on feminism. [...] But over time, it became cramped inside the university, we were something like a circle of interests there, this did not quite suit us. Our goal is to popularise feminist knowledge. (Danilov, 2020)

FEM TALKS describe their feeling with the word "cramped" (*tesno*), as if they experience the *embodied* effect of boundaries pressing on them. They continue by explaining how, in their desire to promote feminist knowledge, they have aspired to create spaces outside institutionalised spaces of teaching and learning:

> It was all the more joyful to meet like-minded people at the faculty and create some kind of safe "islands" - mini-conferences and scientific seminars on feminism. The [FEM TALKS] project was the culmination of our desire to create a feminist space within the university. (Danilov, 2020)

As it does not seem possible to change the university composition, FEM TALKS have aspired to create safer spaces within and near the university: ones that the organizers call "islands" —new territories that are deterritorialised from the institutionalised university spaces. During my fieldwork, I encountered cases where FEM TALKS's outsideness was referred to as "profanation" and "devaluation" of academic knowledge—not so much due to the format as to the teachers' lack of qualification. However, to a great extent, feminist knowledge has historically been produced outside academia in activist groups: "[m]ost of the groundbreaking contributions to feminist theory were made by the women's movement in the 1970s through practice; some of its insights were published in journals, obscure newsletters, and some books" (MacKinnon, 1991, p. 15). Along these lines, FEM TALKS insists that it is possible to produce good knowledge outside institutionalised universities, and that is exactly what they do:

> It seems to me that we and projects similar to ours are proving that a good education can also be obtained outside institutions. This became especially clear after the dismissals of outstanding teachers from the Higher School of Economics. (Danilov, 2020)

By "dismissals of outstanding teachers from the Higher School of Economics," they refer to those who were laid off from the university due to their oppositional political activity—and who subsequently founded the Free University in 2020. This case could be seen as a sign of tightening authoritarian-neoliberal control over academic performance in Russia. At this point in time, the need to teach and learn otherwise—to organise liveable projects outside the authoritarian-neoliberal university—became especially pressing. The Free University proclaimed how they transitioned outside the university controlled by authoritarian-neoliberal state governance: "This is where the paths of the university and the state part" (Free University, n.d.).

The Free University attempts to decompose not only the authoritarian-neoliberal governance that contaminates universities but also to subvert the power of state borders and territorial grip. The Free University imagines itself and builds its infrastructure through connections beyond regional and national boundaries. Existing in the digital space without a physical campus has made the Free University a project with multiple spatialities, as its members are often on the move. When I was taking courses at the Free University, I noticed the geographic mobility of the course participants; this experience was supported by one of the students at the Free University whom I interviewed:

> Of course, it would be cool to see everyone live and all that, but online, of course, has huge advantages, because, for example, our teacher of the "Sociology of nature and city" is from Krasnoyarsk. It's interesting that we already had three lessons, three Thursdays, and it turns out that the first Thursday I was in Berlin, the second Thursday I was in Turkey, and yesterday I was in Novgorod. Another Thursday I will be in St Petersburg—and everything works. Bliss.

Free University activities are attuned to the multiplicity of contexts and spatialities. The charter of the Free University claims: "The Free University is extraterritorial; there are no citizenship restrictions for community members" (Free University, n.d.). This deterritorialisation / extraterritoriality is also proclaimed in the project's manifesto: "We do not have a campus. We will teach from home, we will teach from libraries, we will teach at summer schools" (Free University, n.d.; my emphasis).

Building collegiality, horizontality, and joy

When breaking outside, these projects aim at different translations, most of which revolve around efforts to decompose the vertical power structures strengthened by authoritarian-neoliberal governance and to enrich academia with collegiality and horizontality. As the FEM TALKS organisers emphasize, such translations usually bring about feelings of joy.

> [FEM TALKS] have lectures in the format of parties and our course: they are all about a horizontal and relaxed format of interaction with people. Here you first discuss serious things and then dance to Lana Del Rey with a glass of cider in your hands. You are discussing memes in Zoom before the lecture, while you are waiting for everyone to join. This is the kind of communication that is impossible to imagine in an ordinary university, and the format that eliminates the fear of everything academic. Many wrote to us that initially that they were afraid to take the course because of the fear of not understanding some complex terms and concepts, but later these fears disappeared. And it's cool. I think feminist theory is about that, and not preaching from the tribune. (Danilov, 2020)

FEM TALKS activities embody resistance to institutionalised university hierarchies and power relations through their "horizontal and relaxed format," which is "impossible to imagine in an ordinary university" where knowledge is preached "from the tribune." Hierarchy is translated into collegiality, and the fear propagated by such hierarchies is translated into joy.

One of the course students shared with me in an interview a very joyful account of her participation in the FEM TALKS activities:

> I love them. [...] I enjoy it a lot, I look forward to seeing them every Saturday. There I'm not afraid to look stupid. Especially because there are such topics, you know, as "queer" or "transgender." And I'm just a simple girl, from Novgorod [smiling]. I understand that I am able to ask different, even offensive, controversial questions there because they understand that we are learning. [...] And we communicate with memes, and TikToks, and so forth. In short, there is a very kind atmosphere there.

The student pays a lot of attention to the project's non-hierarchical architecture of teaching and learning. Social media becomes an important socio-material component enabling this project: it helps bypass the hierarchies and, in this sense, further deterritorialises university knowledge, whereby academic life in the sense of collegiality and richness of topics springs up from the ruins of the corporate-authoritarian university. Interestingly, the student not only observes free communication between participants and "the teachers," but also suggests that the boundaries between the elitist and the peripheral are breaking. In her narration, the student ironically mentions that she is "a simple girl" from the small city of Novgorod, thereby contrasting her (peripheral) subject position to the presumably elitist academic (feminist) research. This juxtaposition breaks in the format of FEM TALKS by dismantling the academic hierarchies, making it a site of translating authoritarian-neoliberal hierarchies and control.

Finding freedom

Collegiality and horizontality, as opposed to the authoritarian-neoliberal vertical of control, are often imagined in terms of freedom. The name of the Free University already suggests this aspiration, and the project describes itself as "an independent educational project free of administrative pressure and censorship" (Free University, n.d.). The goal is to build a university anew, freeing teachers from any corporate-authoritarian dictate: "We, professors and teachers at different universities, are joining forces to work with students in a new way" (Free University, n.d.; my emphasis). This newness signifies the attempt to imagine academic life otherwise, to breathe life into higher education that has become synonymous with "bureaucratic indicators, massification, and cheapness of the educational process," as expressed by Viktor Gorbatov, one of the founders of the Free University:

> When, due to COVID-19, when universities were forced to be thrown into the online space fully, it suddenly became especially clear that many of the institutional requirements that we used to take for granted are completely false in terms of goal setting and ridiculous in form. We realised that they are not at all about the quality of education, soft skills, and motivation. Rather, they are about bureaucratic indicators, massification, and cheapness of the educational process. And then we further realised that we could do a lot on our own, if we need a quality education not for show, but for life. (Free University, n.d.)

"Freedom," however, is understood in very particular terms. The Free University does not try to escape the idea of a university as such. Rather, the Free University has built itself in opposition to the institutionalised architecture of corporate-authoritarian knowledge production. The Free University is a translation site where the corporate-authoritarian university is attempted to be recomposed into a liberated university.

When I interviewed one student at the Free University, who had also been a part of other oppositional activist and academic networks, she mentioned that freedom from corporate-authoritarian censorship and bureaucracy was exactly what had attracted her to this project:

> Well, I'm probably attracted to this one because it is free. But not even because of the money, but because [...] your background is not important to them. That is, they are not such bureaucrats. I like this very much. That they don't look at your regalia, at your diplomas; there are no such obstacles. [...] I also really like that the teachers have a position similar to mine. Not like at St Petersburg State University where the teacher kisses the dean's ass, the dean kisses the rector's ass, the rector kisses Putin's ass. That just made me feel sick at St Petersburg State University. And of course, this is one of the main, most significant things for me, that people there [at the Free University] have a connection with reality, that they do not deny it, that... I know that if I join a course on political systems, we will analyse things that are unpleasant for authoritarian regimes. I joined just for this. Because I understand that if I would like to study Political Science or even International Relations at St Petersburg State University, then they will iron out difficulties, and all controversies will be avoided. I do not need it. What I want is the most critical view, the relevant agenda. I just understood that I would find it there [in the Free University], and not in the institution.

The student intertwines several things that became important and attractive to her in the Free University: its "freedom" from bureaucracy ("they don't look at your regalia"), from the authoritarian-neoliberal vertical of power ("the teacher kisses the dean's ass, the dean kisses the rector's ass, the rector kisses Putin's ass"), and from authoritarian-neoliberal depoliticisation ("they will iron out difficulties"). The knowledge in the Free University is openly produced in a politicised environment. The Free University not only creates spaces for critical knowledge but, arguably, creates a sense of community united by the values of freedom from censorship in an authoritarian context where all self-organising has become extremely difficult (cf. Erdem, 2020, p. 320).

Reclaiming the university

When the corporate-authoritarian university has the ability to control the content of studies, the role of the university, and the academics' working conditions, academics arguably feel alienated from their academic life-worlds (Poutanen, 2022; Hall, 2018a; Hall, 2018b). The alternative projects organised by Russian academics and students not only attempt to escape the institutionalised boundaries and subvert its authoritarian-neoliberal control into something joyful, collegial, and horizontal. In these new spaces of translation, the organisers and participants attempt to reclaim what the university is, to take it back from the bureaucratic authoritarian-neoliberal machine of ruination. As the Free University's manifesto claims, "We cannot be expelled from the university because we are the university." (Free University, n.d.)

"We are the university" is a slogan that has been voiced by different academic groups. In the Russian context, the Free University was not the first to apply this slogan. It was taken up even earlier by the Russian students' collective DOXA in 2019. When DOXA's official status as a student organisation was revoked by the university administration due to DOXA's oppositional political activity, the organisation continued without official status. DOXA declared that "the university is a platform that belongs to society, and not to the business reputation, the brand, the vice-rector, the Board of Trustees, or anyone else" (DOXA vygonyayut..., 2019). DOXA resisted authoritarian-neoliberal control over university activities and attempted to reclaim them: "We are the university" became a slogan frequently used in their media publications.

DOXA mobilised the idea of reclaiming the university in the context of protests against the arrest of opposition figure Alexey Navalny in January 2021. DOXA posted a video address where they declared threats by university authorities to expel students for participating in protests as illegal. In that context, they talked about the right of citizens to protest and called for expressing students' political opinions "in any peaceful way" —for example, by becoming a volunteer in a human rights organisation or launching an independent student initiative (Adresant..., 2021). The video address ended with DOXA editors saying, "The state has declared war on youth, but we are the youth, and we will win." The video address was banned by governmental agencies within days, and DOXA editors who appeared in the video were subjected to criminal persecution. However, the slogan "We are the youth" / "Youth is us" (*Molodost' eto mi*) became one of the prominent slogans of DOXA as well as of the student movement more broadly. The identity of youth was mostly constructed around the identity of a student, which DOXA saw as an essential academic subject at a university. DOXA resisted the power of the university to punish and expel students for their participation in the protests and attempted to reclaim their subjectivity as active citizens and university subjects.

Limitations of translations: Intrusive powers of state and capital

Despite the attempts to translate the corporate-authoritarian university into collegiality, freedom, and joy, break free from its control, and reclaim academia, these processes of translation have their limitations. The powers of state and capital continue to have, or even amplify, their grip on academia, preventing possibilities for translation. Breaking free from the state simultaneously means losing material, administrative, and institutional resources, which the state, through its authoritarian-neoliberal governance, monopolises. For example, not being affiliated with a state university prevented the FEM TALKS project from receiving institutional funding. Most of the project activities were performed voluntarily; the organisers sometimes had to donate their own money to the project. For their course on feminist theory, they implemented commercial relations by charging their students fees (Danilov, 2020).

The Free University experienced similar limitations. Due to the lack of institutional support and resources, one of the students noticed how the activities of the Free University, especially in the first rounds of courses, were poorly organised. The number of applications exceeded the capacity of each course several times over, making the selection process laborious; in the context of unstable resources and overlapping projects by the Free University teachers, the organisation was not always smooth. Moreover, there is criticism toward the formation of course groups: while the student, whom I quoted above, appreciated the anti-bureaucratic nature of the Free University, she criticised some courses that did not pay attention to the differences in students' backgrounds, thus making the course content not suitable for everyone.

> What I don't really like is that, to be honest, [the course] is difficult for me. Probably, if I were a teacher, I would not approve my application, because I don't have this background, and it's very difficult for me. [...] In terms of background, there is a heterogeneous group, and we have these two boys for whom, apparently, [this course] is a professional field. [...] In short, these criteria are not very pedagogical. [...] It's rather strange to me why there was an eleventh grader in our group who is not even from a city. There are these two dudes who fucking quote Lacan and Deleuze by heart. I am also there. And we are all different. We are completely different.

While the student first cited freedom from bureaucratic dictates as something attractive, this eventually created tension: such horizontality becomes an obstacle in the context of a course that does not operate under any standards or regulations. The student continues: "But this [Free University], of course, is not a replacement for [institutionalised] academia. Of course not." While new academic life emerges from the ruins in these spaces of translation, the ruins themselves are not abandoned and devoid of life: they still operate and seem necessary for the participants. The ability to translate the authoritarian-neoliberal assemblages is limited. The institutionalised universities hold the power to provide opportunities that other projects still cannot: structured education, funding, resources, and degrees that are recognised on the labour market.

These projects of resistance are not shielded from the oppressive powers of authoritarian states, which tighten their grip on sites of subversion and translation. All three projects intensively relied on digital technologies: deterritorialised spaces where one could presumably escape from the grip of territorial state control and authoritarian-neoliberal governance. But those digital sites of translation also become reterritorialised and infiltrated by the authoritarian and controlling powers of the state. For example, the students at the Free University from Belarus experienced difficulties with internet connection: on several occasions, the authorities shut down the internet to counteract the protests against the falsification of presidential election results in August 2020. This shows that some bodies are not able to escape the territorial grip even with digital technologies that authoritarian regimes are able to control.

The intrusive authoritarian powers of the state further strengthened their grip in March 2023, when the Free University was proclaimed an "undesirable organisation" by the Russian authorities. The status of an undesirable organisation yields an administrative penalty to anyone participating in its activities and criminal prosecution to those involved in organising them. It affected the project's spatiality: for safety reasons, the Academic Board of the Free University decided to stop activities on the territory of the Russian Federation (Zajavlenie..., n.d.). The Russian state's attempt to prevent Free University activities forced the project out of the country: many teachers and students at the Free University relocated abroad. Although the Free University has stated that it wishes to continue its work (Zajavlenie..., n.d.), the possibilities for more liveable translations have been restrained by the authoritarian powers of the state.

Paradoxes of translations

These sites of translation do not subvert authoritarian-neoliberal control into nothingness. The pressure to institutionalise themselves, attach to other sources of resources, and amplify their voices might lead to attachment to other possible projects of power. The idea of assemblages and relationality reminds us that the sites of translation can hardly be shielded from the workings of capitalism and authoritarianism; in acts of patchy translation, they equally might borrow from other regimes of governance which themselves propagate control and dispossession.

The Free University, while trying to escape and resist the authoritarian-neoliberal control of the Russian state, attached itself to the European Union's projects of higher education governance, namely, the Bologna Process. After the Russian government decided to break ties with the Bologna Process in 2022 (Vorob'eva, 2022), the Free University posted an address condemning this: "We believe that this step opposes the interests of students and teachers. It leads to the isolation of Russian universities from the world, the destruction of academic rights and freedoms" (Free University, n.d.). The address further disassociates higher education from state boundaries: "Science should not serve the interests of any state, it is engaged in the search for knowledge. Modern academic science is unthinkable without international cooperation. [...] We declare that we have been and remain part of the international academic community" (Free University, n.d.). A tension is visible here: the idea of a deterritorialised Free University and science intertwine, slightly paradoxically, with attempts to anchor the Free University within the EU's higher education, specifically the Bologna Process. The Free University declared that "[t]he efforts of Free University will be focused on the recognition of our programs within the Bologna system and the development of academic mobility programs" (Free University, n.d.).

Paradoxically, then, while resisting the authoritarian-neoliberal governance of the Russian state, the Free University attached itself to the Bologna Process, which has been characterised as a neoliberal, hegemonic, Eurocentric, and even colonial project in the field of higher education. One of the imaginaries behind the creation of the Bologna Process was the idea of increasing the competitiveness of European economies (Hummel, 2009; Kaya, 2015). This was exactly the reason why the Russian state initially joined the Bologna Process in 2003 (Deriglazova, 2019, p. 346). In the global competition of knowledge economies, the European Union aspired to become the most competitive one in the world through the Bologna Process (Jessop et al., 2008). Figueroa (2010, p. 248) argues that the Eurocentricity of the Bologna Process is rooted in "narrativizing history" within Europe as the creator of progress understood solely in terms of capitalist culture.

Aligning itself with the neoliberal project of the Bologna Process, which the Russian government had initially taken up to increase its state competitiveness, paradoxically becomes a mechanism of resistance against the authoritarian politics of the Russian state in this new temporal context. The translations entail tensions and contradictions: despite the attempts of these projects to break outside of authoritarian-neoliberal control, they might still be entangled in the patchy acts of translation and not fully shielded from the powers of capital and states, which penetrate these projects through their porous boundaries.

Conclusions: Porous boundaries of resistance

There is a wealth of research showing that the penetrative workings of capitalism generate dispossession, alienation, and control. They ruin different areas of life, including that of the university, by building authoritarian-managerial hierarchies and subsuming academic activities to profit-making. However, it is important to recognise that the forces of neoliberal capitalism are not working in isolation. Sometimes they entangle with other oppressive powers, such as authoritarian states. This also creates resistance and attempts to imagine and actualise academia anew. While desires to build alternatives to the neoliberal university are common to many contexts, some scholars, such as those in Russia, also struggle with the dictates of the authoritarian state, as this chapter has shown. Analysing the resistance to the oppressive workings of neoliberal capitalism beyond the contexts of liberal democracies is important: projects of resistance in these cases must navigate through a complex assemblage of oppressive powers, that of global neoliberalisation and the authoritarian state. In this chapter, I have been specifically interested in how resistance to authoritarian-neoliberal control is imagined and acted upon, and how we, as scholars of capitalism, could enrich our understanding of the dynamics of destabilisation, translation, and subversion of these oppressive powers.

By intentionally trying to resist the oppressive workings of the state and capital, the projects of resistance analysed in this chapter become sites for translation. This means that they attempt to replace the vertical of power with collegiality, fear with joy, bureaucratic-administrative dictates with freedom, and separation propagated by state borders with the deterritorialised academic enterprise. However, while resistance is usually articulated through such contrasts and binaries, translations are exactly something different: they are messy and patchy and include tensions, contradictions, and paradoxes.

Although the projects analysed in this chapter were intended to break outside authoritarian-neoliberal dictates, to part ways with the state, and to reclaim the idea of a university beyond institutionalised entities, they had limitations in doing so. The authoritarian state holds control over many of the resources needed for knowledge production and may use its legislative powers to prevent the existence of these projects. While the projects seek to operate beyond control, there is hardly any utopian outside, and the projects might become entangled in other forms of power in the acts of patchy translation. The intrusive powers of state and capital often penetrate these alternative projects through their porous boundaries.

In the complex matrix of authoritarian-neoliberal forms, resistance is necessarily in conversation with the workings of authoritarianism, neoliberalism, and their compositions. The projects analysed in this chapter have been born in the interaction with authoritarian and neoliberal forms of the contemporary university: even when seeking to resist authoritarian-neoliberal control, the latter is the point of departure for their translations. They want to take, reposition, and reclaim the academic world-making projects, to strip the oppressive powers of ownership. However, the projects of resistance are born in and through their relation to the oppressive powers.

The boundaries of these projects are porous, and different elements might leak through them. As I have shown in this chapter, in the void of resources, these projects and sites might need to attach themselves to other powerful orderings. There are diverse capitalisms and neoliberalisms contained by (sometimes opposing each other) states: the Russian authoritarian-neoliberal regime has constructed itself in opposition to the Eurocentric neoliberal project of the European Union. This might create paradoxes in the acts of translation: while resisting one authoritarian-neoliberal composition, such as the Russian state, resistance might come attached to other neoliberal projects, such as the EU's neoliberal Bologna Process. This underscores that translations are messy and incomplete puzzles that patch together different elements. The boundaries are porous. In their multiple compositions, acts of political resistance contribute both to the orderings of neoliberal powers as well as to their subversions.

As capitalism is, in itself, a multitude and hybrid, the very idea of breaking free from all these multiple forms becomes even more problematic. A question remains: how far "outside" neoliberal and/or authoritarian compositions can such projects of translation go? What might be the way to subvert oppressive powers? How drastically can we escape assemblages of control? As capitalism is enabled by diversity and translations, as scholars such as Anna Tsing (2015) or J. K. Gibson-Graham (2006) have shown, the same applies to different forms of resistance. The assemblage perspective suggests replacing the modernist binary of inside and outside and their rigid boundaries with relationality, hybridity, and porosity. Translations are a space of interactions and subversions of meanings that leak into each other through their porous boundaries.

Acknowledgements

I would like to express my gratitude for the enriching and intellectually stimulating environment provided by two research projects: "Towards Good Neighbourliness with Higher Education Cooperation" (Principal Investigator: Sirke Mäkinen, funded by the Kone Foundation, grant number 201608897) and "Assembling Postcapitalist International Political Economy" (Principal Investigator: Anni Kangas, funded by the Academy of Finland, grant number 3121325976). Additionally, I acknowledge the support from the Kone Foundation for the individual research project "Assembling a Postsocialist University: The Politics of Higher Education in Russia" (grant number 202105839).

References

Acuto, M., & Curtis, S. (Eds.). (2014). *Reassembling international theory.* Palgrave Macmillan.

Adresant soobshaet o predstoyashej pobede molodosti [The sender announces the upcoming victory of youth]. (2021, April 14). *Meduza.* Retrieved January 28, 2023, from https://meduza.io/feature/2021/04/14/adresant-soobschaet-o-predstoyaschey-pobede-molodosti

Ashwin, P. (2020). *Transforming university education: A manifesto.* Bloomsbury Academic.

Belina, B., Petzold, T., Schardt, J., & Schipper, S. (2013). Neoliberalising the Fordist university: A tale of two campuses in Frankfurt a.M., Germany. *Antipode, 45*(3), 738–759. https://doi.org/10.1111/j.1467-8330.2012.01054.x

Borovskaia, M. A., Masych, M. A., & Bechvaia, M. R. (2014). An analysis of compensation systems for college and university instructors. *Russian Education & Society, 56*(1), 3–12. https://doi.org/10.2753/RES1060-9393560101

Bruff, I. (2014). The rise of authoritarian neoliberalism. *Rethinking Marxism, 26*(1), 113–129. https://doi.org/10.1080/08935696.2013.843250

Bruff, I., & Tansel, C. B. (2019). Authoritarian neoliberalism: Trajectories of knowledge production and praxis. *Globalizations, 16*(3), 233–244. https://doi.org/10.1080/14747731.2018.1502497

Cannella, G. S., & Koro-Ljungberg, M. (2017). Neoliberalism in higher education: Can we understand? Can we resist and survive? Can we become without neoliberalism? *Cultural Studies ↔ Critical Methodologies, 17*(3), 155–162. https://doi.org/10.1177/1532708617706117

Connell, R. (2019). *The good university: What universities actually do and why it's time for radical change.* Zed Books.

Coşar, S., & Ergül, H. (2015). Free-marketization of academia through authoritarianism: The Bologna Process in Turkey. *Alternate Routes, 26*, 101–124.

Danilov, A. (2020, September 14). Prosto o feminizme: My zapustili obrazovatelnyj proekt FEM TALKS [Simply about feminism: We launched an educational project FEM TALKS]. *Wonderzine.* Retrieved January 28, 2023, from https://www.wonderzine.com/wonderzine/opportunities/partners/252433-fem-talks

Dean, M. (2002). Liberal government and authoritarianism. *Economy and Society, 31*(1), 37–61. https://doi.org/10.1080/03085140120109240

Deleuze, G. (2004). On capitalism and desire. In D. Lapoujade (Ed.), *Desert islands and other texts, 1953–1974* (pp. 262–263). SemiotextI.

Deriglazova, L. (2019). Democrats, authoritarians and the Bologna Process: Universities in Germany, Russia, England and Wales by Judith Marquand (review). *Ab Imperio, 2019*(3), 343–350. https://doi.org/10.1353/imp.2019.0087

DOXA. (n.d.). Retrieved January 28, 2023, from https://doxa.team/

DOXA vygonyayut iz Vyshki [DOXA is kicked out of HSE.]. (2019, December 4). *DOXA*. Retrieved January 28, 2023, from https://doxajournal.ru/doxa_hse_2

Dubrovsky, D., & Kaczmarska, K. (2021). Authoritarian modernisation and academic freedom: The contradictions of internationalisation and "pockets of effectiveness" in Russian higher education. *TranstextIs Transcultures 跨文本跨文化, 16*, 1–20. https://doi.org/10.4000/transtexts.1543

Dönmez, P. E., & Duman, A. (2021). Marketisation of academia and authoritarian governments: The cases of Hungary and Turkey in critical perspective. *Critical Sociology, 47*(7–8), 1127–1145. https://doi.org/10.1177/0896920520976780

Erdem, E. (2020). Free universities as academic commons. In J. Gibson-Graham & K. Dombroski (Eds.), *The handbook of diverse economies* (pp. 316–322). Edward Elgar Publishing. https://doi.org/10.4337/9781788119962.00046

Fabry, A. (2019). *The political economy of Hungary: From state capitalism to authoritarian neoliberalism*. Springer International Publishing. https://doi.org/10.1007/978-3-030-10594-5

Fabry, A., & Sandbeck, S. (2019). Introduction to special issue on 'authoritarian neoliberalism.' *Competition & Change, 23*(2), 109–115. https://doi.org/10.1177/1024529418813827

FEM TALKS. (n.d.). Retrieved January 28, 2023, from https://femtalks.moscow

Figueroa, F. E. (2010). The Bologna Process as a hegemonic tool of Normative Power Europe (NPE): The case of Chilean and Mexican higher education. *Globalisation, Societies and Education, 8*(2), 247–256. https://doi.org/10.1080/14767721003779936

Forrat, N. (2016). The political economy of Russian higher education: Why does Putin support research universities? *Post-Soviet Affairs, 32*(4), 299–337. https://doi.org/10.1080/1060586X.2015.1051749

Free University. (n.d.). Retrieved January 28, 2023, from https://freemoscow.university/

Gataulina, I. (2025 Forthcoming). Neoliberal authoritarianism: An ethnography of Russian universities. Palgrave Macmillian.

Gel'man, V., & Ryzhenkov, S. (2011). Local regimes, sub-national governance and the 'power vertical' in contemporary Russia. *Europe-Asia Studies, 63*(3), 449–465. https://doi.org/10.1080/09668136.2011.557538

Gerashchenko, D. (2022). University leader appointment procedure in Russia: Building a vertical of power in higher education. *Demokratizatsiya, 30*(1), 107–133.

Gibson-Graham, J. K. (2006). *A postcapitalist politics*. University of Minnesota Press.

Giroux, H. A. (2014). *Neoliberalism's war on higher education*. Haymarket Books.

Golubeva, A. (2020, July 8). "Neblagonadezhny, vredyat reputacii." Prepodavatelyam "Vyshki" grozyat sokrasheniya ["Unreliable, damaging reputation." HSE teachers face layoffs]. *BBC News Russkaya sluzhba*. Retrieved January 28, 2023, from https://www.bbc.com/russian/features-53338263

Hall, R. (2018a). On the alienation of academic labour and the possibilities for mass intellectuality. *Triple, 16*(1), 97–113.

Hall, R. (2018b). *The alienated academic: The struggle for autonomy inside the university.* Springer International Publishing. https://doi.org/10.1007/978-3-319-94304-6

Hardt, M., & Negri, A. (2000). *Empire.* Harvard University Press.

Harvey, D. (2005). *A brief history of neoliberalism.* Oxford University Press.

Higgins, V., & Larner, W. (2017). *Assembling neoliberalism: Expertise, practices, subjects.* Palgrave Macmillan US.

Hummel, F. (2009). The neoliberal language of higher education in the EU: An analysis of the Bologna Process. *The Journal of the World Universities Forum, 2*(5), 53–64. https://doi.org/10.18848/1835-2030/CGP/v02i05/56621

Loveday, V. (2018). The neurotic academic: Anxiety, casualisation, and governance in the neoliberalising university. *Journal of Cultural Economy, 11*(2), 154–166. https://doi.org/10.1080/17530350.2018.1426032

Kaya, A. (2015). Critical voices against the Bologna Process in Turkey: Neo-liberal governance in higher education. New Perspectives on Turkey, 52, 105–133. https://doi.org/10.1017/npt.2015.13

Konkurs: Kak s jetim zhit' [Competition: How to live with it]. (2020, October 30). Universitetskaja solidarnost'. Retrieved April 20, 2023, from https://unisolidarity.ru/?p=8634

MacKinnon, C. A. (1991). *Toward a feminist theory of the state.* Harvard University Press.

McCann, L., Granter, E., Hyde, P., & Aroles, J. (2020). 'Upon the gears and upon the wheels': Terror convergence and total administration in the neoliberal university. *Management Learning, 51*(4), 431–451. https://doi.org/10.1177/1350507620924162

Minina, E. (2017). 'Quality revolution' in post-Soviet education in Russia: From control to assurance? *Journal of Education Policy, 32*(2), 176–197. https://doi.org/10.1080/02680939.2016.1250165

Mäkinen, S. (2021). Global university rankings and Russia's quest for national sovereignty. *Comparative Education, 57*(3), 417–434. https://doi.org/10.1080/03050068.2021.1926125

Olssen, M., & Peters, M. A. (2005). Neoliberalism, higher education and the knowledge economy: From the free market to knowledge capitalism. *Journal of Education Policy, 20*(3), 313–345. https://doi.org/10.1080/02680930500108718

Peters, M. A. (2021). Knowledge socialism: The rise of peer production — collegiality, collaboration, and collective intelligence. *Educational Philosophy and Theory, 53*(1), 1–9. https://doi.org/10.1080/00131857.2019.1654375

Poutanen, M. (2022). 'I am done with that now.' Sense of alienations in Finnish academia. *Journal of Education Policy*, 1–19. https://doi.org/10.1080/02680939.2022.2067594

Pyyhtinen, O., Onali, A., Zavos, S., Maija Sutinen, U., & Niina Uusitalo. (2022). The decaying stuff of the Anthropocene. *DigitHUM Revista Digital d'humanitats, 30*. https://doi.org/10.7238/d.voi30.416569

Sidorov, N. (2021, March 5). "Optimizacija" po LIIZhT-ovski (hronika razrushenija gumanitarnogo obrazovanija) ["Optimization" according to St Petersburg State Transport University (chronicle of the destruction of education in humanities)]. *Universitetskaja solidarnost'*. Retrieved April 20, 2023, from https://unisolidarity.ru/?p=8746

Smolentseva, A., Froumin, I., Konstantinovskiy, D. L., & Lisyutkin, M. (2018). Stratification by the state and the market: High participation higher education in Russia. In B. Cantwell, S. Marginson, & A. Smolentseva (Eds.), *Higher participation systems of higher education* (pp. 295–333). Oxford University Press.

Tsing, A. L. (2015). *The mushroom at the end of the world: On the possibility of life in capitalist ruins*. Princeton University Press.

Vorob'eva, I. (2022, May 28). Rossiya vyhodit iz Bolonskoj sistemy: Kogo i kak eto kosnyotsya [Russia exits the Bologna system: Whom and how it will affect]. *RBK*. Retrieved January 28, 2023, from https://www.rbc.ru/spb_sz/28/05/2022/628e29749a794747a1ee085d

VshE lishila zhurnal DOXA statusa studencheskoj organizacii. Pochemu eto vazhno. [The HSE has stripped DOXA of the status of a student organization. Why it is important]. (2019, December 4). *BBC News Russkaya sluzhba*. Retrieved January 28, 2023, from https://www.bbc.com/russian/news-50655236

Wullf-Wathne, M. (2021). Alternatives in the academe: Swimming with absurd flippers. *Gender, Place & Culture, 28*(4), 576–584. https://doi.org/10.1080/0966369X.2020.1784104

Zajavlenie Uchenogo Soveta [Statement of the Academic Board]. (n.d.). *Free University*. Retrieved April 24, 2023, from https://the.freemoscow.university/zayavlenie-uchenogo-soveta/

VERTAISARVIOITU
KOLLEGIALT GRANSKAD
PEER-REVIEWED
www.tsv.fi/tunnus

9

Resisting academic capitalism with a postcapitalist pedagogy

Healthier universities through antihierarchy, communality, and lived alternatives

Iris Pajunen

With this chapter, I contribute to the debates on retheorising capitalism by drafting a suggestion for a postcapitalist pedagogy that examines alternative epistemologies and methodologies, academic citizenship, and practices of resisting academic capitalism. I revisit previous scholarship on academic capitalism, autoethnography as a way of *writing differently*, and then make use of a case study of a three-day "Retheorising Capitalism Funfair" event that took place in Tampere University, Finland, in October 2023. As an undergraduate student, I also suggest that early-career scholarship is a valuable position for unchained and positive reimaginings of academia. It is a novel position locating sites of legitimacy, politics and innovation.

I argue that a postcapitalist pedagogy is a policy encompassing a philosophy of methodological and epistemological diversity, communality and collegiality, as well as inclusion and antihierarchy. It manifests as institutional culture, teaching and learning practices, and knowledge interests. These results may be significant in constituting healthier—and, ironically, more productive —universities, faculty, and students. With this chapter I answer the call for alternatives in the face of the persistent hold of academic capitalism and the intensified challenges to well-being that follow.

Pajunen, I. (2025). Resisting academic capitalism with a postcapitalist pedagogy: Healthier universities through antihierarchy, communality, and lived alternatives. In A. Kangas, I. Gataulina, M. Poutanen, A. I. Rajala & H-E. Ventovirta (Eds.), *Retheorising capitalism* (pp. 183–197). Tampere University Press.
https://doi.org/10.61201/tup.981

Autoethnography as methodology

For the research material, I utilise my personal experiences to derive from them a narrative representing not only myself, but the positionality and relationality of university students more broadly. My own observations are enriched by engaging in dialogue with other scholars in the field through their publications, which helps critically evaluate the Retheorising Capitalism Funfair and my own situatedness. This piece of writing aims to deliver a participant's perspective, and perhaps to stretch the normative boundaries of the genre of academic writing. Arguably, this kind of writing is in itself resistance to academic capitalism and its hierarchies.

My methodology rests on earlier insights of *writing differently*, drawing heavily from the feminist tradition which by nature defies scholarly conventions (e.g., Brigg & Bleiker, 2010; Gilmore et al., 2019; Kociatkiewicz & Kostera, 2023). The point of departure is the recognition that the norms of academic writing and research shape the perception of valid knowledge, teaching and learning. As Lacatus, Schade and Yao (2015, p. 777) put it "methodological choices are ethical choices", which "inform our training, teaching, and disciplinary governance." Therefore, writing differently has political and ethical implications: it aims to broaden, widen and deepen knowledge, and reach new ideas and meanings (Gilmore et al., 2019). This chapter is about writing differently in the sense that it challenges norms both in research and in academia more widely. Moreover, it experiments with and ponders alternatives to academic capitalism, appreciates the perspectives and diversity of academic novices, and concludes with invoking novel practices with a particular emphasis on humane ethics. The chapter is based on my participation at the "Retheorising Capitalism Funfair" event, and I turn to autoethnography as a methodology for locating the sites of politics, resistance, and innovation by systematically, and critically, navigating through my experiences and feelings associated with the event.

Figure 1. Zine-making at the Retheorising Capitalism Funfair event. CC BY-NC-ND Natalia Batrakova, 2023.

Autoethnography bypasses positivist assumptions about knowing and the self, exposes relations of power and legitimacy, and provides perspectives and information otherwise not available. It produces more nuanced, complicated and comprehensive forms of insights, derives from a range of faculties and sources of knowledge, and issues out first-hand information (Brigg & Bleiker, 2010; Buckley, 2015). The force of autoethnography lies in questioning the authority of the seemingly objective neutral and understanding oneself better in the process, leading to a more critical, sophisticated and ethically aware scholar in reproducing and transforming structures of knowledge and power (Löwenheim, 2010). Furthermore, as I suggest here, the social, experimenting, slow, deep, personal, relational and questioning nature of autoethnography challenges the mainstream neoliberal mode of *doing* academia. Considering the aforementioned, autoethnography can be perceived as a "revolutionary form of writing" and methodology (Auchter, 2019, p. 192).

I wish to stress that autoethnography is a complementary expedition alongside more traditional social science approaches, both equally essential. The validity of autoethnographic research should be evaluated in terms of the very process of knowledge production: opening up new hypotheses, identifying research questions, and creating "new and valuable insights for particular knowledge communities" (Brigg & Bleiker, 2010). Following this line, Naumes (2015) provides a simple starting point for the critical examination of autoethnographic research by asking: "[H]ow might the narrative disrupt congruity in political thought and does the narrative incorporate those who have otherwise been left out of political science discourse?" (p. 831). Naturally, autoethnographic research should also be transparent about key choices of selection and interpretation of data and include some self-reflection that is sensitive to cultural and societal contexts in order to provide means for evaluating the relevance of the results (Brigg & Bleiker, 2010). In this research chapter, my unique position as a participant and an undergraduate student helps identify key issues and generate new insights and visions that could challenge and change the present university practices.

Reviewing academic capitalism

Recognising the institutionalisation and normalisation of academic capitalism in various parts of the world's universities, this contribution attempts to draft a postcapitalist pedagogy as an alternative. In the Finnish context, where this autoethnographic inquiry takes place, there has been a qualitative turn towards academic capitalism through many neoliberal reforms and jurisdiction regarding universities and higher education since the 1990s. This reflects the larger pattern of increased market-oriented and neoliberal reasoning by the Finnish state and the Nordic countries in general. However, notable differences in the practices and scales of academic capitalism still occur between disciplines when compared to other countries such as the United States (Kauppinen & Kaidesoja, 2014). Perhaps the main difference is that in Finland the administrative changes towards academic capitalism have been largely top-down policies deriving from, among others, the European Union, the Organisation for Economic Co-operation and Development (OECD), and the philosophies of New Public Management and knowledge-based economy (e.g., Kauppinen & Kaidesoja, 2014; Poutanen 2022). In Finland quantitative productivity indicators are highlighted, and education is increasingly viewed as an individual investment and a commodity (Poutanen, 2023). Poutanen (2023) also argues that universities face a crossfire of growing demands and diminishing funding, while debates continue over possible tuition fees and the overall direction of Finland's higher education policy.

All in all, the concept of academic capitalism describes the globally dominant changes in the context of academic work and policy of higher education. Its most prominent features include growing intertwinement with markets, centrality of technoscience, tightening relationships with multinational corporations and limited funds for discretionary activities (Slaughter & Leslie, 1997). To compensate for the reduction in public funding, faculty and institutions utilise market activities such as tuition fees, patenting, grants, and industry collaborations to secure external funding (e.g., Slaughter & Leslie, 1997). Academic capitalism transforms knowledge into a profitable market contributing to capital accumulation and the changing labour market and economy (Jessop, 2018). Education, knowledge and creativity are no longer being viewed as a common good. Instead, they are commodified with intellectual property rights claimed and traded through exercises of privatisation, hierarchy and exclusion (Jessop, 2018). On the whole, universities and academics have become increasingly entrepreneurial, profit-oriented and operate in a growingly competitive environment (e.g., Ylijoki, 2003; Deem, 2001).

It can be argued that academic capitalism maintains, creates and defends institutional(ised) inequality. It divides educational institutions, faculties and academic workers into ranks (e.g., McNay, 2021; Reitz, 2017; Beatson et al., 2021). Resources are granted unevenly among universities and faculties, favouring institutional prestige next to market-oriented and male-dominated STEM-fields (Science, Technology, Engineering, and Mathematics). Simultaneously, the new system of stratification through competition legitimises positional privilege, wage differences and hierarchies in general (Reitz, 2017). Furthermore, despite the academic profession growing more diverse, women and racial minorities continue to constitute the lowest positions and suffer salary discrimination (Reichman, 2022). Altogether, as with capitalism in general, there seems to be no trickle-down effect (MacNay, 2022).

The negative impacts of academic capitalism also include the growth and intensification of project work, short-term contracts, and external funding, which is deemed to endanger researcher's career prospects, financial safety, and even the quality of their research (Ylijoki, 2003). Furthermore, universities have implemented a more corporate management approach to leadership (Slaughter & Leslie, 1997), which has led to the weakening of "academic citizenship" (Macfarlane, 2005, p. 300) overlooked simply as an issue of administration (Macfarlane, 2005, p. 299). However, it would be pivotal to nurture a culture of collegiality, especially amidst junior faculty, in order to secure sustainability within the academia (Beatson et al., 2021).

Practices of resistance

Remarkably, academic capitalism has caused notable backlash and incentives to pursue alternative forms of work (e.g., Ylijoki, 2003; Collyer, 2015). Alternatives through which academic capitalism can be resisted include, for example, community activism, curiosity-driven research, the mentoring of junior colleagues, intensive interaction with students, intellectual engagement for its own sake and those forms of knowledge production which aim to improve understanding of community issues or the solving of social problems. (Collyer, 2015, p. 325) . Moreover, as Oili-Helena Ylijoki (2003) suggests, project work and partnerships can also be interpreted as a possibility for collective teamwork, collaboration and solidarity opposing individualism.

Besides challenging the working culture of one's own unit or institution, the resistance against neoliberal reforms has also prompted action against national governments in various countries, such as the UCU strikes in the United Kingdom and protest against university privatisation in Greece (The Guardian, 2023; France24, 2024). In Finland, a national walk-out of researchers and university teachers took place in February 2024 organised by Akava, the Confederation of Unions for Professional and Managerial Staff in Finland. This occurred while I was writing this text. The campaign was part of a larger strike wave, united under the apt motto "for a better working life", opposing government reforms that, if implemented, would significantly weaken Finnish labour legislation (Tieteentekijät, n.d.). Additionally, in September 2023, university students mobilised against government education cuts and universities' policy to sell out campus spaces by occupying campuses and camping there overnight for two weeks (e.g., Auranen & Kauppi, 2023; Yle News, 2023).

These examples illustrate that despite the neoliberal reforms taking place in various universities, academic workers and students remain active shapers of the academia driven by their values, interest, aims, and traditions. Importantly, they demonstrate that relations of power and structure are (re)produced and changed through social action. (Ylijoki, 2003; Collyer, 2015.) These observations also speak to the need for (auto) ethnography in recognising the significance of feelings, experiences and individuals in the creation of institutions and institutional cultures.

In the quest for drafting a postcapitalist pedagogy as an alternative to academic capitalism I draw on Latin American and feminist frameworks. In their article Rhoades et al. (2004, p. 326) present three significant alternative projects regarding universities. Firstly, they propose a focus on democratisation and the promotion of increased access to higher education as a public good and as an investment; secondly, strategies for independent social development and community; and thirdly, sovereignty and cultural distinctiveness for universities. This project resonates with Gibson-Graham's,

Cameron's, and Healy's (2013, pp. xviii-xix) postcapitalist proposition for "taking back the economy". This includes:

> surviving together well and equitably; distributing surplus to enrich social and environmental health; encountering others in ways that support their well-being as well as ours; consuming sustainably; caring for...our natural and cultural commons; and investing our wealth in future generations (Gibson-Graham et al., 2013, pp. xviii—xix).

In my reading, the projects outlined by Rhoades et al. (2004) and postcapitalist diverse economy scholars are mutually supportive. I combine the two signposts with the experiences from the Retheorising Capitalism Funfair event, as locating and building on existing forms of alternative economies and revolution is at the heart of postcapitalist politics (Gibson-Graham et al., 2013). The notion of "taking back the economy" (Gibson-Graham et al., 2013) also complements my autoethnographic approach by stressing the significance and power of individual agency.

Retheorising Capitalism Funfair

The "Retheorising Capitalism Funfair" was a three-day event held at Tampere University in October 2023. It was organised by the Academy of Finland funded project *Assembling Postcapitalist International Political Economy*. The event invited students and scholars of International Relations (IR) and International Political Economy (IPE) to rethink capitalism and its aftermath(s) through cultivating alternative academic cultures, epistemologies, and creative workshop methods (Tampere University, n.d.). The program included zine-making (i.e., a small-circulation, self-published DIY leaflets), a movement-based workshop, a relaxation session, capitalism-themed board games, group discussions, a roundtable, as well as keynote presentations on decolonisation, Islamic economic philosophy, and capitalism's spatio-technological infrastructures. Approximately 30 people, both students and staff members, participated in the event. Further analysis of the diversity of the event will be discussed later.

Master-level students could join the Funfair through a 5 ECTS intensive course, which involved completing preassigned readings, writing a learning diary, and participating in the Funfair. As a 21-year-old, second-year bachelor's student, I ended up on the course by a lucky accident. Having spotted an advertisement for the event in an email newsletter, I immediately enrolled feeling very much invested in the topic, excited, and looking forward to the seminar. Blinded by my enthusiasm, I only later reread the practicalities and realised the Funfair was intended for advanced students. Having faced this first academic hierarchy, I sent a follow-up email explaining my motivation to the coordinating teacher and, to my delight, was admitted regardless. Taking on my first master's course made me feel proud, yet slightly nervous and insecure as I knew I would probably be the youngest and most inexperienced one present.

However, regarding autoethnographic research, I now view my position as a "novice" to be a strength as it breaks many norms. As a beginner, my mentality has been less affected by (sub)conscious schemes, habits and commitments, which might lead to fresh viewpoints and insights. Additionally, my lack of experience has led me to draw value also from exposures outside academia, potentially resulting in interesting outcomes. Furthermore, my positionality has allowed me to become easily excited and surprised. Here, I seek support from the feminist notions of "getting lost" as a beginning for subversive research (e.g., Lather 2007). In developing my analysis, I have utilised field notes and my learning diary from the time of the event.

My first, and perhaps the most important point concerns the emphasis placed on alternative epistemologies and methodologies during the event. For a start, naming the event a "Funfair" suggests a focus on enjoying oneself, the company, and the learning process. Overall, the stated aim of implementing these alternative approaches was to find new ways to learn, think and (re)theorise capitalism (Tampere University, n.d.). The methodology involved practical exercises of zine-making and a movement-based workshop. This drastically differs from the mainstream and traditional academic experience, mostly leaning on physically immobile knowledge work executed through listening or reading. Moreover, by centring sociability, the Funfair event proposed a stark contrast to the mass, distance- and independent courses that have been generally predominant in my studies.

Figure 2. A movement-based workshop. CC BY-NC-ND Natalia Batrakova, 2023.

The zine-making also prompted questions of wellbeing and consent. One goal of the Funfair was to produce postcapitalist zines. Crafting was allowed during the presentations, and everyone progressed at their own pace. Some made multiple zines while others did not finish even one. On the last day, everyone was invited to present their work, but no one was forced to do so. There was an open discussion about coping and tiredness, as one participant admitted to not having created anything due to being too exhausted. Despite the idea of everyone producing something, this was accepted, and the hosts agreed that the past three days had been long ones. It felt as if the pressures of productivity, competition, or accomplishment were absent. In my view, more flexibility was granted, and students' anxieties over coping were acknowledged better than usual. According to my experience, these kinds of policies customarily remain superficial and easily yield to the demands of efficiency.

The second significant observation regards the notably low hierarchies and power structures. During the Funfair, scholars, keynote speakers, and students all happily mingled with each other, and, importantly, were encouraged to do so. I found myself discussing hair dyes with an international senior scholar, flirting with a cute fellow-student, falling asleep next to a course mate during the relaxation session, talking to a doctoral researcher about her partner reading aloud for her, crafting with another well-established researcher, having lunch at the cafeteria with peers, exchanging numbers with a new friend, and playing board games in a team dissecting all attending groups. This fusing was further emphasised by the informal logistical arrangements. Instead of traditional lecture halls, the venues were spaces where the furniture could be moved.

Figure 3. Playing capitalism-themed board games. CC BY-NC-ND Natalia Batrakova, 2023.

My third point covers the apparent emphasis on discussion and collegiality. Multiple group discussions were scheduled in the program, there was always time for the audience's questions, and lunch and coffee breaks were adequately long for informal networking. Crafting and playing board games together were ideal impetuses for exchanging thoughts and establishing new connections with others. The genuine interest and appreciation of the participants' input regardless of their academic rank spoke for antiauthoritarianism. In addition, this communality diverged from my preceding experiences of academia as onerously competitive and hierarchical.

The fourth and final remark I wish to raise turns to the evident commitment to diversity. There were many nationalities present, and the speakers were multicultural. Intentionally or not, all the keynote speakers were women. I found this rather exceptional given that IPE has long been one of the most male-dominated fields within IR (Elias & Roberts, 2018). Also, the outward appearance of these women challenged the normative ideas of a "credible academic". Everyone was neatly dressed but allowed their personal style to shine through. There was a young woman of colour in business formal, a middle-aged woman without make-up in a hoodie, and a third woman who represented a bohemian aesthetic with many loose-fitting and layered pieces. Most appeared in colourful and patterned clothing. It felt as if the stylistic choices made by these women opposed the masculinist notions of professionalism that tend to suppress femininity and personality. The example these women posed made me feel more included, confident, and trusting in finding my path and place in academia. I was left feeling empowered.

Not all fun and games

Even though I was deeply impressed with the Funfair, it is worthwhile to also examine it critically to make visible the contradictions and challenges that surround postcapitalist pedagogies. The event challenged academic capitalism in many ways but simultaneously remained entangled with it. This complies with the previous literature reviewed in the theoretical framework section.

Firstly, this was a one-time project that has been enabled by external funding from the Research Council of Finland (RCF). Even though the RCF is a state-funded government agency operating within the Finnish Ministry of Education, Science and Culture, this still reflects a pattern where university operations are increasingly dependent on financing from external agencies such as the government and industry (e.g., Ylijoki, 2003, p. 307). Aligned with the framework of academic capitalism, this may also speak for serving business interest, profit-seeking market mentality, and commodification of knowledge. It may undermine the Research Council's mission of supporting high-quality, diverse, impactful, and responsible Finnish research across all fields of science for the benefit of the whole society (Suomen Akatemia, n.d.). On the one hand, outside funding offers possibilities to conduct free research, while on the other hand it imposes increased competition, as scholars of academic capitalism have noted.

Secondly, some of the cozy spaces were located outside the university campus in the nearby Nokia Arena, a new concert and event hall with 15,000 seats distinctive to the image of the city of Tampere built in 2021. The narratives behind the construction of the Nokia Arena are influenced by neoliberal ideas of creating an urban, dynamic, and lively city centre. This is supported by the symbolic capital of hiring world-class Danish-American architect Daniel Libeskind. Through Nokia Arena, Tampere additionally embraces its roots and legacy of sports success, proudly being home to two long-standing and popular hockey teams. (Leino, 2024.) Notably, this careful orchestration also served to depoliticise the Nokia Arena as a "political-economic megaproject reinforcing large-scale urban regeneration" (Leino, 2024, p. 14).

The fact that the university rents a costly venue in the Nokia Arena in the hopes of attracting visibility and improving its image, while at the same time reducing its original campus spaces to save on operating expenses, appears controversial (e.g., Eskelinen, 2022). It further exemplifies the interweaving between academia and business actors, of a shift away from prioritising student and research needs, and of the demand for universities to brand themselves with nonacademic merits in order to succeed in the current competitive environment. However, hosting the Funfair partly in the distinguished space proved that these aspirations are successful, as the venue was impressive and boosted the overall spirit of the event. Nonetheless, this triumph is accompanied by the loss of pleasant spaces elsewhere, even though they tend to serve a larger crowd of students and staff (instead of limited groups of seminar attendees) on a daily basis at the campus. This again points to internal structures of hierarchy and privilege.

Figure 4. Relaxation session. CC BY-NC-ND Natalia Batrakova, 2023.

Thirdly, a modest distance and distinction between students and scholars remained, and some made more of an effort to overcome it than others. Relatedly, it is important to note here that sociality and sociability are not equally easy, enjoyable or natural for everyone due to differences in personal temperament and upbringing. Additionally, the definition of good social skills varies significantly between cultures. (Keltinkangas-Järvinen, 2010.) I propose that authentic appreciation of diversity fosters collaboration and sociality while acknowledging their intricate limitations as aspirational new norms of pedagogy. Like autoethnography, alternative methodologies may not be suitable for everyone or everything but are nonetheless worthy and complementary in specific endeavors.

Finally, it is worthwhile to note that another student with a different background, interests, opinions, experiences etc. likely would have provided a divergent account of the Funfair. I wish to point out the rather like-minded atmosphere of the Funfair, which was perhaps due to the subject and nature of the event. It is possible that this left no space for dissidence, or made it difficult to express disagreement, which might weaken student and community engagement and reduce diversity. Although I consider the perspective and diversity of an academic novice to be a plus in the context of this autoethnographic inquiry, it may also make me by default easier to impress. However, I have aimed to balance this out with a thorough review and discussion of preceding literature in the field, by strictly following good scientific practice in this research, and by engaging in self-reflection and transparency, which are central elements of a successful autoethnographic methodology.

Towards postcapitalist pedagogies

I propose that a postcapitalist pedagogy harbours a philosophy of *methodological and epistemological diversity, communality and collegiality, as well as inclusion and antihierarchy.* It views universities as infrastructures that support public investment and common good, rather than the neoliberal modus operandi of capital accumulation, productivity and business interests. A postcapitalist pedagogy subsists as an institutional culture, teaching and learning practices, and knowledge interests.

A postcapitalist pedagogy must be fundamentally antihierarchical and committed to demolishing intersectional structures of oppression, as capitalism's prerequisite lies in divisive exploitation. Embracing alternative epistemologies and methodologies assist in this through exposing new ways of asking, searching, knowing—and eventually being. In turn, focusing on diversity and inclusion in terms of the people involved and uplifted in academia attends to the prevalent inequalities within the academic institutions specifically and the society at large.

Figure 5. Participants at the Retheorising Capitalism Funfair event. CC BY-NC-ND Natalia Batrakova, 2023.

An important finding of this chapter is the centrality of building short- and long-term communities within academia. The essence of this also appears to be found in the dismantlement of hierarchies. I derive from this the insight that a postcapitalist pedagogy is in particular a policy that materialises through engagement in practices of resistance and benevolence. These include for example curiosity-driven research, mentoring students and junior colleagues, peer-reviewing, co-operating, volunteering for the community—and even activism (Beatson et al., 2021).

Despite advocating for presence over productivity, an alternative postcapitalist pedagogy does not indicate the erasure of hard work, challenging oneself, ambition, advancement, publicising or conducting first-rate research. Rather, it actually fortifies these by enhancing the well-being of current academic workers and students; improving the integration of junior and early-career scholars; maintaining academia as a desirable work environment; shaping academia and academic success as feasible for a more comprehensive public; and by introducing novel research approaches and aspirations. Ironically, experiences of community, affinity, safety, support, motivation, contentment and continuity are, in fact, likely to simultaneously contribute to neoliberal aims of increased productivity (for example more graduates faster) (e.g., Katz et al., 2019).

Relatedly, traditional and mainstream approaches continue to persist, as differences occur between disciplines, institutions and countries in the experienced benefits, disadvantages, practices, and scales of academic capitalism (e.g., Ylijoki, 2003; Deem, 2010; Kauppinen & Kaidesoja, 2012). Ultimately, a change in mentality and practicalities is indeed a valuable first step in "reframing" the university and studying (Gibson-Graham et al., 2013), but a comprehensive normative shift away from academic capitalism will also require institutional and governmental actions. Nonetheless, in the light of this research, postcapitalist pedagogies can and, de facto, do operate within the neoliberal university.

My autoethnographic expedition showed that students and early-career scholars are a valuable resource for reimagining capitalism, as they raise fresh viewpoints, expose points of congestion and are not limited by habitual normativity or restrictions brought on by the prestige of a senior position. Autoethnography allowed me to produce comprehensive and nuanced understandings, draw from first-hand experiences, entwine them with previous literature on related topics, and locate sites of politics and innovation. Furthermore, autoethnography continues the important legacy of "writing differently", therefore shaping the perception of legitimate knowledge and carrying political and ethical input (Gilmore et al., 2019). These results consolidate the notion that autoethnographic research ought to always be assessed with regard to its contributions to the process of knowledge production (Brigg & Bleiker, 2010). Moreover, this chapter, as a piece of writing, can also be interpreted as an example of a postcapitalist pedagogy, since an autoethnographic expedition conducted from an undergraduate student position challenges the existing knowledge hierarchies.

I argue that the presented results are useful for both defining a postcapitalist pedagogy, and for extending the understanding and meaning of postcapitalism itself. In the 21st century context of persistent neoliberalism, this chapter adds to the existing literature on academic capitalism and postcapitalist politics by using a pedagogical approach and demonstrating alternative modes of actions within academia through a real-life example. These findings are significant for individual experiences of well-being; for the university as an institution; for academia as a place of employment and study; for the validity of knowledge, teaching and learning; and for composing better policy and politics in the future. I conclude with an invitation for further research on the subject and a message of hope for healthier universities through antihierarchy, communality, and lived alternatives.

References

Auchter, J. (2015). Orienting the body: Affective methodology and embodiment. In E. Van Rythoven & M. Sucharov (Eds.), *Methodology and emotion in international relations: Parsing the passions* (pp. 189–204). Routledge. https://doi.org/10.4324/9780429443930-11

Auranen, I., & Kauppi, A. (2023). Leikkauspolitiikka sai opiskelijat liikkeelle. *Visiiri, 6*, 8–9.

Beatson, N. J., Tharapos, M., O'Connell, B. T., de Lange, P., Carr, S., & Copeland, S. (2021). The gradual retreat from academic citizenship. *Higher Education Quarterly, 76*, 715–725. https://doi.org/10.1111/hequ.12341

Brigg, M., & Bleiker, R. (2010). Autoethnographic international relations: Exploring the self as a source of knowledge. *Review of International Studies, 36*, 779–798. https://doi.org/10.1017/S0260210510000689

Buckley, R. (2015). Autoethnography helps analyse emotions. *Frontiers in Psychology, 6*, 209. https://doi.org/10.3389/fpsyg.2015.00209

Collyer, F. M. (2015). Practices of conformity and resistance in the marketisation of the academy: Bourdieu, professionalism, and academic capitalism. *Critical Studies in Education, 56*(3), 315–331. https://doi.org/10.1080/17508487.2014.985690

Deem, R. (2010). Globalisation, new managerialism, academic capitalism and entrepreneurialism in universities: Is the local dimension still important? *Comparative Education, 37*(1), 7–20. https://doi.org/10.1080/03050060020020408

Elias, J., & Roberts, A. (Eds.). (2018). *Handbook on the international political economy of gender*. Edward Elgar Publishing.

Eskelinen, H. (2022, May 24). Yliopiston oma peliareena. *Visiiri*. https://www.visiirilehti.fi/yliopiston-oma-peliareena

France24. (2024, February 8). Greek students step up protests against private university plan. *France24*. https://www.france24.com/en/live-news/20240208-greek-students-step-up-protests-against-private-university-plan

Gibson-Graham, J. K., Cameron, J., & Healy, S. (2013). *Take back the economy: An ethical guide for transforming our communities*. University of Minnesota Press.

Gilmore, S., Harding, N., Helin, J., & Pullen, A. (2019). Writing differently. *Management Learning, 50*(1), 3–10. https://doi.org/10.1177/1350507618811027

Jessop, B. (2018). On academic capitalism. *Critical Policy Studies, 12*(1), 104–109. https://doi.org/10.1080/19460171.2017.1403342

Katz, A. S., Pronk, N. P., McLellan, D., Dennerlein, J., & Katz, J. N. (2019). Perceived workplace health and safety climates: Associations with worker outcomes and productivity. *American Journal of Preventive Medicine, 57*(4), 487–494. https://doi.org/10.1016/j.amepre.2019.06.011

Kauppinen, I., & Kaidesoja, T. (2014). A shift toward academic capitalism in Finland. *Higher Education Policy, 27*, 23–41. https://doi.org/10.1057/hep.2013.28

Keltinkangas-Järvinen, T. (2010). *Sosiaalisuus ja sosiaaliset taidot*. Werner Söderström Osakeyhtiö.

Kociatkiewicz, J., & Kostera, M. (2023). Writing differently: On the constraints and possibilities of presenting research rooted in feminist epistemologies. *Gender, Work, and Organization, 31*(1), 284–304. https://doi.org/10.1111/gwao.13072

Lather, P. (2007). *Getting lost: Feminist efforts toward a double(d) science.* State University of New York Press.

Lacatus, C., Schade, D., & Yao, Y. (2015). Quo vadis IR: Method, methodology, and innovation. *Millennium, 43*(3), 767–778. https://doi.org/10.1177/0305829815587822

Leino, H. (2024). From big apple to home of hockey: How scalar narratives and performative practices work in urban planning. *Planning Practice & Research,* 1–18. https://doi.org/10.1080/02697459.2024.2309408

Löwenheim, O. (2010). The 'I' in IR: An autoethnographic account. *Review of International Studies, 36*(4), 1023–1045. https://doi.org/10.1017/S0260210510000562

Macfarlane, B. (2005). The disengaged academic: The retreat from citizenship. *Higher Education Quarterly, 59*(4), 296–312. https://doi.org/10.1111/j.1468-2273.2005.00299.x

McNay, I. (2022). Academic capitalism, competition, and competence: The impact of student recruitment and research assessment. *Journal of Further and Higher Education, 46*(6), 780–792. https://doi.org/10.1080/0309877X.2021.2003307

Naumes, S. (2015). Is all IR 'I' IR? *Millennium, 43*(3), 820–832. https://doi.org/10.1177/0305829815576820

Poutanen, M. (2022). Competitive knowledge-economies driving new logics in higher education – reflections from a Finnish university merger. *Critical Policy Studies, 17*(3), 390–408. https://doi.org/10.1080/19460171.2022.2124429

Poutanen, M. (2023). Näkyvätkö suomalaisen korkeakoulupolitiikan kristallipallossa lukukausimaksut? *Poliittinen Talous, 11*(1), 46–69. https://doi.org/10.51810/pt.125176

Reichman, H. (2022). Introduction: Academic capitalism and the crisis of the professoriate. *Journal of the Early Republic, 42*(4), 543–555. https://doi.org/10.1353/jer.2022.0072

Reitz, T. (2017). Academic hierarchies in neo-feudal capitalism: How status competition processes trust and facilitates the appropriation of knowledge. *Higher Education, 73*(6), 871–886. https://doi.org/10.1007/s10734-017-0115-3

Rhoades, G., Maladonado-Maladonado, A., Ordorika, I., & Velazquez, M. (2004). Imagining alternativas to global corporate, new economy academic capitalism. *Policy Futures in Education, 2*(2), 316–329. https://doi.org/10.2304/pfie.2004.2.2.6

Slaughter, S., & Leslie, L. L. (1997). *Academic capitalism: Politics, policies, and the entrepreneurial university.* The Johns Hopkins University Press.

Suomen Akatemia. (n.d.). Mikä on Suomen Akatemia. https://www.aka.fi/suomen-akatemian-toiminta/mita-teemme/mika-on-suomen-akatemia/

The Guardian. (2023, January 12). More than 70,000 staff at 150 UK universities to strike for 18 days. *The Guardian.* https://www.theguardian.com/education/2023/jan/12/more-than-70000-staff-at-150-uk-universities-to-strike-for-18-days

Tampere University. (n.d.). Retheorising Capitalism Funfair, Tampere University, 23–25 October. https://projects.tuni.fi/postcape/funfair/

Tieteentekijät. (n.d.). FUURT to participate in Akava's walkout on 6 February 2024. https://tieteentekijat.fi/en/akavas-walkout-on-6-february-2024/

Yle News. (2023, September 19). Helsinki University students stage sit-in against government budget cuts.

10
Capitalism as colonialism as capitalism (and the alternatives)

Sabaheta Ramcilovic-Suominen

It is a well-established position that the European colonial project has played a central role in bringing about the current dominant sociocultural, socioeconomic, and sociopolitical realities and imaginaries—from the way we see and interpret ourselves and the world around us, to the global sociopolitical and socioeconomic institutions (Amin, 2010; Escobar, 2018; Fanon, 1952). The problem is that the majority of the Minority world (i.e., the majority of racially or otherwise privileged people living in the affluent European and settler colonial states) treat the European colonial project as a thing of the past, a historic fact that does not matter now and that nothing can be done about it. This is problematic because, first, colonialism is also the current state of affairs—as we are painfully reminded by the ongoing (plausible) genocide of Palestinians and confiscation of their land by Israel, but fully backed by the former colonial and settler colonial states. Second, because treating colonialism as something that is no longer present and just a part of European "dark history" is a major inhibitor for socioecological justice, transformations, and liberation.

Colonialism produced logics and structures including norms and praxis that are harmful to the web of life, the rest of the living world, land, water, planet itself, and eventually to all humans, as an intrinsic part of the whole. That we are part of and one with 'the rest of life' is something that some of us, faced with the horrendous global socioecological destruction and health crises, are starting to relearn, while others have never forgotten it (for example, see Kimmerer & Artelle [2024]; Wahinkpe Topa (Four Arrows) & Narvaez, [2022]). Colonialism has altered our psyche, the ways we

Ramcilovic-Suominen, S. (2025). Capitalism as colonialism as capitalism (and the alternatives). In A. Kangas, I. Gataulina, M. Poutanen, A. I. Rajala & H-E. Ventovirta (Eds.), *Retheorising capitalism* (pp. 198–218). Tampere University Press. https://doi.org/10.61201/tup.981

think, and the ways we know and understand the world, the ways we see ourselves and our positions in the world and the ways we understand our roles and responsibilities in the web of life.

Capitalism as colonialism as capitalism

Colonialism permeates every aspect of our living, both in the Minority world, or the so-called Global North as well as in Majority world, or the so-called Global South, albeit in starkly different ways, as I will explore in this chapter. My contributions to the debate on capitalism is two-fold. First, I explore the shared temporal and historic coevolutionary pathways of colonialism and capitalism, arguing that the two are inseparable and that one does not exist in isolation of the other (hence, 'capitalism as colonialism as capitalism'). Second, I dwell on the critiques of this colonialism-capitalism nexus, not merely to highlight its socioecological violence and destruction, but also to explore the various strategies to tackle this nexus, exploring their divergences and possibilities for convergence, which I argue is necessary for devising collective responses and shared pathways towards post- and anti- colonialist-capitalist futures. Finally, I emphasise that in this chapter, I focus predominantly on the linkages between capitalism and colonialism to illuminate the colonial roots of capitalism as we know it today. This, however, does not mean that colonialism can only be understood through and/or reduced to capitalism and capitalist violence and exploitation (Tharappel, 2023).

What do you mean when you say capitalism?

The comeback of capitalism in academic and political debates is to its own detriment, as noted by Nancy Fraser (2022) in her book *Cannibal Capitalism*. In the last couple of decades, the term is increasingly discussed in the 'belly of the beast', i.e., the core economies of the European and settler colonial states, including the United States of America (USA), and the United Kingdom (UK). This discursive comeback is associated with the growing concerns about the alarming state of ecosystems, such as the loss of life ('biological diversity'), and the climate change associated risks that are increasingly felt also in the 'core', all of which have been linked to capitalism as the root cause (Fraser, 2022; Harvey, 2014; Hickel & Sullivan, 2023; Moore, 2015). Thus, capitalism has become the mutual target of various movements for justice, be it social, racial, ecological, or climate justice. It unified movements tackling issues beyond the narrowly defined economy, which is quite right considering that rather than being an economic system, capitalism is a (global) social system, where *social* is defined quite broadly, to include race, wealth, ecology, gender, care work, etc.

Fraser (2022) explains this by highlighting the non-economic 'background conditions' on which the economic 'foreground features' of capitalism depend, and without which the economy and profit accumulation are impossible. Those background conditions include: 1. Social reproduction and care work; 2. Earth ecology; 3. Political power; and 4. Racial expropriation. Hence rather than an economic system, capitalism is better framed as a social system, where 'social' also includes the ecological, political, and ideological. It is also central to keep in mind that, due to its shared origin and proximity with European colonial project (see next section), capitalism discriminates when choosing its prey. It bites especially hard the people of specific race, class, gender, religion, historic background, and political affiliation, and the territories where they reside (Danewid, 2023).

Scholars distinguish between several historically specific forms of capitalism, including merchandised, liberal colonial, state managed, and globalising neoliberal, as the latest version (e.g. Fraser, 2022). Others differentiate between markets and trade vis-à-vis capitalism, convincingly arguing that markets and trade have existed for thousands of years before capitalism (i.e. before 15th century) and that:

> What makes capitalism different from most other economic systems in history is that it is organised around the imperative of constant expansion, or 'growth': ever-increasing levels of industrial extraction, production and consumption, which we measure as Gross Domestic Product (GDP) (Hickel, 2020).

This growth-oriented critique of capitalism is most common in degrowth literature (e.g. Schmeltzer et al., 2022) and is commonly positioned in relation to socioecological crises, including the accelerated dying of species, climate change, and associated global inequalities. Kate Raworth (2017), another well-known proponent of postgrowth economics similarly argues that while capitalism is based on private property and markets, private property and markets existed well before the rise of capitalism, and therefore capitalism is more than that.

One feature of capitalism on which scholars commonly agree is capital and/or profit accumulation. Importantly, such accumulation cannot occur in an egalitarian and democratic system where means of production are co-owned, profit equally distributed, and the questions on the use of productive capacities of a society democratically decided upon (Hickel & Sullivan, 2023). These can therefore be considered as antidotes of capitalism, and thus central features for any postcapitalist future scenario. Since its origins in the 15th and 16th centuries, capital accumulation has required access to cheap, confiscated and/or forced labour, raw materials, minerals, and land for agricultural and other 'commodities'. We cannot begin to understand capitalism without going back to the European colonial project, the expansion, exploitation, expropriation, and dehumanisation of the 'other' and the forced imposition on the rest of the world, which led to severe ongoing consequences and violence, as opposed to the more common economic progress and industrialisation in the 'core economies' (Hickel, 2017).

The process that started with mechanisation and externalisation of nature defined in Descartesian way, followed by commodification and appropriation, as well as devaluation and cheapening of nature, land, labour (Patel & Moore, 2017), care work (through the processes of exploitation and/or expropriation (Fraser, 2022)), and finally the dehumanisation required to justify the unjustifiable (Danewid, 2023; Luxemburg, 2015; Rodney, 2018), with the aim of profit accumulation and domination, is what I understand by capitalism as manifested today. The process that destroyed common ownership (Harvey, 2014; Patel & Moore, 2017), the existing ways of doing the economy otherwise (Mignolo, 2011; Mignolo & Walsh, 2018), as well as other ways of social organising, some of which were egalitarian well before the 'invention' of agriculture (Graeber & Wengrow, 2021).

Capital accumulation relies on two interconnected processes: 1. Exploitation, i.e. transfer of value through contractual labour for wages, which workers use to cover their costs of living, while surplus labour time and productivity is captured by capital; and 2. Expropriation, i.e. brutal and forced caesura of time, labour, confiscation of land and resources of the subjugated and/or marginalised people, who gain little or nothing in return, as in the cases of slavery and modern slavery (Fraser, 2022; ILO, 2022; Luxemburg, 2015). Expropriation of the subjugated and marginalised make exploitation of 'free' wage workers profitable, and it makes lavish profit for the capitalist elite. The expropriated subjects are often black, indigenous and people of colour (BIPOC), or otherwise marginalised rural or urban communities in the periphery. Both exploitation and expropriation are necessary, structural, constitutive, and institutionalised elements of the capital, rather than errors or undesired effects. Oppression, violence, marginalisation, appropriation, confiscation, corporate landgrabs, labour-grabs, and structural debt are necessary conditions for capitalism. Capitalism is violent, socioecologically destructive, and racist not by error but by design, which links it with the current socioecological crises, green and (neo) colonialism, imperialism, and racial oppression (Danewid, 2023; Du Bois, 2010; Fraser, 2022; Hickel et al., 2021).

On colonial origins of capitalism, and how it reproduced the polarised racist world we live (in) and manifest today

As capitalism emerged and evolved alongside the European colonial project, justification for the violence, enslavement, and commodification of black and brown bodies, was mediated through false narratives of the supremacy of the white race, leading to racial domination, dehumanisation, and genocides, which became second nature to capitalism (Danewid, 2023; Du Bois, 2010; Wilson, 1996). The rise of early capitalist enterprises, for example, the nutmeg spice trade, is heart wrenchingly described in Amitav Ghosh's (2021) Nutmeg's Curse. Placing economic benefit and profit above human life during colonialism marks the start of capitalism, and is the corner stone for continued oppression, which is the first condition of many wherein colonialism serves capitalism (see the next subsection). While the forms, ownership and to an extent even the colour line of capitalism is evolving and changing the aims and logics remain unchanged. This can be clearly seen with the more recent rise of emerging economies in BRICs (Brazil, Russia, India, and China) (Wilson, 1996).

As white, educated men and women, with legal residence in Finland, and relatively secured and relatively well-paid jobs in the formal economy, we enjoy access to amenities and public services, from education, to healthcare, to paid parental and sick leaves. This stands in contrast to those who for various reasons, including their origin, class, race, citizenship, have no access to such amenities in Finland. This also stands in even starker contrast to the billions of women and men in the global peripheries who are structurally disadvantaged and whose labour is either exploited for meagre wages, or fully expropriated, for the benefits of capitalist elite, but also for the benefit of those of us in the Minority world, including myself. At any given time, I can afford food, clothes, and electronic gadgets, which are grown, extracted, and produced in and by exploited 'others', land, and resources from around the world. Thus, in capitalist society we are structurally conditioned to exploit others, complicit in the existing polarisation and violence against racialised and gendered black and brown bodies.

This polarisation and 'global peripheralisation'—while mostly taken for granted—is constructed over the last 500 years. The polarisation and peripheralisation is directly linked with the internal colonisation and/or marginalisation throughout Sub-Saharan Africa and Latin America, as well as in the settler colonial states, including in the USA, Canada, Australia, New Zealand, and Israel. The violence is specifically targeting black, and/or native and indigenous populations, some of whom are currently being cleansed in masses, under the full sponsorship of the capitalist-colonial allies, USA, UK, Canada, and most of the European Union (EU) member states.

While historically rooted, the exploitation and expropriation of land, resources, and labour continues to the present day (Hickel et al., 2021), in the form of modern slavery, for example in cocoa production (in Côte d'Ivoire and Ghana), textile manufacturing (China, India, Bangladesh), and the mining industry across Sub Saharan Africa and South America. The colonial-capitalist process has captured not only the traditional sectors and discourses, but also those of environmental protection (for example, carbon trading, fence nature protection), all of which are organised around nature commodification and profit accumulation (Fletcher, 2023). As Jason Hickel (2017) shows in his book "The Divide", the great divide is fuelled by structural adjustments of the World Trade Organization (WTO) and the International Monetary Fund (IMF), preventing the countries in the Majority worlds from accessing fair tariffs and providing subsidies to Western economies, while keeping wages low. Low wages and extreme poverty benefit the Empire because they allow for slave workers in various value chains, from agriculture to mineral extraction for electronic devices, electric vehicles, and batteries for solar energies (Almeida et al., 2023).

Economic growth as the latest cloth of the emperor, and the role of the state

Contemporary capitalism manifests and works through economic growth. To show this manifestation of capitalism, I will draw from degrowth literature, even if with few exceptions (e.g., Hickel, 2021a, Schmelzer et al., 2022), the 'mainstream' degrowth literature hardly engages in deeper analysis of colonial-capitalist nexus. This contrasts with the decolonial and postcolonial (Escobar, 2015), and to some extent, the feminist perspectives on degrowth (Dengler & Lang, 2021; Hanaček et al., 2020; Singh, 2019), where the relations between colonialism, capitalism, and economic growth (EG) are central.

Generally, degrowth literature points out that, while capitalism is as old as colonialism, EG is comparatively a recent phenomenon, originating only in the mid-20th century (Schmeltzer et al., 2022). As Schmeltzer et al., (2021) point out, EG was adopted as a political and economic goal only after the introduction of the GDP in the 1930s, and became relevant after the Second World War, especially in the 1950s and 1960s. What distinguishes EG from other earlier forms of capitalism is the freedom of markets (Fraser, 2022). In this context, as well as historically, EG is equated with what Nancy Fraser (2022) refers as the last form of capitalism—globalising neoliberal capitalism.

Free or autonomous markets implies that market signals and monetary flow are used as indicators for deciding on key issues regulating our lives, including how, how much, for whom, by whom the socioecological and productive, as well the biophysical or material capacities are used, produced, and distributed in a society. This, however, does not mean that the state is an innocent observer in this (neo)liberal globalising capitalism. On the contrary, capital has always depended on the state and vice versa (Danewid, 2023; Rodney, 2018). The increased use of state violence against land-, forest-, and environment- defenders, as well as against climate justice movements and movements for liberation, including the Boycott, Divestment and Sanction (BDS), but also pro-Palestinian protests in the EU countries, are only some of the latest examples where the state protects financial and racial capitalism against its citizens.

This includes state-backed violence against pro-Palestinian protests, which has made it plainly obvious that Western states are ready to defend the colonial-capitalist nexus, regardless of their ally Israel mass murdering black and brown bodies. However, as the black Marxist literature reminds us, the state has always been racial state (Danewid, 2023; Du Bois, 2010). Protected by state-sponsored violence and augmented by consumerist ideology and lifestyle, the logic of neoliberal economy quickly led not only to eroding of earth's bearing capacities, but also to disproportionate impacts on racialised, gendered, and marginalised others, leading to unpresented and ever-growing inequalities.

Framing EG as the latest manifestation of capitalism shows the adaptiveness of capitalism, but more importantly how the logics, norms, values, and myths are the hardest to die, especially when militarised and protected by the global hegemonic capitalist-colonialist-statist power. When and if the struggle for global hegemony were historically questioned, for instance during the Cold War, EG was the main political tool of the (Western) states. Embracing EG as their 'new religion' and imposing it onto the rest of the world, just as they did with their old religion through missionaries during colonialism, the latest 'gift' of the West to the rest of the world became the primacy of EG. This 'gifting' process that started in 1960s is similarly violent, even if somewhat more covert.

Narratives of democracy have been important to justify invasion of countries that reject the West's imposition and conditions of free/cheap access to resources and labour, including some—not all—Middle East countries. In cases of democratic states across Africa and South America, democratically elected leaders who mobilised the population towards economic liberation were assassinated and/or removed by military coups, covered up by the narratives of democracy, development, economic growth, and structural adjustment programmes (Hickel, 2017; Hickel & Sullivan, 2021). Effectively the Western states installed a neoliberal state-backed globalising economy, while clashing and smashing any movements for liberation from the hegemony of the West, under the guise of economic progress, democracy, and in some cases the narrative of fighting terrorism. In case of the most recent, and currently ongoing oppression no attempt is made to cover the intention, by this I mean the Israelian plausible genocide in Gaza that killed close to 30.000 people (as of March, 2023). The violence is streamed around the clock globally for nearly half a year at the time of writing, ignoring international rule of law and institutions, such as the United Nations and the International Court of Justice. This sends a message to anyone, but especially the emerging economies, such as BRICs and others, that the imperial capitalist order and global dominance of the West (the USA, UK, the EU, and its allies) is not to be questioned.

Coloniality/ism & decoloniality/ism: Problematising the divide between material/structure & immaterial/symbolic

In decolonial schools of thought, the distinction between *colonisation* and *decolonisation*, vis-à-vis and *coloniality* and *decoloniality* is quite central. *Colonisation, or colonialism* commonly refer to the historical point in time when the Western colonising powers (Spanish, Portuguese, British, French, Belgian, Dutch, German, Danish, among others) seized and occupied half of the planet. Decolonisation in turn refers to the political independence of former colonies and the withdrawal of the occupying European colonising powers. *Coloniality* on the other hand refers to indirect and to a degree hidden means and forms of oppression and domination, including symbolic, cognitive, epistemic, ideational, and discursive. However, all of these are essential for enabling and maintaining the very material, or structural violence of historic colonial powers over politically liberated colonies. *Decoloniality* by extension then refers to the multifaceted process and set of strategies that aim to deconstruct, unlearn, and abolish the harmful narratives that enable coloniality and colonialism.

The common argument when elaborating *Coloniality* and *decoloniality* is that while European colonisation project has mostly—even if not fully—ended approximately 70 years ago, the domination of previous colonial and settler colonial states over the postcolonial ones remained, which is due to the ongoing process of coloniality. Examples of coloniality include universalised hierarchies such as (i) social hierarchies (race, gender, ethnicity), (ii) epistemic hierarchies (different knowledge systems), (iii) institutional and power hierarchies and domination (global institutions regulating finance, trade, economy, such as the WTO, IMF, and World Bank).

Brenny Mendoza (2015, p. 15) defines coloniality as:

> Long standing patterns of power that emerged as a result of colonialism that redefine culture, labour, intersubjective relations, aspirations of the self, common sense, and knowledge production in ways that accredit the superiority of the colonizer. Surviving long after colonialism has been overthrown, coloniality permeates consciousness and social relations in contemporary life

Thus, while coloniality is a result of historic and ongoing colonialism, it is not the same as colonialism. Coloniality is also defined as modernity. Building on Anibal Quijano's (2000) *coloniality of power*, various decolonial thinkers, including Walter Mignolo, Arturo Escobar, Maria Lugones, Nelson Maldonado-Torres, and others, have further illuminated this link between Eurocentric modernity and coloniality. Eurocentric modernity, meaning an ontology that proposes the universality of a singular, one-world world—a world where there is no space for different interpretations, a world based on rationality, individualism, separation, hierarchy, domination, and capitalist accumulation. Quijano's work linking the material (political, economic, existential) with the symbolic (the meaning, the mind, the epistemic) (see also, Fúnez-Flores, 2023) is central for my purpose and argument that the two are co-constructive and inseparable.

Ontology as used here is understood as worlding, so in that sense it is very material and political (de la Cadena & Blaser, 2018). This implies that the current crises of modernity (socioecological crises and injustices), are a direct result of the symbolic and cognitive bias. Modernity as coloniality imposes one dominant view of seeing the world. It is a singular lens to reality, which robs others to live outside of this projected singular reality. It erases plural views and forms of living, being and knowing, and substitutes them by universal, Eurocentric ways (Amin, 2010; Icaza & Vázquez, 2016).

Decoloniality as a scholarly debate has mostly focused on the so-called symbolic or ideational (decoloniality of mind and knowledge), compared to the material and structural, including the struggles for land and life (Tuck & Yang, 2012), even if such debates are often in direct relation to and support of such struggles. However, more often than not, the two strands of literature stand in opposition to one another, forming one *of the major tensions* in decoloniality debate, which is the decoloniality as modernity *vis-à-vis* decoloniality of land, structures of oppression.

Decoloniality of mind/knowledge and the focus on Eurocentric modernity or ontology has been critiqued as co-optation of anti-colonial movements of liberation and indigenous land repatriation (Smith & Lester, 2023; Tuck & Yang, 2012). To my mind the tension is artificial at best and unhelpful at worst, because as I discussed above, the patters of exploitation, domination, and even massacres and genocides require the narrative, the logic, mind/set, and worldviews to legitimise such acts. To be clear, I am not arguing that experiencing, for example, racism verbally vis-à-vis as a violent act of beating by police are equally harmful, but rather that they are part of the one and the same system of oppression—two sides of the same coin, two branches of the same tree. Thus, both should be tackled, not necessarily at the same time or with the same urgency, but both require attention, as they are mutually co-constructive and part of the same struggle for liberation and freedom.

Just as we have established above that because 'capitalism is colonialism is capitalism', the end of it can only come from anti-capitalist-colonialist movements and initiatives, so I argue that because colonialism requires mindsets, logics, philosophies, and knowledges (provisionally referred as 'symbolic'), as well as structure of violence (provisionally referred as 'material'); thus, the anti-colonial and decolonial efforts must work towards the decoloniality of mind/knowledge, and of structure/institutions. Decoloniality can and should include a wide range of strategies that seek to either unlearn or eliminate the various forms of oppressions and dominations—either at an ideational level (mind, language, constructs, categories, and interpretation of reality), or at the level of actual resistance, uprising and movements for liberation. To approach decoloniality in this way is to enable connection and platform for joint action against the same enemy, rather than delegitimising others' efforts, which has mostly been the case until now (Smith & Lester, 2023). In this sense the calls for decoloniality of knowledge, education, academia, science, and curricula—as acts of epistemic disobedience and struggles for epistemic freedom (Ndlovu-Gatsheni, 2021)—stand as extremely relevant, as do the calls for civil disobedience and insurgency for fighting ecological and climate catastrophe and injustices (Dunlap & Tornel, 2023; Sovacool & Dunlap, 2022).

Alternatives and transformative movements and agendas: teasing out the divergence to call for unity and convergence

Alongside decoloniality (See previous section), there is an array of initiatives that recognise the colonial and/or capitalist roots of our socioecological crises, even if not necessarily as two sides of the same coin and/or even if they tend to (over)emphasise one over the other. These initiatives are based on and embedded in one or more of the following traditions and schools of thought: (i) Pluriverse; (ii) Degrowth; and (iii) Marxist approaches. In addition, (iv) Anarchist, and (iv) Feminist approaches contribute immensely to the fight against the ills associated to the colonial-capitalist nexus.

Anarchist approaches frame the state as a colonial construct and violent structure that needs to be challenged and eventually abolished for the freedom and liberation of human and other-than-human populations. It emphasises the importance of self-organisation and autonomous movements for self-sufficiency, liberation, and organisation of social life beyond state (Gelderloos 2022). When compared to degrowth, decoloniality, and pluriverse there are some parallels in aims, but also differences in means (Dunlap, 2022). Specifically, anarchist perspectives challenge the idea that degrowth or any other response to socioecological crises require state-level policy interventions, favouring instead 'bottom up' movement and struggles for liberation.

Feminist approaches highlight the intersectionality between layers of oppression and domination and hegemonies across the board, from human-nature relations to accumulation through various forms of domination (Arruzza et al., 2019; Haraway, 2016; Tsing, 2015); emphasising care as labour, affect, and politics (Puig de la Bellacasa, 2017; Vaittinen & Confortini, 2019). Feminism critiques the lack of acknowledgement and devaluation of reproductive care work, especially but not only by the deemed dispensable 'others' (women, BIPOC, and lower classes) for economic outputs (Fraser, 2022). Linking Marxist and feminist perspectives have illuminated the relations between the multi-layered violence (gender, race, etc.) and the colonial-capitalist regime, highlighting the role patriarchy, racism, and heterosexuality, among others (hooks, 2004). Anarchist and feminist approaches shape others by emphasising their blind spots, and the narrow and shallow scope(s). I refer to some of those critiques in relation to the three transformative blocs covered in the subsequent sections.

Pluriverse as anti-capitalist and anti-colonial response

Pluriverse may refer to multiple ways of thinking, being, knowing, acting, dreaming, existing, living, and dying. It rejects the 'One-world world' meaning the universality of ways and norms of living, relating, knowing, teaching, doing economics, and so on, which have been promoted as universal, modern, or Eurocentric (Amin, 2010). It acknowledges and encourages a world that includes many worlds, as the famous definition of pluriverse goes—"a world where many worlds fit"—initially defined by the Zapatista movement (Escobar, 2018; Mignolo, 2011). As Escobar (2008) explains, pluriverse is different from pluralism, since pluralism is not concerned with how different worlds come into being, and/or come to dominate others, and is therefore apolitical, ignoring the histories and struggles, global and local power relations, worldviews, and praxis. In addition, unlike pluralism, which does not go into the topic of colonia-capitalist violence and oppression, pluriverse is specifically anti-colonial and anti-capitalist, acknowledging, claiming, and owning its normative nature and radical values and principles.

As specifically anti-capitalist, pluriverse puts forth an argument that to liberate from the oppressive and destructive neoliberal, financialising, globalising, capitalist, (neo)colonial system described above, changes are needed at an ontological and practical level. Theoretically, the pluriverse is outlined by decolonial scholars, including Arturo Escobar and Walter Mignolo, while the practical examples of existing initiatives worlding 'a world where many worlds fit' are documented by Kothari et al. (2019).

Pluriverse and decoloniality (of mind, of power, and of land) have many common aspects. Both question the universality of the dominant Eurocentric ontology and the associated development models, critiquing the logics of human-nature duality, (neo) extractivism, consumerism, and those associated with it. Additionally, both focus on the grassroots and community level and are quite closely linked to the postdevelopment school of thought (Escobar, 2015; Garcia-Arias & Schöneberg, 2021). Some scholars have argued that pluriverse, like decoloniality, tends to overemphasise the discursive and/or the so-called 'cultural', compared to the structural, which combined with its emphasis on scattered, local, and place-based responses casts doubt on pluriverse as a viable response to the colonial-capitalist nexus (Garcia-Arias & Schöneberg, 2021; Gills & Hosseini, 2022). Others have questioned it by bringing forth a theory of a 'rich universality', which links universality and solidarity (Heron, 2019).

While in my view the strength of pluriverse is precisely its embeddedness in the local and the grassroot issues and responses, the above critiques point to the important challenge of organising and connecting to build global networks of resistance, which can confront the global capitalist-colonial structures, including gendered and racialised labour expropriation and exploitation, appropriation and accumulation in the global value chains, and the ownership of means of production, which suggests the need for complementarity with other responses and strategies.

Degrowth: Planetary limits and beyond

Unlike decoloniality and pluriverse, until recently degrowth has been a school of thought by and for the 'Global North', i.e. the Minority world. This remains the case in the mainstream literature, despite the emerging scholarship that links postdevelopment, pluriverse, decoloniality, and degrowth (Escobar, 2015; Hanaček et al., 2020; Kothari et al., 2014; Singh, 2019; Trophe, 2024). This later literature highlights the synergies between degrowth and Eastern and Southern philosophies. Pluriverse and decolonial thinking suggest that degrowth is but only one in the pluriverse of alternatives (Kothari et al. 2019), and that it needs convergence with other movements (Nirmal & Rocheleau, 2019) if it is to avoid the tyranny of domination and universalism.

This definition by Jason Hickel (2021b) offers a fair outline of the key qualities of the concept,

> democratically planned reduction of energy and resource throughput designed to bring the economy back into balance with the living world, in a way that reduces inequality and improves human well-being for all, globally.

Degrowth calls for reimagining the meaning of "good life" and for collectively and democratically defined societal boundaries. Further, Hickel and Sullivan (2023) argue that degrowth can be understood as an anti-colonial demand that calls for an end to the colonial appropriation that underpins the capital accumulation in the North at the cost of the South. The implications for the South include, ending structural adjustment programs, cancelling external debt, transferring necessary technologies, and enabling governments to use industrial and fiscal policy for economic sovereignty (Hickel, 2021a). For the time being, framing degrowth as anti-colonial project is unique to a smaller group of scholars, and thus the question of degrowth's super-powers to tackle the colonial-capitalist nexus are worth revisiting. Despite degrowth popularity and undeniable potentials, anarchist, feminist, decolonial/postdevelopment, and Marxists offer various critiques:

(I) anarchist critique: state-based and 'non-reformist reforms' as solutions, as well as insufficient engagement with indigenous resistance and autonomous movements (AKC Collective, 2023; Dunlap, 2022) and co-optation (Spash, 2021),

(II) feminist critique: lack of engagement with social reproduction, expropriation of (care)work (Dengler & Lang, 2021),

(III) postdevelopment and decolonial critique: objectification of rural and/or racialised women and lack of engagement with other intersectional layers of domination (Garcia-Arias & Schöneberg, 2021; Mehta and Harcourt, 2021; Nirmal & Rocheleau, 2019),

(IV) Marxist critiques are many, including degrowth's demand for limiting production, including socialist, centralised and state regulated, its preference for local and/or small-scale operations (Huber 2022a, 2022b); and its engagement with growth, that is seen as obscuring the complexities of power relations, ownership, capital accumulation behind it (Heron, 2022a).

However, far from all Marxists dismiss the idea of degrowth as utopian and/or naive. On the contrary, an eco-socialist and communist version of degrowth is emerging (next sub-section; see also, Saito, 2023). In any case, the so-called 'mainstream' degrowth (with an emphasis on the biophysical limits, socioecological 'metabolism', and the state policy response) has attracted various more and less friendly critiques, including the arguments that it is reformist (AKC Collective, 2023; Garcia-Arias & Schöneberg, 2021) and universalist (Nirmal & Rocheleau, 2019). In their commentary of the "The Case for Degrowth" (Kallis et al., 2020), Garcia-Arias & Schöneberg (2021, p. 4) note: "(the book) proposes a collection of measures within capitalism, to make it greener, progressive, (...) better—seemingly more sustainable—while continuing operating under the capitalist episteme".

Such critiques are instrumental for expanding and diversifying the degrowth movement, resulting in different varieties of degrowth. In the spirit of building synergies, and recognising the significant divergences within degrowth movement, for the purpose of this chapter, I join with Eastwood and Heron (2024) to emphasise degrowth as one of the key responses to socioecological crises and capitalist destruction of life, and that the different views on degrowth are unified by the rejection of growth paradigm, and the imperative of growth at all costs (Schmelzer et al., 2022). Finally, degrowth has won popularity across very different societal groups, from activists to researchers to policy makers, and it might well be that the perceived weakness (the simplification of complex processes behind economic growth, and openness to different ways of affecting change—from grassroot initiatives to social movements to policy), are its strengths when it comes to momentum building. Co-optation in policy circles however remain a challenge ahead (Ramcilovic-Suominen, 2023).

(Eco-)Marxist approaches, their tensions, and synergies

It goes without saying that a text about capitalist-colonialist nexus, polycrises, and alternatives cannot be complete without a section on (Eco-)Marxist views and contributions (Danewid, 2023; Moore, 2015). The core concepts in Marxist tradition, including primitive accumulation, class struggles, modes of production, value creation and exchange, ownership of means of production, and to a various degree integrated issues of race, gender, social reproduction, imperialism, dependency, under-development (depending on the specific variant of Marxism) are central for and in anti-colonial and anti-capitalist alternatives, responses, and struggles.

Significant tensions exist between distinct positions within this bloc. To illustrate this, I will consider the tensions between the (i) *eco-socialist* (Heron, 2022a, b) and (ii) *eco-modernist* position (Huber, 2022a). The former emphasises the importance of national self-determination and sovereignty, the anti-colonial and anti-imperial struggle, and the importance of agrarian question and land reforms (Ajl, 2022b; Heron & Heffron, 2022). The latter emphasises centralised production and control over production relations, as well as green technologies and industry powered by 'renewable' energy. In addition, the (iii) *(Eco)Feminist* (Arruzza et al., 2019) view emphasises care labour and ethics, unpaid care work, mistreatment and exploitation of the least privileged women and men, which applying the Marxist teaching advances an anti-colonial, anti-capitalist, eco-socialist, and anti-racist feminism. Such is at the margins, however, as is shown by the silence of the mainstream white feminism, in the case of Israeli's attack on Gaza, including murder of women and children. Finally, (iv) *Anti-colonial, anti-imperial, and black-Marxism* (Amin, 1990; Danewid, 2023; Du Bois, 2010; Rodney, 2018,) provide invaluable contribution by positioning race in the context of value creation and capitalism, as I touch on in the next section of this chapter. They are central in the debate on colonial-capitalist entanglements and the associated anti-colonial, anti-racist, and anti-imperial responses that deserve an undivided attention in a separate piece of analysis.

Beyond internal disagreements, some of the points that delineate (eco-)Marxist tradition from others examined here include, the centrality of class struggle (i.e., workers vis-à-vis bourgeois class), core and periphery, and value generation and exchange. Such concepts link socioecological crises with labour and trade unions, and position the production, consumption, and inequalities within the global colonial and neocolonial relations and contexts. It is precisely here where synergies are made between the (eco-)Marxist and degrowth as eco-socialist and anti-colonial project. The extent to which labour and trade unions can tackle socioecological issues and inequalities is a different question, especially globally and in the global peripheries. This question calls attention to the tension between job creation and economic growth, which remain key concerns for labour and trade unions, vis-à-vis the socioecological destruction and exploitation in the periphery. Sadly, the green transition stands as the latest example where 'green jobs' prevail at the cost of neocolonial and imperialist capture (Ajl, 2022a). This has resulted in calls for international solidarity with the exploited workers in the periphery, in the eco-socialist varieties of Marxism. Similar solidarity with the periphery is called for in relation to the agrarian question and land reform in the core, which requires attention to agrarian struggles in the periphery (Ajl, 2022b; Heron & Heffron, 2022).

Eco-socialist vs. eco-modernist Marxist positions as an example of internal tensions

As noted above, while there are commonalities between the different Marxist traditions, the differences between the eco-modernist and the eco-socialist positions are quite significant[1]. First, while the proponents of the eco-socialist Marxist strand, who question the unbound production and consumption, and therefore not only the 'who and how', but also the 'how much' of production, and therefore the associated question of (over)consumption, including the overconsumption of the working class in the core economies. The proponents of the eco-modernist strand are less worried about these issues, assuming that growth would automatically be sustainable under socialist economy and modes of production.

This concerns the second point of divergence between the two, which is the eco-modernist over-reliance on green technologies vis-à-vis the eco-socialist reservation in terms of 'technology fixes'. This is quite central, as the eco-modernist view leads to harmful optimism and false solutions, where half-truths are presented as solutions to socioecological crises and inequalities, perpetuating rather than resolving them (Fletcher, 2023). It also risks the continuity of neocolonial and neo-extractivist imperial relations between the core and periphery in the light of 'green transition' (Almeida et. al., 2023; Ramcilovic-Suominen et al., 2022).

The third set of divergences concern the 'core and periphery' debate mentioned above. On the one hand, it is the difference in attention given to the core-periphery debate, with the eco-modernist Marxist position brushing over the debate and focusing mostly on the core economies (Huber, 2022b), vis-à-vis the eco-socialist Marxist position debating the existing predatory and imperial relations of the core over periphery (Heron, 2022a). On the other hand, it is the similarities between the eco-socialist Marxist and degrowth as anti-colonial project (Hickel, 2021a) versus the eco-modernist Marxist views. The former two positions invariably place the debate in the context of 'imperial mode of living' in the core economies on the cost of the periphery (Brand & Wissen, 2021)[2].

---

1 Kai Heron's response (2022a) to Matt Huber's (2022a) 'Mish-Mash Ecologism' offers a good summary of tensions between the eco-modernist vis-à-vis eco-socialist Marxist perspectives.

2 This is far from an exhaustive debate on synergies and differences between 1. degrowth as anti-colonial project and 2. eco-socialist Marxist position, vis-à-vis 3. eco-modernist Marxist position. I invite readers to check out the newly published DeGryter Handbook on Degrowth (Eastwood and Heron 2024), with interesting and more detailed discussions on disagreements and bridges between Degrowth and Marxism, (e.g. Hornborg 2024; Jackson 2024), as well as Kohei Saito's "Marx in the Anthropocene: Towards the idea of Degrowth

The differences as a strength rather than a weakness, and how to nurture political solidarity

My call for convergence of different strategies and responses does not imply that I consider the means less relevant than the aims (see Hamilton & Ramcilovic-Suominen, 2023). It simply means that diverse ways and approaches are applicable in different situations towards the same goal of post-capitalist-colonial futures. One universal way that works in all contexts across the Globe is not possible, and while all presented positions recognise this, they rarely inhabit or manifest this understanding in their recommendations and engagements with one another. In my view, the tendency to seek superiority over other ways, traditions, and approaches is a significant part of what hold us back collectively, and the first thing we must unlearn for collective transformations to post-colonialism-capitalism. After all, if your house was attacked, you do not start arguing about the shape, size, and colours of arrows to use, rather you would use all of them to defend it.

Having said that, the existing rifts between various responses and strategies are not insignificant, and while they may appear to be (only) about the ways they perceive or define problems and possible solutions, these perceptions are based on distinct value systems, and ideologies and therefore they are hard to bridge or compromise. Perhaps one of the rifts that is hardest to bridge is the view on the role of the state. If a tradition or a set of responses consider state as the problem (part and manifestation of colonial-capitalist establishment), it is indeed hard to see how it can join forces with those working through state, and/or aim to better or reform the state, largely within the capitalist boundaries (see previous subsection). Similarly, the tension between (de)coloniality of mind and knowledge versus structures and land, and the tendency to downplay the former by the proponents of the later approach (see previous section) is significant. However, just as there are many ways in which colonial-capitalist system affects different societal groups, there are many ways to respond and fight it. The ways to fight may also depend on personalities. For example, resistance can be manifested in different ways: as silent resistance and refusal (e.g., refusal to consume imported products, or industrially grown meet) or vocal and active resistance (e.g. protests and barricades). Both approaches can be radical and anti-colonial and can lead to elimination of violent practices and regimes, even if not in the same way or at the same speed. Yet, both are fighting the same ill and both can lead to peaceful and liberated future because decolonised minds never seek to colonise, dominate, or oppress others.

Finding common ground and motives between these vastly different ideas is possible as it is necessary if we are to build collective, and democratic responses to the capital-colonial present. Hence, rather than working towards developing new

Communism" (Saito 2023), for discussions on, inter alia: (i) production vs. production *and* consumption; (ii) local and people-driven actions and responses, vs. national/centralised initiatives, (iii) localised and commonly owned supply vs. large-scale, globalised supply chains, (iv) solidarity internationalism vs. an approach to green transition that is likely to lead to (neo)colonial seizure of land, labor and resources from the periphery.

'best solution(s)', we need to shift gears towards building political solidarity between the existing solutions and consequently develop joint collective anti-capitalist imaginaries and structures. All efforts are needed, as long as they work to unsettle, challenge, and eventually abolish the hegemonic colonial-capitalist system that leads to socioecological destruction of human and other-than-human life.

Building solidarity between different and opposing movements and approaches could include: (i) defining joint principles, for example principles of radical democracy, conviviality, and non-duality between human and the rest of nature; (ii) building safe spaces and platforms for engagement where different strategies and praxis can be planned in support of shared anti-colonial, anti-racist and anti-capitalist efforts; and (iii) strategising of responses in relation to scale and context. For instance, in some cases small-scale and local responses might be needed (community gardens, local energy supplies, and other cooperatives), while in others, large-scale corporate and international responses and regulations are better suited (policies and laws to keep corporate actors in check in terms of profit accumulation and/or introducing limits on their material and energy use). To conclude, the solutions are already here, and not only some but all are needed.

References

Ajl, M. (2022a). Everything stays the same while everything changes. *Development and Change, 53*(6), 1398–1420. https://doi.org/10.1111/dech.12719

Ajl, M. (2022b). Land and the US Agrarian South. *Agrarian South: Journal of Political Economy, 11*(1), 158–171. https://doi.org/10.1177/22779760221079891

AKC Collective. (2023). Anarchism and degrowth: deepening degrowth's engagement with autonomous movements. *Degrowth Journal*. https://doi.org/10.36399/Degrowth.001.01.09

Almeida, D. V., Kolinjivadi, V., Ferrando, T., Roy, B., Herrera, H., Gonçalves, M. V., & Van Hecken, G. (2023). The "Greening" of Empire: The European Green Deal as the EU first agenda. *Political Geography, 105*, 102925. https://doi.org/10.1016/j.polgeo.2023.102925

Amin, S. (1990). *Delinking: Towards a polycentric world*. Zed Books.

Amin, S. (2010). *Eurocentrism*. Monthly Review Press.

Arruzza, C., Bhattacharya, T., & Fraser, N. (2019). *Feminism for the 99%*. Verso Books.

Brand, U., & Wissen, M. (2021). *The imperial mode of living: Everyday life and the ecological crisis of capitalism*. Verso Books.

Danewid, I. (2023). *Resisting racial capitalism: An antipolitical theory of refusal*. Cambridge University Press.

De la Cadena, M., & Blaser, M. (Eds.). (2018). *A world of many worlds*. Duke University Press.

Dengler, C., & Lang, M. (2022). Commoning care: Feminist degrowth visions for a socio-ecological transformation. *Feminist Economics, 28*(1), 1–28. https://doi.org/10.1080/13545701.2021.1973108

Du Bois, W. E. B. (2010). *Darkwater: The Givens Collection*. Simon and Schuster.

Dunlap, A. (2022). Recognizing the "De" in degrowth: An anarchist and autonomist angagement with degrowth. *The Anarchist Library*. https://theanarchistlibrary.org/library/alexander-dunlap-recognizing-the-de-in-degrowth

Dunlap, A., & Tornel, C. (2023). Pluralizing energy justice? Towards cultivating an unruly, autonomous and insurrectionary research agenda. *Energy Research & Social Science, 103*, 103217. https://doi.org/10.1016/j.erss.2023.103217

Eastwood, L., & Heron, K. (Eds.). (2024). *De Gruyter handbook of degrowth*. Walter de Gruyter GmbH & Co KG.

Escobar, A. (2015). Degrowth, postdevelopment, and transitions: a preliminary conversation. *Sustainability Science, 10*, 451–462. https://doi.org/10.1007/s11625-015-0307-1

Escobar, A. (2018). *Designs for the pluriverse: Radical interdependence, autonomy, and the making of worlds*. Duke University Press.

Fanon, F. (1952). *Black skin, white Masks*. Grove Press.

Fletcher, R. (2023). *Failing forward: The rise and fall of neoliberal conservation*. University of California Press.

Fraser, N. (2022). *Cannibal capitalism: How our system is devouring democracy, care and the planet – and what we can do about it*. Verso.

Fúnez-Flores, J. I. (2023). Anibal Quijano: (Dis) entangling the geopolitics and coloniality of curriculum. *The Curriculum Journal,* 35(2), 288–306. https://doi.org/10.1002/curj.12345

Garcia-Arias, J., & Schöneberg, J. (2021). Urgencies and imperatives for revolutionary (environmental) transitions: from degrowth and postdevelopment towards the pluriverse? *Environmental Politics,* 30(5), 865-871. https://doi.org/10.1080/09644016.2021.1911443

Gelderloos, P. (2022). *The solutions are already here: Strategies for ecological revolution from below.* Pluto Press.

Ghosh, A. (2021). *The nutmeg's curse: Parables for a planet in crisis.* The University of Chicago Press.

Gills, B., & Hosseini, S. (2022). Pluriversality and beyond: Consolidating radical alternatives to (mal-)development as a commonist project. *Sustainable Science,* 17, 1183–1194. https://doi.org/10.1007/s11625-022-01129-8

Graeber, D., & Wengrow, D. (2021). *The dawn of everything: A new history of humanity.* Penguin.

Hamilton, R. T. V., & Ramcilovic-Suominen, S. (2023). From hegemony-reinforcing to hegemony-transcending transformations: horizons of possibility and strategies of escape. *Sustainability Science, 18*(2), 737–748. https://doi.org/10.1007/s11625-023-01129-8

Hanaček, K., Roy, B., Avila, S., & Kallis, G. (2020). Ecological economics and degrowth: Proposing a future research agenda from the margins. *Ecological Economics, 169,* 106495. https://doi.org/10.1016/j.ecolecon.2019.106495

Haraway, D. J. (2016). *Staying with the trouble: Making kin in the Chthulucene.* Duke University Press.

Harvey, D. (2014). *Seventeen contradictions and the end of capitalism.* Oxford University Press.

Heron, K. (2019). Many struggles, one fight: Deleuze| Guattari, Lacan, and the US Anti-Fracking Movement. A thesis submitted to The University of Manchester for the degree of Doctor of Philosophy in the Faculty of Humanities.

Heron, K. (2022a). The great unfettering. *Sidecar* [Internet], 7. https://newleftreview.org/sidecar/posts/the-great-unfettering

Heron, K. (2022b). War, ecocide and eco-socialist transition. *GND Media.* https://www.gndmedia.co.uk/articles/war-ecocide-ecosocialist-transition

Heron, K., & Heffron, A. (2022). Renewing the Land Question: Against Greengrabbing and Green Colonialism. *New Socialist.* February 20.

Hickel, J. (2017). *The divide: A brief guide to global inequality and its solutions.* Random House.

Hickel, J. (2020). *Less is more: How degrowth will save the world.* Random House.

Hickel, J. (2021a). The anti-colonial politics of degrowth. *Political Geography, 88,* 102404. https://doi.org/10.1016/j.polgeo.2021.102404

Hickel, J. (2021b). What does degrowth mean? A few points of clarification. *Globalizations, 18*(7), 1105–1111. https://doi.org/10.1080/14747731.2020.1812222

Hickel, J., & Sullivan, D. (2023). Capitalism, global poverty, and the case for democratic socialism. *Monthly Review, 75*(3), 99–113. https://doi.org/10.14452/MR-075-03-2023-07_7

Hickel, J., Sullivan, D., & Zoomkawala, H. (2021). Plunder in the post-colonial era: quantifying drain from the global south through unequal exchange, 1960–2018. *New Political Economy, 26*(6), 1030–1047. https://doi.org/10.1080/13563467.2021.1899153

hooks, b. (2004). *The will to change: Men, masculinity, and love.* Atria Books.

Hornborg, A. (2024). Degrowth disagreements with Marxism: Critical perspectives on the fetishisation of value and productivity. In L. Eastwood & K. Heron (Eds.), *De Gruyter handbook of degrowth* (pp. 361–376). Walter de Gruyter GmbH & Co KG. https://doi.org/10.1515/9783110778359-025

Huber, M. (2022a). Mish-mash ecologism. *New Left Review*. https://newleftreview.org/sidecar/posts/mish-mash-ecologism

Huber, M. T. (2022b). *Climate change as class war: Building socialism on a warming planet*. Verso.

Icaza, R., & Vázquez, R. (2016). The coloniality of gender as a radical critique of developmentalism. In W. Harcourt (Ed.), *The Palgrave handbook of gender and development: Critical engagements in feminist theory and practice* (pp. 62–73). Palgrave Macmillan UK.

International Labour Organization. (2022). *Walk Free, and International Organization for Migration (IOM)*, Geneva.

Jackson, J. (2024). Not just newer, but fewer: A bridge between ecomodernism and degrowth? In L. Eastwood & K. Heron (Eds.), *De Gruyter handbook of degrowth* (pp. 123-140). Walter de Gruyter GmbH & Co KG

Kallis, G., Paulson, S., D'Alisa, G., & Demaria, F. (2020). *The case for degrowth*. John Wiley & Sons.

Kimmerer, R. W., & Artelle, K. A. (2024). Time to support Indigenous science. *Science, 383*, 243–243. https://doi.org/10.1126/science.ado0684

Kothari, A., Demaria, F., & Acosta, A. (2014). Buen vivir, degrowth and ecological swaraj: Alternatives to sustainable development and the green economy. *Development, 57*(3), 362–375. https://doi.org/10.1057/dev.2015.24

Kothari, A., Salleh, A., Escobar, A., Demaria, F., & Acosta, A. (2019). *Pluriverse: A post-development dictionary*. Tulika.

Luxemburg, R. (2015). *The accumulation of capital*. Routledge.

Mehta, L., & Harcourt, W. (2021). Beyond limits and scarcity: Feminist and decolonial contributions to degrowth. *Political Geography*, 89, 102411–. https://doi.org/10.1016/j.polgeo.2021.102411

Mendoza, B. (2015). Coloniality of gender and power: From postcoloniality to decoloniality. In L. Disch & M. E. Hawkesworth (Eds.), *The Oxford handbook of feminist theory* (pp. 100–121). Oxford University Press. https://doi.org/10.1093/oxfordhb/9780199328581.013.6

Mignolo, W. (2011). *The darker side of western modernity: Global futures, decolonial options*. Duke University Press.

Mignolo, W. D., & Walsh, C. E. (2018). *On decoloniality: Concepts, analytics, praxis*. Duke University Press.

Moore, J. W. (2015). *Capitalism in the web of life: Ecology and the accumulation of capital*. Verso.

Ndlovu-Gatsheni, S. J. (2021). The cognitive empire, politics of knowledge and African intellectual productions: Reflections on struggles for epistemic freedom and resurgence of decolonisation in the twenty-first century. *Third World Quarterly, 42*(5), 882–901. https://doi.org/10.1080/01436597.2020.1775487

Nirmal, P., & Rocheleau, D. (2019). Decolonising degrowth in the postdevelopment convergence: Questions, experiences, and proposals from two Indigenous territories. *Environment and Planning E: Nature and Space, 2*(3), 465–492. https://doi.org/10.1177/2514848618819478

Patel, R., & Moore, J. W. (2017). *A history of the world in seven cheap things: A guide to capitalism, nature, and the future of the planet*. University of California Press.

Puig de la Bellacasa, M. (2017). *Matters of care: Speculative ethics in more than human worlds*. Minnesota: Minnesota University Press.

Ramcilovic-Suominen, S. (2023). Envisioning just transformations in and beyond the EU bioeconomy: Inspirations from decolonial environmental justice and degrowth. *Sustainability Science, 18*(2), 707–722. https://doi.org/10.1007/s11625-022-01091-5

Ramcilovic-Suominen, S., Kröger, M., & Dressler, W. (2022). From pro-growth and planetary limits to degrowth and decoloniality: An emerging bioeconomy policy and research agenda. *Forest Policy and Economics, 144*, 102819. https://doi.org/10.1016/j.forpol.2022.102819

Raworth, K. (2017). *Doughnut economics: Seven ways to think like a 21st-century economist*. Chelsea Green Publishing.

Rodney, W. (2018). *How Europe underdeveloped Africa*. Verso.

Saito, K. (2023). *Marx in the Anthropocene: Towards the idea of degrowth communism*. Cambridge University Press.

Schmelzer, M., Vetter, A., & Vansintjan, A. (2022). *The future is degrowth: A guide to a world beyond capitalism*. Verso.

Singh, N. (2019). Environmental justice, degrowth and post-capitalist futures. *Ecological Economics, 163*, 138–142. https://doi.org/10.1016/j.ecolecon.2019.05.011

Smith, M. N., & Lester, C. A. (2023). From "dependency" to "decoloniality"? The enduring relevance of materialist political economy and the problems of a "decolonial" alternative. *Social Dynamics, 49*(2), 196–219. https://doi.org/10.1080/02533952.2023.2220588

Sovacool, B. K., & Dunlap, A. (2022). Anarchy, war, or revolt? Radical perspectives for climate protection, insurgency and civil disobedience in a low-carbon era. *Energy Research & Social Science, 86*, 102416. https://doi.org/10.1016/j.erss.2021.102416

Spash, C. L. (2021). Apologists for growth: Passive revolutionaries in a passive revolution. *Globalizations, 18*(7), 1123–1148. https://doi.org/10.1080/14747731.2020.1824864

Tharappel, J. (2023). Imperialism and postcolonialism. In F. Obeng-Odoom (Ed.), *Handbook on alternative global development* (pp. 12–37). Edward Elgar Publishing.

Tsing, A. L. (2015). *The mushroom at the end of the world: On the possibility of life in capitalist ruins*. Princeton University Press.

Tuck, E., & Yang, K. W. (2012). Decolonization is not a metaphor. *Decolonization: Indigeneity, Education & Society, 1*(1), 1–40. https://doi.org/10.5555/decolonization.1.1.1

Quijano, A. (2000). Coloniality of power and Eurocentrism in Latin America. *International Sociology, 15*(2), 215–232. https://doi.org/10.1177/0268580900015002005

Vaittinen, T., & Confortini, C. C. (2019). Introduction: Analysing violences in gendered global health. In T. Vaittinen & C. C. Confortini (Eds.), *Gender, global health, and violence: Feminist perspectives on peace and disease* (pp. 1–21). Rowman & Littlefield.

Wahinkpe Topa (Four Arrows), & Narvaez, D. (2022). *Restoring the kinship worldview: Indigenous voices introduce 28 precepts for rebalancing life on planet Earth*. North Atlantic Books.

Wilson, C. A. (1996). *Racism: From slavery to advanced capitalism*. Sage

11
A theory of fragmentism

Akseli Kettula

After 100 years of market and government failure, it is time for capitalism to take a new path. In this chapter, I present a new theory of fragmentism, which is inspired by the debate on market failure and government failure. It is a new theoretical proposal that shifts the focus from the debate to avoiding the root causes of these failures. In fragmentism, the consolidation of economic power and decision-making leads to unpleasant circumstances and thus must be avoided through vast diversification. Both the private and public sectors are unable to escape these adverse effects, which could be traced back to attributes of systemic risks. These risks exist in the economy regardless. Additionally, fragmentism unleashes what Joseph Schumpeter (1942) called creative destruction and enables Adam Smith's (1776) metaphoric invisible hand to operate in the economy in an unforeseen manner. Thus, the essence of fragmentism is a better-functioning market economy along with mitigating systemic risks. Moreover, there are very concrete examples of why both markets and centrally led economies tend to fail. Thus, why not abandon both if there is an alternative way to manage a capitalistic economy?

This theoretical contribution is developed through the following steps: The chapter begins with a description of the current form of the economy and its flaws. More precisely, current globalisation, consolidation, and multinationals are analysed from the perspectives of economic efficiency, democratic decision-making and, perhaps most importantly, in the context of creative destruction (Schumpeter, 1942) and the invisible hand (Smith, 1776). Then, the chapter shifts the context from the present day to the historical debate between market and government failure while connecting the

Kettula, A. (2025). A theory of fragmentism. In A. Kangas, I. Gataulina, M. Poutanen, A. I. Rajala & H-E. Ventovirta (Eds.), *Retheorising capitalism* (pp. 219–242). Tampere University Press.
https://doi.org/10.61201/tup.981

discussion to events in the past. The aim here is to reveal that pre-fragmentistic ideas have been outlined before but have never broken through to mainstream economics.

After a historical representation, both mainstream alternatives are questioned based on empirical evidence and in relation to theories concerning the chaotic nature of capitalism. Chaos is examined from several different perspectives particularly connecting it to capitalism itself. The purpose here is to illustrate how the invisible hand, combined with the dynamics of creative destruction, could harness chaos to improve the economic wellbeing of society. Moreover, attributes of systemic risks, one of the most essential theoretical pillars behind fragmentism, are examined. After this, it is time to return to the idea of fragmentism. The chapter not only presents a new model or theoretical abstractions of arranging capitalistic economy, but it also offers offers some ideas about implementations in practice. Especially alternative routes for managing publicly owned organisations are examined. This section is followed by clarifications to decrease misunderstandings in the context of the new theoretical concept of fragmentism. The chapter concludes with some final thoughts, presented with an evocative touch.

Today, before, and pre-fragmentistic ideas

The first section consists of two different parts. The first part broadly describes the current form of the economy as flawed. It delineates a perspective of the current economic system, within which the ideas concerning fragmentism are easier to understand. In the second part, the historical debate between market and government failure is considered, while connecting the economic academic discussion to events in the past. The aim here is to reveal that pre-fragmentistic ideas have been outlined before but have never broken through to mainstream economics. Fragmentism is not coming out of nowhere; it has been vastly influenced by economic thinkers throughout history, and they deserve to be mentioned and connected to the great debate concerning failures themselves.

The age of multinationals and consolidation

Since Ronald Reagan and Margaret Thatcher took office at the turn of the 1970s and 1980s, (neo)classical economic policies were dominant in the West until the Great Recession of 2008. This rather long period included some earth-shaking economic and (geo)political transformations. The Soviet Union and the Eastern Bloc collapsed, the European Union expanded rapidly in addition to the, perhaps, most influential process: the globalising economy. The globalising economy is an essential piece of globalisation, which could be described as an expansion of interconnections that exceed geographical boundaries among humans on Tellus (Scholte, 2008). The period from around 1980 can be described as an era of globalisation or, more precisely, the second era of globalisation (Das, 2010). However, the timeline and the process of globalisation itself is under debate. For example, Amartya Sen (2002) sees globalisation as a remarkably older phenomenon, a few millennia at a bare minimum. Although there are, as already mentioned, disagreements with the timeline and periods of globalisation, there is a consensus about living in a globalising era today (e.g., Dreher et al., 2008, p. 5). Thus, in this chapter, the era is defined as the current era of globalisation instead of the second era of globalisation.

In the area of current globalisation, business organisations have consolidated into larger and more powerful units, so-called multinationals. This consolidation has reached a rather extreme form. For example, only five multinationals dominated all major business segments worldwide at the turn of the millennium. Moreover, a single company had over 40 percent market share in one-third of them. (Nolan et al., 2002) Rather understandably, such an accumulation of markets raises discussions concerning the functionality of markets. For example, Crouch (2011) argues against competitive markets and claims that market forces have been hijacked by multinationals, and thus free markets have failed while historically they helped the growth of these organisations. Along with these shifts in the power over the economy, this development has led to situations where systemic risks (presented in section 2.2. below) posed by these entities have increased. Nowadays, there are global giants that could cause an economic disaster in the case of rather long business interruptions—not to mention impairments or bankruptcies. For example, if the operations of Microsoft, Alphabet, or Pfizer pauses, the consequences could be catastrophic.

The development of consolidation has been associated with increased problems of systemic risks. For example, Mühlnickel & Weiß (2015) have made interesting findings from the perspective of financial markets. They discovered a remarkable positive relation between two attributes: consolidations and these risks. Especially non-traditional financial functions, a large portfolio of different insurance segments, and the size of the firm were found to correlate with increased systemic risks (Mühlnickel & Weiß, 2015). In addition to systemic risks, consolidation is sometimes harmful also to others—for consumers and other customers. For example, consolidation development has led to rising insurance costs in the United States (Dafny et al., 2012, pp. 1183–1185).

Furthermore, consolidation concentrates global economic power to even more powerful corporations (e.g., Wu, 2018), and thus to their owners and decision-makers, a small number of influential individuals (e.g., Phillips, 2018). This development makes economic decision-making more undemocratic (e.g., Wilks, 2013). Single international business stars, such as Elon Musk, Warren Buffett, Bill Gates, Mark Zuckerberg, and Jeff Bezos, have become richer and richer (Peterson-Withorn, 2024). Hence, they have enough resources to transform entire industries, such as private motoring and social platforms, in our daily lives. It is rather unheard-of that individuals are competing against each other with space programmes, for instance. Furthermore, projects such as Neuralink and metaverse experiments emphasise the significant power of private businessmen. Even the wealthiest nations might struggle to find finance for such projects while battling against increasing public debt regardless of the will of politicians.

Old classics, such as *Das Kapital* (Marx, 1867), seem to be relevant again. Accumulative asset clusters push the petty bourgeoisie and other smaller owners into the margins. Along with increasing power of multinationals, these power-figures are extreme examples of modern accumulation of capital after the 1970s, which is continuing still after the 2007–2008 financial crisis (e.g., Piketty, 2013; Brancaccio et al., 2018), and the current form of the iron law of oligarchy (Michels, 1911). If undemocratic economic decision-making, the accumulation of capital, and the concentration of power inside organisations are not viewed as problematic, the vast increase of systemic risks among single individuals should at least be concerning. If any of these business stars choose the wrong path for the rest of us, unintentionally or not, the whole society could suffer serious consequences.

Pre-fragmentistic ideas and historical economic selections

Even though concerns about consolidation development have increased in rather recent times, they are not especially new. Relatively recently, Crouch (2011) declared global giants as anti-market actors. However, much earlier, right after the Great Depression of 1929, Henry Calvert Simons (1934), a member of the "Old School of Chicago," wrote an academic essay where he describes giant monopolies, along with other similar organisations, as not only the great enemy of the economy but also "the great enemy of democracy" (Simons, 1934, p. 4). In the essay where he also discusses other themes, such as critique against tariff regulations and practised monetary policies, Simons targets monopolies heavily on several occasions. Monopolies are argued to manipulate prices and incomes, which makes them harmful for society. Power imbalances are seen as a fault of gigantic entities. The very first element of Simons' liberal-sounding programme is the "elimination of private monopoly in all its forms" (p. 17). Rather obviously, acquisitions of monopolistic corporations should be prohibited as well (p. 19). He even manifests that too influential groups, monopolies included, oppress and undermine the economy as competition disappears (p. 4). This sounds rather familiar in the context of this chapter. Today, we face the same problems with economic consolidation, and fragmentism gains its inspiration from them.

However, Simons' views did not have much influence on mainstream economic practices. More precisely, the economic theory that gained traction in the early 20th century was Keynesianism, and the role of central governments was increased. However, the transformation was rather slow. For example, as Renshaw (1999, pp. 342–343) describes, New Deal policies did not increase public deficits in the US remarkably until the Second World War, although public sector spending began to diminish unemployment rates in 1934. However, it was rather impossible to be Keynesian before his *The General Theory of Employment, Interest, and Money* (1936) was published. In Europe, the transition was even slower. Moreover, Keynesian economic policies spread country by country: at first to the United Kingdom, Scandinavia, the Netherlands, and France, followed by others such as Italy and Belgium during the 1950s and 1960s (Maes, 2008). Even though Western societies restricted the role of unregulated markets, large corporations remained large. Thus, the core of Simons' message was ignored.

Later, the existence of large companies—more precisely financial institutions—was criticised by Hyman Minsky. He proposed that private banks should remain small and independent. Furthermore, Minsky argued that other private corporations would not remain large without access to larger financial institutions. Large corporations need larger external funding possibilities. (Minsky, 1986, p. 355)

As mentioned above, the economic mainstream shifted towards an increased role of central governments prompted by the Great Depression. Remarkable public sector driven economic programmes were planned and implemented, such as the New Deal before the Second World War. Internationally, Marshall Aid was launched right after the global devastation. As a clarification, big governments were dominant both in the capitalist world and in authoritarian regimes. The era ended with the Oil Crisis, stagflation, and most importantly, the crisis of the strong presence of the public sector, especially in the United States and the United Kingdom. The *laissez-faire* orientated economic school, the Economic School of Chicago, played an impactful role in the transition and critique against existing economic policies, probably most famously in the context of monetary policy (Reichart & Slifi, 2016; De Long, 2004, p. 84) and antitrust policies in the United States (Bradford, et al., 2020; McKenna 2023). Issues with the inefficiency and negative aspects of policies that restricted market forces empowered ideas related to unregulated market forces. As an illustration, Milton Friedman, one of the 20th century's most prominent defenders of free markets, refers more than a few times to Adam Smith, the inventor of liberal economics and the term invisible hand (Smith, 1776), and calls for a return to the idea of *laissez-faire*, to allow markets to be free, in the same context. (e.g., Friedman & Friedman, 1979; Friedman, 1976)

Like their predecessors, Friedman and others neglected to pay attention to the counterforce of the invisible hand, Chandler's (1978) visible hand. Chandler's seminal observation revealed the great shift from small independent companies to large enterprises with several functions and the increasing power of their managers in the United States already during the 19th century. It is debatable whether free markets are free in an environment where the visible hand rules. Unfortunately, the roles of large corporations in the economy were ignored by Friedman and others, again. Ironically, the very same critique by Simons and Minsky was valid despite the drastic change in Western economies since large were allowed to remain large. Policies before the Great Depression failed in limiting power and adverse effects of large organisations as well as policies before the Oil Crisis. Again, the public debate of economics revolved around the question of which one fails less, the government or the market (e.g., Datta-Chaudhuri, 1990; Keech, et al., 2012; Zerbe & McCurdy, 1999). In this discussion, the focus is not on the size of organisations. Hence, the debate tends to be rather useless and even slightly counterproductive. Fractioning the public or the private sector is not represented as an option for *laissez-faire* and Keynesian economics and has been abandoned to the shadows.

Far more dramatic examples of the failures of central planning appeared in the communist world. Mao's Great Leap Forward and the four-year Red Khmer regime in Cambodia were economic and social disasters, as well as the 1930s Kazakh famine Asharshylyk (e.g., Grantseva Ageeva, 2023) in the Soviet Union, approximately concurrent with Holodomor, the starvation of Ukrainians due to Soviet policies. The status of the Holodomor as a genocide of Ukrainians is under scholarly debate (e.g., Andriewsky, 2015). In addition to offering empirical evidence of the failures of communist experiments, they share a unifying factor with capitalistic economies in the 1970s. In the Oil Crisis, centralised publicly driven decision-making failed to handle stagflation at that time. Fortunately, the consequences of this misjudgement were much less severe than in the other above-mentioned cases. These other cases are illustrations of how consolidated economic decision-making could lead to remarkable catastrophes if economic analysis turned out to be inaccurate or purely false. It must be concluded that arranging the economy should not be in the hands of a few individuals or a single governing body. Furthermore, a constantly continuing discussion about how to organise economics is a necessity to avoid such tragedies.

The everlasting debate

The debate between market failure and government failure has existed for nearly a century, and there is still no winner in terms of which one fails less. In this section, I argue that both fail, and the root causes are, in fact, the same. Moreover, the section examines these causes, systemic risks, and their essence. After examining systemic risks and especially their attributes, the section flows to the areas of complexity and uncertainty. Complexity and uncertainty are viewed as an inevitable part of modern human society. Thus, they must be managed as carefully as possible. Management happens by utilising market forces and creative destruction as widely as possible—but within the scope of good chaos. Due to the key role of good chaos, the definition of good and bad chaos is presented. This section's perspectives and theoretical approaches to society overall are crucial in understanding fragmentism and why this new theoretical proposal is needed to replace the great debate.

Market failure or government failure, or both

As described above, the debate between market failure and government failure has been present in economics literature for decades (e.g., Datta-Chaudhuri, 1990). The debate has heated up again after the Great Recession in 2008 and especially the critics of unrestricted globalised markets have become more active and paid more attention to it (e.g., Stiglitz, 2009). However, as described above, both unrestricted markets and heavily centralised economies tend to fail. Given this, the intention of scholarly discussions and analyses should be to avoid failure, not to debate about which one fails less.

When the focus is turned to Simons' and Minsky's perspectives on large corporations and other dominant entities, the view changes vastly. From time to time, bankruptcies and impairments of large companies, even industries, happen. Moreover, from time to time, bailouts have been in the toolbox of economic policies, despite whichever economic school rules in the Western world. To give examples of this, the American military corporation Lockheed Martin was bailed out in 1971, during a time of Keynesian hegemony, and the German energy giant Uniper was also bailed out in 2022, during the current age of globalisation, after suffering drastically reduced gas exports due to the Russo-Ukrainian war. Bailouts, and ending up in situations where decisions to bail out or not to bail out, are unpleasant and costly in any circumstance (e.g., Sjostrom, 2009). Bailouts are always debatable, but sometimes they seem to be against the common good and not justified whatsoever (e.g., Eidenmueller & Valbuena, 2023). Furthermore, it could be rightfully asked whether bailouts are an ineffective use of resources or not. Since bailouts have become a common practice throughout contemporary Western economic history, they increase moral hazard issues. If profits are privatised and losses socialised, the incentive to limit risks is reduced. Moreover, bailouts are restricting one of the greatest forces of capitalism, Joseph Schumpeter's (1942, pp. 81–86) idea of creative destruction.

Besides purely economic problems, large economic entities face issues in the context of social sustainability and democratic decision-making. In these organisations, like in every other entity where large number of stakeholders do not have access, the economic power is in the hands of a few individuals. This is not a problem if the organisation is not so influential that it impacts a remarkable business segment or the economy overall. However, when this is the case, diversified decision-making disappears. This issue applies regardless of the economic sector, from local retail stores to global consulting.

Moreover, along with moral hazard problems and more generic issues with democratic decision-making, challenges with transparency also occur. Especially nowadays, the decision-making of limited liability companies can be hidden rather effectively, no matter whether the corporation is owned publicly or privately. The current form of the limited liability company still exists and, hence, its issues (Tricker, 2011). Thus, forcing corporations under public ownership does not solve the problem. To give an example, because of drastically failed decisions with questionable securities, the publicly owned Finnish aviation company Finavia suffered losses of 34 million euros (Pietiläinen, 2015). The incident was not given public attention before a pilot, Horst Weckström, filed an investigation request to the Police of Finland (Loponen, 2015; Lehtonen, 2016)

Currently, these issues with the feeling of a lack of control over economic power can translate into politics. For example, the Brexit slogan "Take back control" captures the idea that people feel they do not have it (anymore). The construct of sovereign decision-making carried the popularity of leaving the EU years after the Brexit Referendum (Menon & Wager, 2020, p. 279), and probably still does for those who would still vote to leave the EU. The most frequently mentioned premise to vote for Brexit was "the principle that decisions about the UK should be made in the UK" in surveys right after the Brexit Referendum (Ashcroft, 2016; Richards & Heath, 2018), not in Brussels.

Attributes of systemic risks and their impact

Market and government failure have something critical in common: the root causes of both failures are the same. Failures come from the inability to avoid attributes of systemic risks. Thus, the consequences of failure among certain organisations are too severe. Someone might ask: what are these attributes? Cummins and Weiss (2014, p. 493) have introduced three attributes of systemic risk to academic literature. Originally, these were conceptualised by the Financial Stability Board (2009, p. 9), approximately at the time of the Financial Crisis, which started in December 2007. These attributes are size, interconnectedness, and lack of substitutability. Size is a rather straightforward term that is easily understood. However, interconnectedness and lack of substitutability need to be defined in a more comprehensive manner to avoid misunderstandings. The term interconnectedness describes a situation where the struggling organisation drags other significant organisations or even industries down due to its critical ties with them. For example, financial institutions could be connected in such a manner. It is not about the organisation itself, but instead about dependent entities. If there are no ways to find a replacement for the organisation, it has an attribute which is defined as the lack of substitutability. Usually, organisations managing critical infrastructure have this attribute. For example, power grids could be irreplaceable (e.g., Fairley, 2024).

These three attributes are designed for financial markets. Naturally so since the discussion around industries' risks has traditionally included booms and busts. For example, and perhaps most famously, the idea of the structurally unstable cyclic nature of financial markets has been developed by Hyman Minsky (1980). However, it is reasonable to assume that these are also relevant to other areas of society. If comparing the current era of globalisation to the attributes of systemic risks, it becomes rather obvious that organisations with such attributes exist outside financial markets. Moreover, their impact on the world is indeed not diminishing. On the contrary, global giants such as the aforementioned Microsoft, Alphabet, and Pfizer are even larger, interconnected, and possibly even irreplaceable—at least rapidly, if something bad happens.

Complexity and uncertainty—advantages of market economy

Whether living in a capitalistic economic system or not, humankind must face challenges posed by complexity and uncertainty. In the context of this section, Nassim Nicholas Taleb's (2007, pp. 26–37) concepts of Extremistan and Mediocristan prove helpful. A brief simplified illustration is in order. People previously lived in smaller communities, slowly changing environments with more significant geographical and physical restrictions—hence in Mediocristan. Today, the global world with its turbulent shifts and exponential scalability in critical areas from the economy to scientific citations illustrates the turn towards Extremistan. In our society, uncertainty is faced more widely compared to measurable risk. According to Knight, risk is measurable and thus probabilities of outcomes could be accurately measured, unlike in uncertainty where the lack of information prevents such evaluation (Knight, 1921). To make Taleb's concepts more convincing, empirical observations of even the long-term economy and stock market (e.g. Mandelbrot & Hudson, 2004; Day, 1982) show significant turbulence and irregularities. Mediocristan is absent in these empirical datasets, while Extremistan dominates. These effects are applied—regardless of economic periods, ruling economic schools, and forms of arranging society. Moreover, recent crises, such as the COVID-19 pandemic, demonstrate rather well whether we live in Mediocristan or not.

Even though market failure and government failure exist in Western societies, capitalist systems have a significant advantage over the world of Extremistan, complexity, and uncertainty—and this advantage is market forces. Market forces are dynamic and flexible, and they react rapidly to the changing environment. Furthermore, market forces, when applied properly, diversify decision-making and prevent the adverse accumulation of single wrong decisions. If a few individuals choose inaccurate actions, the whole society does not suffer. Furthermore, the most powerful individuals and organisations have resources to impact collective reallocation over the less powerful after the turmoil. In the context of organising economies, the intention should be to diminish their influence after a crisis, not to foster it.

Consumer markets and business-to-business trade do not require capitalism explicitly. However, capitalism extends market forces to organisations effectively and unleashes Schumpeter's creative destruction. According to Schumpeter (1942, p. 82), creative destruction is a process that "revolutionizes the economic structure from within, incessantly destroying the old one, incessantly creating a new one" and this process "is what capitalism consists in and what every capitalist concern has got to live in." Collective ownership structures have a remarkable problem. They vastly restrict the renewability of organisations, since there is only a little on no competition (e.g., Clark & Wildavsky, 1990). This renewability is essential in the world of Extremistan. It should be possible to establish new organisations without severe restrictions and, perhaps more importantly, to discontinue them without almost any limitations. Unfortunately, the current form of capitalism has failed this principle and approved practices in which discontinuation is sometimes almost impossible, and bailouts happen. Thus, creative destruction is not unleashed in a proper manner.

Interestingly, by combining insights from great, but drastically different, economic thinkers such as Keynes, Schumpeter, and Marx, it is possible to draw a conclusion about the structural instability of capitalism. In Keynesian thinking, instability appears in stochastic and cyclical models. Incremental deviance from the economic equilibrium is the basis of Schumpeterian instability. Marxian instability appears in long-term developments such as the accumulation of capital. (Vercelli, 1985) Structural instability can be harmful in a stable and forecastable environment. However, instability is not a weakness if the environment is unstable and hardly predictable, like today's society seems to be. In fact, structural instability could be used as a tool to survive in a chaotic environment. In this section, chaos is divided into good chaos and bad chaos. Characteristics of these different types of chaos are illustrated below (Figure 1).

Good chaos and bad chaos

Good chaos	Bad chaos
Enables all failures • Creative destruction is unleashed	Disables failures of significant organisations • Creative destruction is drastically limited
Disables uncontrollable growth • Systemically risky organisations and asset accumulations are prevented	Enables uncontrollable growth • Society becomes vulnerable for systemic risks in the context of organisations and capital
Benefits from asset bubbles • Small enough to stimulate growth	Drastically suffers from asset bubbles • Large crashes are harmful for the economy
Uses unstable nature as an advantage • Intrinsically matches with capitalism	At the mercy of unstable nature of capitalism • Is contradictionary for the capitalism itself

Figure 1. Good chaos vs. bad chaos

Usually, and also in this chapter, chaos has been viewed as a negative abstraction that should be feared. However, chaos is a creative force and sometimes leads to progression, prosperity, and development. Good chaos exists, and exploiting it is as important as avoiding undesirable outcomes. For example, the fourth industrial revolution, characterised by a rapid advancement in technology, has had undeniably positive outcomes, regardless of its somewhat chaotic nature. Moreover, it seems that small asset bubbles even stimulate economic growth, while large ones obviously do not (Hirano et al., 2014). The gist of the problem is how to limit the cons of chaos while utilising it with Smith's (1776) invisible hand and Schumpeter's (1942) creative destruction, all while tackling the attributes of systemic risk. In other words, how could societies gain the benefits of chaos by limiting bad storms and cycles to ones in water glasses?

Hyman Minsky's (1986) proposal about limiting corporations to small and medium enterprises while maintaining big government seems like an attractive path to pursue while trying to find a solution. Limiting the size of corporations does increase the workability of both creative destruction and the invisible hand. However, it does not solve the problem of government failure. Thus, Minsky is still lacking the answer to how to avoid failures completely. Is this a dead end? Or is there a way to bypass the problem while limiting chaos and gaining from it?

Fragmentism

The theory of fragmentism, which I develop in this section, is a route to escape the debate between market failure and government failure. It extends Minsky's ideas concerning corporations to the public sector. In fragmentism, the central government has two main economic principles: to maintain both itself and the markets diversified. From the perspective of the public sector, the central government should allocate a great number of economic resources to regional decision-makers and municipalities. Furthermore, the regulation of the central government should give significant freedom to smaller units to use money and provide public services.

Since the power of single private and public organisations has been confined by diversification, the undesired consequences of failures have abated. If failures do not cause such significant risks for society, they could be allowed. Thus, the great force, creative destruction, is unleashed in a much wider manner than before. When creative destruction is unleashed, the moral hazard issues of bailouts diminish. Losses cannot be socialised since society does not suffer remarkably from the impairments of a single organisation. Hence, the management of organisations cannot take excessive risks while chasing profits. Some organisations, such as healthcare services, exist in an environment where failures could have serious and inhumane consequences. To avoid these adverse situations and to enable creative destruction as widely as possible, a shared responsibility through regulation should be adopted. The Finnish employer's pension insurance system is a great example of how to implement shared responsibility without restricting creative destruction. If an insurance company collapses, others are required to carry policyholders' insurance covers (Finnish Government, 2021).

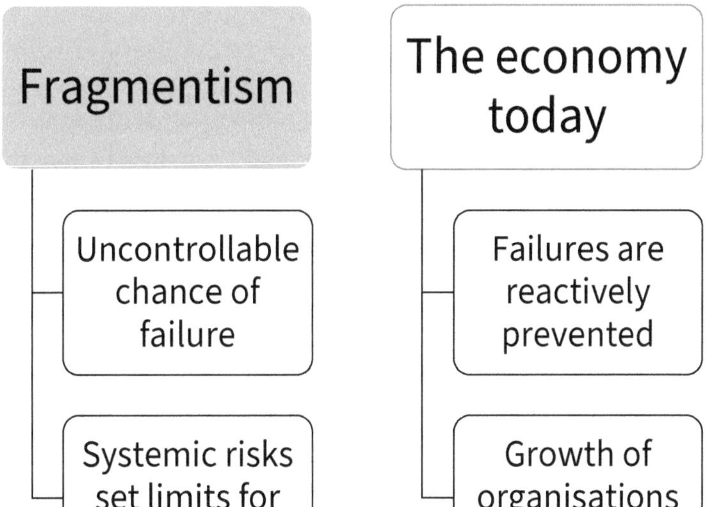

Figure 2. Fragmentism, growth, and failure

Fragmentism, then, turns the current relationship between success and failure upside down (figure 2). It enables the uncontrollable failure of organisations since the adverse effects of the failures are reduced. On the other hand, a key element of fragmentism is the ability to intercept situations where an organisation prospers in an uncontrollable manner. Fragmentism, following three attributes of systemic risks, limits organisations' growth and interconnections, and, if possible, prevents evolutions where organisations become irreplaceable. Hence, if an organisation fails, let it fail; if an organisation prospers, let it prosper—but in a controlled manner. Today, especially due to the remarkable scalability of digital technologies, giant organisations can become uncontrollable in relation to the rest of society. The tail is wagging the dog. In today's economy, organisations do not prosper under control. This leads to circumstances where bailouts might be the only realistic option. There are attempts, nowadays, to avoid these situations by increasing the amount of regulation and supervision. However, this does not reach the root causes like fragmentism does. Furthermore, a heavier burden of regulation and supervision leads to an increasing amount of entry costs (e.g., Gutiérrez & Philippon 2019; Djankov et al., 2002). Thus, they are harmful to the Smithian invisible hand. Moreover, rhetorically, it is possible to ask whether the global giants have more potential to influence regulation than other entities. Unfortunately, the current form of the economic system strengthens the power of huge corporations at the cost of two great forces, those outlined by Schumpeter and Smith.

As to regulation and regulators, fragmentism requires less than the current economy. As described above, the current society must heavily limit markets. While root causes are not recognised and dealt with through proper practices, avoiding bailouts and other negative effects of systemically risky organisations is unsuccessful. Good chaos, creative destruction, and the invisible hand do not explicitly need regulation. In fact, good chaos requires an almost limitless possibility of failure, not more rules. Bad chaos, i.e. systemically risky situations, does need rules. Thus, the core of fragmentistic regulation is prevention: restricting the uncontrollable growth of organisations and their path towards circumstances where they become too interconnected or irreplaceable. If mitigating systemic risks by restricting corporations and public sector entities is executed as carefully as possible, chaos could be used as an advantage. As fragmentism necessarily needs to be implemented against the background of the current society, reactive regulatory mechanisms must be adopted. More precisely, systemically risky companies should be split into smaller entities before fragmentism can be executed successfully. Otherwise, already existing giants remain as they were and invalidate the purpose and logic behind fragmentism.

When markets are more fragmented, there is more supply and demand. Hence, market forces work better overall compared to consolidated markets. Furthermore, like in the context of failure and creative destruction, less regulation is needed. Customers and providers have an opportunity to switch if they are not satisfied with partnerships. Thus, under these conditions, Smith's invisible hand is unleashed in an unforeseen manner. When there is no dependency on certain actors, these actors are unable to exploit their power. Besides restricting the possibility of exploitation, the adverse effect of asymmetric information is also reduced. More rivals and more alternative routes for gathering information can be found. Thus, using asymmetric information for better economic outcomes becomes riskier compared to a situation where there are only a few competitors. Moreover, influential lobbying for public sector decisions becomes significantly harder from the perspective of single entities. There are just more channels to receive adequate knowledge, and thus the power imbalances among producers of information are diminished.

The public sector is not immune to systemic risks and, as illustrated above, even catastrophic decision-making. Hence, if fragmentism is applied in its most complete form, the public sector also needs to be subordinated to the same practices as the private economy. Most straightforwardly, fragmentism is applicable to publicly owned limited liability companies. If the costs of their struggles become too severe, they may also be fractioned into smaller units, if possible. This does not necessarily require the privatisation of these services. Publicly owned organisations are able to compete against each other if circumstances are set properly. Thus, founding more limited liability companies for the public sector in general could be a relevant scenario for implementing fragmentism.

In addition to limited liability companies, keeping the public sector diversified could be done by allocating great amounts of power from larger units to smaller units. In general, this means directing resources from the central government to municipalities and regional governments. Sometimes, sufficient diversification is not achievable without the existing structures of the public sector. In this case, new administrative units are an alternative to consider. If there are simply no sensible options for splitting power organisationally, obligatory and wide stakeholder engagement could be used. Even direct democracy could be applied in the context of the principles of fragmentism.

Through decentralisation, fragmentism can also decrease corruption. However, the relationship between a decentralised economy and corruption is far from linear. On the contrary, if a country struggles with high corruption rates, decentralising public services can lead to even worse outcomes (Freille et al., 2007a). Perhaps the best-known and most influential example is India and its diversification processes (Widmalm, 2008, pp. 55–111). When applying diversification procedures, unitarism has been empirically proven to be extremely useful in the context of decreasing corruption. Moreover, electoral reforms should be halted during the implementation of diversification. Other structural changes do not have the same effect. (Freille et al., 2007b) Regardless of decentralised or centralised decision-making practices, unitarism, or constitutional centralisation, reduces corruption (Gerring & Thacker, 2004). In conclusion, a fully adopted fragmentism requires unitarism, at least to some extent.

Fragmentism resembles the subsidiarity principle but is just extended even further. The principle, according to Føllesdal (1998), "regulates authority within a political order, directing that powers or tasks should rest with the lower-level sub-units of that order unless allocating them to a higher-level central unit would ensure higher comparative efficiency or effectiveness in achieving them." Moreover, it could be interpreted to be included in the United States Bill of Rights as the 10th Amendment (United States Creator, 1789) and is one of the General Principles of the European Union (European Union, 2016, p. 18). Thus, fragmentism helps societies follow one of their own fundamentals in the Western world.

Including active and rather complete public sector decentralisation, fragmentism disperses economic decision-making in the private sector as well. The private sector economy affects society significantly. Thus, enabling more people to get involved in it limits the potential for errors by powerful individuals. Powerful individuals are not that powerful anymore, meaning that they can only mislead smaller organisations to dust, even if their mistakes are drastic. Because the very same diversified form of economy is applied in the public sector, the impact of prominent figures in the public sector vastly reduces, too. Most importantly, in fragmentism, their mistakes do not collapse the economy as a whole. In this system, economic failure can only happen if a remarkable share of decision-makers, whose numbers are increased and extended in the new areas, make severe errors.

If it were completely inevitable that all organisations end up being led by a few, as Michels' (1911) iron law of oligarchy suggests, at least power-figures would rule unsystemically risky organisations. More power-figures leading smaller organisations is a more pleasant outcome than fewer power-figures leading larger ones. Even though this iron law is generally supported by empirical evidence (e.g., Rucht, 1999), it is not seen as "a cascade effect." As Diefenbach (2019) illustrates, there are options to manage the *iron threat of oligarchy,* as he calls it, highlighting the constant presence of the threat and emphasising the importance of active and systematic procedures in various forms as counteractions. Because fragmentism diminishes the impact of the law, it could be seen as another tool to respond to the phenomenon.

The broader vision of diversification is rather simple. However, the principle itself does not yet answer the question of practice. How is diversification executed in fragmentism? What are the criteria that regulators should apply behind the process? To keep the markets diversified, regulators should focus on three attributes causing systemic risks: size, interconnectedness, and lack of substitutability. To diminish the systemic risk of size, officials should limit market shares aggressively whenever possible. Competition regulators already exist. Thus, the kinds of public processes required by fragmentism already exist in some form. If envisioned further, similar public officials could be hired to supervise interconnectedness and the threat of irreplaceability. Furthermore, wide interconnectedness as well as a lack of substitutes should be prevented on a large scale through regulation. There are already tools for monitoring interdependence. They are mostly made for financial markets (e.g., Fry-McKibbin et al., 2018), but there are no obstacles to developing them into a form that is more universally applicable.

The third criterion, lack of substitutes, is intuitively the hardest one to control. In some cases, alternative systems could be built. Secondary roads and powerplants could be used as an example, as well as building a natural gas or biogas network to replace fossil fuels in cars with combustion engines. However, sometimes the attributes of an irreplaceable entity set remarkable challenges for building substitutive systems. They could be simply impossible or too expensive in the context of rational decision-making. For example, constructing a whole new water supply network as a backup appears nearly impossible to execute. Furthermore, some public sector functions, such as the judiciary, can be viewed as irreplaceable. In fragmentism, these exceptions are governed broadly through vast shareholder engagement inspired by the principle of subsidiarity. If, somehow, an industry cannot avoid systemically risky structures to function well, relevant stakeholders, not only shareholders, should be able to widely influence decision-making in private and public organisations. Figure 3 summarises the possible procedures for systemic risk management in practice.

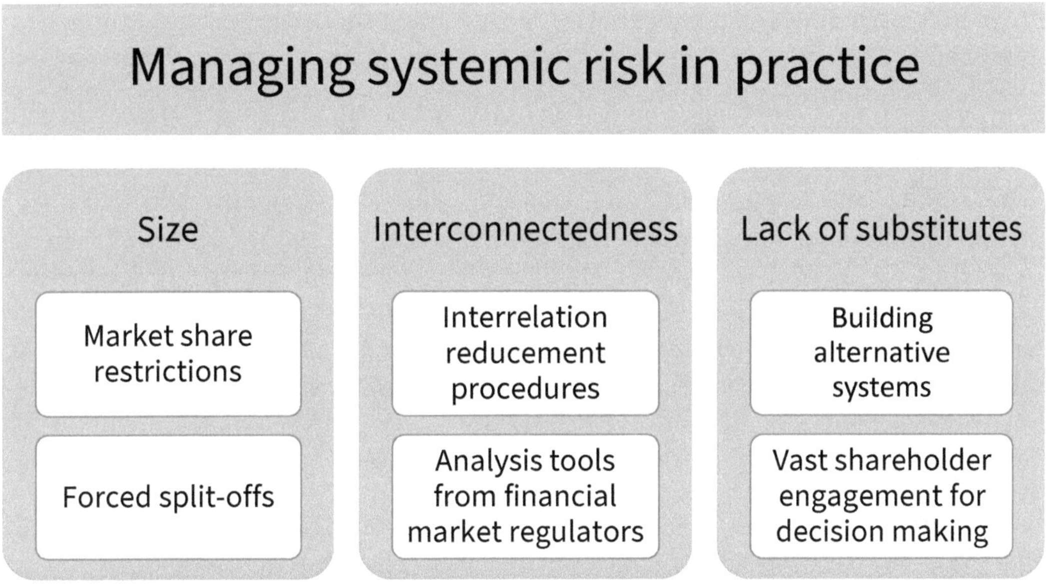

Figure 3. Proposed procedures for managing systemic risks

When observing the lack of resilience in the context of preparing for natural, industrial, or terrorist disasters, Perrow (2007) criticises consolidation development (e.g., pp. 211–247). However, he also offers solutions, and his ideas could be simplified and summarised with the sentence on the very first page: "[W]e should reduce the size of vulnerable targets" (p. 1). For all attributes of systemic risks, a network of small companies introduced by Perrow, could be a fascinating and relevant alternative. The network consists of, obviously, a remarkable number of small firms, but in more detail, it consists of a hub of producers, some distributors, and a vast number of independent suppliers. Most importantly, the solution emphasises restricting interdependencies between organisations. (Perrow, 2007, pp. 302–304) The proposed alternative, while making the economy more resilient to disasters, diminishes attributes of systemic risks at the same time. If companies are small enough, failure is a completely possible outcome. If they are not interconnected with each other, a couple of them cannot drag the whole network down. If the network is well-planned, the risks of a lack of substitutes could also be reduced. Moreover, there is no reason why the concept of the network cannot be extended to the public sector.

Along with being an interesting idea in the context of fragmentism, empirical evidence shows that networks of small firms have been successful in economic development (e.g., Piore & Sabel, 1984). However, this is not a huge surprise in the context of fragmentism. In fragmentism, good chaos, or storms in water glasses, can foster economic wellbeing. Moreover, naturally limiting bad chaos diminishes the harmful side effects of capitalism. Given this, it is rather surprising that these networks have not gained more public attention. When practising fragmentism, they would be a cornerstone of the economy wherever and whenever they could be feasibly structured.

Even though rules and practices of fragmentism are applied, as suggested above, to public and private sectors, there is a threat of remaining systemic risky structures. If a single person, family, investment fund, or any entity has a systemically risky power to influence the economy through ownership, the advantages of fragmentism diminish. Fortunately, financial markets, such as real estates and natural resources, along with other capital-intensive markets, are markets despite their cumulative nature. Hence, the very same procedures presented in figure 3 above are in the toolbox. If a single owner has a share of ownership, which is found to be systemically risky in the context of a certain industry or the economy overall, regulators set obligatory requirements to reduce the amount of shares in a certain period. If a single owner seems to be at the centre of too interconnected financial instruments, such as subprime loans, these instruments are dismantled reasonably. If an owner's capital seems to be irreplaceable for certain industry, alternative capital systems should be put in place, or vast shareholder engagement must be applied.

Overall, financial markets are quick to adjust, and buyers appear when the price is attractive. Due to abolishing systemically risky accumulation of capital, prices drop, since the supply of capital is decreased. Thus, smaller investors and a larger number of individuals have access to the shares, which they previously did not. There is less capital in competing these assets, since systemically risky owners cannot buy and hold them anymore. Marx (1848) himself saw a conflict between capitalists; as the result of the accumulation of capital, more and more smaller capitalists drop to the proletariat inexorably. Incidentally, fragmentism mildly reverses this development and sets limits to the accumulation. Capital cannot be accumulated at the costs of attributes of systemic risks. Thus, these attributes constitute a ceiling that cannot be exceeded. As an annotation, if the ownership structure is too complicated and the owner cannot be identified, regulators should see it automatically as dangerous in the context of systemic risks and treat it accordingly.

If Vercelli's (1985) three elements of structural instability and three attributes of systemic risks are combined according to fragmentism, the conclusion is rather surprising. Using the attributes, all three elements can be detained in the world of good chaos (figure 1). Keynesian stochastic instability is used as an advantage in the form of small asset bubbles. Large bubbles are severely less likely due to vast mitigation of systemic risks. The accumulation of capital is restricted with the attributes of systemic risks—like the adverse effects of creative destruction. The attributes give freedom to these instabilities to do whatever they do—but in water glasses. Individuals, owners, and organisations have the freedom to fail.

For avoiding misunderstandings and some final thoughts

Since fragmentism is a proposal for a new theoretical framework, some clarifications need to be expressed for the sake of avoiding misunderstandings. First, proper diversification requires disconnection from interdependence within industries. Since business segments, such as financial markets, can cause economic turmoil on their own, properly adhering to fragmentism requires practices that prevent society from falling into the interdependency trap.

Second, the fragmentation of the capitalistic world has a slightly more complicated relationship to fragmentism than would be expected at first sight. Fragmentation, which was represented in a framework by Jones and Kierzkowski (1990), means splitting different processes of production into smaller parts, fragments. Thus, it makes supply chains and production more sophisticated and interconnected with certain locations and societies. In fragmentism, fragmentation itself is neither desired nor undesired if it does not lead to circumstances where systemically risky structures are formed. As mentioned above, interconnectedness is one of the key elements of systemic risks. Thus, if there are several alternative suppliers to potentially replace every link in the supply chain, fragmentation is not a problem in and of itself. On the other hand, fragmentation might prove useful in the context of fragmentism, since the concentration of manufacturing processes on a single producer is not an ideal outcome, to say the least.

Some Marxist thinkers, such as Ralph Miliband and David Harvey, have also taken part in the discussion about fragmentation. David Harvey (2001) sees fragmentation as a natural characteristic of capitalism and extends it throughout capitalistic societies due to the accumulation of capital as well as forced and continuous profit seeking. Miliband (1969, 265) argues that fragmentation of economic power is an inaccurate statement and that consolidation of power exists. As a clarification, Harvey does not deny this hypothesis. From the perspective of fragmentism, systemically risky organisations and too powerful individuals are harmful. Thus, if the accumulation of capital leads to their presence, it is undesirable. However, fragmentism does not argue where fragmentation in its various forms exists and where it does not. The focus is on Vercelli's (1985) three elements of instability, not on fragmentation.

Third, it is also crucial to understand that, in fragmentism, the overall proportional size of the public sector is not the most relevant issue. Therefore, fragmentism can be applied by economic liberals as well as by those with leftist orientations. These traditional political perspectives could both find arguments that support a transition towards fragmentism. For economic liberals, fragmentism enables an economy where there is less regulation and intervention. Fragmentism does not imply more regulation, just better regulation. As Simons (1934, p. 3) argues, "[T]he existence (and preservation) of a competitive situation in private industry makes possible a minimizing of the responsibilities of the sovereign state." The vision is to unleash market forces, not to restrict them. Moreover, fragmentism distributes public sector decision-making to smaller units. Hence, in it, there is no one large, centralised government that could disturb the private economy.

For leftist political actors, fragmentism could appear as a solution against the increased power of multinationals. Furthermore, powerful businessmen would be less powerful in fragmentism. Conversely, other people would have more influence in the private sector economy. For example, Ward and Guglielmo's (2021) concept of pop-socialism could apply fragmentism as a tool to activate people through the involvement of private sector decision-making. Proposed procedures for managing systemic risks (figure 3) can be used as a guideline for implementing the involvement soundly—in the context of irreplaceability at least. Moreover, fragmentism offers the left a path to maintain the globalised world while restricting some of its unpleasant consequences, such as the dominance of corporations. There is no need to reverse globalisation if it can be fixed properly.

Extending fragmentistic regulation to capital markets (figure 3) creates an attractive option for the problem of highly concentrated capital. Specific criteria concerning systemically risky ownership are not set in fragmentism. Hence, it is completely possible to limit accumulation, even rather heavily if it is rationalised according to the three attributes of systemic risks. Fragmentism offers tools for the left to pose a challenge to whether traditional conservative economic policies support global corporatism rather than economic freedom. Significant accumulation of wealth and capital has the potential to lead to systemically risky structures and thus hinder the work of creative destruction and the invisible hand.

Fourth, fragmentism recognises the great force of creative destruction as initially theorised by Schumpeter. Therefore, fragmentism is not market socialism. Rather, it is a new theoretically structured form of capitalism. Technically, the form of ownership is irrelevant in fragmentism. It permits private and public ownership. The ownership structure must just allow for the failure of organisations. Consequently, not all global giants are contractionary from the perspective of fragmentism. For example, globally, the automotive industry is very competitive and rather immune to systemic risks. Obviously, territorial issues exist, and they should be dealt with according to the regulative principles of fragmentism. Fragmentism does not dismiss economies of scale and their benefits (e.g., Robinson, 1958, pp. 26–27; McGee, 2014; Caves & Christensen, 1988). Only when the principle of economies of scale conflicts with attributes of systemic risks should fragmentistic regulation be adopted.

Fifth, fragmentism is not ordoliberalism either. Fragmentism is a response to Vercelli's (1985) structural instability by using three attributes of systemic risks

(Financial Stability Board, 2009) as a tool. Furthermore, in fragmentism, the public sector must keep itself diversified. A decentralised state is not necessarily strong. On the contrary, the strong state is seen as an essential part of well-functioning society in ordoliberalism; it must be protected from others, for example, private equity and advocacy groups (Hien, 2013, p. 351). Otherwise, it is “at the mercy of market forces” (Bonefeld 2012, 634) and other threats such as labour unions. In preventing market-dominating positions (Lenel, 1976) and the wide role of the competition authority (Krieger & Nientiendt, 2023), ordoliberalism has undoubtedly similarities compared to fragmentism. However, the attributes of systemic risks, especially interconnectedness and irreplaceability, can exist without market domination. Thus, fragmentism extends the power of regulators to such sectors where ordoliberalistic views do not reach.

Sixth, fragmentism does not explicitly mean radical reforms in the context of globalisation. The interesting point in the current era of globalisation is that only a few multinationals have truly expanded globally. Right after the Great Recession of 2008, Rugman and Verbeke (2009) wrote in *The Oxford Handbook of International Business* that even among the top 500 companies, only nine could be considered *de facto* worldwide when observed in the context of significant sales activity and the number of countries. Furthermore, 320 out of 500 gained more than 80 percent of their revenue from domestic markets. (Rugman & Verbeke, 2009) Thus, even though the idea of restricting the global expansion of business might sound rather radical at first sight, in practice it would only concern a very limited group of organisations. As an annotation, fragmentism is not against globalisation *ipso facto*. On the contrary, fragmentism encourages releasing the forces of the free market and creative destruction as widely as possible.

For almost a century, large organisations and central economic planning have put us in trouble. This has been accompanied by a seemingly everlasting debate about which one fails less: free markets or central economic decision-making. However, both have undoubtedly failed and, ultimately, the root causes are the same. As has been discussed above, three attributes of systemic risks make the economy vulnerable and centralised decision-making dangerous. No more bailouts or unnecessary economic crises are needed. Moreover, socialising losses while privatising profits is not fair. Simultaneously, for a better-functioning economy, the invisible hand and creative destruction should be unleashed, since they deserve to be free. They have been chained by bad chaos in addition to the visible hand, and it is time to end that era. Fragmentism, which enables good chaos, puts Adam Smith, along with Joseph Schumpeter, in the spotlight again.

References

Andriewsky, O. (2015). Towards a decentred history: The study of the Holodomor and Ukrainian historiography. *East/West: Journal of Ukrainian Studies, 2*(1), 18–52. https://doi.org/10.21226/T2301N

Ashcroft, M. (2016, June 24). How the United Kingdom voted on Thursday ... and why. *Lord Ashcroft Polls.* https://lordashcroftpolls.com/2016/06/how-the-united-kingdom-voted-and-why/

Bonefeld, W. (2012). Freedom and the strong state: On German ordoliberalism. *New Political Economy, 17*(5), 633–656. https://doi.org/10.1080/13563467.2012.656082

Bradford, A., Chilton, A. S., & Lancieri, F. M. (2020). The Chicago School's limited influence on international antitrust. *University of Chicago Law Review 87*(2), 297–329. https://doi.org/10.7910/DVN/WB7KPY

Brancaccio, E., Giammetti, R., Lopreite, M., & Puliga, M. (2018). Centralization of capital and financial crisis: A global network analysis of corporate control. *Structural Change and Economic Dynamics 45*(1), 94–104. https://doi.org/10.1016/j.strueco.2018.03.001

Caves, D. W., & Christensen L. R. (1988). The importance of economies of scale, capacity utilization, and density in explaining interindustry differences in productivity growth. *Logistics and Transportation Review 24*(1), 3–32.

Chandler, A. J. (1978). *The visible hand: The managerial revolution in American business.* Belknap Press.

Clark, J., & Wildavsky, A. (1990). Why communism collapses: The moral and material failures of command economies are intertwined. *Journal of Public Policy 10*(4), 361–390. https://doi.org/10.1017/S0143814X0000605X

Crouch, C. (2011). *The strange non-death of neo-liberalism.* John Wiley & Sons, Ltd.

Cummins, J. D., & Weiss, M. A. (2014). Systemic risk and the U.S. insurance sector. *The Journal of Risk and Insurance, 81*(3), 489–527. https://doi.org/10.1111/jori.12039

Dafny, L., Duggan, M., & Subramaniam, R. (2012). Paying a premium on your premium? Consolidation in the US health insurance industry. *American Economic Review, 102*(2), 1161–1185. https://doi.org/10.1257/aer.102.2.1161

Das, D. K. (2010). Globalisation: Past and present. *Economic Affairs, 30*(1), 66–70. https://doi.org/10.1111/j.1468-0270.2009.01976.x

Datta-Chaudhuri, M. (1990). Market failure and government failure. *Journal of Economic Perspectives 4*(3), 25–39. https://doi.org/10.1257/jep.4.3.25

Day, R. (1982). Irregular growth cycles. *The American Economic Review, 72*(3), 406–414. https://doi.org/10.1016/0304-3932(93)90008-4

De Long, J. B. (2000). The triumph of monetarism? *Journal of Economic Perspectives, 14*(1), 83–94. https://doi.org/10.1257/jep.14.1.83

Diefenbach, T. (2019). Why Michels' 'iron law of oligarchy' is not an iron law – and how democratic organisations can stay 'oligarchy-free'. *Organization Studies 40*(4), 545–562. https://doi.org/10.1177/0170840617751007

Djankov, S., La Porta, R., Lopez-de-Silanes, F., & Shleifer, A. (2002). The regulation of entry. *Quarterly Journal of Economics, 117*(1), 1–37. https://doi.org/10.1162/003355302753399436

Dreher, A., Gaston N., & Martens P. (2008). *Measuring globalisation: Gauging its consequences.* Springer.

Fairley, P. (2024, April 15). There is a part of modern life that is so essential armies should never attack it again. *New York Times.* https://www.nytimes.com/2024/04/15/opinion/ukraine-russia-power-grid.html

Financial Stability Board. (2009). *Guidance to assess the systemic importance of financial institutions, markets and instruments: Initial considerations.* https://www.fsb.org/2009/11/r_091107d/

Freille, S., Haque, M. E., & Kneller, R. (2007a). Decentralisation, corruption and economic development. *SSRN.* http://dx.doi.org/10.2139/ssrn.985638

Freille, S., Haque, M. E., & Kneller, R. (2007b). Federalism, decentralisation and corruption. *SSRN.* http://dx.doi.org/10.2139/ssrn.951110

Fry-McKibbin, R., Hsiao, C. Y-L., & Martin, V. L. (2018). *Measuring financial interdependence in asset returns with an application to euro zone equities* (CAMA Working Paper, 5). Centre for Applied Macroeconomic Analysis. https://cama.crawford.anu.edu.au/publication/cama-working-paper-series/12093/measuring-financial-interdependence-asset-returns

Eidenmueller, H. G. M., & Paz Valbuena, J. (2023). Taxes blown in the wind? The Siemens Gamesa bailout. *European Corporate Governance Institute – Law Working Paper, 745*, 1–15. http://dx.doi.org/10.2139/ssrn.4653156

European Union. (2016). 12016M005/2016. *Consolidated version of the Treaty on European Union. Title I – Common Provisions. Article 5 (ex Article 5 TEC).* http://data.europa.eu/eli/treaty/teu_2016/art_5/oj

Finnish Government. (2021). *Hallituksen esitys 28/2021.* Ministry of Justice of Finland. https://www.finlex.fi/fi/esitykset/he/2021/20210028

Friedman, M. (1976). *Adam Smith's relevance for 1976.* University of Chicago.

Friedman, M., & Friedman, R. D. (1979). *Free to choose.* Harcourt.

Føllesdal, A. (1998). Survey article: Subsidiarity. *The Journal of Political Philosophy* 6(2), 190–218. https://doi.org/10.1111/1467-9760.00052

Gerring, J., & Thacker, S.C. (2004). Political institutions and corruption: The role of unitarism and parliamentarism. *British Journal of Political Science (34)*2, 295–330. https://doi.org/10.1017/S0007123404000067

Grantseva Ageeva, V. (2023). *Russia's exceptional role in managing Kazakhstan's postcolonial identity.* Routledge.

Gutiérrez, G., & Philippon, T. (2019). The failure of free entry. *NBER Working Paper, 26001*, 1–48. https://doi.org/10.2139/ssrn.3408936

Harvey, D. (2001). *Spaces of capital: Towards a critical geography.* Routledge.

Hien, J. (2013). The ordoliberalism that never was. *Contemporary Political Theory, 12*(4), 349–358. http://dx.doi.org/10.1057/cpt.2013.19

Hirano T., Inaba, M., & Yanagawa, N. (2014). Asset bubbles and bailouts. *Journal of Monetary Economics, 7*(6), 7189. http://dx.doi.org/10.1016/j.jmoneco.2015.09.008

Jones, R. W., & Kierzkowski, H. (1990). The role of services in production and international trade: A theoretical framework. In R. Jones & A. Krueger (Eds.), *The political economy of international trade* (pp. 233–253). Basil Blackwell.

Keech, W. R., Munger, M. C., & Simon, C. (2012, March 8–11). *Market failure and government failure* [Conference presentation]. World Congress of the Public Choice Societies, Miami, FL, United States.

Keynes, J. M. (1936). *The general theory of employment, interest and money.* Palgrave Macmillan.

Knight, F. H. (1921). *Risk, uncertainty and profit.* The Riverside Press.

Krieger, T., & Nientiedt, D. (2023). The renaissance of ordoliberalism in the 1970s and 1980s. *Constitutional Political Economy,* 1–16. https://doi.org/10.1007/s10602-023-09411-2

Lehtonen, M-O. (2016, September 15). Tämä mies nosti Finavian johdannaiset pöydälle: "Kuka tekee näin idioottimaisia sopimuksia?". *Kauppalehti.* https://www.kauppalehti.fi/uutiset/tama-mies-nosti-finavian-johdannaiset-poydalle-kuka-tekee-nain-idioottimaisia-sopimuksia/38e739d4-ab88-3321-96dc-f0e261d6c9f3

Lenel, H. O. (1976). Perfect and free competition as guiding principles in competition policy towards large enterprises. In A. P. Jacquemin & H. W. de Jong (Eds.), *Markets, corporate behaviour and the state: International aspects of industrial organization* (pp. 316–323). Springer.

Loponen, T. (2015, April 13). Tutkintapyyntö Finavian johdosta. *Koillis-Helsingin Lähitieto.* https://www.lahitieto.fi/2015/04/13/tutkintapyynto-finavian-johdosta/

Maes, I. (2008). The spread of Keynesian economics: A comparison of the Belgian and Italian experiences (1945–1970). *Journal of the History of Economic Thought, 30*(4), 491–509. https://doi.org/10.1017/S105383720800045X

Mandelbrot, B. B., & Hudson, R. L. (2004). *The (mis)behavior of markets: a fractal view of risk, ruin, and reward.* Profile Books.

Marx, K. (1867). *Das Kapital: Kritik der politischen Ökonomie.* Meissner.

Marx, K., & Engels, F. (1848). *The communist manifesto.* Kommunistischer Arbeiterbildungsverein.

McGee, J. (2014). Economies of scale. In C. L. Cooper (Ed.), *Wiley encyclopedia of management* (3rd ed., pp. 1–6). John Wiley & Sons, Ltd.

McKenna, F. (2023, August 7). What made the Chicago School so influential in antitrust policy? *Chicago Booth Review.* https://www.chicagobooth.edu/review/what-made-chicago-school-so-influential-antitrust-policy

Menon A., & Wager, A. (2020). Taking back control: sovereignty as strategy in Brexit politics. *Territory, Politics, Governance, 8*(2), 279–284. https://doi.org/10.1080/21622671.2019.1702895

Michels, R. (1911). *Zur Soziologie des Parteiwesens in der modernen Demokratie; Untersuchungen über die oligarchischen Tendenzen des Gruppenlebens.* Werner Klinkhardt.

Miliband, R. (1969). *The state in capitalist society.* Basic Books.

Minsky, H. (1980). The finance and profits: the changing nature of American business cycles. *The Business Cycle and Public Policy, 1929–80.* 209–244. https://digitalcommons.bard.edu/hm_archive/63

Minsky, H. (1986). *Stabilizing an unstable economy.* McGraw-Hill.

Mühlnickel, J., & Weiß, G. N.F. (2015). Consolidation and systemic risk in the international insurance industry. *Journal of Financial Stability, 18*(1), 187–202. https://doi.org/10.1016/j.jfs.2015.04.005

Nolan, P., Sutherland, D., & Zhang, J. (2002). The challenge of the global business revolution. *Contributions to Political Economy, 21*(1), 91–110. https://doi.org/10.1093/cpe/21.1.91

Perrow, C. (2007). *The next catastrophe.* Princeton University Press.

Peterson-Withorn, C. (2024, April 2). Forbes' 38th annual World's Billionaires List: Facts and figures 2024. *Forbes.* https://www.forbes.com/sites/chasewithorn/2024/04/02/forbes-38th-annual-worlds-billionaires-list-facts-and-figures-2024/

Phillips, P. (2018). *Giants: The global power elite.* Seven Stories Press.

Pietiläinen, T. (2015, November 11). Finavia teki johdannaisilla 34 miljoonan euron tappiot – myönsi isot puutteet riskinhallinnassa. *Helsingin Sanomat.* https://www.hs.fi/talous/art-2000002868751.html

Piketty, T. (2013). *Capital in the twenty-first century.* Harvard University Press.

Piore, M. J., & Sabel. C. F. (1984). *The second industrial divide: Possibilities for prosperity.* Basic Books.

Reichart, A., & Slifi, A. (2016). The influence of monetarism on Federal Reserve policy during the 1980s. *Cahiers d'économie politique (70)*1, 107–150. https://doi.org/10.3917/cep.070.0107

Renshaw, P. (1999). Was there a Keynesian economy in the USA between 1933 and 1945? *Journal of Contemporary History, 34*(3), 337–364. https://doi.org/10.1177/002200949903400302

Richards, L., & Heath, A. (2018). *Sovereignty and co-operation: Different dimensions of Brexit. Brexit and public opinion.* The UK in a Changing Europe. https://ukandeu.ac.uk/wp-content/uploads/2018/01/Public-Opinion.pdf

Robinson, E.A.G. (1958). *The structure of competitive industry.* University of Chicago Press.

Rucht, D. (1999). Linking organization and mobilization: Michels's iron law of oligarchy reconsidered. *Mobilization: An International Quarterly, 4*(2), 151–169. https://doi.org/10.17813/maiq.4.2.l2680365q32h6616

Rugman, A. P., & Verbeke, A. (2009). Competitiveness, and the multinational enterprise. In A. P. Rugman (Ed.), *The Oxford handbook of international Business* (2nd ed., pp. 146–180). Oxford University Press.

Scholte, J. A. (2008). Defining globalisation. *World Economy, 31*(11), 1471–1502. https://doi.org/10.1111/j.1467-9701.2007.01019.x

Schumpeter, J. (1942). *Capitalism, socialism, and democracy.* Harper & Brothers.

Sen, A. (2002). How to judge globalism. *The American Prospect 13*(1). https://prospect.org/features/judge-globalism/

Simons, H. C. (1934). *A positive program for laissez faire.* Chicago University Press.

Sjostrom, W. K. (2009). The AIG bailout. *Washington and Lee Law Review, 66*(1), 943–991. https://scholarlycommons.law.wlu.edu/wlulr/vol66/iss3/2

Smith, A. (1776). *The wealth of nations.* W. Strahan and T. Cadell.

Stiglitz, J. (2009). Government failure vs. market failure: Principles of regulation. In E. J. Balleisen & D. A. Moss (Eds.), *Government and markets toward a new theory of regulation* (1st ed., pp. 13–51). Cambridge University Press

Taleb, N. N. (2007). *The black swan: The impact of the highly improbable.* Random house Inc.

Tricker, R. (2011). Re-inventing the limited liability company. *Corporate Governance: An International Review, (19)*4, 384–393. https://doi.org/10.1111/j.1467-8683.2011.00851.x

United States Creator. (1789). *Bill of Rights*. Library of Congress. https://www.loc.gov/item/2021667570/

Vercelli, A. (1985). Keynes, Schumpeter, Marx and the structural instability of capitalism. *Cahiers d'économie politique, 10–11*, 279–304. https://doi.org/10.3406/cep.1985.1013

Ward, B., & Guglielmo, M. (2021). Pop-socialism: A new radical left politics? Evaluating the rise and fall of the British and Italian left in the anti-austerity age. *The British Journal of Politics and International Relations, 24*(4), 1–16. https://doi.org/10.1177/13691481211044643

Widmalm, S. (2008). *Decentralisation, corruption and social capital: From India to the West.* Sage Publications.

Wilks, S. (2013). *The political power of the business corporation*. Edward Elgar Publishing Limited.

Wu, T. (2018). *The curse of bigness: How corporate giants came to rule the world.* Columbia Global Reports.

Zerbe, R. O., & McCurdy, H. E. (1999). The failure of market failure. *Journal of Policy Analysis and Management, 18*(4), 558–578. https://doi.org/10.1002/(SICI)1520-6688(199923)18:4<558::AID-PAM2>3.0.CO;2-U

Part IV
Reconceptualising

Mikko Poutanen & Iuliia Gataulina

Reconceptualising involves rethinking and redefining existing concepts, theories, or frameworks. Integral to retheorising, reconceptualising as a process often requires exploring alternative viewpoints and questioning established assumptions that may relate, for example, to ontological, ethical, or temporal dimensions of thought. Old concepts and vocabularies can yet be fruitfully repurposed to describe changed circumstances or ways of thinking and being. The chapters in this part of the book propose to retheorise capitalism through reconceptualising the foundations of our analytical work, its temporal, ethical, and ontological dimensions. On one hand, this entails refining the conceptual tools needed to understand the temporal composition of capitalism as a dynamic social system in flux (cf. Sewell, 2008). On the other hand, it involves 'troubling' the onto-epistemological assumptions of theorising: What can the economy—and economic practices—be if we depart from the ontologies of capitalism (cf. Enderle, 2020; Miller, 2013) and instead reconceptualise economies through Indigenous or Islamic ontological systems?

Mariam Khawar's chapter "(Re)theorising heterodoxies: Labour in Islamic economic philosophy" (Chapter 12) reconceptualises capitalism by way of offering a perspective often overlooked: Islamic economic philosophy. The chapter draws on economic philosophy and ethics outlined in Islamic texts and developed by Islamic thinkers to offer a more diverse perspective to capitalism. The chapter further uncovers blind spots regarding gender in Islamic economic philosophy. Khawar connects theology, ethics and economics specifically to the question of labour to argue that Islamic tradition can enrich the diversity of theoretical discussions on capitalism, for instance, by highlighting spiritual emancipation. The chapter further points toward existing tensions between the Global North and South also in terms of analyses of capitalism.

Chapter 13 by Edemilson Paraná, "Financialised digitalisation, digitalised financialisation" reconceptualises a temporal composition of capitalism, which has entered a new stage characterised by neoliberalism, digitalisation, and financialisation, while keeping some of its key elements intact. In other words, Paraná approaches the advanced digitalisation of social processes and interactions as a conceptually distinct type of capitalism. The chapter develops this reconceptualisation by inquiring into the complex interplay of technological dominance and financial hegemony. The chapter exemplifies how enhancing our conceptual ability to better detect ongoing dynamics of transformation within capitalism lends itself to potent retheorisations.

The third chapter in this section, "Re-indigenising kuku (green-lipped mussel) economies in Aotearoa (New Zealand)" (Chapter 14) by Georgia McLellan, Cory Tuhoro-Bodey and Anataia van Leeuwen, argues against misrepresenting the indigenous economies as some variant of capitalism. Through a reconceptualising approach, the chapter reminds us that the capitalocentric understanding of 'the economy' has become intimately entangled with neo-colonial projects of government and resource management. While indigenous economies are undermined by the capitalist economic-social relations, they are not completely subsumed by them. The chapter specifically focuses on the economy of Māori, indigenous peoples of New Zealand. In this chapter, the 'Māori economy' is re-framed and re-indigenised by drawing from a whakapapa indigenous relational episto-methodology.

References

Enderle G. (2000). Whose ethos for public goods in the global economy? An exploration in International Business Ethics. *Business Ethics Quarterly*, 10(1), 131–144. https://doi.org/10.2307/3857700

Miller, E. (2013). Community economy: Ontology, ethics, and politics for radically democratic economic organizing. *Rethinking Marxism, 25*(4), 518–533. https://doi.org/10.1080/08935696.2013.842697

Sewell, W. H. (2008). The temporalities of capitalism. *Socio-Economic Review, 6*(3), 517–537. https://doi.org/10.1093/ser/mwn007

12
(Re)Theorising heterodoxies
Labour in Islamic economic philosophy

Mariam Khawar

The past two decades, marked by ongoing global crises and escalating inequality, have sparked significant discourse advocating for diverse exploration in economic thinking, particularly within the field of global political economy. A fascinating space for such exploration is the discipline of Islamic economics. Since the late 19th century, there has been a notable rise in research interest and subsequent development in modern Islamic economics, particularly in banks and financial institutions throughout the 20th century (Iqbal & Llewellyn, 2002; Iqbal & Mirakhor, 2011; Zaman, 2009). More recently, there has been a surge of interest, coinciding with a global curiosity for heterodox economic thought following the financial crises of the 2000s (Ahmed et al., 2014; Diwany & Ahmad, 2010). However, this research interest has largely neglected the pressing needs for theoretical development, focusing primarily on Islamic financial institutions, banking and related products and regulations. Similarly overlooked is the discourse on meta-theory, addressing issues of ontology, epistemology, and methodology. This chapter is part of a broader research project seeking to explore Islamic economics beyond the conventional categories found within the discipline, which often consist of either apologetics or critiques of capitalism. It aims to foster a more productive exploration of economic philosophy, advocating for advancements in philosophical discourse.

Islamic economics is deeply rooted in the broader worldview and has been part of the Islamic discourse since the very inception of the faith in the 7th century. During the classical period of Islam, which spans roughly from the 8th to the 14th

Khawar, M. (2025). (Re)Theorising heterodoxies: Labour in Islamic economic philosophy. In A. Kangas, I. Gataulina, M. Poutanen, A. I. Rajala & H-E. Ventovirta (Eds.), *Retheorising capitalism* (pp. 245–262). Tampere University Press. https://doi.org/10.61201/tup.981

century, economic thought flourished as part of the broader intellectual and cultural developments of the Islamic world. Prominent scholars such as al-Ghazali (1058–1111), Ibn Khaldun (1332–1406), and Ibn Taymiyyahh (1263–1328) made significant contributions to economic thought during the classical period, addressing issues related to taxation, public finance, property rights, labour, and the role of the state in the economy. In the post-classical period scholars such as Shah Waliullah al-Dihlawi (1703–1762), furthered the intellectual heritage of Islamic economics. From the late 19th to the 20th century Islamic economics played a significant role in the anti-colonial struggles in various Muslim-majority regions during the 20th century. Scholars such as Abul A'la Maududi (1903–1979), Muhammad Baqir al-Sadr (1935–1980), and Ali Shariati (1933–1977) used Islamic economic principles as a framework for resistance against colonial powers and as a means of promoting self-sufficiency and independence.

Though initially a cornerstone in the fight against imperialist oppression, economic thought within Islam has evolved. A cursory examination of current Islamic economic and financial institutions reveals a lack of revolutionary thought or claim. Islamic banks, the primary institutions in this structure, are far from radical. They operate fully within the prevailing structure of the global economic order (Hanieh, 2011). This same trend extends to research, teaching, and practice within the Islamic intellectual sphere. The transformation of Islamic economics from a space of struggle to a sub-category of conventional finance is a noteworthy example of the absorption of alternative economic ideas into neoliberal economics. Unfortunately, this assimilation has been detrimental to the broader tradition of economic thinking within Islam. The singular focus on the development of religiously approved financial instruments, banking practices, profitability without interest rates, and catering to a consumption-centric market has overshadowed other critical areas of inquiry.

To break this impasse, in this chapter, I would like to analyse a pertinent aspect of economic thought: labour. The goal of my research is to bring forth the complexity of Islamic economic philosophy to i) engage anew with neglected theories in Islamic economic thought and ii) introduce Islamic economic philosophy into the discipline of Global Political Economy to broaden the discipline beyond its Eurocentric approaches. Eurocentrism is a worldview that places Europe at the centre of historical, cultural, and intellectual development while marginalising or ignoring the contributions and perspectives of non-European societies and cultures (Amin, 2009). Addressing Eurocentrism in GPE requires a concerted effort to diversify perspectives and critically examine the underlying assumptions and biases inherent in dominant economic theories and narratives.

This piece is part of this multidisciplinary effort. In examining labour from a global political economy perspective, I will endeavour to provide a new understanding of labour in Islamic economic philosophy, one that centralises the humane aspect of work and focuses on work as an aspect of spiritual enlightenment and central to the discussions of a moral, sustainable economy. I believe that theorising Islamic economic philosophy is paramount if we are to understand Islamic economics as an independent economic system rather than a niche in the global capitalist order. In the following sections, I provide a brief history of Islamic economic thought followed by a discussion of labour within Islamic economic discourse. I then harness the concepts of *khilafah* (human agency) in Islamic ethics literature to conclude that labour should be recognised as a pathway to spiritual emancipation and advocate for a more inclusive and emanicipatory approach to Islamic economic philosophy.

Islamic economic thought: A brief history

Muslims believe that Islam encompasses more than just the pursuit of spiritual growth; it encompasses the conduct of worldly affairs as well. As a result, they believe that worldly matters like politics and economics can, and should, be conducted under the auspices of Islam's ethical teachings. This, in turn, led to the emergence of Islamic economics and finance in the post-colonial era of the 1970s. The Quran, the sacred text of Islam and the primary source of Islamic ethics does not cover all the issues that concern a modern economy. However, it does guide on financial matters such as property and inheritance (4:5, 4:12, 2:188, 2:220), and trade and charity (2:271-2:275, 5:55 8:43), thus providing a moral basis for economic conduct for the followers of the faith. It is important to remember that the Quran imagines a society of justice, unity, and order as an ideal (Iqbal & Mirakhor, 2011). The same is true of the functioning of the economy. Islamic scholars have found it possible to create an Islamic economy based on the principles of the Quran.

A significant aspect of Islamic philosophy is its view of the economy as a domain where believers express their moral and spiritual obligations. This concept underpins the notion of the 'economic man' or '*homo Islamicus*' in Islam. The concept of the 'economic man' or '*homo economicus*' refers to a theoretical construct used in classical economics to model human behaviour within economic systems. The economic man is characterised by rationality, self-interest, and utility maximisation. According to this model, individuals make decisions based on a rational assessment of costs and benefits, aiming to maximise their utility or satisfaction. This self-interested behaviour is believed to drive market interactions and allocate resources efficiently within an economy (Demsetz, 2008; Watson, 2011). However, critics argue that real-world decision-making is often influenced by psychological, social, and cultural factors that cannot be fully captured by the rational actor model (Anderson, 2000). According to Islamic teachings, humans are spiritual beings entrusted with the noble role of God's representatives on Earth.

As such, individuals are expected to fulfil their divinely assigned duties to attain enlightenment. These duties extend beyond mere ritualistic practices or adherence to dietary guidelines; they encompass every aspect of one's interactions within society. Islamic jurists aim to guide individuals on how they can fulfil their economic responsibilities as part of this broader framework. Various interpretations exist regarding the principles of Islamic economics; Nurizal (2016) summarises its essence as being rooted in the Quran, the teachings of Prophet Muhammad (*Sunnah*), and reasoned interpretations derived from the works of scholars and contemporary thinkers. Like other fields of Islamic scholarship, there are differing views on the extent of interpretive flexibility allowed. However, a consistent theme is the recognition that economics is inherently ideological, influenced by preconceived notions about human nature and societal organisation (Tripp, 2006). Therefore, Islamic scholars do not rely solely on rational choice to understand economic behaviour but rather perceive the economy as governed by man-made laws. It is implicitly understood that these laws can be inspired by secular or religious codes. Thus, the economy is a social construct governed by socially constructed rules of engagement, there are no similarities drawn in Islamic thought between economic laws and natural laws.

Islamic economists (Chapra, 1999; Siddiqi, 1981) lay down the conceptual framework of Islamic economics by upholding the ethics of a moral economy as the gauge to evaluate economic policies. To operate within the framework of the Islamic system and remain faithful to its epistemological sources, certain guiding principles are followed. The central principle in this context is the concept of *Maqasid-al Sharia*, which translates to the objectives of Sharia or Islamic law. al-Ghazali (1058-1111), renowned theologian, legal theoretician and mystic of Islamic thought provides the quintessential primer on *Maqasid-al Sharia* in his seminal work *Al-Mustasfa min 'Ilm al-Usul* (transl. *The Essentials of Islamic Jurisprudence*: al-Ghazali 1100/2017). This work delves into the principles of Islamic jurisprudence, including the objectives of Sharia. al-Ghazali discusses the objectives of Sharia in the context of safeguarding human well-being and fulfilling fundamental needs, such as preserving life, religion, intellect, progeny, and wealth. These principles extend beyond economics to guide rulings in all areas of jurisprudence and are also significant in the personal lives of Muslims. Siddiqi (2004) contends that these objectives should not be limited to individualistic pursuits but should encompass broader notions such as justice and equity. However, given the inherent vagueness of concepts like justice and equity, they cannot be exhaustively captured in a list. The goal of Islam as a way of life should be the reference point rather than solely that of Islamic Law, especially since many issues, such as inequality, fall outside the purview of law (Dusuki & Abozaid, 2007). Therefore, several scholars, including those mentioned here, assert that reason should be the ultimate guide in ensuring adherence to these principles. This emphasis on reason has contributed to the push for *Ijtihad* (independent legal reasoning) in Islamic economics (Al-Alwani, 2005; Rafikov & Akhmetova, 2020).

The rise of Islamic economic thought as a modern discipline in the 20th century was aided by the changing geopolitical situation between the West and the Middle East. One of the reasons for this was the rise in oil prices during the 1970s (Hanieh, 2020). The goal of developing an Islamic economy was to offer a moral and ethical alternative to capitalism. In this period of anti-colonial struggle, capitalism was seen as the product of the intellectual colonialism of European modernity (Nasr, 1987). Hence, Islamic scholars aimed to create an alternative economic system in which Muslims could integrate their religious beliefs and live out their moral duties in their day-today lives. They were able to create a somewhat flexible version of a moral economy, but it cannot be called an ideal model, largely because it cannot be called complete. Interestingly, over the years research in Islamic thought has moved to specific genres, questions or subjects. Even though Islam remains a fascinating topic of research in the more mainstream universities in the Global North, economic thought has been sparsely discussed. In the post-9/11 world, the Global War on Terror (GWoT) brought renewed attention to specifically the Islamic faith and its relationship with violence, the oppression of women and the denial of human rights (Tabassum, 2019). This may be why there has been little theoretical development of different concepts within the framework of Islamic economics.

Hamid Dabashi (2011) offers an interesting discussion on the emergence of the so-called comprador intellectuals in the post-9/11 era. The idea of comprador intellectuals as individuals who serves the interests of foreign powers or dominant external forces by promoting their ideologies, policies, or cultural values within their own society was first introduced by Fanon (1974). Dabashi (2011) argues that in the decade following 9/11, a great deal of literature was produced by such comprador intellectuals that contributed to the hegemonic narrative that the American media used to promote its imperial and militaristic policies in the Middle East, and Asia. Western powers' tendency to find and empower 'native' informers in the Islamic world led to the emergence of several dubious public intellectuals and dishonest and provocative discourse. The emergence of the Islam-terror conversation in popular media and the academy impacted the research in wider Islamic studies as more attention was being paid to reactionary and apologist accounts as well.

There has been a strong influence of US/European/Western political narratives on discourse within Muslim societies and Islamic scholarship, which is then weaponised by these hegemonic powers. Consequently, research and scholarship that align with the interests of the 'empire' receive more attention, funding, publishing opportunities, and career advancements, often overshadowing other marginalised lines of enquiry. As shown by Dabashi, critical and derogatory examinations of Islam have proven lucrative for many in Europe, academics included. Ideas and terms are co-opted by state and media outlets in the US and other Western countries to further their religious agendas as part of a broader hegemonic mission. Therefore, research rooted in a decolonial and emancipatory perspective within the Islamic tradition is crucial. This becomes especially pertinent in the field of global political economy, where these intersecting ideas elucidate the power dynamics shaping contemporary societies and their interactions.

As such, my own approach falls under Global Political Economy (GPE), which is a multidisciplinary field of study that examines the dynamic interaction between politics and economics on a global scale. It seeks to understand how political institutions, processes, and actors shape economic outcomes, and conversely, how economic forces influence political decisions and structures (O'Brien & Williams, 2016). At its core, GPE investigates the distribution of power and wealth in the international system, analysing how states, international organisations, corporations, and other actors compete, cooperate, and negotiate to advance their interests. It examines how processes such as colonialism, imperialism, neoliberalism, and globalisation have contributed to economic disparities between and within countries. However, it should be noted that even GPE as a discipline remains deeply Eurocentric. Eurocentrism in GPE refers to the tendency within the field to prioritise European perspectives, theories, and experiences, often at the expense of non-European perspectives and voices. Indeed, much of GPE has frequently advocated for, upheld, or glorified Western civilisation as the ultimate standard or ideal reference point (Hobson, 2013). This chapter aims to challenge Eurocentrism in GPE by advocating for diversified perspectives and questioning dominant economic narratives.

Although many scholars in various genres of Islamic studies have focused on imperialism, globalisation and capitalism, there is little synthesis of these in the discourse on Islamic economic philosophy. I would argue that much of the Islamic economics scholarship today is focused on the development of financial products and economic practices yet little space is provided to the power relations between states and institutions. Adam Hanieh (2011, 2020) for one, discusses at length the development of capitalism and Islamic finance in countries in the Gulf Cooperative Council (GCC). Although insightful, this research falls within the discourse in GPE without any connection to Islamic economic philosophy. With this discussion, I aim to break this impasse and provide an interdisciplinary critique that can prove mutually beneficial to both GPE and Islamic economic philosophy. By integrating GPE and Islamic economic philosophy both disciplines can be enriched, though it must be said anyone engaging with such theoretical interaction must be wary of the subsumption of one discourse into another. I am ethically committed to avoiding any such Eurocentric narratives and on the other extreme the political vilification of any Western or European philosophy just for the sake of it. Hence, I will present labour as an example of the theoretical possibilities within Islamic economic philosophy beyond Eurocentric GPE.

Labour in the Islamic tradition

In this introduction to labour in Islam, I will explore key concepts related to the labour market as found in the Islamic tradition. This will be followed by a brief critique of the concept of labour. The goal here is to present an example of a concept that is lacking in Islamic economic philosophy and discuss interventions towards retheorisation. Labour is a fundamental component of any economy. It represents the physical and mental work individuals contribute to create value and generate income. The study of labour is essential for understanding economic systems, as it influences productivity, wages, employment levels, and overall economic growth (Borjas, 2013; Cahuc et al., 2014; McLaughlin, 2019). By delving into the intricacies of labour economics, we gain insights into how individuals make decisions regarding work, how firms hire and compensate employees, and how government policies affect labour market outcomes.

Understanding these dynamics is crucial for policymakers, employers, workers, and researchers seeking to address labour market challenges and promote inclusive and sustainable economic development.

Note that it is almost impossible to summarise the entirety of the literature on the labour market in Islamic economics in the space provided. Muslim scholars' economic perspectives on labour economics have spanned from the 7th century to the emergence of modern economic thought. A variety of Muslim scholars contributed to various economic theories during this period. Examples include al-Ghazali's ([1096] 1993) discussions on market mechanisms and social justice and Ibn Khaldun's (1332-1406) development of the labour theory of value (al-Ghazali, 1096/1993; Ibn-Khaldun, 1377/2015). These theories, rooted in divine laws and spiritual dimensions, aimed at achieving salvation and embodied an ethico-moral socioeconomic context. The ethico-moral ideals in Islam refer to the combination of ethical and moral teachings in Islamic thought. Ethicists such as al-Ghazali construct their ideas of ideal human behaviour in the context of a society where Islamic ethico-moral considerations are primary. Azid and Asutay, (2007) explore this concept further in relation to Islamic economics. In this chapter, I will include elements of the debates around labour that I find most pertinent for the discussion of an emancipatory understanding of the concept.

The Islamic economy is formulated based on the dual relationship between the rights and responsibilities of all the agents involved. For instance, workers and employees are responsible to do right by each other. The Quran and *Sunnah* (the life and conduct of the Prophet Muhammad) provide the guidelines for these while *shariah* (Islamic law), and *fiqh* (jurisprudence) formulate these into practical codes of conduct. The leader of the community (we would equate that with the state today) is meant to act as an arbiter in the economy and ensure that these rights are protected (Azid et al., 2021). It is incumbent upon the worker that he does not shirk his responsibility to fulfil the task that he has been contracted to do. Punctuality, honesty and respect for one's work are paramount in Islamic thought and labour should ensure that they maintain trustworthiness with their employees (Azid, 2005). For an employee to avoid her responsibilities on the job and receive an unjustified wage, is considered *haram* (prohibited and thus sinful). Inversely it will also be considered *haram* for the employer to not pay the just wage for contracted work. In Islamic theory, the employer and employee are viewed as participants in a collaborative effort, each performing distinct tasks yet deserving equal respect (Zaman, 2009). This means that while entrepreneurial abilities are acknowledged in Islam, they are not elevated above other forms of contribution. The employer must feed and clothe his workers or pay enough wages so that they can meet their own needs (Khan, 1975). The work contract between the worker and the employee is supposed to be such that it provides for the basic necessities of the employee. Wages may differ from one place to another based on the economic conditions of the society, but the difference cannot be insurmountable (Mawdudi, 1969/2011).

As such, wages and wage rates then receive attention in Islamic thought. As early as the thirteenth century Ibn Taymiyyah (1263-1328) argued that the state should fix the wages of artisans and cultivators if their services were needed in the economy, but they refused to offer them due to low wages or imperfections in the market (Ibn Taymiyyah, 1982). This wage control was supposed to protect both the employer and the employee from exploitation from the other and ensure the availability of essential goods and services in the market. Contemporary Islamic scholars too have argued for the responsibility of the state to ensure decent wages (Al Faruqi, 1980; Chapra, 1971). On the other hand, some scholars have suggested that the wage rate should be linked to the profit of the employer (Azid, 2005). The ideal wage should be the one that bridges the gap between the living conditions of the employer and the employee. Several scholars are in favour of profit sharing between the worker and the employer as this will increase a worker's interest in the prosperity of the employer (Mawdudi, 1969/2011). This idea is based on the incentivisation of work rather than the mechanisms of the free market that practically coerce workers into labour. Here I am referring to not only the financial hit that the unemployed take but also the social stigma attached to the unemployed. In a similar vein, Iqbal & Mirakhor (2004) contend that firms owned by labour would best embody the principles of Islam.

In Islamic thought, labour is not only a fundamental factor of production but also the main source of value. Even capital is considered to be the embodiment of natural resources and past labour rather than a factor of production in itself (Mannan, 1970). This is different from the Marxist labour theory of value. According to Marx (1867/1992), the value of a commodity is determined by the amount of socially necessary labour time required for its production. In other words, the value of a commodity is not determined by its utility, or the amount of labour put into its production alone, but rather by the average amount of labour time needed to produce it within a given society. Marx argued that under capitalism, workers are paid for their labour power—the ability to work—rather than the full value of the goods and services they produce. The surplus value generated by workers' labour, exceeding the value of their wages, is appropriated by capitalists as profit. This exploitation of labour forms the basis of capitalist accumulation and leads to the inherent contradictions and inequalities within the capitalist system. For Azid et al. (2021), the Marxist labour theory of value is political in that it highlights the struggle between two classes. Such a class division is not found in the Islamic system, as the Quran and the entire ethical system of Islam are built on the equality of people. There is no concept of struggle and distinction between different groups in society. Rather all groups of people are meant to exist in harmony and cooperate. An ideal Islamic economy is designed to encourage generosity and welfare of all as it is only a means to an end: eternal salvation. Here, the normative claims of Islamic thought supersede the economic reality. Instead of observing whether distinctions of class exist in society at all, economic scholars refer to how in an ideal Islamic economy they will not.

With this brief overview of labour in Islam, I return to the key question of this chapter: how can we (re)theorise labour in Islamic economic philosophy? Here the important, perhaps political, element is that I do not deny the differences in power between the workers and capitalists in society. Indeed, laws, regulations and worker action have improved the bargaining power and living standards of labour yet challenges remain. Towards this, let us turn to the literature on ethics in Islamic thought.

Ethics, khilafah and labour

Any discussion of the human in Islamic economic thought must be contextualised in the notion of economic agency in Islamic economics. This concept is cushioned in the theological framework of moral agency or *khilafah* in Islam. This section examines the concept of *khilafah* as portrayed in medieval ethical literature authored by al-Ghazali (2015), Tusi (1964), and al-Davani (1839). The writings of these Islamic scholars continue to exert influence on Islamic thought, both directly and indirectly. Abu Hamid Muhammad ibn Muhammad al-Ghazali (1058–1111), a Persian scholar, was a versatile figure, renowned as a theologian, jurist, and mystic within Islam. Similarly, Muhammad ibn Muhammad ibn al-Hasan al-Tusi, also known as Nasir al-Din Tusi (1201–1274), was a Persian philosopher, theologian, and scientist, celebrated for his contributions to prose, mysticism, and science. Muhammad Ibn Jalal Ad-din Davani (1427–1502/03), hailing from the Kazerun region of Iran, was a jurist and philosopher.

Much like Aristotle and Plato, classical Islamic philosophers placed great emphasis on the pursuit of human happiness (Butterworth, 1983). According to al-Ghazali, ultimate happiness, or *sa'adat* (flourishing), is achieved through adhering closely to the principles of *adl* (justice) and *khilafah* (vicegerency of God). Ibn-e-Sina argued that justice could be attained through moral virtues such as temperance, courage, and practical wisdom (Parens & Macfarland, 2011). These virtues, transcending religious doctrines, were crucial for individual spiritual development and, consequently, communal cohesion and flourishing. In the context of classical ethicists, *khilafah* signified the vicegerency of God, representing the universe's macrocosm within the mortal realm. A person could only reach the enlightenment of *khilafah* by actively engaging with others in society. The soul, referred to as *nafs* (the mystical driving force of life and the source of desire in Islamic theology), must interact with others in the mortal realm to fully realise its ethical self. This engagement occurs in the domestic and the public spheres. As products of their time, these literary works are masculinist in their understanding of and interpretation of *khilafah*. Ayubi (2019) provides valuable insights into the historical and cultural contexts that have shaped gender norms and values within Islamic societies by engaging with classical ethics literature noted above from a feminist critical perspective.

Indeed, classical ethics literature visualises a rather masculinist and elitist world where spiritual enlightenment is limited to only men at least in the public arena. A pious woman can rise to spiritual height, but this level will always be below that of a man. Additionally, the acts that gain her this enlightenment are always in service of her husband and his household whereas for men these acts are to be found in engagement with the wider public sphere and religious/spiritual pursuits. This is contrary to Islamic theology where the centre of human identity is *nafs*. *Nafs* does not have gender, nor does it imply any. However, when the ethicists discuss *nafs,* they differentiate between the *nafs* of men and women thus writing their patriarchy in the texts that they produce. Indeed, the three ethicists begin their treatises with a gender-neutral understanding of *nafs* but end up with a masculinist explanation of its manifestation.

In an earlier work, I discuss the works of al-Ghazali, Tusi and al-Davani and the concept of economic agency and argue for a gendered approach to the idea of economic agency as the *homo Islamicus* is designed as a man. The literature discussed here does not recognise the presence of women in the economy and thus following discourse on economic agency excludes them as well. In my earlier work, I provide a gendered understanding of *khilafah* and argue for the same in Islamic economic philosophy, as gender is an important category of analysis for economic philosophy (Khawar, 2023). Here, I will not discuss the masculinist lenience of our esteemed ethicists in detail. Rather, the discussion is limited to the category of class and its relation to labour.

In premodern Muslim societies, urban centres held significant importance, serving as primary sources of identity and loyalty (Euben, 2008). al-Davani likened the city to a household, while Tusi viewed it as a reflection of individual and household dynamics, suggesting that a virtuous city stems from virtuous individuals and households. Drawing from Ibn Rushd (1126-1198), both ethicists emphasised the role of ethics in politics, highlighting the importance of social order and civic engagement (Butterworth, 1983). Thus, the city became a vital arena for ethical practice, paralleling the significance of the household for virtuous individuals. While these concepts are presented as universal, they were influenced by the civic realities of the ethicists' lives (Ayubi, 2019), who were often supported by court funds. Furthermore, the ethicists envisioned the public sphere as masculine, relegating women to the private sphere, despite the presence of women in various social roles across medieval Islamic societies (Katz, 2014). Hence, not only were these sketches of the ideal city informed by their personal experiences and positionality, but they also reflected what would be the ideal city in their minds.

Cities in the classification provided by Tusi (1964) are divided into four classes, with philosophers comprising the first and highest class and craftsmen and farmers forming the fourth and lowest class. Notably, slaves are absent from these categories, while women are considered a distinct class separate from these classifications of the profession. Interestingly, Tusi does not mention the ruler of the city in this classification, asserting instead that the head of the city is responsible for organising and overseeing all classes to ensure proper political order. This hierarchical arrangement, managed by the ruler, places each group relative to one another, with those deemed fit for authority positioned higher in the city's hierarchy. According to Tusi (1964), suitability for authority is measured by knowledge for the upper class and skill for the lower class. Similarly, al-Davani (1839) presents four categories, with philosophers and knowledge producers in the first category and tradesmen and providers of basic necessities in the last. For al-Davani (1839), a man's distinguishing quality is his spiritual pursuit, he considers saints as the highest-ranking ones due to their unblemished intellect. This intellect, equated with the ability to perceive the Divine Unseen, determines a man's status in society beyond his profession. Men from the middle and lower classes are considered unable to perceive the Divine Unseen, according to these scholars. Moreover, a man's intellect dictates his position within the homosocial hierarchy beyond his occupation.

Rational thought is seen as the factor that propels a man's social standing granting him power and influence. Nonetheless, despite the theoretical importance of intelligence, both Tusi (1964) and al-Davani (1839) acknowledge the possibility for lesser men to hold power based on birth rather than intellectual capacity. Tusi and al-Davani advocate for a nuanced approach to interactions between social classes, emphasising the importance of speaking to others according to their intellectual capacity. When engaging with those of higher status, one should aim to elevate oneself, while maintaining dignity when interacting with those of lower rank. Special etiquette should be observed when conversing with rulers or employers. The underlying principle is to determine how individuals of lower status can be corrected, uplifted, and educated. The efficacy of these interactions defines one's virtues, according to Tusi (1964) and al-Davani (1839). Ultimately, privileged individuals are entrusted with the responsibility of caring for the most marginalised members of society. The ethical framework in Islam emphasises the interconnectedness of worldly affairs and spiritual conduct, underscoring the necessity of virtuous behaviour in interactions with others to attain the rank of vicegerency or *khilafah*. This discussion reveals to us that ethics literature in Islamic tradition views society in clear structures. Here those with authority must manage those without. The descriptions of these relationships of patrimony are not manuals on power relations yet they allude to them.

The ruler is not questioned with revolutionary zeal in these texts. This may be due to the preference for civic order in classical Islamic tradition, where civil war is considered a great evil, a *fitnah*. We must also remember that these texts are directed to the elite man. These discussions are for the benefit of the elite man, although they do speak at length about his moral responsibilities in the home and society. However benevolent these relationships may seem; they are part of a patriarchal status quo. Here patriarchy is protected not only by the exclusion of women from the public space but also by the relegation of men to their birth stations. Indeed, we cannot separate masculinity from class, as class itself is a gendered category where men are assumed to be the agents of their class (Morgan, 2005). In the ethics literature too, we see these class and gender divisions which ultimately cause a deep tension. On one hand, the *nafs* is free of class hierarchies, on the other human engagement is tied to the role that each plays in the social hierarchy. I would argue that this is a quintessential tension in much of Islamic thought. Theologically we want to argue against class and for egalitarianism, if not equality in the Western sense of the term, yet we must attempt to reconcile this ethical principle with the social realities in which we work. It does not help that much of mainstream Islamic thought has become married to the idea of maintaining civic order, which ultimately maintains the status quo. More and more scholarly work today is addressing this issue centralising the need for emancipatory thought and frameworks of analysis (Dabashi, 2008; Esack, 2002; Rahemtulla, 2017). This is my framework of analysis within Islamic economic philosophy as well.

Islamic economic scholars have argued that since the rights of labour have been established by *fiqh*, there is no need for worker action such as strikes in the Islamic system (Azid et al., 2021). Islamic economics is built on the principles of maintenance of responsibilities and rights. These rights and responsibilities operate in the same homosocial categories that are described by the three ethicists mentioned here. However, contemporary Islamic economics does not discuss them exactly in the same way, for instance, none of the economic works noted here speak about removing women from the public space. Yet their omission of the special conditions of women in the domestic and public economy is tantamount to the active erasure of women. Similarly, Islamic economic thought has foregrounded the idea of spiritual fulfilment as the goal of an ethical economy, yet the systematic hindrances placed in the path of the lesser privileged in missing from the discussion. Frankly speaking, we cannot speak about the spiritual fulfilment of the domestic workers in Pakistan (Bhatti, 2023; Mehmood, 2023) and India (Neetha, 2023) or the construction workers in UAE and Saudi Arabia (Human Rights Watch, 2023; Lakhani, 2023) without addressing their material conditions.

These examples clearly show that even if *fiqh* ensures labourers' rights, workers' action will only become unnecessary when the Islamic system is built in a way that makes it impossible to exploit labour. To theorise labour then, we must consider not only the conceptual goals of Islamic economics, but we must also consider contemporary challenges. Indeed, we can repeat one after the other the Prophet's teachings on generous behaviour towards one's hired workers but remaining within that discourse means that we are only speaking from the position of the master. This is the central issue with the ethics literature as well as the economics literature in Islamic thought about labour. We will continuously see that employers are asked to be equitable and just while workers are told to be honest and trustworthy. We are also told what to do when a worker shirks their responsibility. However, we are not told what to do in the face of egregious class repression. Conveniently that is not recognised in the discourse to begin with. With the above discussion, I have attempted to show that class divisions have very much been a part of the patriarchal understanding of Islamic society. Hence, discourse on labour must also incorporate said class discussion.

The inclusion of class in the theory of labour requires an in-depth analysis, carried over at least a few years. I would like to take this space to briefly introduce this with the hope that I can develop this notion in detail over the next few years. As I have noted, *khilafah* is the foundational concept of human action and agency in the mortal world be it domestic or public sphere. This is the key theological responsibility of humans and in Islamic scholarship, it is a foundational theoretical device. Indeed, *khilafah* is an epistemology in itself as knowledge from the Divine is received by positioning oneself in relationship to It via *khilafah*. As is clear from the influential texts produced by al-Ghazali, Tusi and al-Davani, *khilafah* has also informed the perception of social structures in the world. It is a concept further nuanced by Islamic feminist and womanist interpretations which have expanded it beyond its patriarchal readings (Lamrabet, 2015). I have attempted to harness these in towards a gender-sensitive reading of economic agency. Here, we must consider the act of work in conjunction with *khilafah*.

As ethics literature itself points to the centrality of work for the spiritual emancipation of men we must consider work in its nature to be emancipatory. For one's work and related social engagement to be a way to enlightenment, work must be removed from oppressive systems even in the world. Of course, we cannot do that if we do not recognise the oppression written into the codex of work in the capitalist system. Indeed, the global economic system is capitalist, and it is the system within which we are imagining heterodoxies too. How can in Islamic thought we safely deny the presence of class? Especially when class structures are so clearly visible in Muslim-majority countries, even the ones with supposedly Islamic laws. Instead of repeating the rhetoric that there is no class in Islam, we must focus on eliminating class-based power that does exist in society. This ontological shift is necessary and made powerful with the expansion of Islamic scholarship and praxis. If I must aim to achieve *khilafah* as a person born outside the upper class, if I must work and be part of labour, then to achieve *khilafah* I must be an active agent in my liberation. *Khilafah* is not only ruling in the household and society but also work. Thus, to labour is to pursue *khilafah*.

Conclusion

Islamic economics is rooted in Islam which extends beyond spiritual pursuits to encompass worldly affairs such as politics and economics, guided by ethical teachings. Despite the Quran not explicitly addressing all modern economic issues, it offers moral foundations for trade and finance. The rise of Islamic economic thought in the 20th century was catalysed by geopolitical shifts and aimed to provide a moral alternative to capitalism. However, challenges persist, including the marginalisation of Islamic economic philosophy within academia, exacerbated by post-9/11 narratives and Eurocentric biases. Hegemonic domination of global political discourse by European or Western thought has been accompanied by a general hostility towards Islamic episteme that does not comply with the current political narratives of the West. In 2015, when I initially delved into Islamic economics, a colleague questioned whether it was wise to associate the word 'Islamic' so emphatically with my academic pursuits, hinting at the perceived detriment to my career prospects if I were to associate too closely with Islamic thought. This was emblematic of the clear prejudice against Islamic theories/worldviews/epistemologies. Indeed, this has remained. It is visible not only in the elements of Islam that are allowed more berth in academic discourse but also in who and which identity is allowed to take this space of power.

Nonetheless, there is potential for interdisciplinary dialogue between Islamic economics and GPE to enrich both fields, provided it is conducted ethically and avoids the dominance of Western narratives or the assimilation of one discourse into another. To remain clear of both Eurocentric narratives and the unwarranted vilification of Western or European philosophies, I have attempted here a prudent conversation between both traditions. By incorporating Islamic economic philosophy into the framework of GPE I have broadened the perspectives within both Islamic economic philosophy and GPE. The specific concept for such an elaboration here is the idea of labour in Islamic thought. Islamic scholarship has elaborated on employers' and workers' rights and responsibilities, the role of the state in ensuring justice in the labour market, and the determination of wages. Islamic scholarship has also provided a precursor to modern debates on the labour theory of value contrasted with the Marxist labour theory of value. The absence of class struggle within the Islamic framework remains detrimental to the praxis of the emancipatory ethics of the Quran. Despite acknowledging power differentials in society, the focus remains on ideal Islamic principles of harmony, cooperation, and welfare for all.

In this chapter, I have explored the foundational concept of *khilafah* or moral agency in Islam. Through an analysis of medieval ethical literature authored by influential Islamic scholars such as al-Ghazali, Tusi, and al-Davani, we can observe the complexities of *khilafah* and its implications for human action and societal structures. The examination of classical Islamic philosophy reveals a masculinist and elitist interpretation of *khilafah*, wherein spiritual enlightenment and societal engagement are predominantly associated with men, while women are relegated to subordinate roles within the private sphere. This gendered understanding of *khilafah* perpetuates patriarchal norms and excludes women from meaningful participation in the public sphere, despite the theological premise of gender neutrality in human identity. The intersectionality of class and gender in shaping societal structures within the ethics literature is clear to see. Class divisions, often overlooked in mainstream Islamic discourse, intersect with gender hierarchies to reinforce existing power dynamics. The patriarchal understanding of *khilafah* is intertwined with class-based oppression, necessitating a critical revaluation of the concept in Islamic ethics and economics.

Contemporary Islamic economics, while rooted in the principles of justice and spiritual fulfilment, must confront the systemic barriers faced by marginalised groups, here the group in concern is labour. The omission of women from economic discourse and the perpetuation of class-based inequalities underscores the urgent need for a more inclusive and emancipatory approach to Islamic economic philosophy. This chapter proposes the recognition of labour as a pathway to spiritual emancipation. By acknowledging the presence of class divisions and advocating for social justice within Islamic thought, scholars can contribute to the realisation of *khilafah* in both individual and collective spheres. In essence, the pursuit of *khilafah* entails not only ruling in the household and society but also active engagement in the struggle for liberation from oppressive systems. By reimagining work as a means to achieve *khilafah* and advocating for structural change within the global economic system, Islamic scholars and practitioners can work towards a more just and equitable society, grounded in the principles of Islamic ethics and social justice.

References

Abdel Haleem, M. A. (Ed.). (2005). *The Qur'an*. Oxford University Press.
Ahmed, H., Asutay, M., & Wilson, R. (Eds.). (2014). *Islamic banking and financial crisis: Reputation, stability and risks*. Edinburgh University Press. https://doi.org/10.3366/edinburgh/9780748647613.001.0001
al-Davani, J. al-Din. (1839). *Practical philosophy of the Muhammadan people* (W. F. Thompson, Trans.). Oriental Translation Fund.
Al Faruqi, I. R. (1980). Islam and labor. *Islam and a new international economic order: The social dimension*. Symposium on Islam and a New International Economic Order: the Social Dimension, Geneva, 1980, Geneva.
al-Ghazali, A. H. M. (1993). *Revival of religious learnings Vol III: Vol. III* (F. Karim, Trans.). Urdu Bazar. (Original work published 1096)
al-Ghazali, A. H. M. (2015). *The alchemy of happiness* (C. Field, Trans.). Routledge. (Original work published 1100)
Al-Alwani, S. T. J. (2005). The role of Islamic Ijtihad in the regulation and correction of capital markets. In *Issues in Contemporary Islamic Thought* (pp. 129–158). International Institute of Islamic Thought. https://doi.org/10.2307/j.ctvk8w1ww.15
Amin, S. (2009). *Eurocentrism: Modernity, religion, and democracy: a critique of Eurocentrism and culturalism* (2nd ed). Monthly Review Press.
Anderson, E. (2000). Beyond homo economicus: New developments in theories of social norms. *Philosophy & Public Affairs*, 29(2), 170–200. https://doi.org/10.1111/j.1088-4963.2000.00170.x
Ayubi, Z. (2019). *Gendered morality: Classical Islamic ethics of the self, family, and society*. Columbia University Press. https://doi.org/10.1093/jis/etab006
Azid, T. (2005). The concept and nature of labour in Islam: A survey. *Review of Islamic Economics*, 9(2), 93–124.
Azid, T., & Asutay, M. (2007). Does ethico-moral coalition complement to economic coalition? A response in the periphery of Islamic economics. *Humanomics*, *23*(3), 153–173. https://doi.org/10.1108/08288660710779380
Azid, T., Burki, U., Khawaja, M. J., Shirazi, N. S., & Tahir, M. (2021). *Labor economics in an Islamic framework: Theory and practice* (1st ed.). Routledge. https://doi.org/10.4324/9781032019550
Bhatti, N. F. (2023, August 12). Child domestic labour: The worst form of slavery. *The Express Tribune*. https://tribune.com.pk/story/2430576/child-domestic-labour-the-worst-form-of-slavery
Borjas, G. J. (2013). *Labor economics* (6. ed). McGraw-Hill-Irwin.
Butterworth, C. E. (1983). Ethics in medieval Islamic philosophy. *Journal of Religious Ethics, 11*(2), 224–239.
Cahuc, P., Carcillo, S., & Zylberberg, A. (2014). *Labor economics* (Second Edition). MIT Press.
Chapra, M. U. (1971). *The economic system of Islam: A discussion of its goals and nature*. Department of Publications, University of Karachi.

Chapra, M. U. (1999). The need for a new economic system. In T. Niblock (Ed.), *The political economy of the Middle East: Vol. III*. E. Elgar.

Dabashi, H. (2008). *Islamic liberation theology: Resisting the empire* (1. ed). Routledge. https://doi.org/10.4324/9780203928387

Demsetz, H. (2008). *From economic man to economic system: Essays on human behavior and the institutions of capitalism*. Cambridge University Press. https://doi.org/10.1017/CBO9780511510656

Diwany, T. el, & Ahmad, T. (Eds.). (2010). *Islamic banking and finance: What it is and what it could be* (1. ed). Ethical Charitable Trust.

Dusuki, A. W., & Abozaid, A. (2007). A critical appraisal on the challenges of realising Maqasid al-Shariaah in Islamic banking and finance. *International Journal of Economics, Management and Accounting, 15*(2), 143–165. https://doi.org/10.31436/ijema.v15i2.133

Esack, F. (2002). *Qur'an, liberation & pluralism: An Islamic perspective of interreligious solidarity against oppression* (Reprinted 2002 (twice)). Oneworld.

Euben, R. L. (2008). *Journeys to the other shore: Muslim and Western travelers in search of knowledge* (2. print and first paperback print). Princeton University Press.

Fanon, F. (1974). *The wretched of the earth*. Penguin Books.

Hanieh, A. (2011). *Capitalism and class in the Gulf Arab states* (1st ed). Palgrave Macmillan. https://doi.org/10.1057/9780230119604

Hanieh, A. (2020). New geographies of financial power: Global Islamic finance and the Gulf. *Third World Quarterly, 41*(3), 525–546. https://doi.org/10.1080/01436597.2019.1675505

Hobson, J. M. (2013). Part 1 – Revealing the Eurocentric foundations of IPE: A critical historiography of the discipline from the classical to the modern era. *Review of International Political Economy, 20*(5), 1024–1054. https://doi.org/10.1080/09692290.2012.704519

Human Rights Watch. (2023, December 18). Gulf states treat migrant workforce as disposable. *Human Rights Watch*. https://www.hrw.org/news/2023/12/18/gulf-states-treat-migrant-workforce-disposable

Ibn Taymiyya, A. I.-ʿAbd-al-Ḥalīm. (1982). *Public duties in Islam: The institution of the Ḥisba* (M. Holland, Trans.). Islamic Foundation.

Ibn-Khaldun. (2015). *The Muqaddimah: An introduction to history*. Princeton Univeristy Press. (Original work published 1377)

Iqbal, M., & Llewellyn, D. T. (Eds.). (2002). *Islamic banking and finance: New perspectives on profit sharing and risk*. Edward Elgar Publishing. https://doi.org/10.4337/9781843765318

Iqbal, Z., & Mirakhor, A. (2004). Stakeholders model of governance in islamic economic system. *Islamic Economic Studies, 11*(2), 43–63.

Iqbal, Z., & Mirakhor, A. (2011). *An introduction to Islamic finance: Theory and practice* (2. ed). Wiley Asia.

Katz, M. H. (2014). *Women in the mosque: A history of legal thought and social practice*. Columbia University Press. https://doi.org/10.7312/columbia/9780231162661.001.0001

Khan, M. N. (1975). Rights of labour in Islam. *The Voice of Islam, 28*(3), 366–375.

Khawar, M. (2023). Economic agency of women in Islamic economic philosophy: Going beyond economic man and Islamic man. *International Journal of Social Economics, 51*(03), 364–376. https://doi.org/10.1108/IJSE-05-2023-0366

Lakhani, N. (2023, October 20). Migrant workers toil in perilous heat to prepare for Cop28 climate talks in UAE. *The Guardian*. https://www.theguardian.com/environment/2023/oct/20/cop28-migrant-workers-uae-heat-climate-crisis

Lamrabet, A. (2015). An egalitarian reading of the concepts of khilafah, wilayah and qiwamah. In Z. Mir-Hosseini, M. Al-Sharmani, & J. Rumminger (Eds.), *Men in charge? Rethinking authority in Muslim legal tradition* (pp. 118-152). Oneworld Publications.

Mannan, M. A. (1970). *Islamic economics: Theory and practice: A comparative study*. Sh. Muhammad Ashraf.

Marx, K. (1992). *Capital: A critique of political economy*. Penguin books. (Original work published 1867)

Mawdudi, S. A. A. (2011). *First principles of Islamic economics*. The Islamic Foundation. (Original work published 1969)

McLaughlin, K. J. (2019). *Labor economics: Principles in practice* (Second edition). Oxford University Press.

Mehmood, A. (2023, April 16). Domestic workers stuck in poverty. *The Express Tribune*. https://tribune.com.pk/story/2412228/domestic-workers-stuck-in-poverty

Morgan, D. (2005). Class and masculinity. In M. S. Kimmel, J. Hearn, & R. W. Connell (Eds.), *Handbook of Studies on Men & Masculinities* (pp. 165–177). SAGE Publications, Inc. https://doi.org/10.4135/9781452233833.n10

Nasr, S. V. R. (1987). Towards a philosophy of Islamic economics. *The Muslim World, 77*(3–4), 175–196. https://doi.org/10.1111/j.1478-1913.1987.tb02799.x

Neetha, N. (2023, June 19). India's domestic workers: Key issues remain swept aside. *The Hindu Centre for Politics and Public Policy*. https://www.thehinducentre.com/the-arena/indias-domestic-workers-key-issues-remain-swept-aside/article66984860.ece

Nurizal, I. (2016). Scrutinizing the epistemology of Islamic economics: A historical analysis. *TASQAFAH 12*(1), 19–46. https://doi.org/10.21111/tsaqafah.v12i1.367

O'Brien, R., & Williams, M. (2016). *Global political economy: Evolution and dynamics* (5th edition). Red Globe Press.

Parens, J., & Macfarland, J. C. (Eds.). (2011). *Medieval political philosophy: A sourcebook* (2nd ed). Cornell University Press.

Rafikov, I., & Akhmetova, E. (2020). Methodology of integrated knowledge in Islamic economics and finance: Collective ijtihād. *ISRA International Journal of Islamic Finance, 12*(1), 115–129. https://doi.org/10.1108/IJIF-02-2019-0034

Rahemtulla, S. (2017). *Qur'an of the oppressed: Liberation theology and gender justice in Islam* (First edition). Oxford University Press. https://doi.org/10.1093/acprof:oso/9780198796480.001.0001

Siddiqi, M. N. (1981). *Muslim economic thinking: A survey of contemporary literature*. International Centre for Research in Islamic Economics, King Abdul Aziz University.

Tabassum, S. (2019). Bernard Lewis on Islam and violence: A critical appraisal. *Islamic Studies, 58*(1), 9–32.

Tripp, C. (2006). *Islam and the moral economy the challenge of capitalism*. Cambridge University Press. https://doi.org/10.1017/CBO9780511617614

Tusi, N. al-D. M. ibn M. (1964). *The Nasirean ethics* (G. M. Wickens, Trans.). George Allen and Unwin.

Watson, M. (2011). Competing models of socially constructed economic man: Differentiating Defoe's Crusoe from the Robinson of neoclassical economics. *New Political Economy, 16*(5), 609–626. https://doi.org/10.1080/13563467.2011.536209

Zaman, A. (2009). Islamic economics: A survey of the literature: II. *Islamic Studies, 48*(4), 525–566.

VERTAISARVIOITU
KOLLEGIALT GRANSKAD
PEER-REVIEWED
www.tsv.fi/tunnus

13
Financialised digitalisation, digitalised financialisation
The inseparability between technological domination and financial hegemony in contemporary capitalism

Edemilson Paraná

While capitalism retains persistent general and abstract defining characteristics, it is not rigid or unchanging throughout history. Instead, it transforms and evolves. As the most revolutionary mode of production up to its time, capitalism thrives on constant self-revolution, as elucidated by Engels and Marx (2015), Schumpeter (2008), Polanyi (2001), and other thinkers. Mobilising typical aspects, processes, and structures of other modes of production is a resource that capitalism has historically utilised to perpetuate and reshape itself in response to contradictions and limitations. This does not alter the fact that labour exploitation remains a pervasive social reality, profit pursuit is an intrinsic goal, and the valorisation of value, as posited by Marx (1990), remains a central and structuring element of current economic and social dynamics. Nevertheless, while we persist within the capitalist mode of production, there are discernible and consequential shifts occurring that warrant careful examination, as they may signify a transformative phase, altering the organisation and disposition of capitalist relations. The new reproduces itself within the old, and vice versa. Comprehending the nuances of this dialectic process demands meticulous attention and intellectual rigour. This chapter seeks to contribute to such an effort, questioning discontinuities within continuities of capitalism. Adding to the impetus and rationale

Paraná, E. (2025). Financialised digitalisation, digitalised financialisation: The inseparability between technological domination and financial hegemony in contemporary capitalism. In A. Kangas, I. Gataulina, M. Poutanen, A. I. Rajala & H-E. Ventovirta (Eds.), *Retheorising capitalism* (pp. 263–280). Tampere University Press. https://doi.org/10.61201/tup.981

for (re)theorising capitalism, it contends that we are witnessing a phase transition in recent decades. Capitalism is evolving into something markedly different from its previous incarnations.

Just as Keynesian-Fordist welfare capitalism differed from liberal capitalism, which, in turn, diverged from contemporary neoliberal and financialised capitalism, I hypothesise that we are now traversing another threshold into a distinct form of capitalism, still to be defined. This shift is fundamentally driven by the advanced digitalisation of social processes and interactions, suggesting an alternative qualitative mode of operation within socioeconomic relations. If this is to be the case, how and from where to investigate this new phase, moment, or configuration of capitalism? How can we concretely and empirically frame social relations that underpin it? How can we elaborate on the core transformations around digitalisation?

Addressing these questions, I first theoretically characterise capitalism based on two of its current fundamental dimensions, interpreted here through a macrosocial lens: financialisation (Fine, 2014, 2022) and neoliberalism (Harvey, 2005; Duménil and Lévy, 2011). My analysis is rooted in the intersection of these processes, facilitating a deeper understanding of the overarching context within which the phenomena of digitalisation (Matthess & Kunkel, 2020; Gradillas & Thomas, 2023) emerge. From this line of reasoning, I will define financialisation, neoliberalism, and digitalisation along the text in connection to each other. Conceptualising these processes in an interdependent fashion and exploring the theoretical consequences of such crossovers is the main contribution aimed by the text. Assessing these crucial phenomena will allow us to better visualise the complex interplay between technological dominance and financial hegemony in contemporary social (re)production, which in turn adds new elements to the investigation of the mentioned transition to a new stage within capitalism spearheaded by digital transformation.

Although building from and bringing attention to different empirical phenomena, this is essentially a theoretical text. The invitation is to engage in a relational and integrative rereading of contemporary capitalism, considering the overdetermination (Althusser, 2005) between financialisation, neoliberalisation, and digitalisation. Overdetermination, in Althusserian terms, serves as the anchor for the meso-level theoretical inquiry cutting across the entire chapter. It refers to how the contradictions within each social practice shape the overall social structure and, in turn, are influenced by it. This concept affects the dominance, subordination, antagonism, and non-antagonism among contradictions within the dominant structure of a society at any given time. Specifically, overdetermination means that a contradiction reflects its existence within the larger social context, including the influence of other contradictions within that context. It also reflects the uneven development of contradictions within the complex whole of society (Brewster, 2005, p. 253).

From this approach, the conceptual definition of financialisation, neoliberalisation, and digitalisation in relation to each other adds a more nuanced perspective to social science debates about capitalism, as per the objectives of this edited volume. This genetically interdependent conceptual development will then finally lead us to the definition of financialised digitalisation/digitalised financialisation, delineating the inseparability between technological domination and financial hegemony in contemporary capitalism. In the later sections of the text, as an illustration of these theorisations, I engage in some reflections on the relationship between finance and technology, drawing from insights gleaned from recent financial innovations such as cryptocurrencies, blockchain, and NFTs—subjects I have investigated in recent years (Paraná, 2020; Campbell-Verduyn & Paraná, 2021; Rotta & Paraná, 2022). Finally, I will conclude by summarising the main arguments and how they contribute to the (re)theorising capitalism endeavour.

Financialisation, neoliberalism, and digitalisation

The capacity of capitalism to transform itself to maintain capital accumulation can be illustrated by the massive structural changes it has notably undergone since the 1970s. As extensively explored by the literature[1], this period marks the exhaustion of the post-war dominant socio-economic paradigm, the Keynesian-Fordist accumulation regime, as described in the theoretical lexicon of French regulationism (Boyer, 1990). There has been much debate about these 30 golden years (1945–1975), their definition, meaning, rise, and fall, as well as the numerous crises that led to its demise (Chesnais, 2016): accumulation and profitability crises, fiscal crises, regulatory and governmental crises, crises of political and social legitimation, ideological crises (Streeck, 2011). This intricate process can be grasped by the image of a reservoir of transformations and contradictions that, amid intense disputes, will *conform* to a new type of capitalism in the coming decades. As crises are moments prone to (tragic) articulations of socio-economic dynamics, such exhaustion is later followed by a new reinvention of capitalism. No longer coordinated, planned, administered, or socially rooted as immediately before, the new capitalism evolved into increasingly flexible, with accelerated and deterritorialising flows (Deleuze & Guattari, 1983; Boltanski & Chiapelo, 2018).

If the institutional dimension matters, as is the case, the choice of the term *conformation* is here deliberate. It illustrates the joint and interrelated emergence of new political, regulatory, and sociotechnical forms characterising this new era of global capitalism. It is difficult to isolate which processes here are purely political, economic, institutional, material, or subjective. In practice, it is a multidimensional plot that articulates the local, national, and global, the subjective with the material, and the political and economic with the institutional. However, for the purpose of comprehensive organisation and method of presentation, it is convenient to focus on what seems particularly significant for the analysis I offer at this point: the global

1 For Marxist regulationist perspectives on these structural socioeconomic changes, refer to Brunhoff (1986), Harvey (1989), and Jessop (2002). For an institutionalist perspective, see Blyth (2002).

productive restructuring and its correlation with the financialised rearticulation of capitalism beginning in the mid-1970s.

Importantly, this period underwent a new wave of technological advancement: the revolution of microelectronics, robotics, and information and communication technologies (Coriat, 1983; Lojkine, 1992). This led to increased mechanisation and automation of work processes and facilitated the emergence of networked companies, relocation and transnationalisation of production (Coriat, 1990; Shiller, 1999). These transformations were complemented by advancements in logistics, transportation, and particularly, the proliferation of corporate, governmental, and later, personal computing (Castells, 2010).

This is how the creative destruction associated with satellites, mobile telephony, computers and information networks began shaping the path along which the liberalisation of world trade, the establishment of new global value chains (Serfati, 2008; Sturgeon, 2009), financial and banking integration, and increasingly freely interconnected capital flows followed (Chesnais, 1996; Paraná, 2019). Moreover, this procession supported the dismantling of labour protections, capital controls, state discretion in various areas, and recurrent fiscal attacks against citizenship rights—for example in the practical form of austerity politics (Blyth, 2013; Fine & Saad-Filho, 2014).

We can now return to financialisation, defining it, beyond what has been mentioned, from digitalisation. This will enable us to further articulate technological domination and financial hegemony. Financialisation primarily involves unlocking the power of money and finance through the expansion of markets—viewed primarily as a domain of competitive discipline rather than free exchange—into broader areas of social life (Mollo et al., 2022; Bayliss et al., 2024). More abstractly, it refers to the relative autonomy of circulation from production, and the emergence of what Marx (1991) termed "fictitious capital." For Marx, this process is not solely economic. The overall restructuring of capital accumulation to prioritise financial gain, meaning the alignment of the entire productive process with the goals, timelines, and operations of finance, carries far-reaching implications, influencing various aspects of social life, including culture, health, and education (Van der Zwan, 2014; Chiapello, 2017).[2] Developing from Marx's conceptual logic, financialisation, as enhanced autonomisation of money from the productive process, indicates a highly advanced, unconstrained form of capitalism. Financialisation is the result of restrictions on and protections from capitalism being lifted.

Financialisation, is, furthermore, a process without which neoliberalism cannot be conceived, leading us another sensitive point. The successive rounds of privatisation, flexibility, austerity, and dismantling of regulations, protections and forms of political and social compensation, in different fields, are both the cause and consequence of this new social subjectivity. The subjectivity of the self-entrepreneur, who competes

2 For numerous examples of such repercussions in Britain, refer to Bayliss et al. (2024). Furthermore, Cordilha (2021) addresses the financialisation of the public health system in the French case. For an extensive analysis of the financialisation of social policy in the Global South, see Lavinas (2020) and Lavinas (2017).

frenetically in physical or digital markets; of a "sacrificial subject," as Wendy Brown (2015) put it, or the "indebted man" to recall the formulation of Maurizio Lazzarato (2012). The fact is that "neoliberalisation," as David Harvey (2005) highlighted, "meant, in short, the financialisation of everything. This deepened the hold of finance over all other areas of the economy, as well as over the state apparatus and [...] daily life" (p. 33). Financialisation is, therefore, the material truth of neoliberalism as a phase of capitalism. Neoliberalisation and financialisation are, from this point of view, inseparable twins. Once again, this is a process that is both economic and political, something that is revealed with special clarity by its outcomes: a high concentration of income and wealth and, therefore, of social power in the hands of a few. It denotes an increase in inequalities and impoverishment of many, with consequent erosion of social cohesion and escalation of political conflicts (Chagas, 2023).

Financialisation, as the relative autonomy of the financial sphere from the productive sphere, is expressed in the corporate control over the monetary authority, the highly abstract and fictitious nature of the values created by financial markets,[3] and the expansion of the power of financial operators to delimit the contours and directions of the economy by defining which agents, countries, or even what types of transactions can or cannot enter into financial globalisation. These processes cannot be conceived without the objective dismantling and subjective reprogramming of the world of work and collective political action. This is the bridge between neoliberalism as a rationale, practice of government, and subjectivation on the one hand, and neoliberalism as a form of management of the economic system on the other, as a regime of flexible accumulation. This advent, Pierre Bourdieu (2003) lamented early on, jeopardises the very condition of possibility for one of the most distinctive features of modern societies (and earlier forms of capitalism): the relative autonomy of the intellectual, cultural, and political fields. The neoliberalisation of social life subjects other social fields' internal values and particular forms of legitimation to the tabula rasa of market discipline and the immediate economic profit drives (Silva et al., 2025 Forthcoming). In neoliberal-financialised capitalism, everything tends to level out through and from the economic field and its codes.

We can now delve into digitalisation and advanced automation, which stand out as characteristic features of our time. Amidst various catastrophes occurring in different domains, if there's any dimension still holding onto hope for humanity's future, surprisingly, it lies in technology. It would seem remiss to discuss contemporary capitalism without framing it as cognitive (Negri & Vercellone, 2008), digital (Shiller, 1999), informational (Castells, 2010), and more recently, as platformised (Boyer, 2021).[4] Here, new sociotechnical imaginaries of crisis abound, with their ominous techno-

[3] As evident in the emergence of new financial products, including financial derivatives, exchange-traded funds, high-frequency trading, and crypto assets (Paraná, 2019; Rotta & Paraná, 2022).

[4] Thomas Poell, David Nieborg, and José Van Dijck describe platforms as "(re)programmable digital infrastructures that enable and influence personalised interactions among end-users and complementors, facilitated by the systematic collection, algorithmic processing, monetisation, and dissemination of data" (Poell et al., 2019, p. 3). Platformisation, on the other hand, refers to "the infiltration of platforms' infrastructures, economic processes, and regulatory frameworks into various economic sectors and aspects of life. Drawing on the tradi-

political narratives, invoking both horror and fascination: from cryptocurrencies to private manned spaceflights, from artificial intelligence to scientific explorations on man-machine interface.

Moving forward, it is necessary to consider the unique encounter between financialised neoliberal capitalism and the informational revolution, manifested in the digitalisation and expanded platformisation of economic activity (Srnicek, 2017; Poell et al, 2019), particularly in the services sector. This facilitates the formation of financial-informational conglomerates, the so-called Big Techs, among the most highly market-valued companies globally. A notable novelty is that, for a significant portion of these technological giants, the bulk of profits arises from share price and financial assets appreciation rather than direct economic exploitation through their innovative business models. This not only reinforces the trend towards monopolisation but also necessitates these companies becoming monopolies in order to survive and function (Pagano, 2014; Rikap, 2021). Speculation underpinning these mega-corporations, alongside technological leverage, derives precisely from the control power amassed through vast consumer and worker information and their economies of scale—often associated with the network effect (McIntyre & Srinivasan, 2017) and the winner takes all model (Valente, 2021). That is, as the number of users increases, the system becomes even more valuable which, in turn, tends to attract more users, creating structural impediments to new entrants to the market.

Despite representing massive shifts within economic and political power relations, contrary to popular belief, digitalisation, platforms, and advanced automation, while impactful, have not yielded substantial gains in labour productivity or sustained economic growth (Benanav, 2020). Despite financial innovations amplifying financial valorisation, they seem incapable of much else. The so-called fourth industrial revolution (Schwab, 2016) has not ushered in the brilliant future promised in its rhetoric. Instead, digitalisation and platformisation, particularly in the services sector, have become the backbone of intensified exploitation, precariousness, and growing informality in the labour market—a realm marked by high technology paired with low quality of work and life (Scholz, 2016; Tubaro et al., 2020). It turns out that the new digital stage of capitalism is defined by the intensification of its exploitative nature through the lifting of protections and restrictions and the expansion of capital accumulation into new areas.

It is crucial to understand that digitalisation and financialisation are complementary dimensions of the same macrostructural change within capitalism in recent decades (Sadowski, 2020). Recognising this aspect enables us to see beyond low rates of global economic growth, sluggish productivity gains, deepening inequalities, and what is immediately apparent in the so-called secular stagnation (Rawdanowicz et al, 2014; Summers, 2015; Blanchard, 2023)—a context where, paradoxically, the power of money appears immense yet insignificant. Immense in prolonging and sustaining financial

tion of cultural studies, it represents the restructuring of cultural practices and perceptions around platforms" (Poell et al., 2019, p. 5).

profits but insignificant in driving employment, consumption, and production in the real economy.

The digital economy

Having established these broader (macro level) connections, we can now better characterise, at a middle or meso level, what is meant by the term digital economy. The term is somewhat ambiguous, having been defined in diverse ways, often contradicting each other.[5] Considering the context provided earlier, the digital economy, as I refer to it here, encompasses a series of major transformations that have unfolded since the 1970s and 1980s, culminating in the first two decades of the 21st century. Specifically, I highlight the consequences of the revolution brought about by information and communication technologies (ICT), within a context marked by industrial-productive restructuring and the expansion of finance's power over production (financialisation). Adding to that, one can mention other significant political-institutional and cultural transformations related to the neoliberalisation of public life, as discussed earlier. It is within this framework that a new international division of labour emerged, alongside the intensification of economic globalisation, resulting in the establishment of new global value chains and their subsequent geopolitical consequences—such as the re-articulation of American hegemony (Panitch & Gindin 2013), the economic and political rise of China (Majerowicz & Paraná, 2024), and the formation of new geoeconomic blocs. Therefore, characterising the digital economy—this so-called new age of the global economy—focusing solely on the emergence of new technologies, without considering these structural dynamics and their evolution, is insufficient and erroneous.

With that in mind, we can now discuss information and communication technologies and their role in shaping this new phase of the world economy. More so than earlier technologies, ICTs are 'cognitive' technologies (or technologies of cognition). While this description could apply to nearly all technologies, ICTs are particularly effective in reshaping the spatial-temporal dimensions central to individual and social experiences (Harvey, 1989; Paraná, 2019). These technologies condense space into time, facilitating the acceleration and compression of flows, which, in turn, give rise to sociotechnical structures like digital networks and platforms. This enables the increasing codification of human interactions into binary data and information, further deepening the financialisation of social life (Zuboff, 2019). By enhancing control and surveillance, these arrangements make possible the technical decentralisation of nearly everything: work, production, circulation, consumption, financial, and communication flows (Paraná, 2024). However, such technical decentralisation only superficially and momentarily leads to the disintermediation of

---

[5] For surveys and discussion of different definitions of the Digital Economy, refer to OECD (2020) and Williams (2021).

economic practices favouring supposedly distributive, self-governed, and cooperative sharing-economy models. Within a capitalist leitmotiv, the digital economy enforces a brutal concentration of processed information and its political-economic effects. The so-called disruptive processes of digital transformation, where third parties and middlemen are removed from information transaction processes, in fact, rapidly replace old economic and social actors for new ones, reintermediating what was just previously disintermediated (Langley & Leyshon, 2021; Hendrikse et al., 2024). The historical evolution of the internet from a decentralised, non-monetary commons-based communication system into an enclosed webspace controlled by tech giants and big corporate platforms serves as the supreme example (McChesney, 2013).[6]

As I have argued before (Paraná, 2024), the informational co-presence and the rapid acceleration of flows connecting production, circulation, and consumption create a convergence between the pressures of technical-operational decentralisation and the increasing concentration of economic, political and sociotechnical power. This results in a growing divide in the labour market and the expansion of monopolistic tendencies within the platform economy, driven by scale and network effects (Valente, 2021). More specifically, digitalisation supports the growing independence of finance from production, a key aspect of financialisation. By linking various locations and social spheres, speeding up processes, and capitalising on economic opportunities from data and information, digital technologies infuse every socio-economic process they engage with financial speculative dynamics. This process gives rise to numerous social tensions. That includes increased inequalities, disruptions in the labour market due to advanced automation, data privacy and data security issues, challenges to technological, fiscal, and financial-monetary sovereignty of nation-states, frictions in global value chains, transformations of the public sphere with its disorganising political impacts, and geoeconomic conflicts.

Once characterised the main features of the digital economy, we can now delve into the strategic resources of this new techno-economic paradigm (Perez, 2010). These are the computational processing capacity, production, storage, and cataloguing of data on an exponential scale, connectivity technologies and the effective combination of these factors through algorithms, programmes, and applications. Equally important is the vast physical infrastructure supporting it: fibre-optic cables and networks, antennas, satellites, routers, microchips, mechanical components, data and processing centres, and new energy sources, comprising a large "global system of machinery" (Majerowicz, 2021), distributed across different sectors, companies, and countries. These sociotechnical infrastructures, without which global society is no longer able to function properly, demonstrate that even in a supposedly virtual world,

---

[6] As I elaborate on in the following section, the internet is currently transitioning from a previous non-corporatised commons-oriented stage to a stage dominated by platformisation, which intensifies its monetisation. In simple terms, capitalist appropriation is expanding into areas that were previously not subject to such appropriation. Just as private property encloses common lands, the digital economy is undergoing a similar process. The same is true for cryptocurrencies: while some enthusiasts may have initially viewed them as a democratic tool, they have evolved into a realm where exploitation, speculation, and consequently financialisation are dominant.

the spatial and territorial dimensions of power remain central (Graham, 2018; Qiu, 2023). These evolving developments extend rapidly across various fields—civil and military, productive, financial, entertainment, and communication—leading some (Schwab, 2016) to characterise it as a new industrial revolution, where boundaries between the online and offline worlds, and between physical, biological, and digital spheres, become even more blurred.

Cementing already existing international division of labour and global value chains, the global south enters a dependent position into this dynamic (Jin, 2013; Couldry & Mejias, 2019). Let us take Brazil, a significant emerging power, as an example. Despite having the sixth-largest population in the world and ranking as the 9th-largest economy, the country represents the world's fourth-largest consumer market for digital goods and services (Pochmann, 2023). Brazilians are primarily (and disproportionally big) consumers of digital services and providers of cheap information, data, and digital labour. For this reason, even with such a thriving digital market, they have inserted themselves into this dynamic in a still subordinate manner, at the expense of the growing economic complexity and other economic opportunities that this new economic paradigm could bring them.

Some developments in the digital economy considering the relationship between finance and technology

Having understood that, we can now return to our guiding questions: How and from where to investigate this phase, moment, or configuration of capitalism broadly and abstractly defined here? How can we concretely and empirically frame the relationships between neoliberalism and financialisation? How, within this framework, to elaborate on the transformations around digitalisation?

A promising approach involves identifying research objects strategically positioned within such connections to investigate the tendencies and countertrends they uncover. That is, research objects characterised by an especially contradictory or paradoxical nature. The idea is that these objects, situated at the frontier or limit, may be less obvious in terms of their definitions and characterisations, enabling us to pose new questions and make new discoveries, thereby deepening our understanding of capitalism in our time. More objectively, the plasticity of the reconfiguration of the circuits of capital in the face of the role of credit, on the one hand, and of scientific-technological development, on the other, as sources, at the same time, of expansion and crisis of the capitalist system in the face of the limits that its development imposes on itself, appear, at this juncture, as a particularly fruitful research endeavour.

Marx says in the third volume of *Capital* (1991) that "capitalist production constantly strives to overcome these [its] immanent barriers, but it overcomes them only by means that set up the barriers afresh and on a more powerful scale" (p. 358). In this regard, credit and finance, on the one hand, and science and technology, on the other, perhaps configure the two main levers of contemporary capitalism. This has been particularly evident since the great financial crisis of 2008,[7] when a massive influx of cheap money into the beleaguered banking sector bolstered tech-oriented venture capital (Srnicek, 2017). Finance and technology are ways to discount the future in the present, of expanding the limits and barriers to valorisation, of recomposing, reorganising, and advancing productive forces (Marx, 1991; da Motta e Albuquerque, 2023). Hence, it is basically around this articulation that I first investigated what I called Digitalised Finance (the relationship between the development of information and communication technologies and the process of financialisation of the world economy), the digitalisation of capital markets and their social consequences (Paraná, 2019), and then the digitalisation of money and monetary-financial innovations such as Bitcoin (Paraná, 2020).

Cryptocurrencies may serve as illuminating examples of this development. Bitcoin, which came into existence in 2009 (Golumbia, 2016), is likely the most recognised and established cryptocurrency. As reviewed by Rotta and Paraná (2022), "the consensus in the extant scholarship is that Bitcoin is neither money nor currency with general social acceptance but is rather an asset mainly used as a vehicle for speculative investments" (p. 3). It also functions as a limited medium of exchange. Due to its strong demand for transferring payments and settling transactions across international borders, as well as its use in online transactions, speculation, tax evasion, wealth protection, and ransomware payments, Bitcoin has steadily gained importance in the modern economy. Cryptocurrencies also embody the technological and financialised aspect typical of the new form of digital economy. But are cryptocurrencies really innovative and significant when it comes to retheorising capitalism more deeply, and if so, how?

The starting point for such an understanding is the correct characterisation of its nature. Cryptocurrency is not money and there is nothing to indicate that, if its current configurations are maintained, it will be. Money, in the full sense of the term, is the socially accepted and recognised vehicle for abstracting wealth, the general equivalent, the universal mechanism for representing and realising value (Brunhoff, 2015). As such, it implies political, social, and economic prerequisites that no cryptocurrency is or will be able to meet in advanced capitalism, at least not in its current form of existence: private, restricted, unregulated, environmentally unsustainable, and highly volatile (Paraná, 2020).

Cryptocurrency is, at heart, a digital commodity, that is, an artefact produced digitally to be exchanged on the market for profit.[8] The significant point, however,

[7] For further discussions of the 2008 crisis as a watershed moment in the contemporary economy, refer to Blyth (2013) and Tooze (2018).

[8] For a conceptualisation and discussion of cryptocurrency as a commodity, refer to Rotta and Paraná (2022). By extending the Classical Political Economy approach and the New Interpretation of the labour theory of value (and rent) to the domain of digital commodities, we demonstrate that Bitcoin is a digital commodity with value but no value-added. We show that both the production of and speculation in Bitcoin draw from the existing global pool of value-added. We argue that Bitcoin mining is an automated reproduction process that requires no direct (living) labour and, as such, generates no new value. Across sectors, Bitcoin mining redistributes

is how this digital commodity is produced, the mechanism that allows it to conform to this variant of a digital thing. Here lies the main novelty that this technological innovation brings about: the technical feasibility of an operationally solid form of private ownership of digital things without the need for direct legal action by the state. That is, the possibility of reproducing in the virtual world the rivalry of use and ownership—as well as the eventual scarcity—typical of physical goods. It is, therefore, a technology of disintermediation (meaning the elimination of monetary and financial intermediaries, third parties, or middlemen), which allows information goods to be locked up and privatised in a completely new way. All its other functions, uses, and forms of existence are subject to this technical feature—as a means of exchange in restricted spaces, as a speculative asset, as financial innovation, and as an enabler of illicit businesses, among others.

Intangible products, such as information and knowledge, are challenging to fully encapsulate within the framework of market logic and private property. This challenge arises because, once created, the barriers to access and the costs of reproducing these goods are typically minimal (Rotta & Paraná, 2022). Since the widespread adoption of the internet, digital enterprises have grappled with this issue, experimenting with various models and, where possible, relying on state intervention to enforce private property rights over intellectual, cognitive, or informational assets. This ongoing conflict sees new forms of control constantly met with corresponding acts of resistance. The platformisation of the internet, which confines it within corporate-controlled spaces of flows and interactions, along with the rise of asset tokenisation,[9] represents significant strategic advancements—especially when combined—towards the necessary enclosure and privatisation required to fully extend the logic of capital into the digital-information realm (Paraná, 2024).

It is true that cryptocurrencies, due to their anonymous and unregulated nature, represent an attractive vehicle for illegal and criminal activities, currency evasion, and tax avoidance, contributing to reinforcing the parallel economy of wealth hiding and tax havens that has advanced enormously in the last decades (Zucman, 2015). It would be equally correct to characterise them as another form of speculative asset, which, in the context of the financialisation of everything, rises and falls in price to the taste of the search for quick and deterritorialised profits, in a global macroeconomic situation that encourages and supports such kinds of economic behaviour. Nor would it be a mistake to characterise it as another technical-institutional innovation in the financial world, with important impacts on it, even with regard to the role of financial

---

pre-existing wealth and value-added, while miners with greater computational power compete to appropriate mining profits within the blockchain. The Bitcoin blockchain thereby creates rivalry in both the ownership and use of the digital commodity through non-legal mechanisms. This approach, we believe, can be further extended to the broader domain of automated digital commodities that are reproducible without the expenditure of direct, living labour.

[9] Asset tokenisation involves converting the ownership rights of an asset into a digital token, which can then be stored, sold, and exchanged on a Blockchain. These tokens represent the ownership of the original asset. Asset tokenisation enables direct peer-to-peer trading of conventional and non-conventional assets, eliminating the need for intermediaries.

institutions and states in monetary-financial dynamics. However, for this all to be valid, cryptocurrencies must first be a new form of technical-operational support for the private ownership of digital products. While the aforementioned aspects are certainly important, this is the central element. Here lies the fundamental milestone of this new round of technological leverage in the digital economy: the search for new businesses, new frontiers for the private appropriation of what tends to be captured with greater difficulty by commodification processes, that is, art, knowledge and information—also encompassing software and platforms, games and networks.

The creation of spurious new forms of digital products can be additionally illustrated by the rise of the NFT—the Non-Fungible Token (Sadowski & Beegle, 2023; Crandall, 2023), that can be directly related to cryptocurrencies. NFTs are cryptographic assets residing on Blockchain networks, serving as digital representations of unique items such as artworks, digital media, or content. Each NFT functions as an immutable digital record verifying ownership and authenticity of the associated asset, whether tangible or digital. These tokens possess inherent features, including cryptographic validation, exclusivity, and seamless transferability. The process of NFT creation, known as minting, entails executing a blockchain transaction detailing token specifications, which subsequently triggers a smart contract function to instantiate the token and assign it to its owner. NFTs can represent a diverse array of assets, spanning digital art, collectible items, multimedia content, and event tickets.

It is crucial to understand how the digital process of enclosure and commodification unfolds in practice, particularly concerning bitcoins and NFTs. This process is enabled by Blockchain, a pivotal technology in cryptocurrencies. Blockchain facilitates collaborative, technically decentralised, public, and auditable recording of information, removing the need for a central transaction settler and bookkeeper. This distributed and collaborative self-management within a network, based on the computing power of its participants, forms the basis for cryptographically recording certain digital information as unique—such as a unit of Bitcoin being non-reproducible. This capability allows for the proliferation of tokens and cryptoassets, transforming almost anything into a unique and transactional symbol. As a result, one of the primary features of this innovation is its ability to commodify intangible objects by assigning them some monetary value. Blockchain technically allows for conferring unique and transactional value upon virtually anything.

The developments and consequences that cryptocurrencies have been producing since their appearance mainly stem from this effect—the emergence of their public and distributed cryptographic registry technology. From the new local and alternative digital currencies to the elaborations around the new central bank digital currencies, from fintech and open banking to the new NFT markets, here lies the engine and vector of the centrifugal force of disintermediation (which does not mean the same as deconcentration—in fact, it could be just the opposite of that) and, above all, commodification (or tokenisation, assetisation, if you will) that the cryptographic world imposes on the space that crosses, in an increasingly intricate way, finance and technology in contemporary digital capitalism. This is how, strictly framed in a systemic reading, the study of an object like Bitcoin, among many other challenging analogous developments, can help us see something more about what emerges as fundamental around the relationships established contemporaneously between technological domination and financial hegemony.

Financialised digitalisation and the (re)theorisation of capitalism

Capitalism evolves by circumventing contradictions through the creation of new contradictions, perpetuating the hegemony of capital as a social relation. This entails the valorisation of value through labour exploitation, driving social (re)production and distribution towards endless accumulation, extraction, and expropriation of social and natural environments to the point of exhaustion. Furthermore, this process instigates structural changes in other social relations and the overall economy, underscoring the historical nature of capitalism's perpetual transformation. This is its revolutionary form alluded to at the beginning of this chapter. Yet, these transformations are underpinned by continuities or adaptations of core exploitation relations, allowing for variances in the capitalist mode of production across space and time, each shaped by historical, cultural, and geographical particularities. When *(re)theorising capitalism*, it is crucial to scrutinise structural discontinuities within continuities and vice versa.

This chapter has examined global capitalism from an abstract and macro perspective, illuminating the interconnectedness of neoliberalisation, financialisation, and digitalisation in defining its current phase. Emphasising the overdetermination of these transformations, the primary argument posits that the system is entering a new stage propelled by digital transformation, where the convergence of intensified technological domination and financial hegemony assumes particular significance. Understanding such a convergence is vital for comprehending the revitalisation of capitalism in the digital age, here conceptualised as financialised digitalisation (or digitalised financialisation).

Regarding the investigation of transitions within capitalism and this specific phase transition, I proposed focusing on the interplay between finance and technology as a strategic entry point since these are powerful means of expanding the limits and barriers to valorisation, spearheading the reorganisation of productive forces within capitalism. I then moved to more concrete manifestations of this proposal by highlighting how research objects such as digital finance, cryptocurrencies, and NFT can serve as valuable starting points for gathering empirical evidence about current capitalist contradictions.

In addressing the financialised technologisation of social life characteristic of this contemporary form of transitional capitalism, I underscored some of the overarching trends emerging from the examination of such phenomena, including social acceleration tied to the compression of spatiotemporal flows, the escalating strategic significance of property over production and products, and the growing social influence of data and information. In essence, a new configuration, increasingly pervasive, facilitating the utilisation of technical decentralisation for economic and political concentration. That is why, following these trends, particularly since the mid-2000s, it is no longer feasible to discuss financialisation without considering digitalisation (or platformisation) and vice versa.

When it comes to the social consequences of these transformations, the compulsive anticipation of the future in the present—a hallmark of capital valorisation anchored in property title possession, where value primarily depends on speculative future profitability—establishes a state of economic exception, a perpetual crisis, constantly teetering on the brink of imminent collapse. This imposition of finance's short-term, deregulating, and deterritorialising temporality across all economic domains forcefully constrains the horizon of capital accumulation and, consequently, the horizon of social possibilities, including the potential for social and political imagination concerning alternative futures, making the case for reimagining society beyond capitalism even more pressing.

These are not inevitable forces. Pertaining to the objects examined in this chapter, ongoing disputes, such as emerging new configurations of digital, community, state, or individual sovereignty persist (Campbell-Verduyn & Paraná, 2021). The same applies to the role of digital and cryptographic technologies in debates over individual and collective, public and private coordination, privacy, and transparency (Nardelli et al., 2023).

In summary, alternative possibilities can emerge from the distributive force of the digital world without privatisation, individualisation, and commodification of everything becoming the sole viable path, though this seems unlikely at present. Nevertheless, achieving this necessitates a rigorous understanding of the situation and steadfast political action in favour of new egalitarian, democratic, and public-oriented progressive configurations for such technologies and their applications (Dyer-Whiteford, 2020; Woodcock, 2021). For this reason, attaining a thorough understanding of the principal trends in today's capitalism is a crucial first step in this direction.

References

Althusser, L. (2005). *For Marx.* Verso.

Bayliss, K., Fine, B., Robertson, M., & Saad-Filho, A. (2024). Reports of my death are greatly exaggerated: The persistence of neoliberalism in Britain. *European Journal of Social Theory, 0*(0). https://doi.org/10.1177/13684310241241800

Benanav, A. (2020). *Automation and the future of work.* Verso.

Blanchard, O. (2023, January 24). Secular stagnation is not over. *Peterson Institute for International Economics.* https://www.piie.com/blogs/realtime-economics/secular-stagnation-not-over

Blyth, M. (2002). *Great transformations: Economic ideas and institutional change in the twentieth century.* Cambridge University Press. https://doi.org/10.1017/CBO9781139087230

Blyth, M. (2013). *Austerity: The history of a dangerous idea.* Oxford University Press.

Boltanski, L., & Chiapello, E. (2018). *The new spirit of capitalism.* Verso.

Bourdieu, P. (2003). *Firing back: Against the tyranny of the market.* Verso.

Boyer, R. (1990). *The regulation school: A critical introduction.* Columbia University Press.

Boyer, R. (2022). Platform capitalism: A socio-economic analysis. *Socio-Economic Review, 20*(4), 1857–1879. https://doi.org/10.1093/ser/mwaa055

Brewster, B. (2005). Glossary. In: Althusser, L. (2005). *For Marx* (pp. 249–257). Verso.

Brown, W. (2015). *Undoing the demos: Neoliberalism's stealth revolution.* Zone Books.

Brunhoff, S. (1986). *L'heure du marché.* PUF.

Brunhoff, S. (2015). *Marx on money.* Verso.

Campbell-Verduyn, M., & Paraná, E. (2021, November 13). Cryptocurrencies and the need to wrestle with multiple sovereignties in the blockchain age. *Trends.* https://trendsresearch.org/insight/cryptocurrencies-and-the-need-to-wrestle-with-multiple-sovereignties-in-the-blockchain-age/

Castells, M. (2010). *The information age: Economy, society and culture Volume 1: The rise of the network society.* Wiley Blackwell.

Chagas, V. (2023). Far-right memespheres and platform affordances: The effects of environmental opacity on the spread of extremist memes on Twitter and WhatsApp. *Journal of Applied Communication Research, 51*(6), 702–719. https://doi.org/10.1080/00909882.2024.2355114

Chesnais, F. (Ed.). (1996). *La mondialisation financière: Genèse, coût, enjeux.* Syros.

Chesnais, F. (2016). *Finance capital today.* Brill.

Chiapello, E. (2017). La financiarisation des politiques publiques. *Mondes en Développement, 178*(2), 23–40. https://doi.org/10.3917/med.178.0023

Coriat, B. (1983). *La robotique.* La Découverte/Maspéro.

Coriat, B. (1990). *L'atelier et le robot: Essai sur le fordisme et la production de masse à l'âge de l'électronique.* Christian Bourgois éditeur.

Couldry, N., & Mejias, U. A. (2019). Data colonialism: Rethinking Big Data's relation to the contemporary subject. *Television & New Media, 20*(4), 336–349. https://doi.org/10.1177/1527476418796632

Crandall, J. (2023). Living on the block: How equitable is tokenized equity? *Big Data & Society, 10*(2). https://doi.org/10.1177/20539517231208455

da Motta e Albuquerque, E. (2023). *Technological revolutions and the periphery: Understanding global development through regional lenses*. Springer. https://doi.org/10.1007/978-3-031-43436-5

Deleuze, G., & Guattari, F. (1983). *Anti-Oedipus: Capitalism and schizophrenia*. University of Minnesota Press.

Duménil, G., & Lévy, D. (2011). *The crisis of neoliberalism*. Harvard University Press.

Dyer-Whiteford, N. (2020). Left populism and platform capitalism. *tripleC: Communication, Capitalism & Critique, 18*(1), 116–131. https://doi.org/10.31269/triplec.v18i1.1130

Engels, F., & Marx, K. (2015). *The communist manifesto*. Penguin Classics.

Fine, B. (2022). From Marxist political economy to financialization or is it the other way about? In D. Fasenfest (Ed.), *Marx matters* (pp. 43–66). Brill. https://doi.org/10.1163/9789004504790_004

Fine, B. (2013–14). Financialisation from a Marxist perspective. *International Journal of Political Economy, 42*(4), 47–66. https://doi.org/10.2753/IJP0891-1916420403

Fine, B., & Saad-Filho, A. (2014). Politics of neoliberal development: Washington Consensus and post-Washington Consensus. In H. Weber (Ed.), *Politics of neoliberalism* (pp. 154–166). Routledge.

Golumbia, D. (2016). *The politics of Bitcoin: Software as right-wing extremism*. University of Minnesota Press.

Gradillas, M., & Thomas, L. D. W. (2023). Distinguishing digitization and digitalization: A systematic review and conceptual framework. *Journal of Product Innovation Management*, 1–32. https://doi.org/10.1111/jpim.12690

Graham, M. (2018). The virtual palimpsest of the global city network. In X. Ren & R. Keil (Eds.), *The globalizing cities reader* (pp. 198–204). Routledge.

Harvey, D. (1989). *The condition of postmodernity*. Blackwell.

Harvey, D. (2005). *A brief history of neoliberalism*. Oxford University Press.

Hendrikse, R., Bassens, D., & Rossiter, A. (2024). Rebooting Amsterdam for the age of Big Tech: Platform capitalism, reintermediation, and financial-center change. *Geoforum, 148*. https://doi.org/10.1016/j.geoforum.2023.103894

Jessop, B. (2002). *The future of the capitalist state*. Polity Press.

Jin, D. Y. (2013). The construction of platform imperialism in the globalization era. *tripleC: Communication, Capitalism & Critique, 11*(1), 145–172. https://doi.org/10.31269/triplec.v11i1.458

Langley, P., & Leyshon, A. (2021). The platform political economy of FinTech: Reintermediation, consolidation and capitalisation. *New Political Economy, 26*(3), 376–388. https://doi.org/10.1080/13563467.2020.1766432

Lavinas, L. (2017). *The takeover of social policy by financialization: The Brazilian paradox*. Palgrave Macmillan.

Lavinas, L. (2020). The collateralization of social policy by financial markets in the global South. In P. Mader, D. Mertens, & N. Van der Zwan (Eds.), *The Routledge international handbook of financialization* (pp. 312–323). Routledge.

Lazzarato, M. (2012). *The making of the indebted man*. Semiotext(e).

Lojkine, J. (1992). *La révolution infirnatuinnelle*. Presses Universitaires France.

Majerowicz, E. (2021). As tecnologias da informação e comunicação enquanto sistema tecnológico e de maquinaria: Implicações para as dinâmicas concorrenciais. *Texto para Discussão. UFRN. DEPEC, Natal, 005*, jul.

Majerowicz, E., & Paraná, E. (Eds.). (2024). *China in contemporary capitalism*. Brill.

Marx, K. (1990). *Capital: Volume I*. Penguin Classics.

Marx, K. (1991). *Capital: Volume III*. Penguin Classics.

Matthess, M., & Kunkel, S. (2020). Structural change and digitalization in developing countries: Conceptually linking the two transformations. *Technology in Society, 63*. https://doi.org/10.1016/j.techsoc.2020.101428

McChesney, R. W. (2013). *Digital disconnect: How capitalism is turning the internet against democracy*. New Press.

McIntyre, D., & Srinivasan, A. (2017). Networks, platforms, and strategy: Emerging views and next steps. *Strategic Management Journal, 38*(1), 141–160. https://doi.org/10.1002/smj.2596

Mollo, M. L. R., Dourado, F. F., & Paraná, E. (2022). Financialisation as the development of fictitious capital in developing and developed economies. *Cambridge Journal of Economics, 46*(5), 955–976. https://doi.org/10.1093/cje/beac041

Nardelli, P. H., Gória Silva, P. E., Siljak, H., & Narayanan, A. (2023). Cyber-physical decentralized planning for communizing. *Competition & Change, 0*(0). https://doi.org/10.1177/10245294231213141

Negri, A., & Vercellone, C. (2008). Le rapport capital/travail dans le capitalisme cognitif. *Multitudes, 32*(1), 39–50. https://doi.org/10.3917/mult.032.0039

OECD. (2020). *A roadmap toward a common framework for measuring the digital economy*. Report for the G20 digital economy task force. https://www.itu.int/en/ITU-D/Statistics/Documents/publications/OECDRoadmapDigitalEconomy2020.pdf

Pagano, U. (2014). The crisis of intellectual monopoly capitalism. *Cambridge Journal of Economics, 38*(6), 1409–1429. https://doi.org/10.1093/cje/beu025

Paraná, E. (2019). *Digitalized finance: Financial capitalism and informational revolution*. Brill.

Paraná, E. (2020). *Bitcoin: A utopia tecnocrática do dinheiro apolítico*. Autonomia Literária.

Paraná, E. (2024). Platform studies and the finance-technology nexus: For a "genetic" approach. *Platforms & Society*, 1. https://doi.org/10.1177/29768624241286779

Perez, C. (2010). Technological revolutions and techno-economic paradigms. *Cambridge Journal of Economics, 34*, 185–202. https://doi.org/10.1093/cje/bep051

Pochmann, M. (2023, April 04). A urgente reindustrialização na era digital. *Outras Palavras*. https://outraspalavras.net/crise-brasileira/a-necessaria-reindustrializacao-na-era-digital/

Poell, T., Nieborg, D., & van Dijck, J. (2019). Platformisation. *Internet Policy Review*, 8(4). https://doi.org/10.14763/2019.4.1425

Polanyi, K. (2001). *The great transformation: The political and economic origins of our time*. Beacon Press.

Qiu, J. L. (2023). Three approaches to platform studies: Cobweb, billiard balls, and ant societies. *Social Media + Society*, 9(3). https://doi.org/10.1177/20563051231193304

Rawdanowicz, Ł., Bouis, R., Inaba, K-I., & Christensen, A.K. (2014). Secular stagnation: Evidence and implications for economic policy. *OECD Economics Department Working Papers, 1169*. OECD Publishing. https://doi.org/10.1787/5jxvgg6q27vd-en

Rikap, C. (2021). *Capitalism, power and innovation: Intellectual monopoly capitalism uncovered*. Routledge. https://doi.org/10.4324/9780429341489

Rotta, T. N., & Paraná, E. (2022). Bitcoin as a digital commodity. *New Political Economy, 27*(6), 1046–1061. https://doi.org/10.1080/13563467.2022.2054966

Sadowski, J. (2020). The internet of landlords: Digital platforms and new mechanisms of rentier capitalism. *Antipode, 52*(2), 562–580. https://doi.org/10.1177/20539517231159629

Sadowski, J., & Beegle, K. (2023). Expansive and extractive networks of web3. *Big Data & Society, 10*(1). https://doi.org/10.1177/20539517231159629

Serfati, C. (2008). Financial dimensions of transnational corporations, global value chain and technological innovation. *Journal of Innovation Economics & Management, 2*(2), 35–61. https://doi.org/10.3917/jie.002.0035

Scholz, T. (2016). *Platform cooperativism. Challenging the corporate sharing economy*. Rosa Luxemburg Foundation. https://rosalux.nyc/wp-content/uploads/2020/11/RLS-NYC_platformcoop.pdf

Schwab, K. (2016). *The fourth industrial revolution*. World Economic Forum.

Schumpeter, J. A. (2008). *Capitalism, socialism, and democracy*. HarperCollins.

Shiller, D. (1999). *Digital capitalism*. MIT Press.

Silva, L. T., Paraná, E., & Pimenta, A. M. (2025 Forthcoming). From Althusser to Foucault, and back: State, discipline and governmentality in the crisis of neoliberalism. *Historical Materialism*.

Srnicek, N. (2017). *Platform capitalism*. Polity Press.

Streeck, W. (2011). The crises of democratic capitalism. *New Left Review, 71*, 5–29.

Sturgeon, T. J. (2009). From commodity chains to value chains: Interdisciplinary theory building in an age of globalization. In J. Bair (Ed.), *Frontiers of commodity chain research* (pp. 110–135). Stanford University Press.

Summers, L. H. (2015). Demand side secular stagnation. *American Economic Review, 105*(5), 60–65. https://doi.org/10.1257/aer.p20151103

Tooze, A. (2018). *Crashed: How a decade of financial crises changed the world*. Viking.

Tubaro, P., Casilli, A. A., & Coville, M. (2020). The trainer, the verifier, the imitator: Three ways in which human platform workers support artificial intelligence. *Big Data & Society, 7*(1). https://doi.org/10.1177/2053951720919776

Valente, J. C. L. (2021). *From online platforms to digital monopolies: Technology, information and power*. Brill.

Van der Zwan, N. (2014). Making sense of financialization. *Socio-Economic Review, 12*(1), 99–129. https://doi.org/10.1093/ser/mwt020

Williams, L. D. (2021). Concepts of digital economy and industry 4.0 in intelligent and information systems. *International Journal of Intelligent Networks, 2*, 122–129. https://doi.org/10.1016/j.ijin.2021.09.002

Woodcock, J. (2021). *Fight against platform capitalism: An inquiry into the global struggles of the gig economy*. University of Westminster Press. https://doi.org/10.16997/book51

Zuboff, S. (2019). *The age of surveillance capitalism: The fight for a human future at the new frontier of power*. PublicAffairs.

Zucman, G. (2015). *The hidden wealth of nations: The scourge of tax havens*. The University of Chicago Press. https://doi.org/10.7208/chicago/9780226245560.001.0001

14
Re-indigenising kuku (green-lipped mussel) economies in Aotearoa (New Zealand)

Georgia McLellan, Cory Tuhoro-Bodey & Anataia van Leeuwen

Dominant[1] conceptualisations of modern-day Indigenous economies commonly misrepresent the underlying forms of these economies as some variant of capitalism. Competing mobilisations of 'the economy' are bound into different political projects, visions of national futures, and understandings of related possibilities. State agencies and allied actors, such as management consultancies, are actively defining and working to grow a singular homogenous and essentialised Māori (Indigenous people of New Zealand)[2] economy. This conception assembles actors, resources, social relations, meanings, and objectives into analogues of dominant understandings of 'the Māori economy'. While Indigenous economies involve capitalist practices, they are not entirely capitalocentric. In Aotearoa, for example, there is a significant debate about what is meant by 'the Māori economy' at a time when the nation is waking up to the importance of Māori assets, investments, and aspirations. The asset base of 'the Māori economy' is currently estimated to be approximately $70 billion (Nana et al., 2021). This number is significant because it highlights the importance of Māori ownership and financial activities. However, making this claim as an analytical conclusion or ontological fact is problematic. Not only is it fraught with inaccuracy,

[1] The use of "dominant" throughout this Chapter is inspired by Liboiron (2021) who distinguishes *dominant science* from *western science* to address uneven power relations and highlight the fact that not all western science is dominant. The same goes for economies. Not all western conceptualisations of economies are dominant, for example, Gibson-Graham's (2005, 2008) diverse economies and community econoimes scholarship.

[2] Translations of te reo Māori words are provided in parentheses on first use. All te reo translations are tailored for their specific context within this Chapter and may not serve well as universal definitions.

McLellan, G., Tuhoro-Bodey, C. & van Leeuwen, A. (2025). Re-indigenising kuku (green-lipped mussel) economies in Aotearoa (New Zealand). In A. Kangas, I. Gataulina, M. Poutanen, A. I. Rajala & H-E. Ventovirta (Eds.), *Retheorising capitalism* (pp. 281–300). Tampere University Press. https://doi.org/10.61201/tup.981

but it is a distraction that misses much of what economy 'is', what is special about Māori economy, and works to deny the rights and possibilities of Māori economic self-determination.

The widely touted idea of 'the Māori economy' requires re-framing to better reflect Māori economic thought and practice and to inform and actualise thriving Māori and national futures. A productive and politically fertile starting point is to recognise that Māori economies, as a sphere of social practice, are always multiple (Amoamo et al., 2018; Scobie & Sturman, 2024), have distinctive foundations, and produce diverse material worlds. To understand Māori economies as a distinctive form of social practice and approach to mobilising resources to enhance livelihoods requires a different conceptual starting point. Recent scholarship argues that this starting point must lie in Māori worlds (Amoamo et al., 2018; Dell et al., 2018; Tau & Rout, 2018).

Māori economic scholars and development practitioners are adding new elements to the critical literature, calling for alternative theories of economy and their enactment (Amoamo et al., 2018; Bargh, 2011, 2012; Dell et al., 2018). These different calls for re-imagining and taking back the economy begin from a shared position that economy is a set of social practices that mobilise and steward resources to generate livelihoods. For example, Amoamo (2018) drew on Mitchell (2008) to re-frame Māori economies as the "diverse processes and interrelations through which we [Māori] constitute livelihoods" (p. 70). This reading of economy as process and practice differs markedly from the dominant, scientised conception of 'the economy', as an independent sphere of action composed of products and the acts and moments of their production, distribution, consumption, and conversion into finance for reinvestment. 'The economy' in these terms can be represented by objective measures and managed by economic expertise to yield or even maximise growth. Indeed, Mitchell (1995) argues that 'the economy' as a concept is less an objective and independent sphere in its own right and is more the outcome of a project to rekindle growth by targeted government investment during the great depression.

Although it is clear that as a category of power-knowledge, 'the economy' has become intimately entangled in neo-colonial projects of government and resource management, our interest in this Chapter on Whakatōhea kuku economies lies less in why the term 'economy' came to be used in dominant economics and more in how reclaiming economy as social process (Amoamo et al., 2018; Mitchell, 1995, 1998, 2008) can help direct attention to the distinctiveness and potentiality of Māori economies. Using a whakapapa (commonly simplified as genealogy, whakapapa is a Māori epistemology which sees all things and beings as interconnected) framework as a guiding methodology (McLellan et al., 2025 Forthcoming), this Chapter explores the social relations and practices involved in gathering and harvesting kuku and the various ways kuku enhance the livelihoods of the descendants of Whakatōhea (a tribe situated on the east coast of New Zealand). Kuku (green-lipped mussels) are a shellfish native to Aotearoa. Kuku have been harvested by Māori groups for hundreds of years and are now intensively farmed throughout Aotearoa. We use the case of kuku economies to illustrate the value of a radical, Indigenous theorisation of economy that begins from the position that Māori economies have distinctive foundations, ideologies, objectives, and social relations and materialise in multiple, often misrecognised, forms. Māori economic development and the resourcing of thriving Māori futures requires a radical re-thinking of the economy.

We start by teasing out key insights from efforts to re-imagine and re-enact economy from both Timothy Mitchell's (1995) insights on the subject and diverse economies' traditions (Gibson-Graham, 2006, 2008; Gibson-Graham et al., 2013) in the global literature. This literature offers an important language of difference which Māori economies scholars draw upon. It is also part of a wider project to 'take back the economy' from the interests and expertise vested in mainstream conceptions of the economy, a project that can be mobilised to support Māori aspirations, and to which Māori economies scholarship can bring inspiration, credibility, and authority. Māori economies scholarship has much to say about 'taking back the economy' (Gibson-Graham et al., 2013) and enabling the possibility of a new world (Roelvink et al., 2015). This is most clearly apparent in the work of Māori scholars on diverse economies (Amoamo et al., 2018; Bargh, 2011, 2012; Bargh & Otter, 2009). It is also evident in the notion of economies of mana (Henare, 2014; Scobie & Sturman, 2020) as a way of capturing the distinctive social relations that underpin Māori economies.

Re-imagining economies

The notion of a singular and quantifiable Māori economy has gained momentum in Aotearoa alongside the increase in economic assets controlled by Māori within trusts and incorporations (Nana et al., 2021). This growing asset base has become valuable to the public and private sectors in Aotearoa as it has the potential to generate revenue streams (Fitzherbert, 2015). However, Māori scholars (Amoamo et al., 2018; Bargh & Otter, 2009; Dell et al., 2018; Tau & Rout, 2018) have highlighted the capiotalocentric nature of what is represented as 'the Māori economy' in private and public sector reporting (Chapman Tripp, 2018; Chen, 2023; Klynveld Peat Marwick Goerdeler New Zealand, 2016; Māori Economic Development Panel, 2012). They insist that this representation of 'the Māori economy' as a quantifiable asset devoid of meaning and place-based relations obscures the diversity of Māori economies and their underlying social relations. Such measures subsume the complex realities of Māori livelihoods and "contradict the heterogeneity of how Māori think about themselves, ... how they see themselves connected to resources available to them ... and therefore how they use those resources" (Amoamo et al., 2018, p. 68). Māori scholars (Amoamo et al., 2018; Dell et al., 2018) have called for a re-conceptualisation of Māori economies away from dominant understandings and towards one grounded in Māori worlds that recognises the multiplicity of the actualised economies in which Māori participate and control.

This challenge echoes a broad and epistemologically diverse critique of the dominant conceptualisations of economy in the global literature. As Jones (2019) puts it:

> The domain of the 'economic' is much broader than the blinkered boundaries of what is too often taken unproblematically as capitalism. There is no singular 'economy', a monolithic entity that organises the provision of needs and wants through market exchange. Rather, economies exist in the plural, embedded in social systems, and refer to the diverse ways in which communities meet material needs and labour to make a livelihood. (p. 12)

Mitchell (1995) posited that the notion of 'the economy' emerged in the 1930s, displacing earlier conceptions that focused less on measuring production and more on the "proper husbanding and circulation of goods" (p. 9). Altman (2009), similarly accents "the complex set of activities or social relations" (p. 1) that underpin production, distribution and consumption rather than production itself, while the diverse economies tradition goes further to argue that the capitalist practices are not the singular or even dominant form of livelihood generation globally (Gibson-Graham, 2006, 2008, 2020; Gibson-Graham et al., 2013).

Diverse economies scholars provide useful ways of re-thinking capitalism and economies more generally (Gibson-Graham, 2006, 2008, 2020; Gibson-Graham et al., 2013). They understand and examine capitalism in terms of capitalist practices, for example, waged labour, commodity production, private enterprise, private property and institutional finance (Gibson-Graham, 2020). Diverse economies scholars also coined the term capitalocentrism, which they use to describe the dominance of capitalist practices within modern economies (Gibson-Graham, 2006). Capitalocentrism privileges supply and demand, capital accumulation and individual self-interest while undermining diverse economic practices (Gibson-Graham, 2020). Diverse economies scholars broaden understandings of economy by highlighting the diversity of economic practices which generate livelihoods (Gibson-Graham & Miller, 2015).

A number of Māori scholars have drawn on diverse and community economies scholarship to help articulate their re-imaginings of Māori economies (Amoamo et al., 2018; Bargh, 2011, 2012, 2014; Bargh & Otter, 2009). Diverse economies approaches encourage scholars to acknowledge activities that are often hidden and marginalised through a dominant lens, for example, non-capitalist processes and practices, and previously existing connections between social and economic worlds that have been extracted and abstracted through capitalocentrism. Māori scholars have increasingly come to argue that Māori economies are inherently diverse (Amoamo et al., 2018; Bargh, 2011, 2012, 2014).

Indigenous scholars have interpreted Indigenous economies in much the same way.

For example, Sámi scholar Kuokkanen (2011) understands economy as practices based on commitments to long-term mutually supportive relationships between humans and nature—reciprocity and intergenerational sustainability rather than profit and self-interest. Antoinette Helmer in Kuokkanen (2011) positions land nature and social relations at the centre of Indigenous economies: "Profit to Natives means a good life derived from the land and sea, that's what we are all about ... The land we hold in trust is our wealth. It is the only wealth we could pass on to our children." (p. 1).

The notion of mobilising and stewarding resources for generating livelihoods is central within Indigenous economic understandings. Kuokkanen (2011) states that economies revolve around "the sustenance of individuals, families and the community" (p. 215) and Droz (2019) posits that economy means "the way a people provide for themselves to live and thrive" (para. 2). Similarly, Māori scholars Amoamo et al. (2018) posit economy as the "diverse processes and interrelations through which we constitute livelihoods" (p. 70). Below, we discuss the strategies that Māori scholars have used to reimagine Māori-led economies.

Re-imagining Māori-led economies

Māori scholars Dell et al. (2018) and Amoamo et al. (2018) posit that if we are going to think about development in Māori worlds and resourcing Māori economic futures, we need to understand Māori economies in a way that aligns with a Māori-orientated outlook. Dell et al. (2018) construct a research agenda for re-framing Māori economies: "we need to re-imagine and redefine our future based on authentic Māori values, world views and capabilities" (p. 60). Amoamo et al. (2018) present a set of strategies for re-imagining Māori economies as grounded in people and livelihoods and suggest that borrowing diverse economic perspectives from Gibson-Graham (2006) will lead to alternative "development pathways that increase Indigenous wellbeing" (Amoamo et al., 2018, p. 70). Amoamo et al. (2018) state that we need to start thinking about Māori economies in a way that works to highlight the "Māori communities that maintain consistency of mātauranga (Māori knowledge) and tikanga (Māori customs)" and that reinstating knowledge back into conceptualisations of Māori economies will open up pathways to explore the multi-dimensionality of Māori economies (p. 67). One example of how these strategies might hold together is found in Henare's (2014) economies of mana. Mana in its broader meaning can be understood as "the potent human state with the profound ability to impact upon, affect and form the lives of others" (Dell, 2017, p. 93). However, it is more commonly defined as prestige, authority, and influence.

Economies of mana: A central concept

Mānuka Henare (2014) conceptualised traditional Māori economies as economies of mana. Dell et al. (2018), who worked closely with Henare, define the economy of mana as "An economic system in which decisions regarding investment, production, consumption and wealth distribution are influenced by the interplay of mana enhancing interactions between people and the environment" (p. 55).

Economies of mana revolve around a particular set of values which differ significantly from those within modern-day dominant economies. Henare (2014) posited that the main intent of actions within the economy of mana was to enhance the mana of others, whether they be human or more-than-human. Within the economy of mana, economic activity is driven by "spiritual, ecological, social and cultural considerations that allow for re-distribution", which differs greatly from dominant understandings of economy as defined by "resource scarcity, constraint and inefficiency" (Henare, 2014, pp. 65–66). The economy of mana prioritises well-being over profit maximisation and is not subject to capitalocentrism or uneven power relations (Henare, 2014). The idea of an economy of mana provides an alternative, non-capitalist lens through which to view Māori economies. It focuses attention first and foremost on practices and what underpins them, rather than financial measures and production-oriented, scalar, or commodity-based boundaries. Māori economies materialise around relations of mana. In what follows, we use the case of Whakatōhea kuku economies to extend this conceptualisation to an additional set of dimensions that we argue underpin Māori economies.

Thinking through economies with whakapapa-guided methodology

Whakatōhea are an iwi (Māori tribe) consisting of six sub-tribes situated on the east coast of Te-Ika-a-Māui (The North Island) in Aotearoa. Whakatōhea descendants have a longstanding whakapapa-based relationship with kuku, and kuku have enhanced their livelihoods for a very long time (Lyall, 1979; McLellan, 2020; Walker, 2007). Kuku are regarded as one of *Ngā Tamahine a Te Whakatōhea* (the daughters of Whakatōhea), along with pipi (a type of shellfish), and cockles (Waka huia, 2014). Whakatōhea descendants have always gathered kuku in their tribal area and it is still common practice to gather kuku today (McLellan, 2020; Walker, 2007). Te Tāwharau o Te Whakatōhea (hereafter TTW) is the entity responsible for managing Whakatōhea post-settlement assets. TTW controls aquaculture space off the coast of Ōpōtiki, a town within the Whakatōhea tribal area. They also hold partial ownership of Whakatōhea Mussels Ōpōtiki Limited, which operates both the TTW kuku farm and a kuku processing factory in Ōpōtiki (McLellan, 2020).

This chapter forms part of the lead author's PhD thesis. As a Whakatōhea descendant, she is ancestrally connected to the case study area, research participants, and the kuku themselves. For her, this research represents a return home to learn, reconnect and repair lost relations rather than simply collect data. Her ancestral connections also shape her exploration and examination of Whakatōhea kuku economies. While there are tensions surrounding large-scale kuku production in the Whakatōhea area, she takes a measured approach to analysing these issues because the industry is owned (partially), operated and staffed by her relations, and emerged from her ancestors' aspirations. Though these tensions are discussed within her PhD thesis, this Chapter focuses specifically on the kuku processes and practices which generate livelihoods for Whakatōhea people.

In her PhD thesis, the lead author develops a whakapapa methodology to examine Whakatōhea kuku economies from a Māori perspective. Whakapapa is commonly thought of as physical genealogical connections, but it is better understood in practice as a lens through which Māori see the world (Mikaere, 2011). The concept draws connections between all phenomena that have ever existed and ever will exist (Mikaere, 2011). The whakapapa methodology draws from key pieces of whakapapa literature, namely Painting and Burgess (2020). It consists of four key tenets for prefiguring Indigenous Māori economies.

The first key tenet is Dimensions. Whakapapa, while often understood through the metaphor of layering (Mikaere, 2011; Painting & Burgess, 2020; Roberts, 2013), is better conceptualised as multi-dimensional as it paints the world as intimately connected across multiple temporalities and networks of relations. This dimensionality enables whakapapa to function as a transformative economic methodology that paints economies as multi-dimensional and enables the uncovering of these dimensions.

Key tenet two is multiple temporalities. Through a whakapapa lens, time is circular (Lo & Houkamau, 2012; Painting & Burgess, 2020). This means that past and future economies are just as important as contemporary ones, and the aspirations and practices of ancestors and descendants play a key role in contemporary economies.

Key tenet three is connections and relationships. Whakapapa positions all human and non-human phenomena that have ever existed and ever will exist within an interconnected network (Painting & Burgess, 2020). Therefore, through a whakapapa lens, Māori economies are understood as infinitely connected and in relation, both within themselves and to other phenomena. Examining and acknowledging these relations, especially those with more-than-human phenomena, can help to re-indigenise Māori economies.

The final key tenet is obligations. A whakapapa lens suggests that through knowing our relations to other phenomena, we can come to know our obligations toward them (Forster, 2019; Mikaere, 2011; Painting & Burgess, 2020; Scobie et al., 2023). When viewed through a whakapapa lens, Māori economies consist of specific sets of intersecting obligations. The whakapapa methodology guided data collection processes for this research project.

Before primary data collection, the lead author, with the support of three summer scholar research assistants, two of which are named as co-authors, undertook a secondary source analysis. Paying particular attention to the key tenets of the whakapapa methodology, the team reviewed various documents, including academic publications, newspaper articles, and documentaries, to explore Māori relationships with kuku over time. This first research phase provided a single layer of information about how kuku have historically contributed to Māori livelihoods. The lead author then spent several months collecting primary data in Ōpōtiki examining Whakatōhea kuku economies through a whakapapa lens. Primary data was collected via field notes, a questionnaire and informal interviews.

The whakapapa methodology encouraged both the lead author and the research participants to consider the diverse dimensions of livelihood creation within Whakatōhea kuku economies. The lead author also used the whakapapa methodology to conduct thematic data analysis and explore the various dimensions of livelihood creation within Whakatōhea kuku economies over time. The following section discusses these dimensions. Because this Chapter is part of a book published on the other side of the world in a place that is far removed from Whakatōhea and Whakatōhea people, we have left participant quotes out of this book Chapter. This is out of respect for participant kōrero (conversations) which we treat as taonga (treasured phenomena). All contributions to the findings section are referenced with a participant's name or pseudonym.

Dimensions of Whakatōhea kuku economies

We worked with participants to identify the various ways in which kuku have enhanced the livelihoods of Whakatōhea descendants over time paying particular attention to the non-dominant forms of economy as "hidden, alternative and informal types of economy ... have more impact on social well-being than capitalism does" (Amoamo et al., 2018, p. 70). The ten dimensions of Whakatōhea kuku economies which are defined and discussed below are taha tinana (physical wellbeing), taha hinengaro (intellectual wellbeing), taha wairua (spiritual wellbeing), mana (authority and prestige), rauemi (resource or material), manaakitanga (hospitality and generosity), mauri (life force), whanaungatanga (relationship building), kaitiakitanga (environmental stewardship) and pūtea (money). Below, we will give an account of Whakatōhea kuku economies, focusing on these ten dimensions, which together form a set of practice-based understandings of economy that move beyond descriptions of diverse understandings of Māori economies in the literature and are grounded in real-world relations.

Taha tinana (physical wellbeing)

Taha tinana can be translated as *physical wellbeing*. Kuku, in their various forms, have long played a role in enhancing the taha tinana of Whakatōhea. Kuku are a healthy source of protein and, over time, have been considered a staple part of the Whakatōhea diet, especially for Whakatōhea ancestors who enjoyed them regularly (McLellan, 2020; Walker, 2007). One research participant reminisced about diving for kuku and cooking them on the beach as a child (Participant 6 Questionnaire, 2022). Whakatōhea descendants have always gathered kuku from various locations around the Whakatōhea area and can now purchase them directly from the local Ōpōtiki supermarket and other seafood distributors in the area. Whakatōhea Mussels Ōpotiki Limited sell kuku throughout Aotearoa, so Whakatōhea families living outside the area can purchase them. Preserving kuku was common practice for Whakatōhea ancestors; they would soak them in water or dry them out and preserve them in fat and some Whakatōhea families still ferment kuku today (Participant 6 Questionnaire, 2022).

In addition to being a reliable source of protein, kuku also uplift Whakatōhea taha tinana through their medicinal properties. Kuku oil and powder are well-known nutraceuticals used worldwide to treat arthritis (Cobb & Ernst, 2006). Whakatōhea ancestors utilised kuku for their medicinal properties long before they were produced for global markets. For example, one participant remembered one of her kuia (female elders) taking kuku to treat her swollen feet (Participant M Interview, 2022). Another participant discussed the benefits of the physical exercise that comes with diving for kuku and how it nourishes their taha tinana (Kimberley Maxwell Interview, 2022).

Taha hinengaro (intellectual wellbeing)

Kuku enhance Whakatōhea taha hinengaro or intellectual well-being as they provide an opportunity for holding and sharing mātauranga-a-Whakatōhea (knowledge specific to Whakatōhea) and other forms of knowledge. Mātauranga-ā-Whakatōhea regarding kuku includes intergenerational knowledge of different kuku gathering locations and the different types of kuku found across their coastal marine area (Danny Arapera Paruru Interview, 2022).

Whakatōhea knowledge surrounding the kuku is embedded in Whakatōhea oral histories and proverbs. A well-known Whakatōhea proverb pertains to *Ngā Tamahine ā Te Whakatōhea* and refers to pipi (a type of shellfish), cockle, and kuku (Participant B Interview, 2022). Whakatōhea also hold intergenerational knowledge around gathering and managing kuku, including information about invasive species (Whetu Walker Interview, 2022). There is an important emphasis within Whakatōhea placed on sharing kuku-related knowledge with future generations, and there are increasing concerns around the potential loss of this knowledge (Whetu Walker Interview, 2022). Teaching others how to harvest and manage kuku is one way for Whakatōhea to maintain this knowledge. Whakatōhea descendants see kuku harvesting not only as a way to gather food but also as a way to enhance the taha hinengaro of others (Danny Paruru Questionnaire, 2022).

The recent kuku venture also provides a unique opportunity for Whakatōhea descendants to implement and share mātauranga-ā-Whakatōhea. Elders, for example, used traditional Whakatōhea knowledge to establish the boundaries of the original kuku farm in the area (Danny Arapera Paruru Interview, 2022). Another participant, whose father was a prominent figure in the establishment of the Whakatōhea kuku venture, discussed his father's vision for the Whakatōhea kuku farm and the importance of Whakatōhea collective taha hinengaro in setting up the kuku venture (Participant T Interview, 2023). Today, the kuku venture and Whakatōhea Mussels Ōpotiki Limited provide an important opportunity for Whakatōhea descendants to connect with and learn about kuku.

In terms of other forms of knowledge dissemination, the kuku venture has increased the amount of research and science activity in the Whakatōhea area. The Moana Project Aotearoa, for example, partnered with Whakatōhea and aimed to improve understandings of ocean circulation, connectivity, and marine heatwaves in Aotearoa. Since their establishment, Whakatōhea Mussels Ōpotiki Limited has also generated valuable intellectual property in relation to open ocean kuku farming, such as storm survival and spat catching technology (Open Ocean Whakatōhea Mussels, 2020).

Alongside providing opportunities for enhancing science and innovation activities in the area, the kuku venture has also provided an opportunity for Whakatōhea to increase their financial knowledge, as Whakatōhea families and individuals were able to purchase shares in Whakatōhea Mussels Ōpotiki Limited. One Whakatōhea participant discussed how they used this opportunity to teach their descendants about financial growth (Participant R Interview, 2023).

Taha wairua (spiritual wellbeing)

Kuku enhance the wairua of Whakatōhea people. Wairua can be loosely translated as spirit; however, this does not capture the full meaning of the term (Valentine et al., 2017). Royal (2003), for example, describes wairua as the source of being and life and a reflection of universal consciousness. Whakatōhea have a special wairua-based whakapapa relationship with kuku (Michelle Mills Interview, 2022), which has enhanced livelihoods over time. This whakapapa-based relationship means that many Whakatōhea people consider kuku to be a taonga (treasured phenomena) (Kimberley Maxwell Interview, 2022). These significant relations fundamentally change Whakatōhea responsibilities and obligations towards kuku, so much so that they are treated more like people than animals or objects (Danny Arapera Paruru Interview, 2022). Gathering, consuming, and working with kuku is a way for the people of Whakatōhea to honour this relationship and re-connect with kuku, the Whakatōhea area, and the natural environment. These interactions also provide a connection back to Hinemoana (a god of the ocean) and Tangaroa (a god of the ocean) which ultimately uplifts Whakatōhea taha wairua (Kimberley Maxwell Interview, 2022).

Mana (prestige, authority and influence)

The Whakatōhea kuku venture is a vital source of mana for Whakatōhea descendants. The venture represents the materialisation of a dream that Whakatōhea elders held for decades (McLellan, 2020). There is a certain sense of pride that comes with being associated with Whakatōhea Mussels Ōpotiki Limited and the exportation of kuku grown in the Whakatōhea marine area. Whakatōhea also draw a sense of mana from the innovative nature of the venture and the new technologies involved (Graeme Riesterer Interview, 2022). Furthermore, the process of preparing kuku both in the factory and within a marae (Māori village) setting is an important job that can also enhance mana (Kimberley Maxwell Interview, 2022).

Rauemi (resource or material)

Kuku contribute to Whakatōhea livelihoods through their use as rauemi which can be translated as *resource* or *material*. The kuku shell has been used as an essential resource by Māori for a very long time (Wassilieff, 2006), for example, it is one of the main tools used in Māori flax weaving (Whetu Walker Interview, 2022). One participant had a memory of her elder, weaving with the kuku shell, using the shell to scrape the fibre from the flax (Hineatua Parkinson Interview, 2022). Hineatua Parkinson (2022) also emphasised the importance of connection between weavers and their kuku shell.

Kuku are also used for catching and preparing food. One survey participant mentioned that their elders used kuku as burley and bait for catching fish (Participant 3 Questionnaire, 2022). Kuku shells can be used as cutting tools when gathering seafood, such as eels (Billy Waugh Interview, 2022). Many participants discussed how they use kuku shells as utensils, with one participant reporting how their family uses the kuku shell to cut open babies' gums when they are teething to shorten their teething period and prevent fever (Participant O Interview, 2023). Hineatua Parkinson (2022) reminisced about their earliest memory of using a kuku shell: to scrape the hair off pigs and prepare them for cooking.

Manaakitanga (hospitality and generosity)

Kuku provide opportunities for Whakatōhea descendants to share and receive manaakitanga in diverse ways. The word manaakitanga is commonly translated as hospitality and generosity. Manaakitanga is about being a generous host towards your guests and working to uplift their mana. Food is often used as a vessel for sharing manaakitanga (Mika, 2013). Danny Paruru noted that wild kuku embody manaakitanga because the time and effort required to collect them elevates their significance as an offering (Danny Arapera Paruru Interview, 2022). The establishment of Whakatōhea Mussels Ōpotiki Limited offers an alternative way of gifting kuku for those who are unable to gather them. This activates a different kind of manaakitanga but still offers an important way to honour others (Danny Arapera Paruru Interview, 2022).

Along with providing kuku for purchase, the kuku venture provides other opportunities for practicing manaakitanga. For example, Whakatōhea Fisheries Trust (the company which manages Whakatōhea fisheries assets), Whakatōhea Mussels Ōpotiki Limited, and Te Ohu Kaimoana (an organisation which manages Māori fisheries assets) have arranged to provide kuku for significant Whakatōhea events such as meetings and funerals. This means that the company is able to care for Whakatōhea families during times of grieving (Danny Arapera Paruru Interview, 2022). Manaakitanga is also evident in the everyday operations of the Whakatōhea kuku factory; staff are given one free meal while on shift, and Whakatōhea descendants are provided with employment opportunities that they may not have had access to if: a) Whakatōhea Mussels Ōpotiki Limited didn't exist and b) TTW did not play such a significant role in the operations of the company.

Mauri (life force)

Mauri is commonly known as life force (Morgan, 2009) or vitality. It represents the life-supporting capacity of all beings (Rout et al., 2021). Kuku enhance the Mauri of Whakatōhea descendants in several ways. Firstly, simply eating kuku has the potential to uplift mauri. Participant Kimberley Maxwell discussed how consuming kuku or seeing kuku in the supermarket or out in the environment allowed her to feel grounded and reminded her of home, uplifting her mauri (Kimberley Maxwell Interview, 2022).

Whakatōhea Mussels Ōpotiki Limited provides further opportunities to access kuku and uplift the mauri of Whakatōhea. One participant mentioned that revenue from the kuku venture could potentially enhance mauri in other areas, such as health and education for Whakatōhea descendants (Hineatua Parkinson Interview, 2022). The kuku venture enhances access to farmed kuku in the region and in turn has the potential to reduce harvesting pressure on wild stocks, enhancing their mauri and their ability to provide for future generations (Danny Arapera Paruru Interview, 2022).

Kuku enhance the mauri of their environment; they are filter feeders and can clean their surrounding water by filtering heavy metals (Participant I Interview, 2022). Kuku shells can be used as a garden fertiliser (Kings Plant Barn, 2023), enhancing the mauri of their surrounding soil (Participant O Interview, 2023). Whakatōhea descendants also use a common kuku predator, the Pātangaroa (eleven-armed sea starts) as a kind of fertiliser. Whetu Walker dries out the Pātangaroa, mulches them with the lawn mower and fertilisers the garden with them (Whetu Walker Interview, 2022).

Kuku also enhance the mauri of their surrounding environments by providing habitats for other species. Kuku beds and farms provide settlement spaces and food sources for larvae and other small sea creatures (Participant I Interview, 2022). Some of these benefits are already evident in the Whakatōhea area as the number of fish has increased since the establishment of the kuku farm (McLellan, 2020). Furthermore, aquaculture farms are more environmentally friendly and produce less greenhouse gas emissions than land-based farms (Yaghubi et al., 2021).

Whanaungatanga (relationship building)

Whanaungatanga can be defined as relationship-building. Painting and Burgess (2020) interpret whanaungatanga as "being in good relation" (p. 210) with both human and more-than-human kin. Kuku provide Whakatōhea descendants with opportunities for enacting whanaungatanga. Kimberley Maxwell, for example, often gathers and prepares kuku with her family, and to her, kuku represent family connections (Kimberley Maxwell Interview, 2022). The process of managing and stewarding kuku in the Whakatōhea area is generally something that is done with others and can strengthen bonds between family members.

The kuku venture has provided opportunities for Whakatōhea descendants to re-connect to the Whakatōhea area. Wharengaro Tapara-Kurei, a fresh productions supervisor at the Whakatōhea kuku factory, returned home to Ōpōtiki from Rekohu (Chatham Islands) because of the growing kuku industry (Wharengaro Tapara-Kurei Interview, 2022). She hopes that Whakatōhea descendants will continue to live in Ōpotiki and work in the kuku factory (Wharengaro Tapara-Kurei Interview, 2022).

Finally, the exportation of kuku around Aotearoa and the world has been a way for some Whakatōhea families, who live outside of the area, to connect with kuku and Whakatōhea. In this way, the commodification of kuku has provided a space for descendants to re-connect with their Whakatōhea-tanga in new ways (Hineatua Parkinson Interview, 2022).

Kaitiakitanga (environmental stewardship)

Forster (2019, p. 9) defined kaitiakitanga as "the obligation arising from the kin relationship to nurture or care for a person or thing". In the context of Whakatōhea kuku economies, Whakatōhea descendants carry out kaitiakitanga to maintain the mauri of kuku, tend *"to their taha tinana, taha hinengaro and taha wairua"* and to ensure that the quality of kuku passed on to future generations is as good or better than it is currently (Whakatōhea Iwi, 1993, p. 9). Kaitiakitanga is a crucial dimension within Whakatōhea kuku economies because the wellbeing of Whakatōhea taonga is a reflection of the wellbeing of Whakatōhea descendants and vice versa (Whakatōhea Iwi, 1993). If Whakatōhea descendants do not carry out their kaitiakitanga obligations towards kuku, then kuku will never be able to return the favour and enhance Whakatōhea livelihoods. The ability of kuku to enhance the livelihoods of Whakatōhea descendants is dependent on Whakatōhea descendants carrying out their kaitiakitanga obligations.

Pūtea (money)

Kuku enhance livelihoods through financial benefits or pūtea which can be translated as money. There are various ways in which Whakatōhea descendants receive pūtea through the kuku venture. Firstly, TTW receives lease payments through their majority ownership of Eastern Sea Farms. Secondly, TTW benefits from their partial (9.28%) (New Zealand Companies Office, 2024) ownership of Whakatōhea Mussels Ōpotiki Limited, which operates within the Whakatōhea sea space and in the Whakatōhea kuku factory. Thirdly, several Whakatōhea families and individuals own shares in Whakatōhea Mussels Ōpotiki Limited, which is currently 56.10% owned by private shareholders, not all of whom are of Whakatōhea descent (Simmons Corporate Finance, 2023).

In addition to providing pūtea through investment, the kuku venture also provides Whakatōhea descendants with pūtea through employment opportunities. Whakatōhea Mussels Ōpotiki Limited employs Whakatōhea descendants, Ōpōtiki locals, and seasonal workers (Ōpōtiki District Council, 2023). Participant B emphasised the importance of the kuku venture as central to the financial and cultural economy of Whakatōhea. They also reiterated the importance of Whakatōhea Mussels Ōpotiki Limited in the Opotiki job market (Participant B Interview, 2022). Whakatōhea Mussels Ōpotiki Limited provides an alternative employment option in a job market that has long been dominated by precarious employment within the kiwifruit industry.

In Ōpōtiki, several other types of businesses are needed to service the kuku industry, which means it has bolstered employment numbers within other industries in the district (Ōpōtiki District Council, 2023). Construction of the Ōpōtiki harbour has also spurred growth in the region (Ōpōtiki District Council, 2023). The Ōpōtiki CBD renewal which sits alongside the harbour construction will create even more jobs in the region (Ōpōtiki District Council, 2023).

Recently, there has been a high amount of investment in the Whakatōhea region due to the establishment and growth of the kuku industry. The New Zealand Government, for example, is Whakatōhea Mussels Ōpotiki Limited's largest shareholder, owning 33.99% of shares (Simmons Corporate Finance, 2023). In 2020, Ōpōtiki District Council received $79.4 million in funding through the Provincial Growth Fund. This funding combined with the $20 million obtained through the Regional Infrastructure Fund in 2013 has enabled the construction of the new Ōpōtiki harbour (Ōpōtiki District Council, 2023). Alongside the construction of the harbour, there are also plans in place for a privately funded marine and industrial zone and expansion plans for residential development in Ōpōtiki (Ōpōtiki District Council, 2023), which will undoubtedly create employment and financial growth in the region.

Diverse kuku economies

The discussion above illustrates that economies are less about financially derived output and more about how resources are organised to enhance livelihoods. Thinking about economy in its original sense as livelihood creation enables the rich diversity of processes and practices involved in modern day economies to emerge. The above empirical analysis speaks to the ways in which kuku have generated livelihoods for Whakatōhea descendants over time. It demonstrates the diverse and multi-temporal plurality of Whakatōhea kuku economies. It is not an all-encompassing depiction, but rather an attempt to describe what these economies look like on the ground.

Māori economic value is generated through a diversity of processes and practices, some of which sit within, and some of which sit outside of financial markets. Kuku gathering is a key non-financial practice which generates a diversity of value for Whakatōhea people. However, there is also a diversity of value generated from the kuku venture, for example, employment at the Whakatōhea kuku factory has provided opportunities for Whakatōhea members to move home and re-connect with their Whakatōhea-tanga (Whakatōhea ways of being and doing). The exploration above shows how value generated within Māori economies is not categorically bound to distinct financial and non-financial boundaries; rather, it flows across these boundaries in complex and inter-connected ways. Examining Whakatōhea kuku economies solely through a dominant lens overlooks the broader ways that kuku generate livelihoods for Whakatōhea. Similarly, failing to recognise the diversity of value generated through financial practices provides an incomplete understanding of Māori economies.

This particular grounded account of diverse Māori economies where capitalist practices are not the dominant form of livelihood creation provides a distinctly Indigenous case to the diverse economies and community economies literature (Gibson-Graham, 2006, 2008; Gibson-Graham et al., 2013). Furthermore it enriches diverse Māori economies literature by demonstrating how livelihood-generating activities, that are often hidden and marginalised within dominant accounts of economy (Amoamo et al., 2018; Bargh, 2011, 2012; Gibson-Graham, 2006, 2008; Gibson-Graham et al., 2013), materialise within everyday Māori economies. Two key insights which derive from this work are discussed below.

Economy as process, practice, and place

The findings above exemplify a grounded account of how Whakatōhea kuku economies are generated through practices and processes in place. By speaking to the various ways that Whakatōhea descendants draw value from kuku, we are able to demonstrate how kuku generate livelihoods for Whakatōhea, the specific processes and practices that generate this livelihood and the importance of the role of place in these relations.

Whakatōhea kuku economies consist of diverse pathways of value creation driven by unique processes and practices which are grounded in place and founded upon longstanding relations with human and more-than-human kin. Place plays a central role in Whakatōhea kuku economies. For Whakatōhea, gathering wild kuku in their tribal area not only provides a healthy source of protein but also a platform to connect with living and non-living and human and non-human relations. The continuity of Whakatōhea descendants gathering and farming kuku in their ancestral waters means something that adds value to Whakatōhea livelihoods. Consuming or growing kuku from somewhere else cannot generate the same kind of value.

The depiction of Whakatōhea kuku economies above, situates theoretical understandings of economy as process and practice within a grounded economy which is connected to both capitalist practices and Indigenous economic traditions. We contribute to the Māori economies, Indigenous economies and alternative economies scholarship a particular place-based understanding of the processes and practices which generate livelihoods.

Whakapapa as a lens for understanding Māori economic relations

A whakapapa methodology pays particular attention to the connections and relations between all phenomena (Painting & Burgess, 2020). When examining Māori economies through a whakapapa lens, the diverse processes and practices that form economies and the value drawn from them are intimately connected and in relation. These processes and practices have a specific set of connections and relations that stretch into the future and the past and often go unseen when examining economies through a dominant lens.

A whakapapa lens provides a number of significant insights for examining contemporary Māori economies. For example, it enables us to see how both financial and non-financial practices generate a diversity of livelihood values within Māori economies. It also points to the importance of temporality and place for generating value within Māori economies - for example, for Whakatōhea descendants, gathering kuku from the same rocks as their ancestors carries profound significance as it connects them to both their ancestors and their ancestral place. Whakapapa also enables us to see important connections that might otherwise remain hidden when examining economies from conventional non-Māori perspectives. For example, the availability of farmed Whakatōhea kuku from local suppliers in Ōpōtiki reduces harvesting pressure on wild kuku populations, allowing them to replenish and remain available for future generations. Whakapapa further draws attention to the relations between financial and non-financial kuku practices—acknowledging that these kuku share the same waters and ecological systems. These relations are important for understanding how different dimensions of economies exist in relation.

The application of whakapapa as an analytical framework has significant implications for how Māori economies are understood and governed. Seeing Māori economies as intimately connected and in relation can transform how decision-makers conceptualise and enact these economies into the future. While diverse economies approaches have provided useful insights for Māori economies scholars to draw upon (Amoamo et al., 2018; Bargh, 2011, 2012), whakapapa offers a more appropriate and distinctly Indigenous framework for understanding Māori economies. Transitioning to using Indigenous frameworks for conceptualising Māori economies will allow Māori economies scholars to move beyond the limitations of non-Māori approaches and better understand and examine Māori economies.

This Chapter set out to think about Māori economies differently by using a whakapapa-based methodology and adopting diverse perspectives of economy from the literature. This whakapapa lens helped us see the diverse value exchanges involved in Whakatōhea kuku economies. Ultimately, we painted a picture of Whakatōhea economies based on the generation of livelihoods which demonstrates two key insights for re-Indigenising Māori economies: a) the processes and practices which make up Māori economies and generate Māori livelihoods are always grounded in place and b) Whakapapa is a useful framework for understanding Māori economies in a way that is grounded in te ao Māori (the Māori world).

While this Chapter highlights the positive aspects of the Whakatōhea kuku industry through its focus on livelihood generation, the key insight for Whakatōhea people is that wild kuku stocks are central to our kuku economies. Wild kuku stocks and our associated practices with them, although not included within dominant understandings of economies, form the essential foundation of Whakatōhea kuku economies. The physical act of gathering, stewarding, and eating kuku enhances livelihoods in ways that purchasing kuku within capitalist markets does not allow. A majority of the value derived from Whakatōhea kuku economies will be lost if Whakatōhea descendants can no longer access wild kuku stocks in the Whakatōhea area.

This particular account of Whakatōhea kuku economies enables Māori decision makers (tribal leaders and policy makers) to think differently about Māori economies. Although Māori economies can derive a lot of value from capitalist practices, value generated from being in good relation with taonga generates a different kind of livelihood - one that is deeply embedded in Māori relations with place. In documenting the diversity of practices that create value within Whakatōhea kuku economies, we have generated pathways for diverse economic futuring and opened opportunities for re-indigenising Māori economic processes, practices and relations.

Acknowledgements

We would like to express our sincere gratitude to all the participants who generously contributed to this chapter and to the broader scope of the lead author's PhD thesis. Additionally, we extend our heartfelt appreciation to all those who graciously hosted and welcomed the lead author during her PhD fieldwork. We would also like to acknowledge the lead author's PhD supervisors, Dr. Emma Sharp, Professor Nicolas Lewis, Dr. Kiri Dell and Professor John Reid for their invaluable guidance, unwavering support, and insightful feedback throughout the development of this chapter. Their expertise and mentorship have been instrumental in shaping the direction and quality of our work. Special thanks are also due to Tai Wright, whose dedicated mahi (work) as a research assistant significantly contributed to the fruition of this chapter. We would like to extend our gratitude to the High-Value Nutrition National Science Challenge for providing the lead author's PhD scholarship funding, without which this research would not have been possible. Their support has been instrumental in enabling this pursuit of knowledge.

References

Altman, J. (2009). The hybrid economy and anthropological engagements with policy discourse: A brief reflection. *The Australian Journal of Anthropology, 20*(3), 318–329. https://doi.org/10.1111/j.1757-6547.2009.00039.x

Amoamo, M., Ruwhiu, D., & Carter, L. (2018). Framing the Māori economy: The complex business of Māori business. *MAI Journal: A New Zealand Journal of Indigenous Scholarship, 7*(1), 66–78. https://doi.org/10.20507/maijournal.2018.7.1.6

Bargh, M. (2011). The triumph of Maori entrepreneurs or diverse economies? *Aboriginal Policy Studies, 1*(3), 53–69. https://doi.org/10.5663/aps.v1i3.12560

Bargh, M. (2012). Rethinking and re-shaping indigenous economies: Māori geothermal energy enterprises. *Journal of Enterprising Communities People and Places in the Global Economy, 6*(3), 271–283. https://doi.org/10.1108/17506201211258423

Bargh, M. (2014). A Blue Economy for Aotearoa New Zealand? *Environment, Development and Sustainability, 16*(3), 459–470. https://doi.org/10.1007/s10668-013-9487-4

Bargh, M., & Otter, J. (2009). Progressive spaces of neoliberalism in Aotearoa: A genealogy and critique. *Asia Pacific Viewpoint, 50*(2), 154–165. https://doi.org/10.1111/j.1467-8373.2009.01390.x

Chapman Tripp. (2018). *Te Ao Māori—Trends and insights.*

Chen, L. (2023). *Do performance metrics of self-identifying Māori firms differ from non-Māori firms?* [Master's Thesis]. Victoria University of Wellington. https://doi.org/10.26686/wgtn.22592182

Dell, K. (2017). *Te Hokinga ki te Ūkaipō—Disrupted Māori Management Theory* [Doctoral dissertation]. The University of Auckland.

Dell, K., Staniland, N., & Nicholson, A. (2018). Economy of Mana: Where to next? *MAI Journal: A New Zealand Journal of Indigenous Scholarship*, *7*(1), 51–65. https://doi.org/10.20507/maijournal.2018.7.1.5

Droz, P. (2019, January 30). *Rebuilding Indigenous economies and remembering how to creatively thrive*. Native Indian Collective. https://ndncollective.org/rebuilding-indigenous-economies-and-remembering-how-to-creatively-thrive%EF%BB%BF/

Fitzherbert, S. (2015). *Geographies of economy-making: the articulation and circulation of taewa Māori across Aotearoa New Zealand* [Doctor of Philosophy]. The University of Auckland.

Forster, M. (2019). He tātai whenua: Environmental genealogies. *Genealogy*, *3*(3), 42. https://doi.org/10.3390/genealogy3030042

Gibson-Graham, J. K. (2005). Surplus possibilities: Postdevelopment and community economies. *Singapore Journal of Tropical Geography*, *26*(1), 4–26. https://doi.org/10.1111/j.0129-7619.2005.00198.x

Gibson-Graham, J. K. (2006). *The end of capitalism (as we knew it): A feminist critique of political economy*. University of Minnesota Press.

Gibson-Graham, J. K. (2008). Diverse economies: performative practices for "other worlds." *Progress in Human Geography*, *32*(5), 613–632. https://doi.org/10.1177/0309132508090821

Gibson-Graham, J. K. (2020). Introduction to the handbook of diverse economies: Inventory as ethical intervention. In J. K. Gibson-Graham & K. Dombroski (Eds.), *The handbook of diverse economies* (pp. 1–24). Edward Elgar Publishing Limited.

Gibson-Graham, J. K., Cameron, J., & Healy, S. (2013). *Take back the economy: An ethical guide for transforming our communities*. University of Minnesota Press.

Gibson-Graham, J. K., & Miller, E. (2015). Economy as ecological livelihood. In K. Gibson, D. B. Rose, & R. Fincher (Eds.), *Manifesto for Living in the Anthropocene* (pp. 7–16). Punctum Books. https://www.jstor.org/stable/j.ctv1r787bz

Henare, M. (2014). The Economy of Mana. In D. Cooke, C. Hill, P. Baskett, & R. Irwin (Eds.), *Beyond the free market: Rebuilding a just society in New Zealand* (pp. 65–69). Dunmore.

Jones, B. M. (2019). (com)post-capitalism. *Environmental Humanities*, *11*(1), 3–26. https://doi.org/10.1215/22011919-7349347

Kings Plant Barn. (2023). *Aquaticus organic soil & plant conditioner (mussel shell) - 5kg*. Kings Plant Barn. https://www.kings.co.nz/aquaticus-organic-soil-plant-conditioner-mussel-shell-5kg-209710

Klynveld Peat Marwick Goerdeler New Zealand. (2016). *Māui Rau - Adapting in a changing world*. https://assets.kpmg.com/content/dam/kpmg/pdf/2016/05/KPMG-Maui-Rau-nz.pdf

Kuokkanen, R. (2011). Indigenous economies, theories of subsistence, and women: Exploring the social economy model for indigenous governance. *American Indian Quarterly*, *35*(2), 215–240. https://doi.org/10.5250/amerindiquar.35.2.0215

Liboiron, M. (2021). *Pollution is colonialism*. Duke University Press.

Lo, K. D., & Houkamau, C. (2012). Exploring the cultural origins of differences in time orientation between European New Zealanders and Māori. *The New Zealand Journal of Human Resources Management, 12*(3), 105–123. https://repository.usfca.edu/cgi/viewcontent.cgi?article=1009&context=olc

Lyall, A. (1979). *Whakatōhea of Ōpōtiki.* Reed.

Māori Economic Development Panel. (2012). *He Kai Kei Aku Ringa - The Crown-Māori economic growth partnership.* Māori Economic Development Panel.

McLellan, G., Sharp, E., Dell, K., Lewis, N., & Reid, J. (2025 Forthcoming). Whakapapa as an Episto-Methodological Framework for Conceptualising Māori Economies. *MAI Journal A New Zealand Journal of Indigenous Scholarship.*

McLellan, Georgia. (2020). *Balancing Moni Hua and Mana Motuhake: Iwi commercial food ventures and Māori food sovereignty: A Whakatōhea case study* [Master's thesis]. The University of Auckland]. https://researchspace.auckland.ac.nz/handle/2292/52486

Mika, J. (2013). *Manaakitanga: Is generosity killing Māori enterprises?* Australian Centre for Entrepreneurship Research Exchange Conference, Sydney.

Mikaere, A. (2011). *Colonising myths—Māori realities—He Rukuruku Whakaaro.* Huia.

Mitchell, T. (1995, November). *Origins and limits of the modern idea of the economy.* Seminar on Social Movements, the Advanced Study Center of the International Institute, University of Michigan. https://blogs.cuit.columbia.edu/tm2421/files/2018/01/Mitchell-1995.pdf

Mitchell, T. (1998). Fixing the economy. *Cultural Studies, 12*(1), 82–101. https://doi.org/10.1080/095023898335627

Mitchell, T. (2008). Rethinking economy. *Geoforum; Journal of Physical, Human, and Regional Geosciences, 39*(3), 1116–1121. https://doi.org/10.1016/j.geoforum.2006.11.022

Nana, G., Reid, A., Schulze, H., Dixon, H., Green, S., & Riley, H. (2021). *Te Ōhanga Māori 2018—The Māori Economy 2018.* Business and Economic Research. https://berl.co.nz/sites/default/files/2021-01/Te%20%C5%8Changa%20M%C4%81ori%202018.pdf

New Zealand Companies Office. (2024). *Whakatōhea mussels Ōpōtiki limited shareholdings.* New Zealand Companies Register. https://app.companiesoffice.govt.nz/companies/app/ui/pages/companies/5351102/shareholdings

Open Ocean Whakatōhea Mussels. (2020). *Whakatōhea Mussels (Ōpōtiki) Limited: Food processing factory and marine farm development—Final business case.* https://www.mbie.govt.nz/dmsdocument/16364-business-case-whakatohea-mussels-opotiki-pdf

Ōpōtiki District Council. (2023). *Te Ara Moana a Toi.* https://www.odc.govt.nz/repository/libraries/id:2bpcqtp1b1cxby3k9b0b/hierarchy/sitecollectiondocuments/our-council/Reports%20%26%20Studies/Reports/Te%20Ara%20Moana%20a%20Toi%20-%20Initial%20Benefits%20Assessment.pdf

Painting, T. K., & Burgess, H. (2020). Onamata, anamata: A whakapapa perspective of Māori futurisms. In A.-M. Murtola & S. Walsh (Eds.), *Whose futures?* (pp. 207–233). Economic and Social Research Aotearoa. http://mediacentre.maramatanga.ac.nz/content/onamata-anamata-whakapapa-perspective-m-ori-futurisms

Roberts, M. (2013). Ways of seeing: Whakapapa. *Sites: A Journal of Social Anthropology and Cultural Studies, 10*(1), 93–120. https://doi.org/10.11157/sites-vol10iss1id236

Roelvink, G., St. Martin, K., & Gibson-Graham, J. K. (2015). *Making other worlds possible: Performing diverse economies.* University of Minnesota Press.

Royal, T. C. (2003). *The woven universe: selected writings of Rev. Māori Marsden* (p. 187). Estate of Rev. Māori Marsden.

Scobie, M., Lee, B., & Smyth, S. (2020). Grounded accountability and Indigenous self-determination. *Critical Perspectives on Accounting, 92*, 102198. https://doi.org/10.1016/j.cpa.2020.102198

Scobie, M., & Sturman, A. (2020). Economies of Mana and Mahi beyond the crisis. *New Zealand Journal of Employment Relations, 45*(2), 77–88. https://doi.org/10.24135/nzjer.v45i2.22

Scobie, M., & Sturman, A. (2024). *The economic possibilities of decolonisation*. Bridget Williams Books.

Simmons Corporate Finance. (2023). *Whakatōhea Mussels (Ōpōtiki) Limited Independent Advisors Report*. https://www.takeovers.govt.nz/assets/Transactions/Whakatohea-Mussels-Opotiki-Limited-2023-Independent-Advisers-Report.pdf

Tau, T. M., & Rout, M. (2018). The tribal economy. *The Journal of New Zealand Studies, NS27*, 92–109. https://ojs.victoria.ac.nz/jnzs/article/view/5178/4596

Waka huia [@wakahuiatvnz]. (2014, September 21). *Profile of Te Kahautu Maxwell, an academic who grew up in Opotiki* [Video]. YouTube. https://www.youtube.com/watch?v=bz7ALUnfleo

Walker, R. (2007). Ōpōtiki-Mai-Tawhiti: Capital of Whakatōhea. Penguin Books.

Whakatōhea Iwi. (1993). *Tawharau o nga hapū o Whakatōhea - Whakatōhea Resource Management Plan*. https://www.whakatane.govt.nz/sites/www.whakatane.govt.nz/files/documents/tawharu_o_nga_hapu_o_whakatohea_resource_management_plan.pdf

Yaghubi, E., Carboni, S., Snipe, R. M. J., Shaw, C. S., Fyfe, J. J., Smith, C. M., Kaur, G., Tan, S.-Y., & Hamilton, D. L. (2021). Farmed mussels: A nutritive protein source, rich in omega-3 fatty acids, with a low environmental footprint. *Nutrients, 13*(4), 1124. https://doi.org/10.3390/nu13041124

Dialogue
Strings of retheorising capitalism

Iuliia Gataulina, Anni Kangas, Mikko Poutanen & Henna-Elise Ventovirta

In collaboration with: Kelly Dombroski, Leo Hwang, Akseli Kettula, Mariam Khawar, Aviv Kruglanski, Heather McLean, Georgia McLellan, Molly Mullen, Maria Mäensivu, Iris Pajunen, Edemilson Paraná, Sabaheta Ramcilovic-Suominen, Anna Ilona Rajala, Kerry Woodward & Mark Young

The chapters in this edited volume cover multiple empirical topics and draw from a variety of approaches. This closing dialogue attempts to portray this chorus of voices and relate it to the ethos of engaged pluralism, which was discussed in the prologue to the book and which offers a way to appreciate the richness of the approaches included. The dialogue is the result of a collective endeavour where we invited each author to contribute a 'snippet' or a short paragraph elucidating their understanding of capitalism and the need to retheorise it. With the help of these snippets, and in response to the reviewers' demand for more coherence, we aimed to weave together the diverse perspectives on capitalism presented throughout the book.

The dialogue is an attempt to pull the strings of difference together while, at the same time, resisting the urge to force them into a tight knot. Strings, after all, may entangle without binding. An effort to weave together various strands without creating a tight knot results in a rich tapestry of approaches. To be clear, it is not an attempt to merge theories and approaches that are ontologically incompatible. Indeed, this resulting pluralism may not always be harmonious as the interplay of varied ontological, epistemological, and cosmological assumptions can sometimes lead to discord and tension.

Gataulina, I., Kangas, A., Poutanen, M. & Ventovirta, H-E in collaboration with the chapter authors (2025). Dialogue: Strings of retheorising capitalism. In A. Kangas, I. Gataulina, M. Poutanen, A. I. Rajala & H-E Ventovirta (Eds.), Retheorising capitalism (pp. 301-313). Tampere University Press.
https://doi.org/10.61201/tup.981

Similarly, on the pages of this book, diverse perspectives engage in meaningful dialogue, respecting differences without enforcing sameness under exclusionary definitions. The diversity of viewpoints offered by the contributors grapples with the pluralism of capitalism and its retheorisations. In doing so, it also sidesteps conventional expectations of objective inquiry, giving room for advocacy, even activism. Retheorising capitalism, this reminds us, is not only theory but practice as engaged pluralism might mean not only engaging with different theoretical approaches but also with society (Box-Steffensmeier, 2022).

Below, we reflect on the vibrant threads of thought that weave through this edited collection. One of the strings in this rich tapestry suggests that capitalism is an economic system and retheorising means detecting its contemporary compositions. Other snippets indicate that a way to retheorise capitalism is by shattering the capitalocentrism of our thinking and making way for other types of economic practices under our analytical gaze. Retheorisation might also imply thinking about the economy through different ontological lenses altogether. It is also possible to see capitalism as a political and social system, rather than a purely economic one. Finally, we can see the work of (re)theorising as an affective labour of nurturing hope and solidarities.

An evolving economic system

For some of the authors, capitalism is an economic system, and retheorising it is a matter of inquiring what shapes this system currently takes. Contributions that resonate with this string indicate that among the key elements of this system are not only private property, competitive markets, and the generation of wealth through reinvestment of profit (i.e. accumulation) but also labour exploitation and economic inequalities. However, while its main elements may remain intact, capitalism is seen to evolve over time, taking different temporal forms. In their snippets, the authors emphasise that capitalism is dynamic and adaptive. The drive to retheorise may arise from the belief that capitalism is transitioning into a new phase marked, for example, by intensifying precarity and commodification of data as suggested in the following snippet:

Edemilson Paraná

> I view capitalism as a dynamic, self-transforming system that evolves by adapting to contradictions while preserving its core elements—labour exploitation, profit pursuit, and value valorisation. This transformation is framed as dialectical, with the old and new continuously shaping each other. Recent shifts suggest capitalism is entering a distinct phase defined by financialisation, neoliberalism, and digitalisation. These interconnected processes amplify financial hegemony and technological domination, restructuring social relations and intensifying capital's reach into new

> domains, including digital platforms and informational goods. My chapter's main thrust argues for retheorising capitalism to capture its evolving configurations, highlighting the systemic interplay between finance and technology. It introduces the concept of "financialised digitalisation" to describe the fusion of financial practices with digital advancements, evident in phenomena like cryptocurrencies and platform monopolies. The chapter adopts a theoretical lens, emphasising overdetermination, where contradictions within capitalism mutually influence and reshape its broader structure. By exploring these processes, my chapter aims to deepen understanding of capitalism's current phase, marked by heightened inequality, precarious labour, and the commodification of data. It concludes by stressing the need for political action to envision alternatives, leveraging digital potential for equitable and democratic societal arrangements.

The dynamic and adaptive nature of the capitalist system, this approach suggests, allows it to evolve and take on different forms over time. On the one hand, this very adaptability can perpetuate instability, as the system continuously adjusts to shifting conditions, creating new contradictions and crises. On the other hand, the instability of the capitalist economic system and the variability of its composition may also be understood as a sign of adaptability and creativity. The dynamic character of market forces may also be viewed as a strength in an inherently unstable environment. Retheorising capitalism, then, may mean thinking of new ways to recalibrate the economic and political system to the flexible and rapidly changing environments of today's interconnected world. It is about finding ways to "fix" capitalism or applying its forces properly, as the following snippet suggests:

Akseli Kettula

> The point of departure of my contribution is that capitalism, as an economic system, is structurally unstable. In Keynesian thinking, instability appears in stochastic and cyclical models. Incremental deviance from the economic equilibrium is the basis of Schumpeterian instability. Marxian instability appears in long-term developments such as the accumulation of capital (Vercelli, 1985). Structural instability can be harmful in a stable and forecastable environment. However, instability is not a weakness if the environment is not stable and hardly predictable, as today's society seems to be. In fact, structural instability could be used as a tool to survive in a chaotic environment.
>
> Even though market failure and government failure exist, capitalist systems have a significant advantage against complexity and uncertainty—and this advantage is market forces. Market forces are dynamic and flexible and react rapidly to the changing environment. Furthermore, market forces, when applied properly, diversify decision-making and prevent the adverse accumulation of single wrong decisions. The gist is how to limit the adverse

effects of capitalism and foster its strengths. A theory of fragmentism is a suggestion to solve these issues and approaches capitalism from a new theoretical angle—in the context of three criteria of systemic risks: size, interconnectedness, and lack of substitutes.

A more-than-capitalist and diverse economy

In several contributions in this volume, retheorising means showcasing the economic diversity not only of capitalism but also beyond capitalism or capitalist practices. This means rejecting the centrality of capitalism and portraying the economy in all its multiplicity. It involves transcending 'capitalocentrism' that characterises much of the contemporary theorising on the economy in order to destabilise the hegemony and centrality of capitalist practices in our thinking. If we want to imagine and enact alternatives, as the snippet below suggests, we need to pay attention to the various ways of doing economy that are already present:

Heather McLean, Molly Mullen, Aviv Kruglanski, Leo Hwang, Kelly Dombroski

Diverse economies approaches refuse to theorise 'capitalism' as an 'ism'. Instead, drawing on a poststructuralist interpretation of Marx's modes of production, diverse economies approaches theorise capitalist practices of surplus appropriation as just one mode of production in use in contemporary economies (Gibson-Graham, 1996, 2008). Limiting the definition of 'capitalist' to an enterprise where surplus is appropriated and distributed by a capitalist or group of capitalists (shareholders) is an intentional political decision (Gibson-Graham, 2006). Limiting the definition of capitalist practices or economies in such a way has the performative effect of opening up our understanding of the economy as a diverse, overlapping mess of 'more-than-capitalist' economic practices (Gibson-Graham and Dombroski, 2020). What is the point of such a limitation, in the face of decades of social science research showing how culture, economics and markets are more and more intermeshed in something called capitalism? The point is to avoid what Gibson-Graham call 'capitalocentrism', a thinking tendency that places capitalism as the ever-present 'norm' against which all other economic practices are defined and incorporated. Drawing on nonbinary feminist and queer thinking such as Eve Sedgwick (1994), diverse economies work invites us to consider and value all the many ways in which our economies are not capitalist—not as a bury-your-head-in-the-sand strategy, but as a strategy for opening up the possibilities of what a postcapitalist economy can be, building on what is already present. Such an approach to theorising capitalism decentres capitalist economic practices as the necessary norm, a tendency which is often present even in leftist and radical circles. It bursts open the space of the economy into a complex array of surplus distribution practices including gifting, looting, state subsidies, Indigenous exchange, and so on.

Our chapter seeks to apply this same refusal to the project of retheorising capitalism in this book, but to extend it further. We extend this by expanding the (already explosive) diverse economies economic imaginary away from formal, rationalised explanations of what does and does not count as capitalist, anticapitalist, postcapitalist and whose surplus goes where and to whom. Instead, we move forward through tentatively sensing a multiplicity of postcapitalist economies in the here and now, in our artistic and embodied practices. We consider theory as an artistic practice, and consider artistic practice as theorising. So, for us, the question is not so much how we theorise capitalism, but why we might choose not to, and sense our way forward into postcapitalist possibilities.

Retheorising, in this sense, also means reconsidering what the term 'theory' stands for. It may involve moving away from rationalised and formal understandings of theory, incorporating art into theorising, or, as suggested above, thinking about new ways of actually 'sensing' the diversity of economies. Besides recognising how capitalism is positioned as the constant standard and how scholarly practices contribute to this, it may mean identifying and exploring sites where diverse economic practices already persist, as suggested in the following response:

Kerry Woodward

My work is heavily influenced by community/diverse economies as well as relational onto-epistemologies, particularly those expressed in material semiotics (i.e. Bruno Latour, Annmarie Mol, John Law, Donna Haraway, Karen Barad). As such, I'm drawn to thinking about capitalist relations and how capitalism as a hegemonic mode of knowing, being and doing is performed. My chapter on farming and economic diversity reflects this approach to understanding and engaging with capitalism as it challenges a hegemonic narrative that agriculture is inevitably capitalist, or that alternative agricultural systems or practices must resist and supplant capitalism. Instead, I offer an ethnographic account illuminating the diverse economic relations that constitutes one farm in southeastern Australia. I aim to subvert capitalocentrism/plantationocentrism by highlighting ways in which the farm is already bound up with other-than-capitalist economic relations. Though, I also acknowledge that capitalist relations remain entangled with the farm, and so point to the problem of binaries in thinking about farming and agriculture that cares for the needs of people and all the others that we share the planet with.

Although capitalism might seem like an insurmountable 'ism' or a monolithic entity, one way to highlight its diverse and plural character is by showing its dependence on noncapitalist forms of life. By practising the "art of noticing" (Tsing, 2015), we can become aware that capitalist practices often rely on social relations that are not necessarily capitalist. However, the following snippet proposes that working with the concepts of diversity or pluralism—while also recognising the pitfalls of capitalocentrism—should not mean losing sight of the fact that many key social dynamics of our time are intricately linked to the history, present, and future of what we may still refer to as "capitalism": colonial logics, extractivist practices, and profit-making impulses:

Anna Ilona Rajala

> Capitalism is currently the dominant economic system globally, but by no means is it homogeneous or an insurmountable monolith. Neither is it self-sufficient: it depends upon noncapitalist forms of economy (Tsing, 2015). Therefore, theorising and retheorising capitalism today requires creative thinking concerning some of the most pressing issues we are facing. Two such issues I address in my chapter are global inequality of health and wealth, and the planetary crisis. While neither of these necessarily follows only from capitalism as an economic system, it is undeniable that profit-seeking, extractivism, and the violent and racist colonial legacy of western wealth are tied to the history, present, and future of capitalism. Behind such injustice, there are always conscious and active decisions and policies that knowingly accept that some life, whether human or more-than-human, is worth less than others.

As seen through various contributions on (re)theorising capitalism, even when the diversity of capitalist arrangements and practices is the common starting point, the question of diversity can be approached from multiple angles. One author responded to our request to clarify how they understood capitalism by highlighting that there are indeed many entry points through which capitalism can be examined. While this may appear troubling to those who prefer clear and deterministic definitions, the snippet suggests that since capitalism itself manifests in multiple forms, it is essential to allow pluralist definitions and approaches to coexist and flourish in scholarly efforts. Only the cognitive tendency to view the world in fragmented terms prevents us from approaching capitalism simultaneously as a system of exploitation, a personal experience, a form of everyday life, or something that can be understood in relation to specific historical events as suggested here:

Sabaheta Ramcilovic-Suominen

> The traditional definition of capitalism as a form of class exploitation for profit and financial asset accumulation stands valid. Yet, as:

i. capitalism enters everyday life, politics, and the geopolitics of the everyday;
ii. its genealogy can clearly be traced in relation to major historical events, including colonialism, as well as iii. the phenomena that define our science and technology, reason and logic (i.e. the Renaissance) —

there are many entry points to define and frame capitalism. For those who love deterministic definitions, this is not helpful, but to give a clear, single definition to a relatively speaking rather 'all-inclusive' phenomenon is not only unhelpful but can be harmful to our analytical inquiry and our ways of thinking. Thus, the way I approach capitalism is in an intentionally pluralistic manner, able to accommodate not only the specific context in which it is observed but also the personal and collective experiences and relations to capitalism of the observer. This is recognising, at the same time, that such definitions might be mutually contradictory (e.g. capitalism as only an economic and political phenomenon vs. capitalism as a culture). However, this apparent contradiction is not absolute but emerges from the cognitive constraints and fragmented ways of seeing reality in categories and separation, rather than in relations and as relations.

So, capitalism is and can be defined as relations of exploitation, which can be approached/framed in ways that emphasise its exploitation of (i) material or physical (including biological, organic or animated, or otherwise), (ii) immaterial or socially constructed (e.g. political systems, states, trade), and (iii) moral (norms, principles, virtue, and ethics) 'resources' for the purpose of class- and identity-based profit accumulation. In so saying, I realise the limits of categorisation of material, immaterial, and moral—since again they too exist in relation to one another, and thus at an absolute or fundamental level, they do not exist as separate entities.

The ontological plurality of capitalism

In some of the snippets, the diversity of capitalism and the imperative to retheorise it are understood in the context of challenging the Euro- or Westcentric assumptions prevalent in much scholarly thinking on capitalism. Offering other ontological openings and cosmological commitments, these contributions also seek to imagine and enact the economy differently, inviting us to see instances where capitalism exists alongside other kinds of economic practices, without entirely subsuming or excluding them. For example, Indigenous relational ontologies cast the meaning of 'economy' and its relation to other aspects of life in a new light. Retheorising, understood in this way, not only opens up new possibilities for enacting the economy but also gives visibility to economic practices and agency to economic actors that the coloniality of the capitalist system has been threatening to destroy but that continue to persist alongside and intertwined with colonial-capitalist relations, as suggested in the response below:

Georgia McLellan

My drive to retheorise capitalism stems from my decolonial research context and the imperative to challenge existing power structures. In contemporary Māori economies, this power manifests as capitalism's dominance over conceptualisations of Māori economy. The term 'Māori economy' has become synonymous with monetary value and profit maximisation, as evidenced by the $70 billion asset valuation. This narrow financial focus not only obscures the sophisticated economic systems Māori maintained prior to colonisation but also the diversity that exists within modern-day Māori economies. My chapter demonstrates this contemporary economic diversity by examining Whakatōhea kuku economy as a set of dimensions that enhance Whakatōhea livelihoods. These dimensions reveal how value generation within contemporary Māori economies extends far beyond financial measures.

Indigenous relational ontologies offer crucial insights for retheorising capitalism. Whakapapa, for example, positions everything and everyone that has ever existed and will exist in an ever-expanding web of connections. Through this lens, capitalism is not the antithesis of Māori ways of being but rather part of our contemporary economic relations. Understanding these connections helps challenge the dominance of capitalism and demonstrates how Māori ways of being can thrive alongside colonial-capitalist relations.

The Whakatōhea kuku venture exemplifies this complexity. Whilst it operates within capitalist frameworks, it simultaneously offers opportunities for practising manaakitanga and sharing mātauranga. Retheorising capitalism requires moving beyond binary oppositions between Indigenous and capitalist economic systems. However, Māori economies fundamentally rely on key relations that exist outside the bounds of capitalist imaginaries.

However, it is important to understand that just because capitalism has a role in Māori resurgence and contemporary economic relations, it doesn't necessarily play a dominant role in thriving Māori futures. My chapter illustrates the diverse noncapitalist practices that generate livelihoods within Māori communities. These practices depend on maintaining relational well-being between Māori communities and their kin. The practice of kaitiakitanga, for instance, is essential for maintaining the mauri of kuku and ensuring their continued ability to enhance Whakatōhea wellbeing. This relational wellbeing exists at odds with capitalist environmental relations that centre on wealth accumulation and resource exploitation. My analysis of Whakatōhea kuku economy ultimately demonstrates the importance of navigating both capitalist and diverse economic systems whilst uplifting indigenous relations upon which indigenous livelihoods depend.

Another author responded to our question with a snippet underscoring that while capitalism is a system of inequalities, class divisions, and economic exploitation, integrating Islamic ethical concepts into efforts to theorise the economy has the potential to achieve not just social justice but also spiritual fulfilment. The value premises of the economy change, reminding us that critiques of capitalism often fall into the same Eurocentric logic as the capitalist system itself. Therefore, to retheorise capitalism, we need other concepts, ontologies, and cosmologies. Islamic economic philosophy, for example, allows us to put spiritual virtues and ethos at the centre of our (re)theorising work, as suggested in the following snippet:

Mariam Khawar

> My chapter offers a critique and reimagining of capitalism through the lens of Islamic economic philosophy, rooted in ethical and spiritual values. In my chapter, capitalism is understood as a system defined by inherent inequalities, perpetuated primarily through class divisions and economic exploitation. The chapter advocates for a retheorisation of capitalism, moving beyond the Eurocentric narratives of global political economy. This entails an intersectional approach integrating Islamic ethical concepts, particularly khilafah, to provide a more inclusive and just framework for understanding labour and economic structures.
>
> The need to rethink capitalism stems from its failure to address systemic inequalities and spiritual alienation. Islamic economics offers a rich tradition that critiques the commodification of labour and redefines work as a path to spiritual emancipation, advocating for a moral economy. This underscores the inadequacies of both capitalist exploitation and the current Islamic economic framework, which has been co-opted into neoliberalism.
>
> In the chapter, I explain further how labour is a key element of economic and spiritual life and argue for integrating the emancipatory ethics of Islam into modern economic thought in favour of structural changes that recognise labour as central to achieving social justice and spiritual fulfilment. While this thinking may seem radical from a contemporary perspective, the chapter shows the deep traditions of this mode of thinking.

A political and social system

However, capitalism is not merely a type, practice, or aspect of the economy. One way to appreciate its diversity is to remind ourselves that while it may make sense to conceptualise capitalism as a system, it is a system shaped and underpinned by political, cultural, and social dynamics. Retheorising capitalism, then, means analysing the intersections of capitalist, social, and political dynamics. This is also a moral imperative as it enables us to recognise the structures of power and marginalisation that examining capitalism solely as an economic system may obscure, as suggested in the following snippet and the related chapter:

Maria Mäensivu

> My understanding of capitalism is that it is an economic system based on the accumulation of wealth, ownership of private property, and free markets driven by demand and supply. However, capitalism does not exist in a vacuum and is intertwined with other social and political dynamics such as neoliberalism, racism, and class divisions. While capitalism thrives on the maximisation of profits, it relies on structures of power and marginalisation to uphold it. Therefore, only looking at capitalism from an economic perspective blinds us to the ethical and moral questions it raises. We need to theorise capitalism through its many intersections with other social systems.

Another response to our question of what capitalism is and why it should be retheorised similarly suggests that instead of rationalising capitalism as an economic system, its political, cultural, and social dimensions merit attention. The practice of viewing capitalism solely as an economic system, this author suggests, is ideological. If capitalism is treated as an economic system, its political power is disguised. The snippet suggests that this way of approaching capitalism may also lead us to appreciate its temporal diversity, in the sense of deeply embedded traits of feudal power reemerging from behind the ideological narrative of a transition from the feudal to the capitalist system:

Mark L. Young

> Capitalism and feudalism are assumed to be historically discrete social formations, an illusion facilitated by the common perception that capitalism is a mere economic system. But this chapter has demonstrated how vestiges of feudalism persist in the institution of employment—relations of power which influence and shape other political and social institutions in the reproduction of a capitalist culture. More than economic, capitalism is political in its demands, cultural in its legitimation, and social in its influence. Yet, when the economic dimensions of capitalism are emphasised and rationalised, capitalism's role as a sociopolitical power is obscured. My chapter has shown how the authoritative regime of employment engenders submission to authority and conformity to workplace logic and economistic ideology. Wherever the economistic principles of capitalism become rationalised certitudes, the political functioning of capitalism recedes from view. Wherever the justification of extreme inequality becomes a self-evident truth, the brute force of feudal power is dissolved before the gentle reflection of free will and consent. Capitalism's political power is disguised

as economic necessity. But if we look beneath its ideological mask, we may retheorise capitalism as a sociopolitical formation which, like feudalism, confers power on the few as it dominates the many.

Another author's snippet also underscores the multiplicity of capitalism, implying that it is best examined beyond the realm of the economic. Here, the assumption is that capitalist logics have infiltrated other realms of social life, as a result of which various oppressive forces reinforce each other. This snippet illustrates this by underscoring the importance of examining the entanglements of authoritarianism and capitalism, and how certain affinities between these logics allow them to forge alliances:

Iuliia Gataulina

For me, the starting point for retheorising capitalism implies seeing its workings in all their multiplicity. I am particularly interested in what capitalism means when it couples with other oppressive forces, for example, an authoritarian state. Capitalism is more than economic production. The rationalities of growth, competitiveness, efficiency, and profit maximisation have promptly entered other areas of social life through global neoliberalisation, reshaping not only economics but also politics and governance. Different oppressive forces which propagate extraction and dispossession often reinforce and breed on each other. I am working within the scholarly tradition which tries to oppose the ideas that neoliberal capitalism brings about freedom; rather, I am tracing how the penetration of neoliberal capitalist governance into different spheres of social and political life prompts the solidification of managerialism, vertical power structures, and the erosion of the commons. In this light, neoliberal capitalism and its political tokens should be analysed as a global endeavour, albeit in different shapes when, for example, coupled with different compositions of governance, such as authoritarian states of the Global East.

Equally, it is crucial to proceed with the intellectual project of how we can imagine economics and politics in a more just way. For that, collaboration and dialogue between emancipatory theory and practice are required.

Hope

Working in the spirit of engaged pluralism can also uncover untypical locations for retheorising. For example, retheorising capitalism can occur as we, as variously positioned academic citizens, engage in our mundane academic labour in mindful ways. Affective labour of hope and inspiration or practices that nurture solidarities and connections and prevent us from collapsing into despair can also be understood as retheorising. This understanding of capitalism is reflected in the snippet from one of the contributors, who takes an anticapitalist position. Capitalism is defined as a system of exploitation, the dismantling of which is required to achieve global well-being. Retheorising capitalism, then, is about identifying and acting in sites of resistance and reimagination, as suggested here:

Iris Pajunen

I understand capitalism first and foremost as a system or philosophy of exploitation. In my view, capitalism often seems to be at the core of all that is evil and wrong with the world. This means that global wellbeing, world peace, and climate change mitigation cannot be achieved without disposing of capitalism. Therefore, I believe that retheorising capitalism is also retheorising hope—hope for alternatives, change, and improvement. I engage in anticapitalism and have participated in this book project to fight hopelessness.

One of the goals and effects of capitalism is that it feels overpowering and appears to have no alternatives. I believe that the way to approach its retheorisation is by implementing a bottom-up approach. This prevents being totally frozen by fear and instead influences the spheres you can and already are in. This is also why, as a university student, I wrote my chapter about academic capitalism and emphasised the importance of academic citizenship and communality. Firstly, democratic policies at universities often repel and resist academic capitalism and exploitation, and vice versa. Secondly, if we more carefully recognise the importance of different communities and the potential of anticapitalist influence in those spheres, the mobilisation can move from marginal to massive.

My position in this book project as an undergraduate student and a first-time author concretely demonstrates my idea of taking action where I can (the university/academia) and retheorising capitalism and hope simultaneously. I do this by locating sites of politics, resistance, reimagination, alternatives, and legitimacy through an autoethnographic methodology as a novice. To conclude, I would like to share that the exact reason I was so excited about the Retheorising Capitalism Funfair, an academic conference and a student course held at Tampere University on 23–25 October in 2023, which paved the way for this publication, is that it has been my inspiration for this entire journey. The event fought hopelessness and portrayed alternatives. The Funfair is proof that influencing your spheres works, hope and alternatives exist, and change is possible—and this is the message I want to share with my chapter.

References

Box-Steffensmeier, J. M. (2022). Engaged pluralism: The importance of commitment. Perspectives on Politics 20(1): 9–21. https://doi.org/10.1017/S1537592721003856

Gibson-Graham, J. (1996). The end of capitalism (as we knew it): A feminist critique of political economy. University of Minnesota Press.

Gibson-Graham, J. K. (2006). A postcapitalist politics. University of Minnesota Press.

Gibson-Graham, J.K. (2008). Diverse economies: performative practices for other worlds. Progress in Human Geography, 32(5), 613–632. https://doi.org/10.1177/0309132508090821

Gibson-Graham, J. K., & Dombroski, K. (2020). Introduction to the Handbook of diverse economies: Inventorying as ethical intervention. In J. K. Gibson-Graham & K. Dombroski (Eds.), The handbook of diverse economies (pp. 1–25). Edward Elgar.

Sedgwick, E. K. (1994). Tendencies. Routledge.

Tsing, A. L. (2015). The mushroom at the end of the world: on the possibility of life in capitalist ruins. Princeton University Press.

Vercelli, A. (1985). Keynes, Schumpeter, Marx and the structural instability of capitalism. Cahiers d'économie politique, 10–11, 279–304. https://doi.org/10.3406/cep.1985.1013

Contributors

Kelly Dombroski is Professor of Geography in the School of People, Environment and Planning at Te Kunenga ki Pūrehuroa Massey University in Aotearoa New Zealand. She carries out research that supports a transition to postcarbon and postcapitalist economies that better enable the wellbeing of people and planet. She holds a Rutherford Discovery Fellowship entitled *Transitioning to caring economies through transformative community investment* which builds on her work with communities in Aotearoa New Zealand and throughout Asia-Pacific. She uses action research, ethnographic, and feminist methodologies. A member of the Community Economies Institute, she is co-editor (with JK Gibson-Graham) of *The Handbook of Diverse Economies* (Edward Elgar, 2020) and author of *Caring for Life: A postdevelopment politics of infant hygiene* (UMP 2024). She is a Pākehā of Scottish, Irish and English descent and lives with her family in Manawatū in the north island of Aotearoa New Zealand.

ORCID 0000-0003-2975-962X

Iuliia Gataulina is a Postdoctoral Research Fellow in International Relations at Tampere University. Her doctoral dissertation, *De/re/composing authoritarian-neoliberal assemblages: Ethnography of Russian universities and beyond*, conceptualised the workings of neoliberalism beyond the Global North, specifically investigating how neoliberal reforms can reinforce the authoritarian state governance. Her postdoctoral project, *Pluriversal waters: Tracing hydro-ontologies across colonial-extractivist assemblages*, continues to investigate the political implications of capitalism, i.e., its connection to the colonial extractivist practices beyond the East-West divide and human-nonhuman interactions.

ORCID 0000-0001-8980-9428

Leo L. Hwang is the Assistant Academic Dean in the College of Natural Sciences at the University of Massachusetts, Amherst. Dr. Hwang earned his Ph.D. in Geosciences and an M.F.A. in fiction writing from the University of Massachusetts, and his B.A. in English and Fine Arts from the University of the South. His work has appeared in *The Racial Equity & Justice Institute Practitioner Handbook, The Handbook of Diverse Economies, The SAGE International Encyclopedia of Travel and Tourism, Rethinking Marxism, Solidarity Economy I: Building Alternatives for People and Planet, The Massachusetts* Review, *Glimmer Train Stories, Fiction, Gulf Coast* and other journals. He has taught at the University of Massachusetts; Mount Holyoke College; Greenfield Community College; and Westfield State University; and served as Dean of Humanities, Engineering, Math, and Science at Greenfield Community College. He plays guitar in Vimana and The Warblers, and bass in the Original Cowards.

ORCID 0000-0002-0730-6737

Anni Kangas is a University Lecturer in International Relations at Tampere University, Finland. In her research, she is inspired to explore the intersections of global political economy and art—as research material, method, or pedagogy. Kangas has previously researched and published on topics such as the interplay of economic nationalism and neoliberalism, global cities, and the dynamics of global labor migration.

ORCID 0000-0002-5794-5625

Akseli Kettula is Doctoral Researcher (Business Studies, Insurance and Risk Management) in the Faculty of Management and Business, Tampere University. Currently, Kettula is advancing his doctoral thesis entitled *Understanding impairments—characteristics and prevention in the perspective of insurance industry.* Along with grinding his thesis, he is heavily involved in teaching and stakeholder activity. As a side hustle, the author loves political economy and more explicitly, learning from unstable and chaotic nature of our society. In the dark corners of his research chamber, Kettula has developed the Theory of Fragmentism inspired especially by discussions with his friends Eetu Aumala and Miika Askeli. Due to a strong encouragement by his wife, the answer for a call of abstracts was sent to this book's editors. Besides academic ambitions, Kettula is a partner of Mission Grey startup (a combination of geopolitics, risk management and AI), a founding member of Euga Male Voice Choir, happy dad, and hopefully lovely husband.

ORCID 0000-0002-8267-1048

Mariam Khawar is a Doctoral Researcher at the University of Helsinki in the discipline of Global Politics. Her research focuses on the theoretical development of Islamic economic philosophy. This interdisciplinary project benefits from the diverse fields of political economy, global politics, Islamic philosophy, and theology.

ORCID 0000-0003-0977-5788

Aviv Kruglanski has a background in art and activism having formed part of activist/artist group Las Agencias and the Yomango. He co-developed arts-based techniques for collaborative neighbourhood work (including Documentary Embroidery with Vahida Ramujkic). He has a PhD in management from the University of Hull focusing on alternative forms of organizing. He is core-group member of a wonderful academic organisation called the Community Economies Institute. He believes in learning through doing, with others.

ORCID 0000-0002-4735-6608

Anataia van Leeuwen (Ngāti Tamaoho) is an Honours student in the School of Environment at The University of Auckland and an environmental consultant.

Heather McLean is an Assistant Professor in Environmental Studies and Human Geography at Athabasca University, an online university in Northern Alberta. As a white settler of Scottish and English descent living on unceded Indigenous land, she works from feminist, queer, and anti-colonial paradigms in a range of collaborative research projects. Her current research investigates accelerating gentrification and precarious work in small cities in so-called British Columbia. She also engages in arts-based research creation projects with artists to investigate climate crisis and mutual aid.

Georgia McLellan (Whakatōhea & Ngāi Te Rangi) is a PhD student in the School of Environment at The University of Auckland and a Research officer in the Business School at Massey University. Georgia is a critical indigenous economic geographer, and her PhD is focused on Whakatōhea (her tribes) kuku (green-lipped mussel) economies.

ORCID 0000-0001-7684-3141

Molly Mullen is a Senior Lecturer at Waipapa Taumata Rau/University of Auckland. She has a professional background in children's theatre, youth theatre, applied theatre and theatre and arts education. Much of her research now focuses on the intersection of policy, funding and practice in applied theatre and other socially engaged art-making. She has published extensively on this topic, including a book, *Applied Theatre: Economies*, with Bloomsbury. She also works on participatory research and creative practice projects that explore the themes of place, ecology, economy and wellbeing, and is co-editor of *Research in Drama Education: The Journal of Applied Theatre and Performance.*

ORCID 0000-0001-6567-3116

Maria Mäensivu is a Master's Student in International Relations at Tampere University, Finland. They have a long history in practicing multiple forms of art such as circus, music, and visual arts. Having had the privilege of receiving art education, Mäensivu wishes to further explore and expand the communication between arts and academia as well as to bring forth the emancipatory and political potential of art in marginalised spaces.

Iris Pajunen is a Finnish-Palestinian International Relations Student and an activist. She is doing her Bachelor's Degree at Tampere University, in the faculty of Management and Business. In her studies she focuses on peace and conflict research, gender studies and political philosophy.

ORCID 0009-0002-1182-1536

Edemilson Paraná is an Associate Professor in the Department of Social Sciences at LUT University, Finland. He has taught at the University of Brasília and the Federal University of Ceará, Brazil, and held research fellowships at the Institute of Applied Economic Research (IPEA, Brazil), the Brazilian National Council for Scientific and Technological Development (CNPq), and the Wales Institute of Social and Economic Research and Data (WISERD)/Cardiff University. He holds a Ph.D. and an MSc in Sociology from the University of Brasília, Brazil. Edemilson has lectured and published in the areas of Political Economy, Economic Sociology, and Social Theory. His research interests include digital economy, digital finance, financialisation, and the political economy of Artificial Intelligence.

ORCID 0000-0003-3487-9677

Mikko Poutanen is a Postdoctoral Researcher in the Faculty of Management and Business, under the Politics Unit, at Tampere University, Finland. His research focus is currently on higher education policy and the political economy of higher education, outlining how higher education is changing at the level of institutions and individual academics due to new policy priorities. These shifts reflect political and economic (and discursive) power in society. He is currently also involved in revitalising alienation theory.

ORCID 0000-0002-1914-9345

Anna Ilona Rajala is a critical theorist and social scientist with a background in physiotherapy. She defended her PhD thesis at the University of Brighton (UK) in 2021 on physiotherapy ethics and the relationship between theory and practice in Theodor W. Adorno's thinking. Her postdoctoral research at the University of the Arts Helsinki focused on aesthetic experience in Adorno's philosophy and narrative medicine. Her current three-year Research Council of Finland postdoctoral fellowship at Tampere University focuses on the politics and bioethics of excrement and abjection.

ORCID 0000-0002-9349-1958

Sabaheta Ramcilovic-Suominen is Associate Research Professor and Research Council of Finland Fellow at the Natural Resources Institute Finland, Luke. She is a Docent of global environmental justice at the University of Eastern Finland. She applies political ecology, decolonial and degrowth lenses to explore socioecological (in)justice and transformations. She studies international and EU driven policy and governance instruments, such as those promoting green economy, bioeconomy, carbon forestry and forest legality, and how they influence the historically and currently marginalized, dispossessed and made vulnerable human and other-than-human communities and natures. In her forthcoming edited book *Socioecological Transformations,* she explores the linkages between personal, collective, and structural change and transformations.

ORCID 0000-0002-3209-545X

Cory Tuhoro-Bodey (Ngāti Maniapoto) is an Undergrad student studying a conjoint degree of Global Studies and Science at the University of Auckland.

Tiina Vaittinen is a feminist political economist and peace researcher specialised in planetary political economies of care. She has researched, for example, the ethics of global nurse migration, political economies and ethics of old age care, and developed theories of feminist care ethics, vulnerability and corporeal relatedness. In her most recent project, she mapped the global political economies of the adult incontinence pad, as a case study of how the material needs of care could be fit within the planetary boundaries. She has published widely, and co-edits the *Edinburgh Feminist Studies on Peace, Justice and Violence* for Edinburgh University Press. Exploring openings to post-capitalism within the capitalist system, also in her own practices of making a living, Tiina has recently left the neoliberal university, to establish a purpose-driven changemaking consultancy, The GoodMess, that seeks to promote just sustainability transitions in social and health care. She's also affiliated with the WHO Collaboration Centre on Health in All Policies and Social Determinants of Health in Tampere University.

ORCID 0000-0002-8349-1487

Henna-Elise Ventovirta is a Doctoral Researcher in International Relations at Tampere University. Her ethnographic research focuses on the corporeal resistance practices of the international climate justice movement exploring politics of embodied emotions in climate crisis, and the emergence of diverse economies and caring practices at the international climate action camps. Henna-Elise is also a dance artist, which informs her approach to embodied practices in her research. Moreover, Henna-Elise is a founding member of the Berlin-based groups *Kipppunkt Kollektiv—education for climate justice*, and *Urgent Bodies—activating corporeality for political change.*

ORCID 0000-0001-7740-4167

Kerry Woodward lives and works in Narrm/Melbourne, Australia. Kerry's research focuses on food, care, farming and postcapitalist identities and practices. This chapter is based on their PhD research exploring how vegetable farms are made by human/earth-kin collectives and are sites of more-than-human caring. Beyond this, Kerry is currently exploring practices that cultivate belonging for both humans and earth-kin and how we can care-fully make homes on our ailing planet together.

ORCID 0000-0001-8187-7151

Mark L. Young is an independent scholar of early American history whose work has recently appeared in the *Journal of the Early Republic.* His former experience as a business owner and employer led him to research the legitimation and development of modern wage labour and its psychosocial impact in Western culture.

ORCID 0009-0009-6200-8466

Tampere University Press
Kalevantie 5 (PL 617)
33014 Tampereen yliopisto
FINLAND

email: tup@tuni.fi
https://edition.fi/tup
https://isni.org/isni/0000000507168743